History and Modern Media

History and Modern Media

A Personal Journey

John Mraz

VANDERBILT UNIVERSITY PRESS
Nashville

First printing 2021

Library of Congress Cataloging-in-Publication Data

Names: Mraz, John, author.
Title: History and modern media : a personal journey / John Mraz.
Description: Nashville : Vanderbilt University Press, [2021] | Includes bibliographical references.
Identifiers: LCCN 2020051355 (print) | LCCN 2020051356 (ebook) | ISBN 9780826501455 (hardcover) | ISBN 9780826501448 (paperback) | ISBN 9780826501462 (epub) | ISBN 9780826501479 (pdf)
Subjects: LCSH: Photography in historiography. | Historical films. | Pictures as information resources—Mexico. | History—Methodology.
Classification: LCC D16.155 .M73 2021 (print) | LCC D16.155 (ebook) | DDC 907.2—dc 23

LC record available at https://lccn.loc.gov/2020051355
LC ebook record available at https://lccn.loc.gov/2020051356

To my mentors from yesterday: Jesús Chavarría, Paul Vanderwood, Janey Place, and Mike Weaver.

And my hopes for tomorrow: Nicolás Ortiz Mraz and Maiala Freyria Meza

Contents

Acknowledgments

This book has been fifty years in the making, and my debts are many. I am grateful, first of all, to faculty members who believed in me enough to help me get over the first hurdle at two universities of California, UC Santa Barbara and UC Santa Cruz, including Jesús Chavarría, Ed Loomis, Carroll Pursell, David Sweet, Julianne Burton, Janey Place, and Jim Borchert. The collective projects in which I collaborated with fellow students were crucial in defining what I have become, and I hope that Chuck Churchill, Rick Chiles, Ray Tracy, Joyce Baker, Perry Kaufman, Roger Nelson, and Robert Chacanaca enjoyed it as much as I did. In Mexico, the visionary administrators who hired me or invited me carry out projects have been fundamental in allowing me to express myself and develop this innovative way of doing history, among them, Enrique Suárez Gaona, Alfonso Vélez Pliego, Eleazar López Zamora, Pati Mendoza, Luis Ignacio Sainz, and Tere Márquez.

The generosity of and interaction with my colleagues in Mexican photohistory have been pivotal in developing this new discipline. I am particularly grateful to Miguel Ángel Berumen, Bernardo "Tigre" García Díaz, Rebeca Monroy, Rosa Casanova, Alberto del Castillo, Daniel Escorza, Pati Massé, Ariel Arnal, Mayra Mendoza, Paulina Michel, Ángel Miquel, Poncho Morales, Ernesto Peñaloza, Jaime Vélez Storey, Samuel Villela, Carlos Córdoba, Fernando Aguayo, José Antonio Rodríguez, Arturo Ávila, Emma Cecilia García, Lilia Martínez, Claudia Canales, "Jimmy" Montañez Pérez, and the "team" of Abraham Nahón and Judith Romero. I have also benefitted from interaction with Latin American colleagues Ana María Mauad of Brazil, Magdalena Broquetas of Uruguay, Andrés Garay of Peru, and

Cora Gamarnick of Argentina, as well as Catalan colleagues José María Caparrós-Lera, Magí Crusells, and Rafael de España.

Juan Carlos Valdez, Director of the Fototeca Nacional-INAH was particularly helpful in providing images during the COVID-19 lockdown in Mexico and has been a constant interlocutor.

I thank Rubén Gallo for inviting me to Princeton University's Program in Latin American Studies, where the libraries aided me in this study, and interaction with Marni Sandweiss was important. I am also grateful to the Harry Ransom Center for granting me a David Douglas Duncan Endowment for Photojournalism/Andrew W. Mellon Foundation Research Fellowship (Harry Ransom Center, University of Texas, 2013).

I am indebted to the many institutions and individual photographers who have made this work possible by providing their images.

Conversations with Fernando Osorio have been useful in developing the methodology of analyzing genres and functions, and the first place I experimented with this method was at the magnificent Centro de Fotografía de Montevideo, at the invitation of its director, Daniel Sosa.

A special thanks to Sam Abrams, who keeps insisting that I read great fiction such as the powerfully anticolonialist *Heart of Darkness*.

Working in the Instituto de Ciencias Sociales y Humanidades "Alfonso Vélez Pliego" of the Benemérita Universidad Autónoma de Puebla under directors such as Alfonso, Roberto Vélez Pliego, Abraham Grajales, and Francisco Vélez Pliego has provided me with intellectual sustenance and the freedom to explore my chosen field of study.

I thank Zachery Gresham and Ignacio Sánchez Pardo for their enthusiastic response to my work, which has been important in completing this book under the difficult conditions in which we find ourselves.

As always, Eli Bartra has been there to criticize my facile interpretations, to pick me up when I fall down, and to bring love into my life.

Introduction

Reminiscences on the Voyage from an Audiovisual Periphery toward a Disciplinary Center

Once you had locked into language, all you could do was shuffle the greasy pack of a few thousand words that millions of people had used before. There might be moments of freshness, not because the life of the world has been successfully translated but because a new life has been made out of this thought stuff. But before the thoughts got mixed up with words, it wasn't as if the dazzle of the world hadn't been exploding in the sky of his attention. **Edward St. Aubyn**

It seemed so obvious. Even back in 1970 it began to be as evident as it is today: we live in a hyper-audiovisual world whose webs of significance are increasingly spun by modern (technical) media: photography, cinema, television, and digital imagery and sounds. Although this metamorphosis began in the mid-nineteenth century, it is something historians have in general given little serious attention. Nonetheless, it would be difficult to overstate the importance of these media, which have completely transformed the exchange of information and our entire audiovisual environment; philosopher Vilém Flusser asserted that the invention of technical images may be as great a revolution as that of lineal writing, around 32,000 BC.[1]

The vast majority of people now learn about the "past" from technical images and sounds—including academics, beyond their immediate areas of specialization—whether in films, on television, in picture books and illustrated magazines, or through some other form of modern visual culture.[2] My focus in this book is on "modern" media, rather those technologies that I would describe as "postmodern": ICT (information and communication technologies) including the Internet and the forms of social communication it has spawned, among them Twitter, Facebook, Instagram, and WhatsApp. Although I utilize the Internet as an indispensable research tool, my work has largely been confined to photography and cinema.

Despite the extraordinary transformation wrought by technical images and sounds, a mutual antipathy has almost always existed—and continues to reign—between the world of professional historians and those who produce popular audiovisual history. Historians have shown a reticence to rigorously employ photographs and films, though this seems to be less true in Mexico and Brazil than among historians from the United States and the United Kingdom. This resistance is curious: as photohistorian Liliana Gómez-Popescu argued, "Images have always provided important insights into history and were accepted as equal to other written source materials. This is certainly true for those historians who work on antiquity or the early modern period, and the medievalists. Yet, with the chemical-technological invention of photography in the 1830s this relationship seems to have experienced serious frictions."[3]

When compared with other fields of study, historians' resistance to modern media is particularly pronounced. Two of the most important scholars of visual culture and photography have provided testimony to the conspicuous absence of image study in history departments. In an overview that examines the development of visually oriented programs, James Elkins states that a "bewildering number of departments offer visual studies courses," and cites ten such areas, among which we find the "usual suspects" such as art history and comparative literature, but no history departments.[4] Ariel Azoulay finds the same situation as does Elkins, noting the inclusion of photographic studies beyond the art paradigm in six disciplines, including sociology and anthropology, but does not mention history.[5]

At the same time, those who work in a wider context with images (cineastes, curators, publishers) have often had little use for professional historians, though the representation of yesteryear is lucrative, to judge from the public interest. For example, some 40 percent of films have been set in the past.[6] Although this statistic was derived from a study of US films made between 1950 and 1961, one reason to suspect that it may be generally applicable is the fact that six of the movies that have won Oscars for Best Film in the past fifteen years are "historical," a percentage exactly equal to that produced by the long-term study. Of course, Hollywood has rarely shown interest in exploring what sorts of options might be available to seriously and/or experimentally depict former times. The same general comments could be extended to the picture history books produced for coffee tables or many of the exhibits mounted that attract those always curious consumers of the heretofore.

Was it not obvious that, among those interested in doing professional history, there should be some concerned to explore visuality (and audiovisuality) within a disciplinary framework, rather than from an illustrationist bent? As Hayden White observed in 1988:

> All too often, historians treat photographic, cinematic, and video data as if they could be read in the same way as a written document. We are inclined to treat the imagistic experience as if it were at best a complement of verbal evidence, rather than as a supplement, which is to say, a discourse in its own right and one capable of telling us things about its referents that are both different from what can be told in verbal discourse and also of a kind that can only be told by means of visual images.[7]

The opening epigraph by St. Aubyn makes clear that words are conventional symbols for similarities: *tree*, for example, describes a woody perennial plant with one main stem that develops many branches. The difference between words and photographs is illustrated in the fact that you cannot photograph the concept *tree*, you can only photograph a particular tree. Thus, a photo is by its nature a document of a specific scene, a particular fraction of a second, a unique history. For Roland Barthes, a photograph "is the absolute Particular, the sovereign Contingency, matte and somehow stupid, the *This* (this photograph, and not Photography), in short, what Lacan calls the *Tuché*, the Occasion, the Encounter, the Real, in its indefatigable expression."[8]

My trip toward figuring out how modern media relates to our ability to think about that "other country" of the "world we have lost" began inauspiciously.[9] In 1961, I started out poorly on my undergraduate odyssey. Coming from a well-off family, I had the luxury to attend, and then drop out, be expelled, or simply disappear from three different colleges in quick succession. With few options, I entered into the army voluntarily in 1963, where I matured; I also managed to see Europe, avoid being drafted (and perhaps sent to Vietnam), and have the GI Bill for higher education. I'd worked at a variety of jobs, among them in a steel mill and on dam construction, so I was ready to study when I finally returned to college in 1966. I got good grades and entered directly from undergraduate studies into the history doctoral program at the University of California at Santa Barbara in 1970.

In that same year, I had an epiphany that changed my life forever when I made my first audiovisual production, *The History of Mexico as Seen by the Muralists*. It was probably pretty awful, but I created it with the paintings of Diego Rivera, José Clemente Orozco, and David Alfaro Siqueiros that I encountered in the university's slide library, coupled with texts from Octavio Paz and other Mexican writers, and a sound track that included "Cristo Redentor" by Donald Byrd (the first and last time I used music in an ahistorical way). In the ensuing years I made around twenty-five audiovisuals, a medium that today seems antiquated, but that was fundamental in learning how to think in terms of linking images, words, and music.

I also began to discover how to research and develop visual and audial sources, and to accumulate a vast archive of photographs and other images, both in my mind as well as slides of the pictures. I was hooked: the mix of images and sounds was so immediately and sensually powerful that it bowled over my former approaches to history, and from that moment on I decided that I would spend my life doing (or at least trying to do) history with modern media. I showed the production in classes around the university, where the pictures, voices, and music produced an affective response and awakened interest. Some historians who have turned toward this method find that their audience research confirm this. As Barbara Franco found, "people were better able to engage in critical analysis of history after they had made an emotional connection to people or events of the past. Rather than thinking of emotion and reason as two separate tracks, we came to understand that emotional engagement often preceded critical analysis and understanding."[10]

Back in the early 1970s, educators in all fields were struggling over how to incorporate photographs, films, and television into their different disciplines. Visual anthropologist Sol Worth argued for their "psychological primacy, sociocultural primacy, communicative primacy (particularly as compared to words), and sensual primacy," fearing that for many students in traditional classrooms "tedium is the message."[11] The "visual turn" that was just beginning to take place produced some truly transformative works. John Berger's affirmation—"seeing comes before words"—with which he opens his pioneering book *Ways of Seeing*, was a defining contribution.[12] Another was the contention of Rudolf Arnheim, an art and film theorist, that, "truly productive thinking in whatever area of cognition takes place in the realm of imagery."[13] Susan Sontag's articles in the *New York Review of Books*, later published in book form, were vital in broadening the discussion of photography beyond the art paradigm.[14]

A new "climate of opinion" was coming into being and, as Carl Becker observed, "Whether arguments command assent or not depends less upon the logic that conveys them than upon the climate of opinion in which they are sustained."[15] In engaging with visuality, I drew upon my work in intellectual history. I placed the argument of Immanuel Kant—that we perceive the world through "a priori" categories of perception—into a Marxist perspective.[16] Linking those two philosophies enabled me to understand that we see the world through the lenses of our class, race, gender, the historical moment in which we have been given to live, and the degree to which we have been able to construct our own coherent and critical consciousness; these are our filters.

I discovered that I had an affinity for imagery; I could spend hours poring over photographs, and my work tended more and more to initiate with pictures. As I have grown into this new discipline I find that the lectures I give and the works I write always begin with images; rather than composing a text and then looking for pictures to illustrate my points, I form the visual discourse and then fill in the words with which to explain it. I have undertaken research projects stimulated by the discovery of archival photographs, as well as by curating photo exhibits. I might say that I work from a "visual standpoint epistemology," paraphrasing the feminist philosopher Sandra Harding.[17] Historians' acceptance of this novel approach to doing history has been a long time coming, but the recognition that we must somehow incorporate modern media is apparent. Peter Burke pointed to the need to develop methods: "New sources require their own forms of source criticism, and the rules for reading pictures as historical evidence, to take just one example, are still unclear."[18] His book *Eyewitnessing* is a most useful introduction to utilizing paintings as a source of socio-cultural history, but unfortunately, even this brilliant historian comes up short when attempting to deal with photography and cinema, where he demonstrates little knowledge of the extensive bibliography on those media. His comments on photography focus largely on how individuals are reduced to types: "the middle class taking photographs of workers, the police taking photographs of criminals and the sane taking photographs of the insane—generally concentrated on traits which they considered to be typical, reducing individual people to specimens of types."[19] While this is one aspect of particular photographic genres, the enormous mass of vernacular photographs do not follow this description, and it is the role of photohistorians to bring specificity and contextuality to their studies. The few pages he dedicates to film provide little insight into the "usual suspects" he briefly mentions, among them: *The Battle of Algiers* (Pontecorvo, 1966), *The Return of Martin Guerre* (Wajda, 1983), and *La historia official* (Puenzo, 1984).[20] Burke's failure to adequately address technical media demonstrates the significant difficulties in engaging with these communication forms.

Being able to incorporate modern media into doing history is crucial to communicating about the differences we discover in past societies. We are caged within an increasingly perpetual present that makes it difficult if not impossible to think in terms of alternative ways of living. We are conditioned to believe that the way we live right now and here is the only option. This is dangerous, and the otherness of the past is one of the most important things we can discover there. It is a "common sense" notion that "human nature" is the same everywhere and in all times, because we have the same basic needs: we need to eat, drink, be sheltered from the elements, and reproduce our species. Nonetheless, the social arrangements we live within in order to meet those needs vary greatly, and that makes us think quite differently about ourselves and others. The idea that people marry for love, for instance, is a very modern notion, and love itself is not an unproblematic concept.[21] Anthropology offers spatial examples of other possibilities, drawing on the varieties of existing cultures around the world. However, such options are fast disappearing; as anthropologist Gregory Bateson remarked some fifty years ago: "The world is flattening out."[22] History can provide not only examples of other ways to live, it can also enable us to think beyond the "short-termism" that is so deeply ingrained in contemporary culture.[23] Further, the study of history teaches us two fundamental lessons. The first is that we have been formed in particular ways by the times through which we have lived. The second is that, if we are products of our environments, we can therefore create new situations that can produce new human beings.

Moreover, the question of how to incorporate "the technological quantum leap of the world wide web and a collaterally looming paradigm shift within history studies" is larger than the discipline itself; as visual historian Gerhard Paul argued, it is "more than an additive expansion of the canon of historical studies or the history of visual media."[24] We have a vital and urgent necessity to develop a visual literacy that will enable us to understand how technical images are mediating, even determining, our ways of seeing the world around us and, hence, our decisions. Flusser asserts polemically in his article, "Photography and History," that photos are less important as images of the past than as projections of the future: "Photographs are programmed to model the future behavior of their addressees. Yet, they are not only models of behavior, but also models of perception and experience."[25] For example, the well-known 1953 Nacho López photo (Figure 24) that I discuss in Chapter 2 not only preserves an instance of the *piropo* (the catcall that men feel free to impose upon women in public spaces) that celebrates—in both form and content—Mexican hyper-machismo, it also continues to teach men how to look at and act around women, based on the credibility of photography.

Because we believe them to be real, technical images provide "life plans for their recipients."[26] This is particularly so in the way they manipulate our sexuality.[27] As historian Michael Roth observed, "The images teach us how to love and how to hate: they teach us about our bodies and about the bodies we want."[28] I will illustrate this point with a highly personal experience. In 2016, I was trying to express to a young student who was interviewing me how crucial it is to learn how to decipher modern media, above all for the ways in which they plant desideratum in our very being. I suddenly became aware of how my decision to marry my first wife, Ulla, a Swedish woman, had resulted to some extent from an advertisement for Noxema shaving cream that was popular in 1967. That was, perhaps not coincidentally, the precise point in which we married and began to live a difficult ten-year attempt to work it out. In that ad, a beautiful blond model faking a Swedish accent urged men to "Take it off. Take it all off."[29] Thanks to the Internet, the interviewer found that ad and included it in her article. I was able to relive the experience with different eyes, which was painful, if most instructive.

It is crucial to understand that we are living within a system dominated by capitalist and patriarchal propaganda that is carried out largely through technical images and sounds, and with which we are assailed constantly. As Berger remarked, "We are surrounded by photographic images which constitute a global system of misinformation: the system known as publicity proliferating consumerist lies."[30] The marketplace mentality has become the new grand narrative: "a single, universal story of liberty and prosperity, the global victory of the market."[31] And, as the former president of Uruguay, and one of the exemplary men of our time, José Mujica explained, "When you buy something, you are not buying it with money, you are buying it with the time you had to invest to make that money. And the only thing you cannot buy is time."[32] Noam Chomsky outlined the political function of this system:

> The major propaganda systems that we face now, mostly growing out of the huge public relations industry, were developed quite consciously about a century ago in the freest countries in the world, Britain and the United States, because of a very clear and articulated recognition that people had gained so many rights that it was hard to suppress them by force. So you had to try to control their attitudes and beliefs and or divert them somehow. As the

> economist Paul Nystrom argued, you have to try to fabricate consumers and create wants so people will be trapped.[33]

Given this situation of what I would describe as "mind control," my work as a historian has focused on developing a critical engagement with modern media, so that we can gain power over the representation of the past and the present. This is necessary because these media have been important in forming not only a consumerist mentality, but also the militarist vision necessary to hold the imperialist structure in place. As journalist Michael Herr observed about the Vietnam occupation, "I kept thinking about all the kids who got wiped out by seventeen years of war movies before coming to Vietnam to get wiped out for good."[34]

Cinema is the most accepted of the modern media in academia, as can be seen in the establishment of film studies programs; it is also that with which historians have most engaged. However, in this book, I have focused on photography for several reasons. Most importantly, photographs are the basic unit of modern and postmodern media, an unrecognized centrality they have long held and that the appearance of networked, digitally shared "social photography" only increases.[35] Learning to really see photographs is the first step toward analyzing technical images, but photos are also the most difficult medium to study because their meaning depends on their functions in the narratives within which they have been embedded. This is the field in which I have worked most since I moved to Mexico. It is also a discipline that has been much less explored, in part because the history of photography is generally conceived to belong within art history; I argue in Chapter 3 that this is a misconception created by the material interests involved. In fact, rather than seeing photography as some sort of peripheral medium, we should understand it as the center of our ways of knowing about the world within which we live. I have had the feeling that in working with Mexican and other Latin American colleagues we have been inventing methods to incorporate photography rigorously into doing history.

Perception appears to be objective in a way that words do not. Today, if visual evidence does not exist of something, it didn't happen. As Sontag noted, "Atrocities that are not secured in our minds by well-known photographic images, or of which we simply had very few images . . . seem more remote. . . . Photographs that everyone recognizes are now a constituent part of what a society chooses to think about, or declares that it has chosen to think about."[36] Certainly, it could be argued that sight has been the sense most developed by technology, as we can see in micro, macro, and astronomical photography, among many other instances. Seeing is the central metaphor for understanding in the scopic regimes of Western culture.[37] This is not so for indigenous Australians; "In Aboriginal languages, it is hearing, not vision, which is extended to denote *know*, *think*, or *remember*, while *see* is more like to be used for specific forms of social interaction (*flirt with*, *love*, *supervise/oversee*)."[38]

In the first chapter, I discuss directing historical documentaries, an endeavor in which I continue to work. However, I do not address myself to the issues of oral history that such filmmaking necessarily raises; the field is too large and complex to undertake within my limited discussion of making documentaries. Moreover, I have not opened up any new research in analyzing fictional historical cinema in this book. My work in studying movies set in the past has been sporadic since around 1990, so what I have to say about it is already largely in print. I have not kept up with the ever-growing bibliography enough to feel safe in going beyond the ideas spelled out in the several path-breaking books written by Robert Rosenstone.[39] Film studies have experienced much growth over the past forty years, in part—I suspect—because it is easier to analyze cinema due to its narrative structure. While photos can be placed within a narrative, I have not yet seen a convincing argument that a photograph in itself offers what I would describe as a narrative. Historians have been using cinema as a source material since the 1970s. Unfortunately, in some cases the studies have limited themselves to saying "that's not history," rather than asking more difficult questions about the specific contributions the film medium could make to representing the past.

I have interwoven my experiences of attempting to do history with modern media, first in US academia and then in Mexican institutions, together with the research I have carried out, because in many instances they are inseparable. In the case of the US, the battles I fought to do what I desired forced me to hone my arguments, as well as develop new ones. The investigations I undertook—that I hoped would convince the skeptics—existed in large part thanks to the support provided by certain faculty. In Mexico, the various invitations I have received to make cinema, mount photo exhibits, and write on visual history have mediated my work in very particular ways that I describe below. Certainly, the two photographic genres I examine at length are a direct expression of the focus I have developed on how to study imperial and neocolonizing, as well as subaltern and decolonizing, imagery. The description of how I got to where I am in terms of being able to decipher this photography seems to me to be a fundamental part of the analysis I carry out.

In 1990, a US graduate student called me to ask what my advice would be about making films as a historian. I said, "Just do it," echoing the Nike advertisement that was then popular.[40] As I explained to him, it takes time to develop the skills to really see visual images, to find and copy them on slides or shoot them with film and video, as well as to link them with words and music. The only way to do that is to jump into it and begin learning, because the structures of consciousness that are created by and that produce texts are different than those shaped by and utilizing modern media. He began to describe the difficulties he faced in having to finish a dissertation and look for a job. I replied that once he had finished his dissertation and turned it into a book, found a position, developed his courses, and gotten the tenure that would be required to allow him the autonomy to explore modern media, he would probably not have the time to learn those skills.

In a sense, this book is for that fellow, and all the other historians—as well as scholars from other disciplines—who have asked me over the years how they can work with the media of our age. I don't know if my caller ever got a position or tenure, but today there is a growing army of innovative historians who want to rigorously employ modern media in their investigations and teaching, knowing how important it can be in their classes both in terms of giving entertaining classes as well as allowing students to do their projects with the media they know intimately; many of these colleagues feel marginalized within the strictures of US academia. To all it is clear we must drag history study into the modern era. To that end, I have described some of the resistance I found in US universities to the use of modern media in teaching and researching the past. I have also tried to give examples of how my own struggle eventually led to a situation where I could carry out my work with the same autonomy and respect that traditional historians receive. Further, this work is an attempt to incite younger historians, who grew up with the new technologies, to engage with them. That decision could open doors to employment beyond the much-contested classroom spaces for semi-employed adjunct faculty and indebted PhD candidates struggling to find jobs. Even as a graduate student, I was often able to supplement my teaching assistant salary with projects developing visual teaching resources.

On coming to Mexico, I was able to enter immediately into television, and all the subsequent work for which I have been hired has been directly related to visual projects. Discovering and developing the audiovisual side to this discipline was my salvation, for I would have been a mediocre historian had I not found a field I loved. Working in multimedia history has opened up opportunities that I could not have imagined when I was in graduate school. I have been invited to write and collaborate in books and journals, as well as serve as to serve as guest editor for special issues on modern media, and to direct videotapes. I have also been offered visiting positions in universities around the world to teach in a wide variety of disciplines (history, art history, film studies). My work has created possibilities outside academia, in the public sphere, as a curator, audiovisual director, and a cineaste. Further, I have a position as a research professor in the Benemérita Universidad Autónoma de Puebla (BUAP), and I have been able to solidify that with historical cinematic productions, which are recognized as books by the Sistema Nacional de Investigadores providing you substantiate the research that went into their making.[41]

I have the advantage of working in Mexico, where I found a greater acceptance for and interest in these forms of doing history. In this book, I have tried to provide some insight into what it means to live in this culture, in which I feel more at home than in my country of origin. Until recently, I thought of myself as a "dual citizen" after acquiring Mexican nationality in 2009, but the election of Donald Trump left me feeling even more estranged from the US just as the recent election of Andrés Manuel López Obrador has made me proud to be a Mexican. Now, I live, write, and use modern media as a Latin American. Walter Mignolo said that the anchor of a decolonial worldview is, "I am where I do and think"; I would add: and where I work for the salaries that are paid in this country, and not as a foreign executive of a multinational corporation, or with a fellowship from abroad.[42] In part, I was inspired to enter into this risky business of incorporating my own experiences by the memoirs of anthropologist Howard Campbell on the years he spent in Oaxaca. I felt a particular empathy with his description of the integration of social, intellectual, and political life: "In the salon atmosphere of the Zapotec cantinas, I felt a camaraderie I have seldom experienced among U.S. intellectuals. The Juchitán intellectual milieu, whatever its flaws may have been, was less alienated than the U.S. academic scene."[43]

As did Campbell, I have also found that my interaction with Mexican photographers, photojournalists, filmmakers, academics, artists, cartoonists, writers, and political activists is constant and face-to-face. Moreover, there is a sense that ideas and creative activities can make a difference, despite the long party dictatorship of the PRIAN.[44] The election of López Obrador demonstrates that such hopes are not futile. And, although I find much of the postmodern narcissism and obscurantism that dominates US and British universities to be objectionable, it has at least opened up the opportunity to write what is in some ways an academic autobiography, stimulated by the examples set by extraordinary historians such as Eric Hobsbawm, Robert Rosenstone, and Richard Morse, though I would certainly not put myself in their league.[45]

CONCLUSION

This book begins (and ends) as an autobiography, and there are elements interlaced throughout, but the emphasis falls upon how we can incorporate photographic images rigorously. My own general methodology can be described in the following way: in order to understand how meanings are generated from without, we reconstruct their contexts of production and dissemination; to understand how photos "mean" from within, we contrast them to other, similar, photos. My past contributions have focused largely on photojournalism, and it was through my efforts in studying that complex field that I came upon a method that may be useful to integrating photos into the historical discipline, that of defining them within genres and then analyzing the varied functions the photographs serve therein. However, before entering into that discussion, Chapter 2 offers a general overview of how to incorporate photographs into the study of the past, and what historians bring to the study of this medium. Chapter 3 opens up the discussion of genre and function by demonstrating how this method developed over years of studying photojournalism. In Chapter 4, Indianist imagery is analyzed in terms of how it incarnates the perspective of imperial, neocolonializing, and decolonizing photography. Chapter 5 offers a history of leftist photography in Mexico, through an analysis of worker, laborist, and feminist imagery, as well as by considering the anti-imperialist photography of Rodrigo Moya. Whether the method will yield fruit for today's and future historians, I cannot say. However, my hope is to discover some of the right questions, and perhaps even offer one or another answer. As the Cuban poet José Lezama Lima wrote: "Human greatness is the arrow's flight, not the bull's-eye."[46]

Part I. Cinehistories

CHAPTER 1

Doing History with Light and Sound

From Compilation Films to Interview-Based Documentaries

Watching a coast as it slips by the sea is like thinking about an enigma. There it is before you—smiling, frowning, inviting, grand, mean, insipid or savage, and always mute with an air of whispering, "Come and find out." **Joseph Conrad**

Back in the early 1960s, the renowned cinehistorian Jay Leyda decided to write about *compilation films*, a now-familiar form and concept. However, he opens his book by describing his surprise at what he encountered, "When I fixed upon this subject I was somewhat taken aback by the fact that there was no name for it." He invented *compilation films*, but even he felt that it was "an awkward, incomprehensible and unacceptable term for this form."[1] I believe that it is quite meaningful that those of us who wish to do history of and with modern media are constantly frustrated when we try to define with words that which we are attempting to do. I began my odyssey employing the term *audiovisual history*, but it brings too readily to mind the boring informational and propagandist movies that many of us were subjected to in high school. It does not convey the seriousness with which today's historians struggle to carry out research and tell our stories about the past through the media of our age.

After moving to Mexico in 1981, I abandoned the word *audiovisual* and attempted to redeem the widely employed term *historia gráfica* from its commonly accepted meaning in that country, where it refers to works that are almost always illustrationist and officialist politico-military histories of Great Men and their heroic deeds in forging the nation.[2] Moreover, *historia gráfica*, or *visual history* (yet another option), refers only to the ocular element, leaving aside the sound track.[3] In a moment of despair, I decided that *photo-phonic history* (*historia fotofónica*) was a solution, but this term is even more unwieldy, unintelligible and, frankly, ugly than *compilation films*.

How are we to describe our role in doing history with and of modern media? We could employ *multimedia*, as did a couple of British historians, although it calls to mind many of the secondary school associations with audiovisual.[4] I sense that these problems of nomenclature will only be resolved as we proceed in our efforts to bring the study and recounting of history into today's context of technical images and sounds. For the present, I will limit myself to defining historians who work rigorously with photographs as *photohistorians*. While I recognize in the next chapter that there are two different approaches—doing histories *with* photographs and doing history *of* photographs—there is often so much overlap between these tasks in the actual investigations that it makes sense to describe the discipline as *photohistory*.

In this chapter, I will avoid the larger issues raised by the multiple forms of modern media and confine myself to attempting to determine how we should describe history as done with pictures in movement accompanied by a sound track. Calling them *motion pictures* sounds awfully dated, and to say *movies* plays into the hands of those colleagues who have ridiculed our efforts, often with the rejoinder, "I like to go to the movies too, but that's not history." We are no longer making *films* because they are not made on celluloid, and by the same token neither are we producing *videotapes*. I think the solution is to describe them in the format in which they were presented, but to talk of the area in general as *cinehistory* that is to say, "history in movement."[5] Hence, I would describe any historian who tries to do history with cinema, and/or analyzes the ways it has been done by other directors, as a *cinehistorian*.

COMPILATION CINEMA

Compilation films are made up of pre-existing shots that are edited into a new work, which "has to indicate that the film used originated at some time in the past."[6] The compilation utilizes the documentary aura of the footage, which is carved by the director-editor into a new and essentially independent work that reflects his or her own purpose and ideology. An oft-cited early example is *Spain* (1939), created by Esther Schub, a Soviet director and editor who was a friend of Sergei Eisenstein, and "brought intelligence, taste and a sense of social responsibility into this generally despised employment [editing]"; Leyda described the film as a masterpiece: "Its brilliant execution is all to communicate a feeling, an experience—akin to a great work of history, not objective or rounded, but personal and passionate."[7] Here, it is important to understand that his strategy was designed to convey history in a new way, not simply apply the media to producing more lucrative costume dramas.

Making historical documentaries with already-existing imagery and sounds is a widely practiced genre today. The works have been realized with widely varying degrees of success in somehow bridging the demands of historians and those of a public (including historians) that expects a certain level of production quality and esthetic power. The capacity to say what you want to say with cinema bears a direct relation to the technical infrastructure available. I often compare writing and mediamaking by describing my experiences of editing the videotape *Innovating Nicaragua/Nicaragua innovando* (1986–87). The low-budget equipment on which I could afford to rent editing time was a "straight-cut" system that was incapable of doing a dissolve. Hence, I could not say whatever it is that a dissolve (or any other special effect) says—which will vary according to the context in which it is used. This is a situation somewhat akin to a writer being told that he or she could not use a comma. The audience expectations created by well-financed and technologically advanced "perfect cinema" pose a formidable competition that we, as cinehistorians, find very difficult to meet in terms of technical quality, although digitalization is transforming this situation.[8]

The US media has been prolific in producing long-running series of historical compilation documentaries. Unsurprisingly, the first was composed of war footage. *Victory at Sea* was an enormously popular commercial television series made up of World War II imagery, and its twenty-six individual segments "reached more human beings than any other motion picture or TV series in history."[9] The fact that it began to be broadcast in 1952–1953, during the Korean War—and in the midst of the Cold War—indicates that it was intended to foster militarism among the populace. Another US television series of note, *The Civil War*, was broadcast on the Public Broadcasting Service during 1990, and depicted combat in a decidedly less triumphalist tone. Ken Burns directed the nine-segment narrative on the 1861–1865 conflict that "was seen by more viewers than any other program in the history of the PBS."[10] It became a noteworthy cultural event and was the work that has most provoked US historians to grapple critically with the issues raised by cinehistory, at least as practiced by Burns.[11]

A French historical compilation, Marcel Ophuls's *The Sorrow and the Pity* (1969), utilized documentary footage of World War II to powerfully debunk the myth of French resistance to Nazi occupation. This work also caused a cultural stir and was banned from French television until 1982, although I am unaware if French historians were as moved as their US colleagues to enter into the polemic. While both US series are well-produced cinematic reflections on the past, they fall short of *The Sorrow and the Pity* as cinehistory, for its narrative complexity makes it one of the preeminent examples of this genre.

DOING HISTORICAL CINEMA

Ophuls's masterpiece came to the University of California at Santa Barbara in the early 1970s, and I was no doubt inspired by it when I began to make Super 8mm compilation films in 1972. The first was *Coming Apart: America in the 1960s*, for which I teamed up with two fellow history graduate students, Joyce Baker and Perry Kaufman.[12] It was largely composed of photographs we shot from magazines such as *Life* and *Look*, as well as from coffee-table tomes; we tried to dynamize the images by zooming in and out (a common curse of beginning filmmakers), and panning when possible. The technical resources were primitive, and a major problem was lighting the images: as incredible as it seems today, UCSB had no copy stands, let alone equipment for animating still photos. We had to borrow stage lamps from the theater arts department and set them up around a cafeteria table on which we filmed. They were very hot, so shooting under them was quite uncomfortable, and we often touched the delicate lamps, burning ourselves and shorting them out, as we tried to move the heavy bound magazines into positions that would allow us to shoot the photos.

We obtained moving footage by filming documentary video off a television screen, such as Martin Luther King's speech the night before he was killed. Unfortunately, the lack of synchronization between the videotape and the Super 8mm film caused black bands to roll across the screen when those parts were projected. We used 1960's music, and dubbed in contemporary speeches. We eschewed omniscient narration, in part because it would have sounded like so many of the boring documentaries we knew too well. And it might have been difficult for the three of us to agree on a voice-over narrative given the passionate disagreements we often had in those effervescent days. Nonetheless, we worked well together in our collaborative endeavor, which was characteristic of the late 1960s and early 1970s. The work was edited in the rapid-fire style of television commercials, a poor model for doing good cinehistory.

The film was accepted at an academic congress: the Pacific Coast Branch meeting of the American Historical Association. This was something extraordinary for graduate students in those days, because we were vetoed from participating in conferences. We also showed the film to other groups around Santa Barbara. We did not know how to place the sound track on the film, so the relation between the images and the sound track changed every time it was shown: the film always moved at twenty-four frames a second, thanks to the sprocket holes, but the audio tape stretched. The result was always aleatoric, and sometimes surprisingly incisive; at other times it was unfortunate.

I had found what I most loved doing, so in 1973 I co-directed another Super 8mm compilation film, *Cracks in the Wall: America/the Fifties*, with another history graduate student who was an expert in sound recording, Ray Tracy, as well as an undergraduate, Roger Nelson.[13] I was working as a teaching assistant in a large US-history course, and the idea occurred to me that we could use a section of the class to make a film that focused on the 1950s; the professor, Carroll Pursell, backed the project. We announced the section in the large lecture class and attracted a group of students who found that more interesting than participating in section discussions. Again we made extensive use of popular illustrated magazines and published photography; the sound track was composed of interviews with people who lived through the era, and music from the 1950s.

The most intriguing part of the film was utilizing home movie footage shot by my father years before. For example, when we focused on US imperialism and the constant public mobilization it required, we incorporated color 8mm footage of my brother and I playing at war, fully decked out in army surplus uniforms from World War II and the Korean conflict. Our shirts and jackets were overlaid with sewed-on, many-hued insignia of different outfits and ranks. Atop this attire, we wore cartridge belts for firearms from pistols to machine guns, first aid kits carried by medics, gas mask containers, and other equipment. We had helmets on our heads (both plastic liner and steel shell), and we were fully armed with toy rifles and pistols. Willing cannon fodder for US neocolonialism, our warrior-like jumping about—shooting and hiding and falling as if dead—was interspersed with still photographs from illustrated magazines that documented US invasions worldwide, linking the generalized militarization of that society to the domestic acceptance of imperial policy.

My memory is that I hit upon this esthetic strategy intuitively. The footage seemed to cry out for inclusion, offering the opportunity to recontextualize it and compelling spectators to look at familiar scenes in significantly different ways, as well as making their minds more alert to the larger purport of what was happening in these old home movies. As cinehistorian Bill Nichols has commented, "The core idea of the compilation film revolves around not only montage and photomontage but also *ostranenie*. . . . The 'making strange' of things familiar": "An 'aha' moment occurs when something familiar and known is seen in an unfamiliar, new way."[14] This was a largely unexplored esthetic strategy in US documentaries, with the exception of Emile de Antonio's works, and perhaps I could claim it as an example of self-reflexivity, a distanciation à la Jean-Luc Godard. Home movies have more recently become a rich source of experimentation in independent cinema, as the widely recognized *Stories We Tell* (Polley, 2012) demonstrated. I continue to believe that family images—still and moving, real or faux (as in some moments of *Stories*)—can provide an invaluable source to audiovisual historians. The use we made of the footage was certainly in line with the critical component of Leyda's conception, which was also an element of the Frankfort School's insistence on transforming the unapparent and unconscious into visible consciousness. Leyda cites Siegfried Kracauer: "The most familiar, that which continues to condition our involuntary reactions and spontaneous impulses, is thus made to appear as the most alien."[15]

The sound track for *Cracks in the Wall* was composed of interviews and music from the period, which were mixed together and juxtaposed with the images; again, we avoided the omniscient narrator. Having discovered that we could put the track on the Super 8mm print in Los Angeles, we left behind the aleatoricism of the earlier effort. The most entertaining snippet of sound was provided by actress Jane Wyatt, the devoted wife and mother figure from the very popular television show *Father Knows Best* (1954–1960). At one point, she reflected upon that patriarchal and Pollyannish series, saying that, though the show might appear ingenuous from the perspective of the 1970s, "I thought it was real." We used that statement a couple of times to great ironic effect.

We were invited to show the film at a historical conference, the Anglo-American Historical Convention, by Patrick Griffin, a history professor at California State University at Long Beach who had begun making films and knew of our efforts.[16] On reflection, I believe that the fact that he worked in a university of lesser prestige (in his case, a California State University rather than a University of California) was perhaps one reason he felt free to explore alternative modes of doing history (although he soon left academia). Given the composition of and prestige among their faculties, I believe that the great universities of the world will be among the last to open themselves to modern media. We wrote up the experiment for *The History Teacher*, a journal that had demonstrated a developing interest in new forms of history, so we got both a congress and a publication out of the experience; again, this was then most unusual for those still in graduate school.[17] In fact, shortly after this experience we proposed a panel on historical photographs to another congress and were rebuffed when we were "unmasked" as graduate students.

The notion of making the unseen visible was a key element of a third (and final) Super 8mm movie. While filming during road trips down to Mexico City in the early 1970s, I was shocked by what I then described as the "magnitude of American advertising, dress styles, and the whole host of goods and services which dominate the physical and psychological landscape of Mexico today."[18] I wasn't sure what to do with the footage until I ran across mention of a Basil Wright documentary, *Song of Ceylon* (1934), which mixed seventeenth-century travel accounts with contemporary footage. Inspired by Wright's example, I decided to make a film that would attest to the continuity of neocolonialism in Mexico, and invited a fellow history graduate student, Rick Chiles, to join me in shooting the still photographs and editing the film. We named it *Todo es más sabroso con . . . : An Historical Film-Essay on the Continuity of Neo-Colonialism in Mexico*, a title inspired by an advertising slogan that was painted all over Mexico: *TODO ES MÁS SABROSO CON PEPSI COLA* (Everything tastes better with Pepsi Cola). In writing up the experience of making the film, we explained the decision to make a "film-essay" as inspired by the example of German filmmaker Hans Richter, who argued that the simple chronological approach of most documentaries was not useful for the analyses he wished to carry out. He felt that "the film-essay can employ an incomparably greater reservoir of expressive means than can the pure documentary film," and that "the task given this sort of documentary film is to portray a concept. Even what is invisible must be made visible."[19]

The idea of our film was to make apparent the persistence of neocolonialism as composed of visual and audial manifestations. We drew visual data for this film from two different time periods, Porfirian Mexico (1876–1911) and the early 1970s. Still photographs from the *Porfiriato* were copied from a wide variety of illustrated travelers' and entrepreneurs' accounts of that period, which depicted European dress styles and modern modes of transportation, as well as neocolonial architecture and entertainment; those images were set in juxtaposition to my moving footage from the early seventies (all shot at least two hundred miles inside the border). Audial data consisted of two elements. Spoken commentary was taken from descriptions of early nineteenth-century excursions made by foreign scientists and businessmen such as Carl Sartorius, who documented the onset of globalization and neocolonialism by remarking on the way wealthy women's dress was "prescribed by the mighty decrees of Parisian tailors and dressmakers" and emphasizing the few gains that the traveled elite brought back with them:

> The young dandies who frequently visit the United States, France or England for a year, and as traveled lions return to their admiring cousins, instead of sound information, which might render their country good service, bring with them naught but a new dance, a bold cut for a dress or a frock coat; and all the fashionable world dances and dresses in the same manner.[20]

The music progressed chronologically. The nineteenth century was represented in Joseph Haydn's classical compositions, popular around the early independence period, and *Lucia di Lammermore*, the opera by Gaetano Donizetti performed in Mexico City in 1841. Placing the images and texts within a twentieth-century context was accomplished through Jacques Offenbach's *Gaîté Parisienne*, which became popular as the setting for the can-can in midcentury, and we ended with the Beatles song "With a Little Help from My Friends," sung in Spanish by Los Ángeles, a Mexican group, which provided a particularly sardonic touch.

We were able to get the film accepted at the 1974 congress of the Pacific Coast Council on Latin American Studies, where it was critiqued by professors E. Bradford Burns and Paul Vanderwood for what they perceived to be its Marxist politics. I polemically countered (tongue-in-cheek) that it was completely objective, since the narration and imagery were purely documentary; there was no omniscient commentary. The exchange was good-natured, for Burns was one of the first historians to take seriously the question of what film could offer the historical discipline (something that must have derived in part from his position at UCLA, one of the first universities to offer a doctorate in film studies), and Vanderwood was also beginning to explore the rigorous use of visual resources. We were later able to publish our reflections on the film in the PCCLAS journal.

DOING A HISTORICAL FILM AS A DISSERTATION

As I began to work more in using technical media to do history, my experiences—and those of some established historians who were also starting to dip their toes in those disdained waters—kept telling me that this was not only that to which I felt most attracted, but also an area badly in need of examples of how to do it in a truly rigorous manner. The die was cast: I had to find a way to explain to the history department why it was important to incorporate the use of modern media in this discipline. Today this might be included in one of the few visual studies departments, but that is such an amorphous field that I have my fears such a route could lack the training required by the historical discipline.[21] I started developing a thesis project for which the making of a film would somehow be justified, thinking that if I could demonstrate that there were certain things cinema offered that were different from the written word, I would be permitted to make a movie as a dissertation.

I decided that the film would be on La Decena Trágica, the Tragic Ten Days of February 9–19, 1913, in Mexico City, during which Victoriano Huerta overthrew the democratically elected government of Francisco I. Madero. I supported my proposal with a variety of propositions. One was that film could portray time differently than the written word. Hence, it could convey the sensation of being caught within an historical event such as the Decena Trágica where the experience of time was crucial to the decisions people made—for example, in understanding the pressure on the populace of Mexico City to accept Huerta's dictatorship. Obviously, this was before the widespread use of videocassettes, DVDs, and the whole gamut of modern home viewing technology that now gives viewers the same sort of control we have long had over reading.

I also based my position on theoretical and scientific work that was just beginning to appear. I cited the postmodern proposition of Hayden White's *Metahistory*, which—in asserting that history writing followed a "precritically accepted paradigm"—seemed at least to hint at the possibility of alternative forms of narration such as cinema.[22] Another recourse to vindicate audiovisual history was the "split brain" research of neuropsychologists such as Robert Sperry (awarded the Nobel Prize in 1981). One of his students, Michael Gazzaniga, was a professor at UCSB and had just published *The Bisected Brain*. A student of Gazzaniga was a good friend, and we often discussed this groundbreaking research that appeared to affirm that one side of the brain—the left—was good at verbal and analytic tasks, while the other was the seat of creative endeavors and spatial orientation. It seemed logical to me that we ought to employ both sides in doing history.

My thesis director, Jesús Chavarría, was a demanding though constant ally, as well as my only real mentor, both academically and politically. It was he who in large part transformed my worldview from the one I had inherited as a privileged member of the upper-middle class, concerned only with feathering my nest, to eventually becoming a Marxist capable of understanding the oppression under which the great majority of people in the world live. Of course, the larger contexts of protests against the Vietnam War, as well as the cultural aspects of the "Peace & Love" movement, had also been crucial in opening my mind. A pivotal event in my conversion to critical thinking had occurred in 1966 when I was at Orange Coast College. I went to a lecture given by members of the Newport Beach Police Department in which they expounded upon the horrors of marijuana. I'd smoked grass in Mexico City in 1962 and enjoyed it. When I came back to California in 1966 I discovered that its use had become widespread among the young, and I returned to smoking it. I carried out research for a term paper on marijuana: how it became illegal and the limited health hazards it posed; with that information in hand, I confronted the police at the end of their talk. As we argued, one blurted out, "I bet you're against the Vietnam War too." I hadn't really thought about the war, especially while I was in the army or working on dam construction in Eastern Washington, but I suddenly felt I should become more informed.

One real turning point of consciousness was experiencing the overreaction of the police and National Guard during the 1970 Isla Vista riots, when residents were indiscriminately clubbed and gassed in what was described as a breakdown in orthodox law enforcement worse than the 1968 Chicago convention. In fact, it was so extreme that conservative intellectual William F. Buckley was moved to describe it as "what would seem to be utterly senseless examples of repression."[23] I still retained some faith in the US, so I wrote a letter to Governor Ronald Reagan hoping that I could somehow communicate the state terror that had been loosed on our community; I received a letter in return thanking me for supporting his position in sending in the Guard and assuring me that "law and order" would be established by any means available. Living during 1974–75 with my friend US historian Chuck Churchill was an education in itself, as we constantly discussed the importance of developing a critical consciousness of oppression and exploitation, as well as the need to find ways of struggling against it. I remember a fellow student in Latin American history moving over into European studies in this period. When I asked him why he had done so, he replied that you have to be either an apologist for multinational corporations or a Marxist if you are going to work on Latin America, and he didn't want to be either. As John Womack observed, "I believe that most of the people who've gone to Latin America to study its history . . . come back reds of one kind or another."[24]

In studying Latin American history under Jesús, I found that a materialist method that employed concepts such as neocolonialism explained the "underdevelopment" of that area more clearly than did other approaches. Jesús was eventually denied tenure, and I am convinced that it was because he was a Marxist; he published a fine study of José Carlos Mariategui, but to no avail.[25] Some think that US universities are leftist, but that has never been my experience. There is much more mind control in US academia than in Mexican public universities (private colleges in Mexico are, with few exceptions, reactionary business schools). I am reminded of this difference when I go up to give lectures in the US. After one talk on Cuban photography, the professor who had invited me said that she could never say in her class the sort of things I had just expressed; she would be denied tenure. As that lecture was roundly criticized from completely opposite ideological standpoints, in the Casa de las Américas in Havana and at the University of Miami, I felt that I was probably walking a middle ground of some objectivity.

At one point around 1973 I was ready to leave the doctorate, move to Los Angeles, and try to make educational films, but Jesús was a battler and argued that staying in academia would permit me to do what I wanted. He was a founder and director of the Chicano Studies Research Center, the first such entity in the country (alongside that of UCLA). He was also instrumental in writing the "Plan de Santa Bárbara," considered to be the manifesto of Chicano studies, and he participated in establishing the Department of Chicano Studies.[26] He contended that if I fought it out, we could eventually win. Our intense, ongoing discussions forced me to define my interests and hone my arguments, until I could finally say, "This is what I want and am going to do: Latin American history through modern media."

Despite Jesús' support, my theoretical ratiocinations crashed upon academia's harsh shoals when I went to discuss my proposal for the film on the Tragic Ten Days with the director of the history graduate program. I was still quite innocent of the sort of reactions that can occur among scholars when they feel threatened by something new in their field. The director was a relatively honest person and, though others might have preferred to leave me with the appearance of accommodation, he could hardly restrain himself when we began talking. In a flash, he lost his temper and loudly asserted, "You are not going to make a laughingstock of this department," a phrase he repeated with great vehemence. I could see that there was little point in continuing our discussion, so I muttered an excuse and left his office. I flew up the stairs to Jesús' office, where he nonchalantly assured me that there was little to worry about. Then his office door burst open, and the director strode in, shouting his now well-worn phrase.

The history department finally resolved the issue with what they must have felt was a compromise. I was awarded a Regents' Fellowship for 1974–75 and informed that I should prepare myself for the Master's exam. I had entered directly into the doctorate program, but I was now to be sent away from UCSB with a "terminal" Master's degree; given my lack of options, it sounded much like terminal cancer. Time may have been on my side, but history—at least insofar as it was practiced in academia—decidedly was not. In fact, a lot of experimentation with the "visual turn" was going on at that time by professors in the UC and California State University systems. Vanderwood and Burns were writing on cinema, while Griffin, Carlos Cortés, and Leon Campbell were making films as well as reflecting on the issue.[27] All of them—especially Vanderwood—were very supportive of my struggle to do history with modern media. Cortés had his reservations about the possibilities that such work would ever be accepted by history departments. He had co-directed a 16 mm film, *Northwest from Tumacacori* (1972), about the string of Spanish missions, and commented emphatically that he would never make another film, because it was twice the work of writing a book, and he got no professional credit at all.

My last academic year at UCSB was important in bringing to fruition several projects. Thanks to a teaching grant Jesús procured, I made three audiovisual productions on the social and political history of Latin America: *Broken Spears, 1450–1783*; *The Two Ways, 1775–1910*; and *Dependency and Nationalism, 1885–1974*. They were composed of around one thousand slides, so I had pretty much copied all the visual material that was available in the UCSB library. I accompanied the images with appropriate Latin American music and texts developed from a variety of documentary sources. I also created an audiovisual production with colleagues, *The Great Depression*, and we were eventually able to show it at the National Convention of the Association for Educational Communications and Technology. At one point on the sound track, a woman being interviewed broke down crying upon remembering the hard times, saying through her tears, "I wouldn't want to have to go through that again"; it provided a moving testimony together with the dramatic pictures of photographers such as Dorothea Lange and Walker Evans.

Imagery from the Farm Security Administration (FSA) also formed part of my first photography exhibit, *Visions of History*, curated together with fellow history graduate students. It was intentionally polemic, contrasting photos of the Great Depression in the US with those of revolutions in

Mexico, Russia, China, and Cuba. It was exhibited at UCSB and later at UCSC. I believe that this is a very important form of visual history, with its own possibilities and limitations. As I was later to learn in Mexico with exhibits on the New Photojournalism and the Mexican Revolution, the time constraints under which a curator operates make it impossible to dedicate the years to research that a historian would under normal conditions. That caveat notwithstanding, it is crucial to produce a lasting product such as a book or a cinema production out of the curatorial experience because once an exhibit has been taken down, it essentially ceases to exist, as did *Visions of History*, although not before causing a controversy in the UC Santa Cruz newspaper when I mounted it there.

In my last year at UCSB I learned a lot about using images and participant narratives to teach history in the first classes I gave, which were in Ventura Community College in 1974–1975. I quickly became convinced that pictures were essential to teaching because I had a night class from eight to eleven p.m., composed largely of adults. They were firemen and secretaries, policemen and housewives, people who would come in after working all day. The very first night I got up to lecture them from behind the speaker's podium—as I had seen my professors do—and their eyes began to drop like shutters. So I decided that for the next session we were going to first talk about the assigned reading, then go and get some coffee. On returning to the classroom, I turned out the lights and showed them slides of Civil War photographs and engravings while reading accounts about that conflict—for example, letters from prisoners in Andersonville. They loved it. From then on that became my method for teaching history, because it offered the possibility for students to relate to something concrete that they could see for themselves, as well as hear through personal accounts, rather than listening to a professor expound about topics that the students had no background with which to interact. I believe that one of the principle problems in teaching is resistance; images let students see things for themselves and, as the images sparked their interest, they began to ask questions. I'd found one way of avoiding what Paul Tillich called "the fatal pedagogical error": "to throw answers like stones at the heads of those who have not yet asked the question."[28]

CONTINUING THE STRUGGLE AT UCSC

Despite my work in doing history with technical media, I was constantly frustrated in my attempts to communicate to historians what I was trying to do. Moreover, in that moment I had no idea what would become of my life when the one-year fellowship ran out; academia seemed closed to my efforts, and the only option appeared to be teaching at the high school level. However, my luck suddenly changed: in a conversation with David Sweet, then an assistant professor at UC Santa Cruz, Jesús described the battles we had waged—and lost. Sweet suggested that I come there to continue my education. Unfortunately, the dean of graduate studies was much against my entering, arguing that I was an aging and problematic student who would never amount to anything and would most likely never even finish a dissertation (something I was fortunately told long after).

The moment was such that new history journals were appearing with an interest in modern media. I was able to publish articles on the representation of history in the Cuban movie *Lucía* (Solás, 1968) in *Film & History*, and two co-authored reflections on making historical films that were printed in other publications.[29] This was something very unusual for graduate students at that time, and although both of my "sponsors" were assistant professors (Julianne Burton was the other), and therefore had little power within UCSC, those publications provided the "proof" necessary for me to be accepted in the largely nonexistent history doctorate. That experience taught me something I always emphasize in talking with young professors and graduate students who want to work in modern media, citing Bob Dylan: "To live outside the law you must be honest."[30] If you are doing something new, you have to produce more than scholars who are following beaten paths in order to convince your peers that your work is of professional quality.

At UCSC, I initially continued in my efforts to make a film for my dissertation. However, a conversation with a professor whom I had asked to serve on my committee gave me pause when he provided the most intelligent negative response to my thesis proposal. At my invitation, he replied that he had never made a film and so could not adequately judge what sort of research was necessary in order for it to be accepted as a dissertation. I finally comprehended that it would be a long uphill battle from a vulnerable and debilitated position, which I would almost surely lose. The cost of making a 16 mm film was another consideration. I was barely making ends meet, so the idea of spending a lot of time looking for money seemed absurd. I am reminded of what Orson Welles (a ridiculous comparison) said about his career, when he reflected that he hadn't spent his life directing films, but rather in looking for the money to make them.

Perhaps most importantly, I understood that I could not change anything from outside the professorial ranks. I had to get through (or over) the wall and change it from the inside, as a faculty member. I believed that the same process had to occur in audiovisual history that was at that moment (around 1975) taking place in the study of film: the first generation of doctorates in cinema history, theory, and criticism had been formed under the guidance of professors from comparative literature and theater arts. However, once those students got their degrees, they founded film studies departments. I imagined (and continue to do so) that if enough historians became interested in producing studies utilizing modern media, the situation would change, as is happening today (at least in Mexico and Brazil). I began to think about doing a thesis that would be acceptable to get that degree.

My move away from making historical movies to studying the cinematic representation of history on commercial screens was decided at my qualifying exams in June 1976. As we were finishing up, Burton made the suggestion that I undertake a dissertation on historical depictions in Cuban cinema, a topic about which I had already published and that was a fulcrum of the academic interest that was developing around the New Latin American Cinema. I accepted the idea because it seemed an attractive and possibly innovative project, as well as one that would be acceptable to the history department as a form of cultural history. Nonetheless, I was constantly reminded by Sweet that the degree was to be in history, not film studies: "What you write might have a lot to say to people interested in Cuban cinema, but what you have to worry about is whether it says anything to historians."[31] I never questioned his wisdom on this point. He was right, and that demand required me to develop the appropriate method for making the dissertation properly historical.

I spent five years at UCSC, mainly working in film studies. Sweet was always the director of my dissertation, and I had much interaction with Burton, who was becoming well known in studies on the New Latin American Cinema. However, the professor I worked with most was Janey Place, who was one of the first in the US to get a PhD in cinema studies. She focused on visual style, principally that of John Ford's films, and I found myself most comfortable in bringing to bear that form of analysis as I made frame enlargements from different Cuban films to offer as research supporting my analyses. For me, films are first and foremost visual experiences; as director Douglas Sirk observed, "The angles are the director's thoughts. The lighting is his philosophy."[32] On working with Janey, I felt that I had acquired a method for my madness, and I finally finished my dissertation—based largely on the visual methods I learned from her—in 1986, after I had moved to Mexico.

My work in analyzing historical films has almost always been undertaken from an ocular perspective. While at UCSC, I made hundreds of frame enlargements from Cuban films, rolling the 16 mm movies from one reel to another and using a special plastic camera to reproduce the frames. Today, making "film grabs" from digitalized material is very easy with a computer, and I am a bit surprised that more colleagues do not employ that as a mode of analysis. I utilized the frame enlargements to study the film *Lucía*, demonstrating how human relations between women, between men and women, and among the races were visually depicted. Then I pointed out how high angle and mirror shots were fundamental in the development of the narrative. I discussed the incorporation of documentary style and moved on to consider how the different themes of the three segments were structured visually.[33] The other film I studied in depth was the remarkable *Memories of Underdevelopment* (Gutiérrez Alea, 1967), for which I did a video deconstruction.[34] I continued to apply this method to Mexican cinema, above all in comparing the representation of the revolution by Fernando de Fuentes with that of Emilio Fernández and Gabriel Figueroa; and I eventually included the Cuban work as well.[35]

The tricky thing about the visual is that it looks so easy. People think that anyone can take pictures, and that anyone can analyze them. Janey recounted an experience she had about dissecting visual style when she was studying for her PhD at UCLA. She had argued that there is a visual hint of a romantic atmosphere between John Wayne's character and his brother's wife in John Ford's *The Searchers* (1956). Her thesis director said that was nonsense. So Janey showed the film to him without sound, demonstrating how the wife touches John Wayne's coat in an endearing way. She proved her point, but her thesis director disdained her research, saying that it was obvious. Well, it was apparent once he was shown it, though it certainly wasn't before. That is what is difficult about visual analysis. It looks easy, but the moment that you have to sit down and write in a disciplined way about the visual structures of cinema and photography, there is nothing easy about it.

I continued to direct modern media productions while at UCSC. Sweet was crucial in orienting my ocular work toward social history. He was much impressed by the slides I had brought from UCSB, but equally appalled by the fact that I had not annotated the images in terms of where, when, who, and what was depicted, as well as the source from whence they had been taken. He said I would quickly forget all that information, and he was right. However, since the purpose of the slides was to make the shows, I probably would not have been able to meet the deadlines had I taken the time to transcribe the pertinent information. This problem often occurs in doing history with modern media: we are compiling material for specific projects, such as a cinema production or a photo exhibit, and don't have the time to extract all the data. I spent the next several years finding the books from which I had made the images and filling in note cards with that data.

David organized a showing of one of my audiovisuals about recent Latin American history, *Dependency and Nationalism, 1885–1974*, and invited the history faculty. Only one fellow came, a senior professor who was known to be highly intelligent but very sardonic. After I presented the production, he sat back and observed acidly that it might be a nice little appetizer, but one would hardly want to call it history. I was stunned into silence by his criticism: What could I say? How could I reach across that intellectual chasm to make him understand how important it is to include modern media in our histories? Most importantly, how was I to receive the necessary criticism to develop this sub-discipline, if it was simply discarded at the outset?

In 1976, Sweet was awarded a teaching grant to make nine visual presentations of eighty slides each for his classes on Latin American history. He wanted the presentations to be about Argentina, Bolivia, Chile, Cuba, the Dominican Republic, Guatemala, Haiti, Nicaragua, and Uruguay. It was a formidable task, and the limited resources of the UCSC library were inadequate. Fortunately, Berkeley was nearby, so I spent much time uncovering the visual materials there and bringing the books with the new images to UCSC to be photographed. The job allowed me to continue to develop an extensive slide collection that I believed would eventually be used in teaching introductory courses on Latin American history. Working with Sweet was very important for developing my knowledge of social history. As I read the books he suggested and worked on the visual presentations, I began to discover the incredible wealth of social and material detail in photographs.

Shortly after arriving in Santa Cruz, I directed an interview-based videotape that focused on medical care in the US: *"That's the medicine business for you, full of no guarantees": A Video-Essay on American Medicine and the Media*, which was mentioned for a Special Jury Award at the 1978 Athens Video Festival. However, my most ambitious project was a videotape production that was to be a long, illustrated interview with Alex Haley. He was very famous in that moment for his book *Roots: The Saga of an American Family*, which was subsequently made into an enormously popular television miniseries.[36] Working with Robert Chacanaca, I rented and requisitioned a full studio setup: two large color cameras mounted on moveable tripods, a host of lighting equipment, and a professional soundboard. The idea was to shoot Haley with the two cameras at the same time, and then to edit the footage, using the best take, and illustrating the text with other visual material. However, for some reason, we could never get the footage from the two cameras to maintain color when editing between them, so the project was scrapped. The only memorable thing about the videotape was the music of Bob Brozman, a wonderful guitarist who went on to international renown; his performance for the tape confirmed my belief in the importance of paying serious attention to the music employed.

The Haley tape was a product of what I described as a "Personal History Project," which I was proposing to UCSC's Oakes College in hopes of creating a position there. Although it certainly didn't seem so at the time, I was very fortunate that proposal was rejected. When I left UCSC in 1980 I had little or no opportunities for a job, because I hadn't finished my dissertation. The move toward neoliberal economics had curtailed university funding, history departments were losing enrollments, and "administrative bloat" was beginning to drain off precious resources, both in the expansion of personnel and in the higher salaries they are paid.[37] Moreover, it was the heyday of Affirmative Action, a program I had seen fundamentally transform the face of US universities from the panorama of old White men that I'd encountered at UCLA in 1961 into a varied and multicolored scene that included women and minorities. In fact, those new faculty had been instrumental in giving me the opportunity to be in academia. Sweet was a White man, but all the other professors who aided me—Chavarría, Place, and Burton—came from the new groups entering the universities. And, while I couldn't convince Herman Blake—the founding provost of Oakes College and the first African American to be hired at UCSC—to incorporate my project as a permanent feature at Oakes, he did give me a year of free housing to develop it. The current backlash against Affirmative Action is reprehensible in a country of so many hues. And if that program hindered to some extent my access to US academia in that moment, I was later presented with more interesting opportunities.

I moved to Berkeley in 1980, going off into an ill-defined future. My last meeting with Sweet featured him insinuating that I was a "fraud." I could not really dispute that because, after a second lustrum of postgraduate studies in search of a history doctorate, I had little more in terms of credentials than those with which I had arrived at UCSC (though I had passed my qualifying exams, and I'd certainly acquired a lot of knowledge that would prove useful in the future). An old friend from UCSB hired me to make ethnographic videos on schools in the Bay Area for the Multi-Ethnic School Environments Project, Far West Laboratory for Educational Research and Development. That was my "day job," but I was more excited about being part of a video collective, Grand Illusions, which was dedicated to making organizing videotapes for workers on strike, as well as for the solidarity movement with the revolutionaries in El Salvador.

The transformative event of my year in the Bay Area was meeting Eli Bartra, who was visiting a friend in San Francisco in the fall of 1980. She accompanied me on a shoot for the tape we were making for the striking restaurant and hotel workers of Local 2 union, and we spent a week together. In February 1981, my connections with radical media groups led to an invitation to smuggle in sound equipment for La Peña Morelos in Tepito, a "heart" of Mexico City noted for its cultural heights and criminal depths. I'd been in black market activities in Italy while in the army—more for the adventure than the money (and the hotel room in Iesolo where the manager took the cigarettes, clothing, and records I brought in exchange). I figured that the only thing that could happen to me in Mexico was that the sound equipment would be taken away. And that's what happened; the two huge speakers and a very large soundboard I brought with me were immediately confiscated. The next week passed in a surreal situation typical of Mexico. The days were spent going from one government office to another, and the nights consisted of Paralympic athletes coming in their wheelchairs to scold me for not bribing the customs officials. I tried to explain that I was not given any money, and that I was poor, a story that did not go down well among *Tepiteños*. I finally got hold of Eli and ended up in Coyoacán with her. There, the idea was born of my moving to Mexico, and when I did so my background in modern media was most helpful for me in getting work. I experienced in my own skin how visual studies can offer many possibilities beyond teaching.

LIVING IN MEXICO

On the morning of July 14, 1981, I arrived in Mexico City with a camera and about three hundred dollars in my pocket, to live with someone with whom I had spent a total of some fifteen days. Although I did not yet know it, I was a visual person coming into contact with an eminently ocular culture. From the very beginning, I encountered the importance of personal connections that so characterizes Mexican society. As Steven Zamora, the first Hispanic dean of the Law Center at the University of Houston, articulately expressed, "Talking with Mexicans about networking would be like talking to fish about water."[38] Tired of battling in universities over the past ten years, I was uncertain where to look for work until Eli asked whether I wouldn't like a job in television. She had a good friend who produced programs for the Secretariat of Public Education (SEP), and thought that there might be a possibility of working for him. We walked over to the Churubusco Studios and met with Vicente Silva. I hardly spoke Spanish, so after a few minutes, Vicente switched to English as he showed me the different options among the various series he produced. I indicated that one of them, *Como jugando*—a program that showed children working as if they were playing, had the sort of documentary style to which I was most accustomed. He then asked me whether I wanted to be a director or producer.

Absolutely stunned by the opportunity offered me so soon after getting off the plane, I managed to control my reaction long enough to say "director." Vicente looked at the tape I had been making in San Francisco for the multi-ethnic research project and—after a quick minute—determined "production." I was just delighted to have a job. I travelled around Mexico with the unit for *Como jugando*, working with more-established directors such as Sergio Olhovich, as well as younger filmmakers Raúl Busteros and José Luis García Agraz. I became friends with them, particularly with cinematographer Jack Lach, during the evenings we spent drinking together; Jack and I remained close, and later collaborated in producing a demo for a planned historical reconstruction. As 1981 drew to a close, Vicente called me in and told me that I would not be able to continue working for him, because his entire production unit was now going to dedicate itself to the presidential campaign of Miguel de la Madrid, and they couldn't have a gringo circulating in that atmosphere. I thanked him profusely for the opportunity he had given me to learn Spanish, earn some money, and begin to know the country in which I had come to live.

WORKING IN LABOR HISTORY

I threw myself into this chaotic, sensual culture, and felt much at home in a liberating society that allowed me to express my own anarchy. After leaving television, I floundered about for a bit, but personal connections came once again to my aid when Eli told me that a friend at the Universidad Autónoma Metropolitana-Xochimilco had mentioned that there was an opening in the publications area of the Centro de Estudios Históricos del Movimiento Obrero Mexicano (CEHSMO), which was founded and directed by Enrique Suárez Gaona. I met with him a few days later, and after he had looked at my curriculum, he asked why I would want to work in publications; I responded that I needed a job in order to continue living in Mexico. He then questioned whether I wouldn't prefer to be CEHSMO's Coordinador de Historia Gráfica. I was flabbergasted at the opportunity, and it was my first experience with what I call Mexico's "enlightened administrators," individuals who have vision and a good deal of autonomy that they employ to carry out projects rather than to enrich themselves (as too often also seems to have been the case in Mexico). Enrique said, "Well, now you're the coordinator. I'm glad that's settled. It's almost time for the World Cup games to begin; get your stuff and come on home with me to watch the games and eat."[39] Well, we went to drink and then eat while watching the games. This became a pattern during the Cup: I would arrive around ten in the morning and work for a while in the photo archive. Enrique came in around noon, carried out whatever administrative tasks he had to, and then we would leave around two or so to go drink and eat together at his house. I was as entranced by the Mexican integration of social life and work as I was astounded by the possibility of being in charge of a photographic archive and using images to explore ways of doing history.

In my experience, drinking is a fundamental aspect of male bonding in Mexico. Once Enrique and I began to drink together seriously, I was in his inner circle: we were invited to parties in the home of he and his wife, and they came to the gatherings that Eli and I organized. I enthusiastically entered into my duties: developing the photographic archive and publishing articles. But it was the combination of the social connection and my work ethic that was definitive in gaining Enrique's confidence. I was an immigrant with no "golden parachute," but I was also working at what I most loved. The year or so I was in CEHSMO was crucial in introducing me to Mexican photographic archives. I would spend the day in the Archivo General de la Nación (AGN), making copies of the images in the Departamento de Trabajo, and afternoons researching in the Hermanos Mayo archive. In both cases, photographs were just beginning to become accessible for study. The DT-AGN photos had been ripped out of the original files and thrown into a dusty box, where I found and began to relate them to the cases they pictured; the Mayo archive had not yet entered into the AGN.

Working in these archives was a dream come true, but I also had an experience that began to teach me the limits of what was permitted in state-funded institutions such as CEHSMO. One of my assignments was to curate an exposition, *El Movimiento Obrero Mexicano, 1857–1980*. It was exhibited around Mexico and in Cuba, a country with whom CEHSMO, and some leftist PRI administrators such as Enrique, then had very close relations. However, I quickly became aware of the limits of officialist leftists when I proposed to include some images by the Hermanos Mayo of the 1958–59 strikes. All photos in which the army was pictured were immediately eliminated by the director. I could show the strikers in action, and even include repression by the police, but the Mexican army was then as untouchable as was the president; both would remain so for many years. CEHSMO was dependent upon the Secretary of Labor, and Enrique had managed to avoid stepping on the toes of the party dictatorship by essentially sticking to the early periods of labor organization, up through the *Porfiriato* and the early postrevolution. I began to think that a return to academia would give me more freedom, despite the fact that working for government-run enterprises such as SEP television and CEHSMO was certainly more interesting than anything I had previously envisioned.

Whatever doubts I was experiencing about continuing in CEHSMO quickly became irrelevant, because the ten-year run of the Center ended with Miguel de la Madrid's presidency (1982–86). Enrique told me to take the photo archive, because it would end up in some warehouse and eventually be destroyed. I began casting about for another job in the middle of a brutal transition to a neoliberal economy, including the debt crisis, an inflation rate of 100 percent, the constant devaluations of the peso, and the prerequisite of Mexican citizenship in order to apply for a position. I found myself trapped in the catch-22 of the Mexican immigration system: I could not look for work because I did not have a work permit, and I could not obtain a permit without having a job. I had worked illegally in television and at CEHSMO, but jobs were now so scarce that those opportunities had disappeared, and one of the requirements for a foreigner was that he or she would be engaged in an occupation that could not be carried out by a Mexican. Getting married was one solution, but when Eli and I met with the bureaucrat in charge of authorizing our matrimony, he asked me to prove economic solvency. Eli stated that she would support me until I could get a work permit; his response was: "Aquí no queremos mantenidos" (We don't want any kept men here). Had I been a woman, I would have had no problem getting permission to marry a Mexican, but as a man it was expected that I should be providing for the family. I had a couple of strategies to earn a living: one was to employ my film background to apply for a grant to study Mexican cinema, but this option closed when the UNAM Filmoteca did not support my efforts.

The other possibility was using the CEHSMO archive to open up some sort of position, and after an anguishing year in unemployment during which I often considered returning to the US, I was able to enter the Universidad Autónoma de Puebla (UAP) in 1984. This was again a result of the connections I had as a member of the Bartra family that, in addition to Eli (one of the founders of neo-feminism in the 1970s), also includes the distinguished intellectuals Roger Bartra and Armando Bartra. I was offered a temporary position in the Centro de Investigaciones Históricas del Movimiento Obrero (CIHMO) at that university, and won a tenured post in 1985. Getting a permanent *plaza* in a public Mexican research university is different from the process in the US or the United Kingdom. Although this situation is changing, positions are rarely advertised; moreover, if they are announced, they are often *retratos hablados* (an agreed upon portrait), a job description so limited in terms of field, interest, and historical period so as to be uniquely applicable to the desired candidate. Usually a job seeker proposes (or is invited to propose) a project for which they are hired on a temporary basis. If they show promise, progress in their work, and get along with their colleagues, a permanent *plaza* with a *retrato hablado* will be opened to a competition that they will win and, hence, be granted *definitividad* (tenure).

I began to write articles about doing history with photographs, using some of the images that I had collected while at CEHSMO. One essay was published in a magazine of some circulation and importance, *Nexos*, which was the first time I participated as a "public intellectual" in Mexico.[40] It appeared shortly before Russell Jacoby's well-known book *The Last Intellectuals* signaled a significant transformation among US scholars. Jacoby asserted that they had formerly directed themselves to an educated public, but with their increasing incorporation into academia, questions of tenure and academic recognition became more important than being involved in cultural politics.[41] For me, it was an extraordinary and unique experience to feel that I was part of a larger cultural dialogue, beyond academic walls, and during the decade from the mid-1980s to the mid-1990s I participated in many periodicals, especially a very popular Sunday supplement, the magazine *La Jornada Semanal* of the leftist newspaper *La Jornada*.

Aside from the photo archive, I enjoyed another advantage in an academic world that was just beginning to undergo a fundamental transition with the creation of the Sistema Nacional de Investigadores (SNI) in 1984. I held a Master's degree and had passed my qualifying exams for the doctorate, whereas few Mexican academics had doctorates, including historians of such stature as Adolfo Gilly.[42] The great majority of professors had remained at the level of the *licenciatura* (BA), because Mexican universities required a thesis for all degrees. Many found the process of writing a dissertation so onerous that they had little desire—or need—to go on to studies at the level of masters or doctorates. The SNI brought a much-needed reform to the politics of *amigüismo* (connections through friends) within universities—above all those in the provinces, but it also took away the incentive to publish in popular periodicals because articles that aren't peer reviewed were not recognized. At the same time, the cultural supplements of newspapers, which had provided spaces for figures as important as Carlos Monsiváis, began to gradually disappear. However, in the 1980s and 1990s, I was impressed by how much more respect and recognition historians, and all intellectual workers, received in Mexico compared to the US.

Alfonso Vélez Pliego was the UAP rector when I entered, and the most visionary individual I have known. He was directly responsible for saving the colonial buildings of Puebla, buying those in good condition with university funds, and bargaining with Puebla's governors to take over what were essentially ruins, which were then restored beautifully. In 1987, Puebla's historic center was named as a UNESCO World Heritage Cultural Centre, one of the first sites to receive such recognition in Mexico. Alfonso was an internationalist who had recruited a large number of foreigners for the UAP, people who were attracted by the Marxist orientation of his administration, as well as the opportunity to work in research institutes; one of the sterling examples is the philosopher John Holloway, who was enticed to leave the University of Edinburgh.[43]

Alfonso understood that Mexican academia was about to undergo a process of *homologación* that would require university professors to have the higher degrees required in the US. One of his favorite stories was about the time he assembled his upper-level administrators and department directors to treat the issue of how the UAP could open doctorate programs, given the fact that almost no one had such a degree. At one point, one of the attendees suggested that they all award one another doctorates, and then proceed from there. For Alfonso, part of the solution was to import academics with those degrees, and that played a role in my acceptance in CIHMO-UAP with my project to carry out a visual history of Mexican workers. There, I quickly became involved in a video project on the history of the Mexican railroad workers, together with Gloria Tirado, who worked in that field. We asked for funding to make a videotape, but by the time it arrived, inflation and devaluations had so reduced its value that it served only to buy the ¾-inch tapes for the interviews. Without money to continue the project, the tapes were put away for three years.

In the meantime, I settled into my position as a research professor in CIHMO and developed friendships with *Poblanos*, usually over cantina tables. We would gather at Vittorio's, a bar-restaurant in the center's famous *portales* (archways) around two or so to begin our *pachanga* (party). When Alfonso was rector, he could always be found there after midday, where he would attend to any questions or confrontations that presented themselves; a far cry from today when the rectors hide themselves amid their bodyguards. We rarely ate more than *antojitos* (snacks) at Vittorio's and would sometimes drink until eight p.m., when we would suddenly decide to dine, although finding a restaurant that would accept a bunch of drunken *vagos* (bums, as we called ourselves) was not always easy; at times we partied until the early morning. At one point, when I had returned from a particularly long night in Puebla, Eli said that I was going to lose my job if I continued in this lifestyle. I told her that I was drinking with the very people that would have to fire me.

One of the keenest observers of drinking in Mexico is Tim Mitchell.[44] He cited a British social anthropologist who wrote of the heavy drinking at Mexican fiestas that "it is merely patronizing to leave exotic ethnographic models of the world uncriticized, as if their possessors were children who could be left to play forever in an enchanted garden of their own devising."[45] Mitchell critiqued that position, contrasting the approach to drinking in Mexico and the US:

> This brings us right back to the classic contrast between the biomedical and anthropological perspectives—the former very attuned to the health costs of drinking, the latter to the benefits: communitas, peer respect, redistribution of wealth, male-bonding, procreation, stress-relief, ecstasy. And note: we are the ones living in an "enchanted garden" if we think that it will be easy to persuade certain groups to adopt different time-mapping strategies. It is quite easy, by contrast, to see how scandalous a guiltlessly hedonistic or death-welcoming culture might be for a culture as medicalized and death-fearing as our own [the US], characterized by the compulsive search for longevity and more time.[46]

Death is near and ever-present in Mexico, and I find that it makes you live with greater passion and commitment; an intense life is preferable to a long one. It is somehow comforting to reside among people who seem to have found a way of incorporating our greatest fear in an acceptance that can border on the festive at times. After the earthquake of September 19, 2017, a Portuguese woman was interviewed on television. She said that she had been living in Mexico City for four years, but had not really known the country until the earthquake and its aftermath. She was overwhelmed by the solidarity among citizens who immediately stepped up to help victims, noting that there was not a lot of crying and sniveling, just a wealth of positive energy among people who did what had to be done by incorporating it as a social experience. She summed it up: "These people really know how to live."[47]

Another recent example of how death is viewed in Mexico was provided by Oscar-winning director Guillermo del Toro. A reporter asked him about his worldview: "You really understand how to look into the shadow side, the darker side of human nature and fantasy and terror. But you also are a really joyful and loving person. So, how do you find that balance?" Del Toro's impromptu response is articulate:

> I'm Mexican. And, no one loves life more than we do in a way because we are so conscious about death. So, the preciousness of life stands side by side to the one place that we are all going. Let's say, everybody in this planet boarded a train whose final destination is death. So [on] this train we're going to live, we're going to have beauty, and love and freedom. I think that when you eliminate one of the two sides of the equation, it's a pamphlet. When you take into account the dark to tell [about] the life, its reality.[48]

How do we account for the particular social construction of death that we find in Mexico, such that André Breton was moved to make his oft-cited remark, "The power of conciliation of life and death is, without any doubt, Mexico's principle appeal"?[49] The founder of Surrealism was writing during the late 1930s when the postrevolutionary cultural effervescence created a "gay familiarity with death [that] became a cornerstone of national identity."[50] However, the initial sources of this worldview may well be related to Nahuatl ideas about death, as in the writings of ancient Mexico's greatest poet, Netzhualcoyotl, who insistently emphasized that we are on earth for only a brief time: "All the earth is a grave and nothing escapes it; nothing is so perfect that it does not descend to its tomb."[51] Further, Aztec use of human sacrifice as a calculated instrument of their statecraft must be taken into account; one historian estimated that in 1487, more than eighty thousand individuals were killed over the course of four days.[52] The effects of the Spanish conquest were another contributing factor. Following their defeat, Amerindians experienced the sixteenth-century holocaust in which scholars have estimated that between half and 90 percent of the indigenous population was wiped out.[53] Among the fruits that such devastation produced was a daily familiarity with death, which was no doubt an element contributing to extensive alcohol consumption; as one historian remarked, "Few peoples in the whole of history were more prone to drunkenness than the Indians of the Spanish colony."[54] Further, Mexico's independence was attained only after a long, bloody, and destructive war in which around 10 percent of the population died, certainly a higher proportion than was the case in any other such movement in the New World.[55]

The Spanish brought their own particular perspective on death. As Hans Magnus Enzenberger observed, "In Spain, death is like a friend, a comrade, a worker you know from the field, the workshop. When he comes you don't make a great fuss because of him."[56] The hybridity of these cultures was consolidated into a singularly Mexican perspective by the revolution in which it is estimated that between 2,000,000 and 3,500,000 people died out of a population of fifteen million.[57] One scholar asserted, "Death emerged as a national totem in the aftermath of the Mexican Revolution. . . . For the artists of the 1920s, the symbolic valence of the Mexican's intimacy with death was antithetical to the violence of colonialism, imperialism, and capitalist exploitation."[58] In the 1980s, intellectuals Roger Bartra and Carlos Monsiváis critiqued these ideas, arguing that it was a mythology rather than an expression of popular culture. Bartra described the idea of Mexicans' so-called indifference to death as "A myth that has two sources: the religious fatality that sponsors a miserable life as well as the contempt of the powerful for workers' lives."[59] Both Bartra and Monsiváis assert that the idea was codified by Octavio Paz, among others, and later "transformed into an object of mass consumption and tourist art."[60]

While I believe that both Bartra's and Monsiváis' critiques are useful, I would argue from personal experience that, though Mexicans are certainly not "indifferent" to death, they have a profoundly distinct relationship with it from the denial and invisibility practiced in European and US culture since the end of the nineteenth century. One recent manifestation in Mexico of this socially and politically structured phenomenon is the spectacular growth of the Santa Muerte cult since the beginning of this century. This saint's immense attraction is derived in part, as anthropologist Wil Pansters argues, from "her great equalizing capacity, all the more so in a society as deeply unequal as neoliberal Mexico, for death undoes the differences between rich and poor."[61] The extraordinary attachment of Mexicans to the Day of the Dead, a tradition that began during the colonial period, is evidence of a long-term propinquity with *la madre Matiana*, just one of the numerous nicknames that are used to describe *la igualadora*.[62] As US and European societies have begun to reject the norms of medicalization and a refusal to accept death, looking instead to create different approaches to dealing with this fact of life, Mexican celebrations such as the *Día de Muertos* have acquired substantial international standing.

SHOOTING IN NICARAGUA

In 1986, Alfonso Vélez sent me to Nicaragua to make a video with the Sandinista Ministerio del Interior. His decision to send a gringo was an example of his internationalism because the US government had just given the Contra one hundred million dollars. On arriving in Managua, I asked the Nicaraguan producers what the video was to be about; they replied that I was the *videoasta* and could focus on any theme, but we had to remain in Managua because they could not provide forces to protect me from the Contra outside of the city. I was given a professional crew, equipment, and ¾-inch tapes, and had ten days to shoot the material that I took back to Mexico for editing. Prior experience had taught me that it was possible to shoot for ten days and have nothing that could be made into a work. I needed a central thread, and initially thought about making a work of denunciation, focusing on the Contra's atrocities. However, on my first day in Managua I heard of the Innovator's Movement, which was part of the Sandinista Workers' Center. I realized in a flash what I already knew from working on Cuban cinema: the extraordinary energy that is loosed in a revolutionary situation, where a spirit of exaltation and hope permeates society, and I decided that the Innovators would be the center of the production. In the videotape, *Innovating Nicaragua/Nicaragua innovando*, this movement is represented by laborers who fashion industrial replacement parts to circumvent the US blockade, and in the creativity displayed to meet daily needs of transportation, childcare, clothing, and food supply in the face of armed aggression.

Having lived in Mexico for several years, I was acquainted with the daily improvisation that is required in neocolonial societies; the concept of "innovation" seemed to be the revolutionary extension of improvisation. The effervescence I discovered as I filmed reminded me of Lee Lockwood's description of life after the triumph of the Cuban Revolution: "It was a fabulous time, one of those rare, magical moments of history when cynics are transformed into romantics and romantics into fanatics, and everything seems possible."[63] I shot in factories and stores and on the street for ten days, interviewing Nicaraguans from different levels of society, as well as capturing the murals denouncing imperialist intervention by representing the US as a figure of death draped in the stars and stripes. I also collected record albums for the sound track, and the music was copyright free, which allowed for greater choice. On returning to Mexico, I edited the tape very cheaply on a straight cut system that had many limitations. One reviewer of the Nicaraguan tape felt that its technical shortcomings represented a certain authenticity: "The charm of the movie is that it looks as if it were made as part of the same innovator's project. . . . Maybe you have to love Nicaragua to love this film with its . . . homemade character. But it is real. It is the way Nicaragua is."[64] In spite of its inadequacies, the videotape was bought by Cuban television, received some awards, and is distributed by the Cinema Guild (US), Macondo/Zafra (Latin America), and La Médiathèque des Trois Mondes (Europe).[65]

My Nicaraguan experience brought me up against my limitations as a leftist intellectual.[66] We were placed in the luxurious Hotel Internacional, which had been Somoza's bunker. There, we spent the nights drinking and dancing. On the first evening I got into a conversation with a correspondent from *In These Times*, a progressive US magazine. He had not been able to get a credential to the congress to which I was nominally attached, which dealt with autonomy for the Mosquito Coast. Since I was not going to be attending the congress, I gave him my credential, without understanding that it was the essential identification for entering the hotel. The next morning my Nicaraguan producer asked me where my credential was, and I said I must have misplaced it. He knew where it was: the Sandinistas had taken it away from the ITT correspondent when he tried to enter the congress because he was suspected of being a CIA agent. I doubted that, but spent the next week in the hotel trying to explain my lack of discipline to very young Sandinistas. My assertion that I had never been told that the credential was crucial fell on ears unacquainted with the casual way we deal with academic congress identifications. After a week, I was approached by one of the young attendants and told that my interview was set up with Tomás Borge, the minister of the Interior, whose department had given me the equipment. I felt that I had been treated unfairly and told her I would not interview Borge until they gave me back my credential. We were at an impasse until my hotel roommate, Edgar Bravo, one of the surviving members of a Colombian guerrilla force (then a UAP faculty member), stood up for me: "The *compañero* is a revolutionary who made a mistake, but he deserves to have his credential returned."[67] Coming from a man with four or five bullet holes in his body, his opinion carried weight. The Sandinistas had probably had me checked out by Cuban security, so my credential was returned and the interview took place.

In 1987, I returned to the videotape on the Mexican railroad workers, stimulated by its acceptance in that year's congress of the American Historical Association; it was to be part of a session dedicated to my work on what I then called *videohistory*, a most uncommon opportunity. I found the money to shoot two days of interviews with communist militants, railroad workers, and the directors of the short-lived Workers' Administration (1938–40) under President Lázaro Cárdenas. I was able to edit the tape at night in the studio of the Puebla state television system—if the governor had not given a speech that day; if he had, then his speech had to be edited, and I returned home with my box of tapes to wait until the next night. I found a music expert and was eventually able to finish the production *Made on Rails: A History of the Mexican Railroad Workers/Hechos sobre los rieles: Una historia de los ferrocarrileros mexicanos*, and it was shown at the AHA congress. Paul Vanderwood closed his review of the railroaders' tape and *Innovating Nicaragua* by expressing "admiration for a colleague who with little budget but with much ingenuity is 'writing' history through a medium which is generally appreciated but less well understood."[68]

MAKING INTERVIEW-BASED DOCUMENTARIES

My videotapes on Nicaragua and the history of the railroad workers fall into the category that Nichols calls "interactive documentaries," in which "the filmmaker and social actors acknowledge one another overtly in conversation, participatory actions, or interviews."[69] However, since the concept *interactive* has come to mean something very different in today's Internet world, I have decided to call this form *interview-based*, although it is far from felicitous. The narrative form of these productions is constructed from interviews, though they all also include much compilation material: still imagery such as photographs, posters, and magazines share screen time with documentary and fictional film footage. Given the possibility of having lengthy interviews and discussions thanks to lightweight digital equipment, it is clear that this is a fundamental style for doing cinehistories.

What are the implications of choosing this form? Although a history forged exclusively from informants may appear to be more objective—as in *cinema verité* (the very name itself points to the danger)—it is not; in fact, the very credibility that informants lend to the work may tend to interfere with the critical perspective which every good history ought to awaken in its audience. It may be difficult to get beyond or behind the vision of the interviewed; thus, it becomes the task of the cinehistorian to create a context that will distinguish between *memory* and *history*. Further, it is important to draw attention to some of the structural limitations that one confronts in attempting to do history through interviews. The director of the widely viewed BBC series *The World at War*, Jerry Kuehl, observed that there is a tendency among informants "to replace a candid, private version of events with a softer public version."[70] Interviews might appear to be intimate, but those that are filmed for historical documentaries are really stories recounted for the public, and informants can be quite circumspect.

The restraints particular to recording and recounting the past with cinema will shape that historical discourse in specific ways. What goes on during the conducting of interviews is of great importance to the finished product, and I believe that "rapport"—that delicate, if difficult to describe, relation between interviewer and informant—may well be the primary mediation of an interactive documentary's aesthetic. Often, personal and family relations are indispensable to establishing rapport, as were those of Gloria Tirado with the *ferrocarrileros*. These affinities are the keys that enable individuals to open up in front of the camera: recounting anecdotes, both dramatic and humorous, and talking openly and critically in great detail about the events that they have lived and know.

There is often a political element in establishing relations with informants. In *Made on Rails*, most of the national and local leaders interviewed were members of the Mexican Communist Party, a decision based on our desire to tell a very different story than is available in official histories, whether written or in the mass media. The fact that we came from the University of Puebla, an institution known (in that moment) for its leftist orientation, was important in allowing them to open up to us: they trusted us and believed that the final tape would not betray them.[71] These relationships also provided access to private photographic collections, as informants allowed us to copy their photos and gave us important information about these images that was an integral element of the work.

Poor rapport results not simply in a lack of information, it turns informants into wooden figures whose stiffness interferes with the audience's ability to learn from the stories they are recounting. The presence of the equipment and personnel necessary to film an interview makes it a toilsome task for cinehistorians to foment the necessary rapport for interviews. That situation has "engendered a great deal of controversy" among oral historians, some of whom perceive it as disruptive of the required interpersonal communication with the informants.[72] Utilizing the interview as the narrative structure of a video history does not, however, assign to it a value such that the historian ought to fear "interrupting" the "flow of memory," as some "extreme defenders" of oral history assert.[73]

Further, it has been argued by documentary filmmakers that such a presence can act as a "catalyst," what Jean Rouch described as a "psychoanalytic stimulant," that leads informants to take the situation more seriously and incites them to greater clarity and honesty—they become more, not less, of who they are.[74] This has certainly been one of the major esthetic strategies of Michael Moore, particularly in his first film, *Roger & Me* (1989), when he surprised many "informants" with his bold approach, forcing himself into their lives and his film. During the filming of *Made on Rails*, I attempted to provoke a spontaneous response during the interview with Guillermo

Treviño, which provided an interesting insight into Mexican culture. When I asked Treviño why the repression of the 1959 strike had been so brutal, I did so knowing that he was going to be made uncomfortable at having to answer me, a gringo, that it had been a result of US president Eisenhower's pressure on Mexican President López Mateos. And that is what happened. He said, "Although I'd prefer not to have to say it, I think that the US had a lot to do with what happened."[75] As a Mexican *caballero* of the old school, Treviño did not want to insult his "guest." But as a tireless defender of social justice, he had to answer with what he thought was the truth.

Another problem in this incipient discipline comes from the sort of expectations that we have about what is a good screen presence; that is, the degree to which what we believe to be "good television" determines who we allow to tell the history. This issue of presence revolves around various considerations: for example, does the informant talk too fast or too slow, do they speak clearly or are they difficult to understand, is theirs a popular or an academic language, do you hear the "dental click" characteristic of many older informants, do they move too much, or do they appear to have no energy? Such questions make us aware of the fact that many times the people that appear on the screen to recount historical events are there not because their interpretation is the best but because they have the type of screen presence to which we have become accustomed. Finally, we must not forget the all-too-familiar phenomenon of informants who tell wonderful stories, passionate and colorful and full of anecdotes that illuminate the past and bring it to life . . . until the moment when we turn on the lights to begin recording them. Then, their faces become pallid and their stories monosyllabic. Terrorized by the equipment, they usually cannot appear in the tape. Nonetheless, if it is necessary to be conscious of these structural limitations, it is important to remember that these are among the limits that define interactive documentary cinehistory.

Further, if the use of interviews and a *cinéma vérité* narrative do not necessarily assure greater objectivity, they do allow viewers to see and hear actual participants, and they provide more historical detail. They proportion information about the informants' gender, age, race, and class (something that can be gleaned from their clothing, as well as from their forms of speech).[76] Moreover, interviews can provide access to elements absent from written sources, such as body language and voice intonation, volume, and rhythm; these may tell us more about meaning than about facts.[77] For example, in *Made on Rails*, one of the participants in those strikes (who would spend more than seven years in jail for his role), Miguel Aroche Parra, provided a trenchant description of the significance attached to the greatest setback in the history of Mexican labor when he states that, "The railroaders' defeat in 1959 was a defeat for the labor movement, a defeat for the democratic movement, a defeat for the anti-imperialist movement, a defeat for the peace movement; *that* is the magnitude of the 1959 defeat."[78]

Whether one agrees with Aroche Parra's hyperbole, it is indicative of the psychological impact of that event on its participants, something reinforced by the emotional charge which is expressed in his vehement tone and passionate gestures. Aroche Parra's use of significant pauses, the lowering and raising of his voice, and his sharp physical movements—one hand cutting knife-like into the other as he recounted how US president Eisenhower ordered his Mexican counterpart, López Mateos, to "strike against the labor movement"—are an articulate demonstration of the feelings still generated by those memories. His intonation and movements are also a revealing embodiment of an expressive style typical of Mexican labor militants—an element at once important to understanding the history of the Mexican railroad workers and also impossible to convey except through the medium of an audiovisual interview.

The only major work I have directed in which I did not use interviews as the organizing structure is *Magí Murià*. This project arose when I had the fortune to meet José María Caparrós-Lera, a pioneer in studying film as a source for history and the founder of the Centre for Cinematic Research "Film-Historia" of the Universitat de Barcelona. I met him at the 1989 conference of IAMHIST (International Association for Audio-Visual Media in Historical Research and Education). On arriving, I was approached by the president of that society, who asked me if I could translate a letter into Spanish because, as he explained, "We've got this guy who wants to us to hold one of our conferences in Barcelona. Barcelona, if you can imagine it!"[79] I attempted to explain that Barcelona was a great city, and IAMHIST usually held its conferences in Europe, but he quickly dismissed my remarks, insisting that he needed the letter translated because Caparrós-Lera was simply not getting the message. I accepted, saw that the letter rather cavalierly rejected the proposal, and translated it. Then I looked for Caparrós-Lera in the welcoming reception, introduced myself, and told him of the letter. I described what I perceived as the intention of the association's leadership: "*Te quieren chingar*" (They want to screw you). "They want to do what?" he asked.

Once I explained the Mexican phrase, we immediately became close friends despite the enormous political gulf between him, a member of Opus Dei, and me, a Marxist atheist. He sponsored my application for a sabbatical-year fellowship from Spain's Ministerio de Educación y Cien-

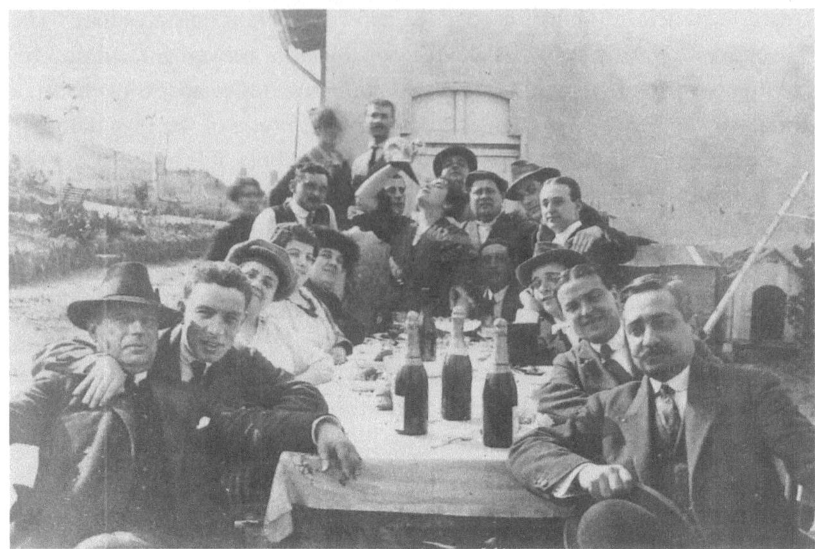

FIGURE 1. Unknown. Magí Murià seated at far right with a film crew; the famous Catalan actor, Margarida Xirgu, is drinking from the *porrón*, a glass bottle with a long cone that ends in a spout. It requires a good deal of dexterity and practice to drink from a *porrón* without spilling it down the front of your shirt. Barcelona, 1916. From *Magí Murià: Un pioner diletant / Magí Murià: Pioneer and Dilettante*; archive of Eli Bartra.

cia, and I spent a most fruitful time in the Centre during 1992–93. He suggested to Eli that she investigate her maternal grandfather, Magí Murià, and we decided to make a videotape to rescue him from the amnesia that surrounded his silent films of the 1910s as well as other cultural activities, from being the editor of the first woman's magazine in Catalan to pioneering the dubbing of foreign films into that language. (See Figure 1.) I was initially discouraged by the paucity of visual materials. Both he and his daughter, Anna, had been refugees from the Spanish Civil War. Hence, we found only nineteen photos of him in her archive, and one of them was so out of focus as to appear absolutely useless.

Nonetheless, I was inspired to make the work by the personal tone that Eli employed in writing about him.[80] I saw that we could construct a "trivocal" texture. In part, a resonance would be created between "informed interviews" at essentially two levels. Experts on Catalan cinema, Joaquim Romaguera i Ramió and Miquel Porter i Moix, provided little-known information about Murià's films. His daughter, Anna Murià, offered a more intimate perspective, although her own knowledge of and position within Catalan culture gave her a particularly privileged viewpoint. The interviews were structured around the third element: the more subjective voice-over "personal narration" that Eli wrote and spoke. For example, at one point she

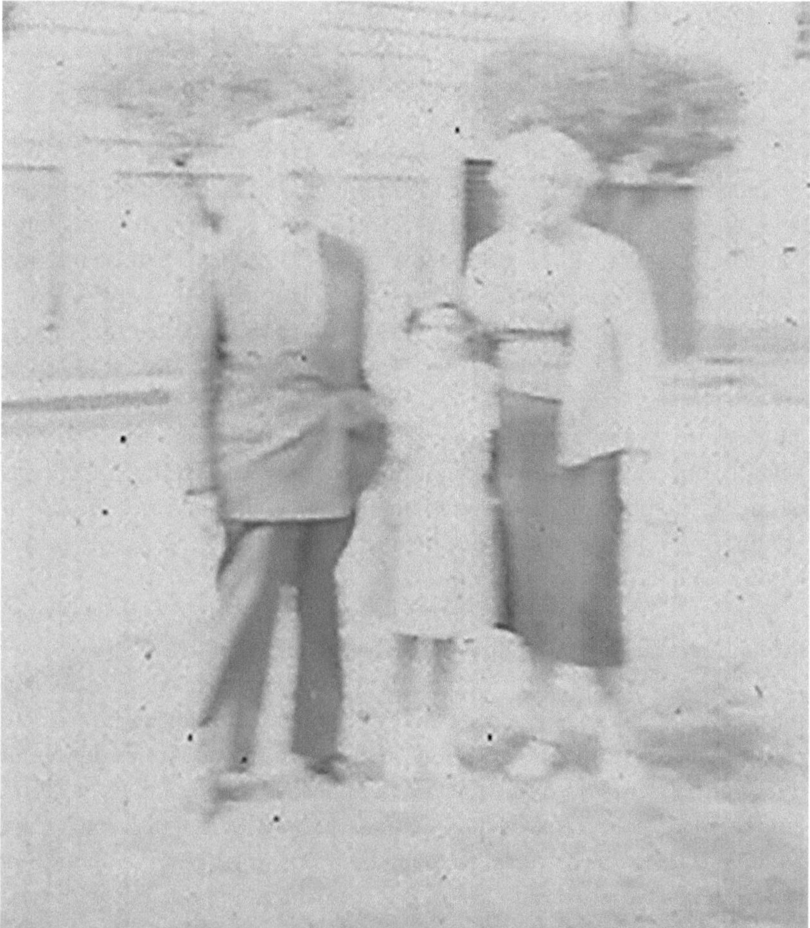

FIGURE 2. Unknown. Magí and Anna Murià with Eli Bartra i Murià, Mexico City, 1958. Archive of Eli Bartra.

asks, "But, what were you, grandfather? A filmmaker? A writer? A journalist? A businessman?"[81]

Magí Murià: Un pioner diletant / Magí Murià: Pioneer and Dilettante begins immediately in this personal tone, visually opening up with a fish-eye lens on Eli's eight-year-old face, which then zooms out to reveal Magí and Anna Murià standing behind her in the blurry photograph that had initially appeared to be of no use. (See Figure 2.) Eli's reflections in Catalan introduce the film and offer a note of self-reflexivity:

> Memory is often like this out-of-focus photograph, and what I remember of my grandfather Magí Murià is as fuzzy as this, the only image in which

> I appear with him and my mother, Anna Murià, in a place long ago and far away, his last exile and my country, Mexico. History has made Murià significant, and so I find myself reconstructing his life from blurred memories, yellowing papers, and pieces of disintegrating film.[82]

Encountering the visual and audial elements of this videotape required research, creativity, and rapport. Anna was quite accustomed to being interviewed on camera, either about her work or that of her late husband, the poet Agustí Bartra. However, Eli used her relationship to surprise Anna at the end of the interview, when she asked her what she felt like in talking about her father. She was at first taken aback, but recovered to articulate what became the closing words of the videotape, "Talking about my father in front of a camera is a new and strange thing that makes me feel a bit disconcerted. I've talked about him privately with family and friends but never in public. But I'm glad to do it because, although we had a lot of arguments, I loved him and love his memory. I'm glad to remember him and what he did."[83]

Rapport with Porter i Moix and Romaguera i Ramió was facilitated through several factors. Catalans are a beleaguered culture and have often been forced by the Spanish state to deny their language. Hence, the fact that the interviews were carried out in Catalan made for an immediate rapport with the film scholars. They were glad to spread knowledge about their culture's cinema, and Romaguera published a book on Magí Murià ten years later.[84] Further, the fact that Eli's parents were well-known Catalan intellectuals was a crucial factor in their opening up in the interviews. Research in a variety of public and private archives provided us with satisfactory still images. However, we were not allowed to make a copy of any of his films, which were being restored in the Filmoteca de Valencia. To resolve that problem, we recreated a short version of *Alma torturada* (1916) made up of what were probably outtakes from that film that we found in the Filmoteca de Barcelona; we structured them based on a published screenplay of the movie.

What I most like to do is to direct modern media productions, but that which least appeals is looking for the money to make them. So, in Mexico, when I am invited to curate exhibits and write books, I look for the possibility of including a production. The short documentary I directed in 2015, *Julio Mayo: Bracero con cámara/Julio Mayo: Bracero with a Camera*, was part of a photographic exhibit, *Braceros vistos por los Hermanos Mayo*.[85] Having accepted the invitation to do the exhibit, I then pushed to do an interview with Julio Mayo, who was ninety-six years old and still very lucid.

The interview lasted more than four hours, out of which I edited the twenty-minute short for the exhibit. Establishing rapport with Julio was no problem. We shared a leftist perspective, and I have interviewed and conversed with him since 1984, at times during long *comidas* and birthday celebrations. Despite my extensive research on the collective, I was surprised to turn up family photos I had never seen, including many of him and other Mayos participating in the Spanish Civil War. I also discovered that after his capture and confinement to forced labor for a couple of years, he eventually joined the world of Spanish cinema and enjoyed quite some success as a photographer who made stills to document prospective sites for films, before he migrated and joined his "brothers" as a photojournalist in Mexico.

THE LESSONS OF CINEHISTORY

What have I learned from my experience as a cinehistorian? In general, I believe that working in modern media has taught me to think differently about doing history, while the historical discipline has enabled me to see multimedia productions in a distinct way. The best thing that I have learned is the value of collective labor, the synergy that comes from working with other people. Doing cinehistory requires collaboration with individuals whose expertise is invaluable. First of all, there are the colleagues in areas about which I am largely ignorant; their knowledge enabled me to direct works without undertaking the years of study that would be otherwise required. Such was the case with Gloria Tirado and Eli Bartra, as well as the music specialists who were hired for each production. Finally, there are the technicians whose knowledge is necessary to be able to "speak" in this new language, and they can sometimes be creative interlocutors. And I have come to value the importance of reflecting on my experiences in doing productions, to defend my work as well as to explain to historians what I am attempting to do.

Many historians are conscious of the necessity to incorporate the new media. The title of a most articulate response to Burns' *The Civil War* was "The Coming Crisis of Academic History." There, historian David Harlan argued for recognition that academic historians' territory had expanded.[86] He asserted that we must be able to "describe the codes and conventions that govern evaluation in each realm," and that "the criteria for evaluating any representation of the past must be both media-specific and genre-specific." For him, "like every other realm, history-on-film has its own areas of expertise, its own methods of representation and its own criteria for determining what counts as good history and what does not."[87]

My adventures in cinehistory have made me aware of the necessity to look for our own esthetic as historians, rather than fall into the rapid-fire form of Hollywood productions and television, made thanks to the technical perfection produced by expensive machines. Personal experiences have been instructive. When *Made on Rails* was shown at the 1987 AHA Congress, the prominent cinehistorian John O'Connor (founder of the journal *Film & History*) commented that the photographs went by too fast to be able to really see them.[88] I remembered that critique in 1993 when I was editing *Magí Murià* in the TV Terrassa studio; the editor and I had constant disagreements about how long an image should remain on the screen. He, a television station editor, felt I was leaving them on too long; I had to fight to ensure the images were up long enough to make my point. It is noteworthy that a renowned film scholar argued that the visual pace of *The Civil War* "limits the readable potential of the photos it displays, if only by cutting down the time of reading and, sometimes, by offering only a detail of the photo."[89]

Finally, I learned to avoid the "illustrationism" that is characteristic of so many works of multimedia history, insisting that a dialectic should always exist between images and sounds. The graphic and audial research is as worthy as investigation in written sources; they must go hand-in-hand. In a discussion about *Made on Rails*, O'Connor was surprised when I informed him that, with few exceptions, the photos utilized in the tape all corresponded to the historical period presented. He found the fact so remarkable that he said some way ought to be found to inform the audience of this. However, this is a constant in my productions, where extensive research in still photos serves to provide sources that can open up a different set of questions and provide elements that might otherwise go unobserved. And I have always worked with experts in the music of the subject covered as well as doing my own research, so that the music has the same historical legitimacy as do the photos and moving footage.

Experience has taught me the value of using photos in place of the reliance on moving footage that we traditionally find in many compilation documentaries. What information is available in moving footage that is not present in photographs? Though recognizing that there are certain elements in documentary footage that are less accessible in stills—body language, for example—a reliance on footage fills up screen time at an alarming rate. This reduces the variety of images, a situation made worse by the fact that the limited amount of footage available necessitates its repeated and stereotypical utilization in different productions. Further, as cinehistorians develop their own esthetic, they can go beyond mere "illustrationism"—

moving from presentation to representation—and allow photographs to offer greater possibilities for bringing the audience into an interpretive tension with the work. Instead of being led along by the nose through a constant alternation of the moving image, the audience will hopefully have the opportunity to view the photos and to reflect on them, as well as on the interpretation that is being offered. One highly experimental example of possibilities is the film *Letter to Jane* (Godard and Gorin, 1972), a fifty-two-minute cinematic essay that is composed of a single news photograph of Jane Fonda in Vietnam and a discussion between Jean-Luc Godard and Jean-Pierre Gorin.

Using still photographs instead of moving footage is a relatively novel tactic, which had few precedents prior to 1960, according to Christian Metz.[90] Leaving aside such experimental works as Tziga Vertov's *The Man with the Movie Camera* (1929), one of the first documentaries to employ this strategy was the Canadian film *City of Gold* (Koenig and Low, 1957), described as "the prototype for all films based on still photographs."[91] When the directors proposed this tactic to the Canadian Film Board, they were met with a resistance that they were fortunately able to overcome by showing the Board how the experiments they were carrying out in dynamizing still photos revealed elements in them of which they had been unaware. *City of Gold* won an Academy Award and opened up new possibilities for filmmakers: "Documentarists the world over began to ransack photographic files."[92]

Other cineastes have made extensive use of photographs. Ken Burns was much influenced by *City of Gold* and has preferred to recount his histories with photos rather than moving footage. As John Tibbets has asserted, "By re-framing a photograph, or examining the mise-en-scène of a given image, or breaking it up into details, or juxtaposing it with other images, or by providing aural clues, Burns compels us to perceive the picture field as an arena of narrative activity, as a constellation of nexes of attention."[93] The influence of Cuban cineaste Santiago Álvarez was paramount for my work. In extraordinarily powerful short documentaries such as *Now* (1965), *LBJ* (1968), and *79 Springtimes* (1969), Álvarez dynamized photographs as a strategy created out of necessity. The US blockade of the island limited access to archival footage and led him to use stills in a highly creative manner.[94]

Family images—still and moving—can provide an invaluable source to cinehistorians. People have made many, many more images of themselves in photographs than on film; these photos are fundamental in trying to tell as truthful a story about them as we can. For example, the fact that working-class couples in the tiny railroad town of Oriental would make

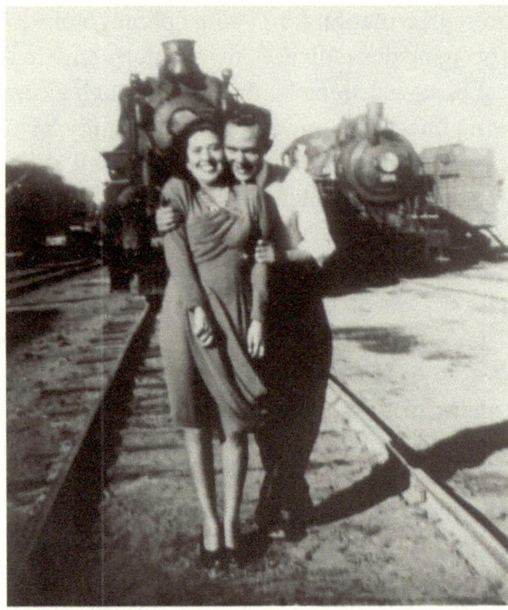

FIGURE 3. Unknown. Couple on train patio, Oriental, Puebla, ca. 1945. From *Made on Rails: A History of the Mexican Railroad Workers / Hechos sobre los rieles: Una historia de los ferrocarrileros mexicanos*; archive of John Mraz.

and preserve images of themselves posing happily in the station patio provides insight into their feelings about being families connected to the *ferrocarriles*: "They show what people were proud of, thought interesting, and what they wanted to show to others."[95] (See Figure 3.)

Photos require a different sort of research than film, one that often brings historians into direct contact with the people whose photos they are reproducing. As we copy and identify the photographs, we hear history told from the mouths of those who have lived and made it. These considerations bring the triangulated relationship of the historian with the sources and the audience into focus: as is the case with the use of interviews, we understand and acknowledge our role as a prism between those who have lived history and those who hear and see it recounted. Finally, it is a good deal cheaper to copy photos than to reproduce film, although digital technology will change this situation to some extent.

It is important to point out that historians who labor in photographic archives engage in essentially the same tasks as those who work with written sources: finding, preserving, and utilizing documents to talk about the past. In general, this is a different situation than that of historians who carry out research in television and film archives, something that can be appreciated in considering Pierre Sorlin's comments on the cinehistorian's role in relation to such footage.

> Audiovisual material[s] . . . completely alter the situation. [H]istorians have no monopoly over the material, nor are they alone in studying and disseminating it. For example, television has made most of the interesting material relating to the Second World War widely available. In this respect, the historian's task is no longer to compile otherwise unknown sources and make them available to all: he must learn instead to use material that is already widely available.[96]

While Sorlin's argument in relation to professional television and film footage is essentially true, this is decidedly not the case with photographs; further, home movie footage is available and will be increasingly so thanks to technology such as smartphones. Extensive research is required in both public and private photo archives in order to unearth and identify images useful to the history that will be recounted. Fortunately, the purchase and preservation of private archives by the government and research institutions is often the direct result of historians' research and lobbying.

Though the visual is necessarily a center of cinehistory, sound is also of fundamental importance. This is true, above all, when the work will be seen on small screens. In general, film has more visual resolution than video and is usually made to be seen on larger screens; in film, the image can "carry" the sound. With smaller screens, it is the opposite: sound is often of greater importance than the visual elements in sustaining the narrative. When I was making the Nicaraguan videotape, the sound technician brought a boom microphone—a mic attached to a long handle that is then put out over the interview—to the first day. I told him I preferred lavalier microphones, which are attached to the front of clothing near the mouth, but they had no such technology. I spot-checked the material that night and found that the sound was unacceptable. I asked him to replace it with hand microphones, which are not particularly esthetic but will provide decent sound quality. While interviews provide the essentials of the story, above all in works that avoid omniscient narration, music is often relegated to a minor role; this is somewhat analogous to the way that "illustrationism" reduces photos to serving as mere decoration. Music is a fundamental tool for recreating past eras, and it must be approached with the same rigor we employ in imagery (and texts). Too often, documentarians fail to carry out the necessary research to encounter music of the period depicted and end up with irrelevant and anachronistic sound.

We live in a hyper-audiovisual world, and I suspect that history will either be done through modern media, or it will be written for small groups of specialists. It is instructive to remember that the study of the classics—

which focuses on the languages, literature, art, history, philosophy, and archeology of ancient Greece and Rome—was the center of university education in the nineteenth century. In the humanities, historical studies replaced the classics during the mid- and later twentieth century, and classics departments were greatly reduced. Today, enrollments in history programs have fallen, in part because students are drawn to the possibility of working in today's media and to contemporary subjects such as communications. This tendency notwithstanding, the enormous popular appeal of histories told through film, photography, video, digitalization, and the Internet makes it clear that there remains a public hunger to know about our pasts.

One advantage of working in newly developing fields is that I am often asked to collaborate in books and journals, as well as invited to serve as guest editor.[97] Nonetheless, an invitation does not necessarily mean your article will accepted, especially if a peer reviewer fears you are trespassing on an area he has staked out. Within largely unestablished terrain such as cinema and photography, I have found two opposing responses by colleagues. One the one hand, we encounter the generosity of those who feel we are opening up uncharted realms together (as was the case with Griffin and Vanderwood, as well as among Mexican photohistorians). On the other hand, one finds recent immigrants to these spaces who feel that they have they have established their authority over them. For the benefit of young scholars who may find themselves stymied by the latter group as they attempt to work in visual culture, I will illustrate one instance of the arbitrariness engaged in by academic journals through a description of my most distasteful experience with US publications. In 1991, I was corresponding with a colleague who was the "visual representative" on the editorial board of a well-established history journal with radical pretensions; he urged me to submit an article on some form of ocular analysis. I sent in my article on videohistory (it was later published in English, Spanish, and Italian).[98] The article coordinator indicated that "the two readers very much liked your essay," but his comments were devastating: "A little knowledge can be a dangerous thing. What is your experience with TV and film? . . . Rosenstone, O'Connor, Toplin, and I (Walkowitz) have made this point earlier and often and in print."[99] This scholar was playing the classic "gatekeeper" role by protecting what he perceived as his turf in cinehistory.[100]

In spite of the mantel in which he draped himself, his work in that field was limited to having worked with a single co-directed film that was in US distribution and published one article on historians as filmmakers, a pedestrian glance at the issue with a bibliography so meager that only one written source about the topic was mentioned, a thin fifty-page "Occasional Paper," *Historians and Filmmakers*.[101] I had directed two videotapes that were in international distribution, and my experience in analyzing cinehistory was much more extensive than his. Moreover, the coordinator was evidently unaware that historians such as Griffin and Cortés had been making historical films in the US since the early 1970s. He also demonstrated an ignorance of the substantial bibliography on film and history that had developed in Europe, Latin America, and among US Latin Americanists in the 1970s and early 1980s. Produced by the parochial and insular nature of intellectual life in the US, his provincial mindset required that I address the bibliography by US scholars on film and history, consult the documentary footage at the Tamiment Library in New York City, and include a whole range of US historical films that were not available in Mexico. He seemed unable to understand the idea that the "transparency" of historical photographs—an issue I discuss in the following chapter—created the possibility of employing them in ways other than representation. I responded by sending my curriculum vitae, noting that it was not my intention to carry out an extensive bibliographic review on film and history but rather to discuss how videohistorians could realize their projects in picturing the past. Further, I also wrote to the editors of the journal, suggesting that having to cite studies by the members of the editorial board could be counterproductive as well as potentially embarrassing. Imperial arrogance reigned: I received no response from any of the participants in this farce.

In the end, perhaps the most important product of my dedication to audiovisual study and production has been the opportunity to develop a critical perspective of those media that so dominate our lives today. The battle is joined: cinehistories will be produced, whether historians do so or not. To some colleagues, certainly, it will seem a weak medium for conveying the complexities of understanding the past, but it is not a question of "translating" a written text into a visual discourse but of exploring the new ways of seeing and talking about that "other country" that this medium makes available. We must not be afraid to experiment with the new opportunities opened by these media. In 1989, Robert Rosenstone created the "Film Reviews" section in the *American Historical Review*, where he insistently argued that he was not interested in the more conventional approach of understanding how a film reflected its historical context but rather in what strategies it employed to do history. The section was discontinued in 2006, but has recently been revived by the editors with the comment, "The scholarly monograph is no longer, if it ever was, the sole outlet for professional historians to disseminate their research and ideas."[102] As

Rosenstone commented in looking back on his experiences, "In the 1970s and 1980s, the growth of visual media reached something of a critical mass that exploded, blowing an (ever so tiny) hole into the world of academia, including that backward-looking discipline, history."[103] His is the most articulate voice on the issues that should be raised by doing cinehistory:

> The question cannot be, Does the historical film convey facts or make arguments as well as written history? Rather, the appropriate questions are: What sort of historical world does each film construct and how does it construct that world? How can we make judgments about the construction? How and what does that historical construction mean to us? After these three questions are answered, we may wish to ask a fourth: How does the historical world on the screen relate to written history?[104]

Finally, people learn from sense experience: the smell of a rose, the stub of a toe, the gaze of a lover. I would argue that there is a sensual expansion obtained by seeing and hearing actual participants talk of their experiences, through looking at photos and footage of events, and in listening to music from the period that provides a stimulation as much intellectual as emotive and esthetic. We witness the living proof of history, a proof which—if it does not provide the same kind of answers—pricks the mind to ask different questions.

Part II. Photohistories

CHAPTER 2

Seeing Photographs Historically

A View from Mexico

It takes work, pious effort, to see what you are looking at. **Don DeLillo**

DOING HISTORY *WITH* AND *OF* PHOTOGRAPHS

For some fifty years I have asked myself what historians bring to the analysis of photographs and what these documents offer us as a new source for studying the past. I finally arrived at a method that heuristically differentiates between what are essentially two approaches to investigating photographs from a historical perspective; in the best of cases, they work dialectically together to deepen the analysis. On the one hand, the focus is on past material cultures, doing history *with* photographs as if they were somehow "transparent" to glean details about material realities, daily life, social relations, mentalities, and popular culture from preserved "traces" of the past that have been left there due to the unique capacity of photographs to be indexes of "that-which-was."[1] On the other hand, the emphasis falls on doing histories *of* photographs, photographers, and/or the media that published them: knowing who took them, how they were made, and having an idea of what the photographer's intentions may have been. This route requires analyzing the ways the imagemakers reflect the mentality of the age in which the photographs were created, the esthetic influences, and the forms in which they appear and reappear, and that provide them with different meanings.

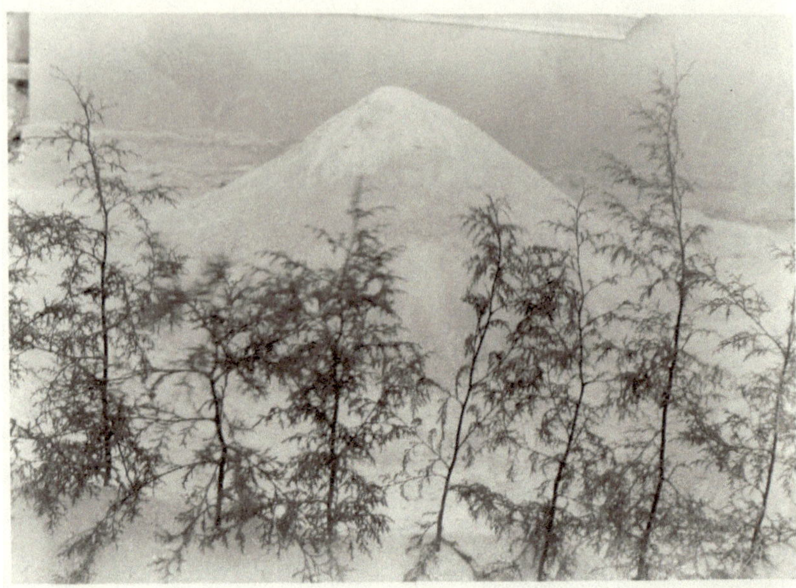

FIGURE 4. Manuel Álvarez Bravo. *Arena y pinitos* (sand and little pine trees), Mexico City, ca. 1920. Archivo Manuel Álvarez Bravo, Copyright Colette Urbajtel.

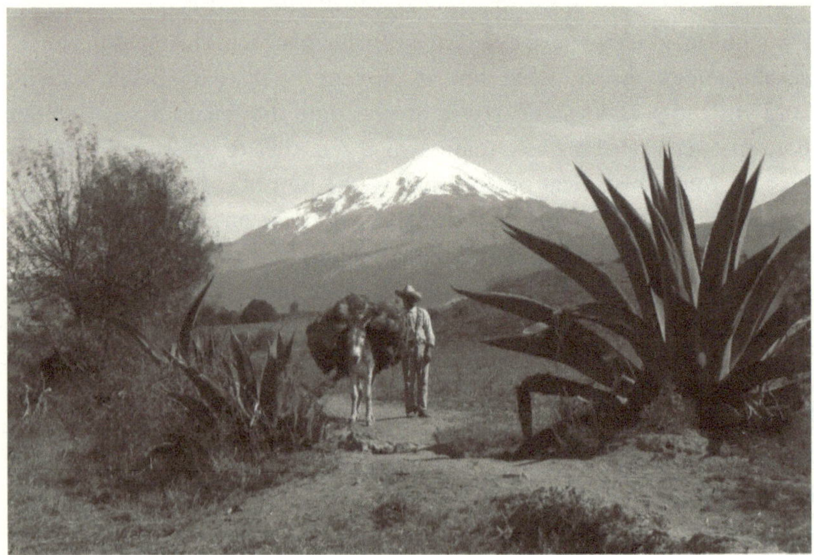

FIGURE 5. Hugo Brehme. *Campesino*, burro, magueys, and Popocateptl, Puebla, ca. 1930. Inv. # 373649, Colección Brehme, SINAFO-Fototeca Nacional del INAH, Secretaría de Cultura.

To the degree that we know who made photos or the different media where they appeared, our understanding of the portrayed objects is deepened, we discover what is present and what is absent as a function of the use(s) for which they were made and published. In knowing what is being pictured, at times without the photographer being aware of doing so, we have a possibility of discovering the author and the interests behind those pictures. As we progress on one side of the equation, it can lead to an advance on the other. Hence, this two-fold approach yields to an increasingly greater depth of examination.

Because in actual practice the two methods often overlap, the distinction is ultimately heuristic and only intended to open up the various possibilities for historicizing photographs. Nonetheless, I think that analyzing the past *with* photographs has an affinity with social history, whereas "deciphering the meaning" of photographs, photographers, or the media through which the images are conveyed seems to me to be a form of cultural history.[2] Perhaps the discipline may best be described as *photohistory*, in which the social and cultural perspectives work together. One problem in exploring the cultural aspect is that—at least in Mexico—we often know neither who took the images, nor why, nor when, nor what it is that appears therein.

This duality of photographs has long been recognized and commented upon. For example, the title of John Szarkowski's 1978 exhibit at the Museum of Modern Art was *Mirrors and Windows*: "In metaphorical terms, the photograph is seen either as a *mirror*——a romantic expression of the photographer's sensibility as it projects itself on the things and sights of this world; or as a *window*——through which the exterior world is explored in all its presence and reality."[3] Rudolf Arnheim described the functions as "the two authenticities of the photographic medium."[4] Roland Barthes argued that, as an "imitative art," photographs are comprised of "two messages: a *denoted* message, which is the *analogon* itself, and a *connoted* message, which is the manner in which the society to a certain extent communicates what it thinks of it."[5] Among the photohistorians who have remarked upon this duality, Boris Kossoy asserted, "The photograph is a double testimony: for that which it shows us of a past scene . . . frozen fragmentarily; and for that which informs us about its author. . . . Two distinct approaches [*vertientes*] of research [are required], although they are not unrelated, because *photographic documents* are at the center of both."[6]

The two approaches would seem to correspond generally to differences between art photography and what we loosely call documentary imagery. We might better describe the latter as "vernacular photography," imagery that has

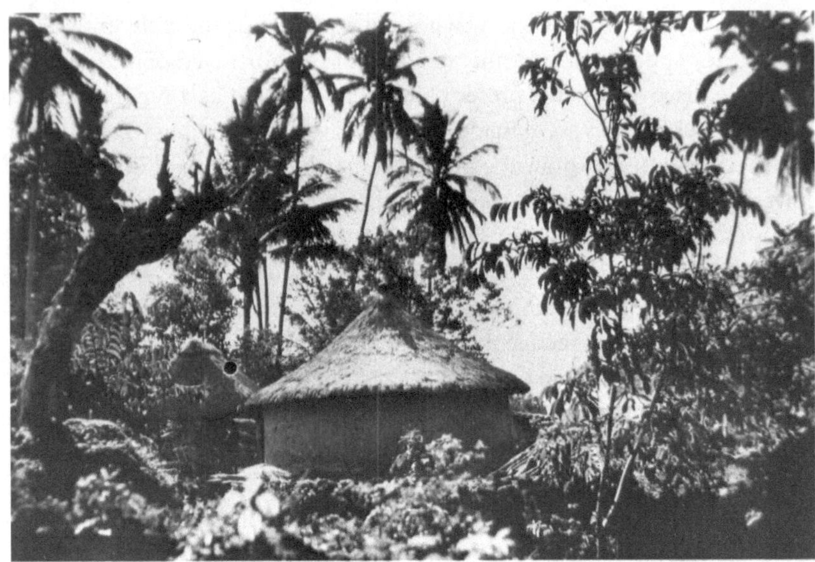

FIGURE 6. Amando Salmerón. Huts in a town of Blacks, Costa Chica, San Nicolás, Guerrero, ca. 1940. Archivo Salmerón. Courtesy of Samuel Villela.

almost always been excluded from histories of the medium, ordinary photographs that have been produced outside of any art-historical considerations; this is by far the great majority of photos that have been taken.[7] A picture made by an artist-photographer will generally tell us more about cultural history. One example is the photograph that Manuel Álvarez Bravo constructed in the early 1920s by making a little pile of sand and sticking some pine twigs in the foreground, *Arena y pinitos* (Sand and little pine trees).[8] (See Figure 4.) This image is of no interest whatsoever for a social historian. However, a historian of photography could well find evidence of the influence of Pictorialism and Japanese art, as well as the re-elaboration of a national symbol (the volcano Popocatepetl). Further, *Arena y pinitos* may well be the first of Álvarez Bravo's photos to take a decolonizing stance, in critiquing Hugo Brehme's picturesque imagery such as that of the all-too-familiar scene of the *campesino*, burro, and maguey set against the backdrop of Popocatepetl. (See Figure 5.) Pictures taken by amateurs, photojournalists, documentarians, and studio photographers will often provide more information about social history than will those of artists. Amando Salmerón, member of a dynasty in Guerrero whose imagery is limited to being essentially of a "testimonial character," recorded the existence of rounded huts that clearly demonstrated an African influence, in a town of Blacks on the coast of Guerrero around 1940; those houses have today completely disappeared.[9] (See Figure 6.)

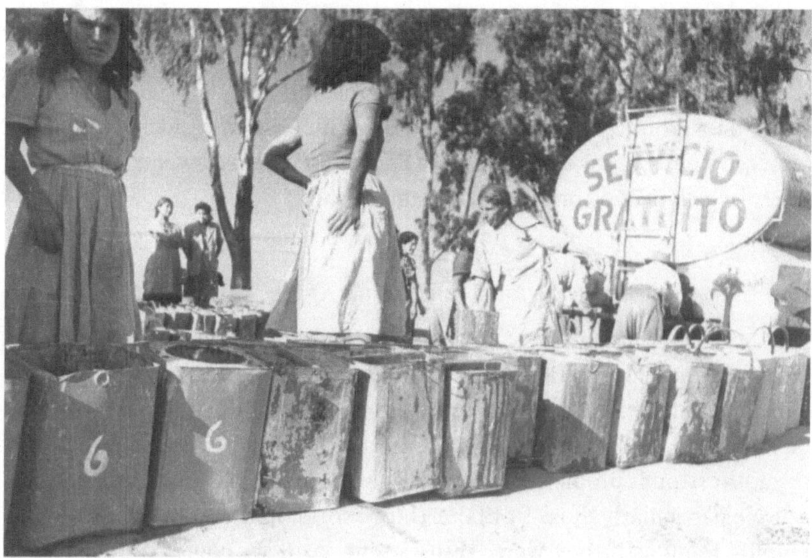

FIGURE 7. Hermanos Mayo. Women awaiting water, Mexico City, ca. 1950. Fondo Hermanos Mayo, Archivo General de la Nación.

The differences between the photographers and photographs notwithstanding, the approaches chosen will ultimately depend upon the questions we bring to interrogating images, as well as the materials we find available for studying them. A picture by the Hermanos Mayo illustrates this point. (See Figure 7.) A low-angle shot of women waiting under a hot sun amid seemingly endless lines of old and rusty tin receptacles for water during the 1950s can be analyzed as a document of one of the ways in which poor women spent their days. It also shows how the proletarian communities were furnished with the precious liquid and is thus a testimony to the way PRI practiced clientelism, for the "Free Service" came courtesy of the city's government. As a source for social history the photo offers a dense representation of daily life, but it can also be studied from the perspective of how the choice of subject and the manner of representation tell us about the Mayo as photographers. They were probably given an order to cover the distribution of water, perhaps for a news story praising the government's concern for the underclasses. However, it would be difficult to employ this particular photo in that task because of several factors. Rather than expressing gratitude, the two women in the foreground testify to the frustration of not having running water in their homes: one stares glumly into the camera, the other holds her arms akimbo in a stance expressing her indignation and exhaustion, even as the angle chosen by Mayo empowers them. In the midground, an old woman struggles to carry the heavy load, a forecasting of what awaits the younger women. The women are enclosed within the tins that dominate the foreground and that can be seen repeated in the background. In terms of the subjects and the way in which they are pictured, the image is a concise articulation of the Mayo's visual critique of the ruling class and concern for the underdogs.

THE "TRANSPARENCY" OF PHOTOGRAPHS

The large Mexican archives contain many photographs about which we have minimal information apart from the places they are stored. Millions of negatives taken by photojournalists can be found in the Archivo General de la Nación (AGN) and the Fototeca Nacional, and in many cases, even the authorship is problematic. This may well be the case in other countries as well, particularly those from the Third World. In these situations, we can employ them as if they were "transparent," as if we could somehow "see through" them to analyze *what* is depicted; this can offer clues about the past that may not be immediately available in other sources.

The idea that photographs document the world in ways very different from other images has circulated since the medium came into being. In an 1839 report to the French Chamber of Deputies supporting a pension as recognition for the technology created by Louis-Jacques-Mandé Daguerre, Dominique François Arago emphasized the "unimaginable precision of detail" obtained.[10] Writing just a year later, Edgar Alan Poe clearly understood the extraordinary importance of the invention: "The Daguerreotyped plate is infinitely (we use the word advisedly) is *infinitely* more accurate in its representation than any painting by human hands"; for Poe, it offered "a more perfect identity of aspect with the thing represented."[11] Photographs made by Jacob Riis that denounced unlivable immigrant housing and by Lewis Hine that decried child labor led to changes in those social conditions. Certainly, their effect depended upon the idea that these images showed "realities" that had been heretofore invisible. Hine may well be considered among the early visual sociologists, a field that was based on photographic transparence.[12]

The challenge to what we might call the "common-sense" view first came from artists, although as early as 1840 Hippolyte Bayard had questioned the notion of photographic reality—and pointed to the problematic nature of captions—in his *Self-Portrait as a Drowned Man*.[13] In 1899, art photographer Alfred Stieglitz inveighed against the ease with which photographs could be made. Perhaps referring to the Kodak motto of that moment—

"You press the button, we do the rest"—Stieglitz decried the "fatal facility" that had placed photography "in the hands of the general public," which led to its having "fallen in disrepute."[14] The described "disrepute" was obviously related to establishing its stature as an art, for Stieglitz's concern was to open the galleries and museums (and the pocketbooks of art patrons) to this new medium. These institutions, along with university art departments, carried out their roles in reducing discussions about photographs to those with an artistic intent, as I discuss in Chapter 3.

Members of the Frankfurt School were the first to articulately argue against confining photography within the art paradigm, asserting that the medium's importance resided precisely in its unique capacity to capture the accidental and spontaneous of the material world. As Walter Benjamin wrote, "Despite all the artistic preparations of the photographer and all the design in the pose of his model, the viewer feels irresistibly compelled to seek out the tiniest spark of accident, the here and now . . . with which actuality has seared, so to speak, the person in the image with reality."[15] In describing a 1843 image made by David Octavius Hill of a fishwife, Benjamin insisted: "The photograph, however, introduces something new and strange: . . . that does not testify merely to the art of the photographer Hill, something that cannot be silenced, obstreperously demanding the name of she who has lived, who even now is still real here and will never entirely perish into 'art.'"[16]

Siegfried Kracauer agreed with Benjamin that approaching photographs as art "threatened to divert the attention from what is really characteristic of the medium . . . [which] is uniquely equipped to record and reveal physical reality."[17] For Kracauer, art provides us with an idealistic conception of the world: "Art proceeds from top to bottom. . . . The real-life material disappears in the artist's conception."[18] In a sense, Kracauer is arguing for the inductive reasoning introduced by Enlightenment thought, as opposed to the deductive method that had preceded it.[19] In order to be true to the materialist implications of the new media of photography and film, "they will certainly not move from a preconceived idea down to the material world in order to implement that idea; conversely, they set out to explore physical data and, taking their cue from them, work their way up to some problem or belief."[20] Gisèle Freund, who studied in the University of Frankfort, also emphasized the importance of photography as a social document, and produced the first doctoral thesis on photography in 1936, as well as the important work *Photography & Society.*[21]

Other ocular theorists joined in recognizing that the photograph is a new and different sign than previous images. The work of André Bazin, a pioneer in thinking critically about cinema, was focused largely on affirming what he described as the medium's objectivity: "Originality in photography as distinct from originality in painting lies in the essentially objective character of photography. For the first time, between the originating object and its reproduction there intervenes only the instrumentality of a nonliving agent."[22] According to the semiotician Charles S. Peirce, all pictures are icons, representations in visual form; however, in linguistic terms, the photograph can be characterized as an *index* as well as an icon.[23] Like the affinity of the fingerprint and the finger that has impressed it, technical images are *traces* of that which was before the camera and reflected the light that was embalmed in representational form. "The photograph is literally an emanation of the referent," observed Barthes.[24]

However, despite the direct existential connection between the object in front of the lens and the resulting photograph, the meaning of the image will be derived from its function.[25] And we want to be careful: the intimate link between this petrified light and "that-which-was" can lead one to confuse the reflected surface of the phenomenal world that is preserved in the photograph with "reality." Reality, of course, is much more complex than the representation of its exterior appearance, as Bertolt Brecht reminded us in his famous formulation from his essay, "The Threepenny Lawsuit": "The photograph of the Krupp works or the AEG reveals almost nothing about these institutions."[26] We might compare a photograph to the ocean: the surface of the ocean is certainly part of its reality, but its depths are very profound, and their reality can hardly be divined by looking at its surface. Its limitations notwithstanding, the photograph—as a technical image and an index—has a dissimilar relation to reality than do other visual media.

Photographs are best described as indexes produced by the light reflected by that which was before the camera. What is the source of the resistance to their capacity to provide a new sort of information about the world around us? I sometimes have the feeling that photographic scholars are ashamed of indexicality; it is too easy and simple, like the idiot savant cousin invited to Thanksgiving dinner. Consider, for example, the extreme position of Spanish photographer and visual theorist Joan Fontcuberta: "Photography always lies, it lies by instinct, it lies because its nature does not permit it to do anything else."[27] In a transparent effort to scandalize, Fontcuberta conflates representation and intentional falsehood. However, this specious and hyperbolic—though nonetheless popular—argument can be easily refuted by recognizing that photography is a medium: simply replace the word *photography* with that of another medium, for example *words*, and the sophistry of such a position becomes evident. Moreover, Fontcuberta's incapacity for thinking clearly is reflected in recurring to the concept of "nature" to make his argument. As Raymond Williams affirmed, "Nature is perhaps the most complex word in the language."[28] Let us for brevity's sake avoid an extended discussion of this concept and content ourselves with Williams' first definition: "The essential quality and character *of* something."

The real *nature* of photography—and what differentiates it from other visual media—is the capacity to produce indexes. The questioning of that attribute stems from the fact that meanings are generated by the contexts created to "explain" photographs. Ariella Azoulay describes this with the metaphor of a paperclip:

> The identification between 'this was there' and 'this is X' can be thought of as a kind of paper clip, a sort of temporary office accessory used at the desk to attach things. . . . When the paper clip, so to speak, solidifies into a representation, anything temporary or contingent is eliminated so that the photograph is reified under one stable representation.[29]

John Berger notes how words and photos work together to create authenticity out of ambiguity:

> All photographs are ambiguous. All photographs have been taken out of a continuity. . . . Discontinuity always produces ambiguity. Yet often this ambiguity is not obvious, for as soon as photographs are used with words, they produce an effect of certainty, even of dogmatic assertion. . . . The photograph begs for an interpretation. . . . And words, which by themselves remain at the level of generalization, are given specific authenticity by the irrefutability of the photograph.[30]

Art historians and curators are less interested in the indexical capacity of photographs than they are in the formal expressivity of individual artists. However, rather than simply focusing on the latter issue, an art historian attempted to deny the importance of photographic indexicality with the familiar "I'll see it when I believe" argument: "We endow [photographs] with the attributes we need them to have. . . . The most significant indexical power of the photograph may consequently lie . . . in the relation between the photograph and its beholder, or user, in what I would like to call a 'performative index' or an 'index of identification.'"[31]

To deny indexicality is like denying climate change, and one powerful source of the rejection of indexicality's pivotal importance comes from the political suppression carried out by imperialist powers and repressive

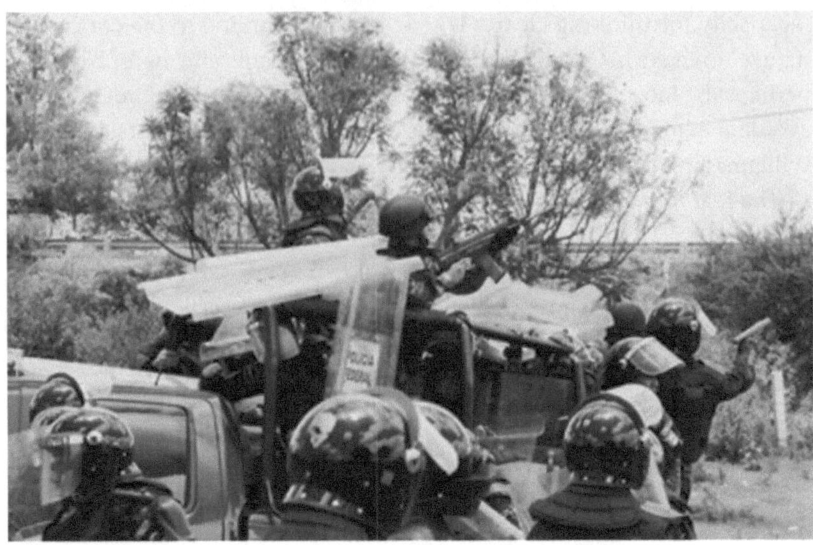

FIGURE 8. Max Nuñez. Armed federal police, Nochixtlán, Oaxaca, 19 June 2016. Courtesy of Max Nuñez/fotoes.mx.

regimes. In the hands of progressive critics and oppressed peoples such as Mexican workers and *campesinos*, as well as Blacks and Latinos in the US, the new medium has provided a tool to "prove" the existence of such things as torture in Abu Ghraib, US police killings of Blacks and Latinos, and the Mexican government's armed repression of protestors. The real problem is that the visual proof of oppression, a sine qua non in today's hyper-visual world, is not always available, and hence did not happen.

There is something new about photography, and it is now clear that digitalization has only made photographs more reliable witnesses than words (above all to anyone who has lived through the Donald Trump presidency). In the beginning, digitalization appeared to threaten photography's credibility, as in one of the first articles to decry this, "Digital Retouching: The End of Photography as Evidence of Anything," published in 1985.[32] However, it has since been discovered that every digital photo comes with its unique "signature" of metadata, which includes the date and time of exposure, the camera's model, the shutter speed, aperture, and lens, among other information.[33] Moreover, the technique of "digital watermarking" can be used to determine whether a digital photo has been subsequently altered.[34]

The importance of these tools can be seen in the case of the photos taken by Max Nuñez of the armed federal police who killed at least six Mexican teachers, and wounded many more in the protest at Nochixtlán, Oaxaca, on June 19, 2016.[35] (See Figure 8.) The Comisión Nacional de Seguridad at first replied to the images by stating categorically, "They are totally false, and do not correspond to the facts."[36] However, the Xinhua News Agency and the Associated Press, which published Nuñez's picture, used the system Exif Tool to examine the original photo, which produced the following analysis: "This image passed all of our forensic tests, so the evidence strongly suggests it is an unmodified original file from a camera."[37] When this test was run on Nuñez's photo that was cropped to focus on the police, and remove the superfluous trees above and around them, it determined that, "Our forensic tests suggest this file has been re-saved since initial capture. Because this file is not a camera original, it is possible that it was modified."[38] Cropping photojournalist images is very common because news photographers work in situations that make it difficult to get the exact framing desirable. However, by providing the original photo and the cropped version it was proved conclusively that the police were armed, and the Mexican government had finally to admit that.

The difference photography makes could be called "transparency," a notion inspired by a theoretical polemic of the 1980s. Philosopher Roger Scruton asserted that the "ideal" photograph is interesting "as a record of how an actual object looked. . . . The photograph is transparent to its subject, and if it holds our interest it does so because it acts as a surrogate for the represented thing."[39] Kendall Walton stated the position even more forcefully: "Photographs are *transparent*. We see the world *through* them."[40] This is because photographs are understood to exist in a "causal relation" to their subjects, whose appearance they reproduce because the light reflected by them imprints itself in the camera; moreover, there is "an affinity between looking at a photograph of something and looking at it directly."[41] For Walton, "The paradigms of transparent pictures would seem to be not the work of professional photographers but casual snapshots and home movies"; I differ from Walton in that I would certainly include photojournalism.[42] Photographs effortlessly capture the most mundane details of ordinary life. For that very reason early artistic photographers who placed their cameras in front of beautiful architecture such as Notre Dame Cathedral in Paris were disappointed when they developed their images and discovered that they had "come away with untidy evidence of building projects, repair work, scaffolding, stonemasons' yards, street trade and tumbledown housing."[43]

PICTURE HISTORIES

The transparency of photographs would seem to offer an ideal means to document the social history of material realities, everyday life, social relations, mentalities, popular culture, and ecological transformations. However, they have not usually been so employed in picture histories, as my studies of Mexican publications—and my more informal research in Brazilian, Colombian, Uruguayan, and Venezuelan productions—leads me to believe.[44] It would appear that that in many Latin American countries, histories of photography that focused on particular authors, largely portraitists or cityscape imagemakers, preceded the production of illustrated histories of past events. Conversely, in Mexico, *historias gráficas* begin to appear during the Mexican Revolution, often funded by leaders who wished to promote themselves. Although the most committed photographers were originally regional studio photographers, many of the photos produced during the revolution were essentially photojournalistic. With the end of the armed struggle, the Casasola Archive began in 1921 to produce what would become a prolific enterprise that would extend far beyond their collection to include an inordinate number of picture histories.

Photohistorian José Antonio Navarrete affirms that the study of particular South American photographers began in the 1940s, although only Gilberto Ferrez became a systematic investigator of photography.[45] I sense that the focus of Brazilian photohistories has largely fallen on the development of cities such as Rio de Janeiro and São Paulo, often on particular photographers such as Marc Ferrez, Augusto Malta, and Militão Augusto de Azevedo. Photohistorians such as Ana Maria Mauad have made great strides in advancing the rigorous study of photography over the past thirty years, and she affirms that the historiography is large and interdisciplinary with interest booming from around 2010 on.[46] Although there are no Colombian equivalents of the massive Casasola *historias gráficas*, one book by Malcolm Deas, *Historia de Colombia a través de la fotografía*, appears to have somewhat addressed that gap.[47] Uruguay has the fortune to have the Centro de Fotografía de Montevideo, from which have flowed rigorous photohistories such as two volumes coordinated largely by Magdalena Broquetas that examine the social uses of photography from 1840 to 1990.[48] There is a twelve-volume *Historia gráfica de Venezuela*, but it follows the usual hagiographic approach of focusing on political leaders, so much so that it is organized around the presidential terms.[49]

One outstanding photohistory was produced in part by Venezuelan institutions: Jorge Luis Gutiérrez's *Fotografía latinoamericana del siglo XIX*.[50] It appears that Gutiérrez abandoned this field without producing any other work, but this apparently little-known photohistory demonstrates a comprehension of both social history and the history of photography in Latin America that few curators possess. Gutiérrez is able to comment as knowledgeably on the "false skies" of Eadweard Muybridge, which the photographer constructed to replace the *cielos lavados* (washed-out skies) produced by the bright tropical sun, as well as on the presence of Blacks in photos by Arturo Booth of the streets of Buenos Aires around 1900, and their disappearance when they were expelled from that city.

A Catalonian series, *Història Gràfica de la Catalunya Contemporània: 1888/1931*, is one of the few works I have examined that not only utilizes photos as a source of social history but also reflects on some of the difficulties posed by such an effort.[51] Edmon Vallès employed both family photo albums and archival imagery to evoke the ambience and ways of rural and urban life, believing that photos are indispensable in this reconstruction. He notes the importance of including the esthetic in photohistories, stating that, "the graphic documents have been chosen in function of their intrinsic expressivity and their documentary importance."[52] He also draws a distinction between his goal and that of illustrated histories, as well as indicating the limitations of his sources:

> The relative importance of the themes is not what they would have in a text in which illustrations were complementing a text. Philosophy, to take one instance, has a very evident transcendence in the life of a people, but it cannot be photographed; we can only show pictures of philosophers. In contrast, balloon contests are much less important, but they are also excellent photographic motifs, and aeronauts are much more suggestive than philosophers.[53]

With few exceptions, I suspect that picture histories throughout the world have often shared a tendency common to the genre: they usually show little respect for what photos could tell us about the past. *Historias gráficas* have a long tradition in Mexico, and at least ten significant series have been produced; some of them have been republished as many as five times on expensive paper, with print runs as big as one hundred thousand. The series produced by the Casasola family are exemplary: *Historia gráfica de la Revolución Mexicana* was expanded and republished many times, eventually reaching 3,760 pages with some 11,500 photographs; *Seis siglos de historia gráfica en México* was also republished several times, arriving at 3,248 pages and around 18,000 images. Other large series include those produced under President Miguel de la Madrid (1982–88): *Memoria y olvido*, a collection of more than twenty assigned "monographs" by various authors; *Así fue la Revolución Mexicana*, a ten-volume sumptuously produced paean to the cataclysm of 1910–1917; *Biografía del poder*, eight gossipy hagiographies of the New Order's heroes; and *Historia gráfica de México*, the obligatorily titled series hurriedly thrown together to take advantage of funds remaining in the final year of the *sexenio* (six-year presidential term), a year known as the *El año de Hidalgo, pendejo el que deje algo* (The year of Hidalgo, anybody who leaves any money in the public coffers is stupid).[54] These voluminous catalogues of photographs could serve historians, both professionals and amateurs, as sources for their studies in social history, although the captions are not completely reliable.

At times, Mexican *historias gráficas* have incorporated important historians such as Lorenzo Meyer, Enrique Florescano, Luis González y González, Javier Garciadiego, Álvaro Matute, and Héctor Aguilar Camín, but their role has been limited to serving as the editors or providing texts. Rafael Samuels noted a similar situation in Britain, where he asserted that photos were treated with greater seriousness in primary and secondary levels than in the universities:

> Schools, under the influence of pedagogies which exalted the "iconic representation," were far more hospitable to the reception of photography—and far more critical and self-aware in their use of it—than university historians who lent their dignity and authority to coffee-table books and Sunday colour supplement articles, but showed no sign of incorporating old photographs into their teaching materials or primary research.[55]

The graphic investigations and the research for the written texts of most illustrated histories produced by professional historians are usually similar to two parallel rails that give the appearance of meeting on the horizon, but never really work together. The scholars who pen the essays and captions have generally had nothing whatsoever to do with the visual investigation, which is often assigned to student assistants. The pictures essentially illustrate texts that have been written completely apart from any questions that could have arisen from searching among old photographs. Moreover, the image research has been limited largely to simply finding pictures—often those previously published—rather than recovering the information that would enable the telling of marvelous stories about the past. The basic tasks of photohistory are essentially the same as historiography: research and documentation. On those happy occasions where visual and written research have somehow functioned together, the mutual benefits make evident that photography ought to be situated in a dialectic relationship with verbal texts, stimulating and orienting research, rather than reduced to being attractive filler sought in a process unrelated to what many historians consider to be the *real* investigation, that carried out in words.

In Mexico, most *historias gráficas* have been epic, totalizing, and officialist. This situation derives in part, no doubt, from the expense in producing them. Books with many images are almost always necessarily mediated by the monies needed to acquire and reproduce photographs in the quality that will communicate their visual wealth of data and expression; with photography, resolution *is* information. The considerable sums required are obtained most easily from the government, with the result that the history promulgated by the vast majority of the series has taken the form of an antiquated nineteenth-century Carlylean worship of Great Men and their politico-military feats.[56] In some Mexican picture histories the percentage of photographs dedicated to these official heroes reaches 75 percent, but it is never less than 50 percent (something I suspect may be true of picture histories in much of the world). What do such images tell us about history? Nothing, other than offering their metatext for analysis: their visual insistence that history was (and implicitly continues to be) made by Great Men. Now, it is certainly true that photographs of human beings can serve to "personify" the past, bringing into view people who are often absent from written documents. But icons of male heroes only nourish the celebrity worship that is itself a product of modern visual culture.

The importance picture histories have had in Mexico has derived from various factors. It is no doubt related to legitimizing the kleptocratic plutocracy of the PRIAN: the party dictatorship and the comprador class that ruled from the official institutionalization of the Revolution in 1946 until its challenge by the victory of Andrés Manuel López Obrador in 2018. The extreme social differences that have characterized the nation throughout its existence have produced a widespread illiteracy or semi-literacy that absolutism has promoted in effect, although its rhetoric of "literacy campaigns" alleges the opposite. Hence, it is my perception that Mexico is primarily a visual culture rather than one of written texts; the recent glut of Oscars and other international awards received by Mexican directors and cinematographers would seem to support such an impression. The proliferation of visual narratives is, as well, a product of the need to construct a national history in opposition to the imperial vision that US media propagates of its southern neighbor as a primitive, corrupt, and lawless society.[57] In that sense, the *historias gráficas* have served to construct a "strong history"; as photohistorian Elizabeth Edwards has affirmed, "Communities which had photographs related to their past were believed to be in a more powerful position in asserting their identities, in negotiating their place in the modern world and in the complex inter-community politics around local leadership and resource ownership."[58]

The development of regional photohistories in Mexico is crucial, and I believe that the next great advance in this discipline will be the investigations carried out beyond the large INAH, AGN, and Mexico City archives. A series produced in the early 1990s, *Veracruz, imágenes de su historia*, broke with the outdated Carlylean model, incorporating the new social and cultural history introduced by the French *Annales* school to examine issues of daily life, material culture, class relations, and mentalities.[59] These works were based on extensive graphic investigation in both public and private (largely family) archives; most importantly, interviews were carried out to "enroot" the images and develop their historical meanings. Some of the volumes, particularly those by Bernardo García Díaz, are outstanding examples of how to do history with photographs. The reproduction quality is high and was probably costly, but it appears that the volumes were self-financing because they sold out quickly. The success of the Veracruz project made it apparent that there may be a methodological (as well as practical) coincidence between the specificities of local history and the particularity of photography.

The first studies on regional photographers examined Romualdo García of Guanajuato (1905–1914) and José Antonio Bustamante Martínez of Fresnillo, Zacatecas (1930–1973).[60] The books, printed respectively in 1980 and 1992, largely reproduce their portraiture, although one or another image of social practices around floods and death are included. A 1998 work on photojournalist Joáquin Santamaría of Veracruz (1912–1950s) provides much more interesting pictures of daily life, work, class relations, prisons, sports, dances, and other activities carried out in the port, with an excellent reproduction.[61] The bilingual texts situate the photographer in his context and carry out a significant analysis of his work. In the same year, anthropologists Blanca Jimenez and Samuel Villela published the work that would be crucial in reorienting research toward regional archives with their study of three generations that labored in the Salmerón family studio in Chilapa, Guerrero (ca.1900 to ca.1980).[62] This book had a major impact on photo studies because the authors were able to identify Amando Salmerón as the personal photographer of Emiliano Zapata, thus opening up the issue of photographers' commitments to different causes. Villela also discovered the only woman to extensively photograph the revolution, Sara Castrejón, who had her studio in Teloloapan, Guerrero (1900–1930).[63] A 2018 study focuses on a couple who photographed in Tlacolula, Oaxaca, Manuel Mandonado Colmenares and his wife, Beatriz Robles (1925–ca.1970).[64] The authors firmly situate the couple within the local, state, and national history, and the photographs document child labor, gender relations, and the

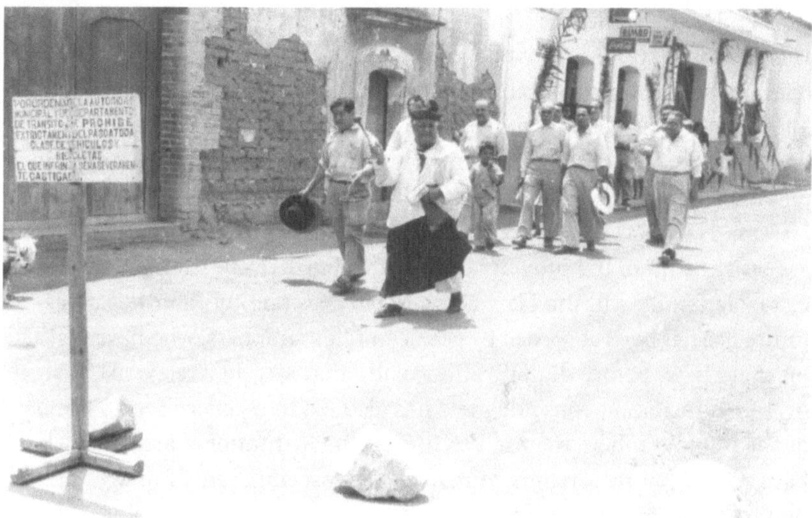

FIGURE 9. Beatriz Robles. Priest blessing a newly paved street, Tlacolula, Oaxaca, 1950s. Acervo Foto Maldonado.

central role of the church in provincial life, as embodied in the image of a priest blessing a newly paved street.[65] (See Figure 9.)

Another recent work came from Cholula, Puebla, and the process by which it came to be offers insight into how books get produced and the way a municipal photo archive is established.[66] The city's mayor decided to bring out a photohistory around families of the region and sent out a call on the social networks for domestic imagery. An announcement was made on the social media site of the municipal government, posters were put up around the city in businesses, and letters were sent to families inviting them to participate. In the beginning, the pictures were to be scanned and returned, but José Zamora believed that they could provide a base for an archive. Many Cholulans donated their images, and the Fototeca de Cholula was founded with the idea of continuing to work in the community. The national infrastructure is vital: Zamora and his team have been trained by the technicians of the Sistema Nacional de Fototecas (SINAFO) in cleaning, stabilizing, and digitalizing photos, as well as methods for cataloguing. The Fototeca now holds more than six hundred images and grows daily; it is currently in the process of producing another work. There is reason to believe that municipal archives should thrive under the government of López Obrador, as he is decentralizing cultural funding away from Mexico City and toward the regions.

Despite the limitations of most as photohistories, the national *historias gráficas* have probably been important in creating a relatively unique consciousness of incorporating the visual in Mexican historical narratives. The State has purchased archives and provides for their conservation; the five million negatives of the Hermanos Mayo (preserved in the AGN since 1982), and the 350,000 negatives in the Casasola Archive (bought for the Sistema Nacional de Fototecas in 1976 and now almost fully digitalized), are only the tip of the proverbial iceberg.[67] Further, the example set by the Casasola family and the Hermanos Mayo of retaining their negatives for future use has been absorbed by Mexican photographers, who have insisted on that right (before digitalization made that largely irrelevant).[68] Moreover, this historical consciousness has also led to a generosity on the part of the photographers themselves, and of the institutional archives, which have permitted researchers to investigate vast numbers of images and to publish them at reasonable rates.

According to Navarrete, in 2003 Mexico was the leader in Latin American photographic studies, followed by Argentina and Brazil.[69] More recently, a scholar observed of the Mexican scene that it is marked by "an unusually numerous community of scholars of photography, who are supported by an outstanding structure."[70] Universities and other degree-granting institutions—among them the Instituto Mora, the INAH and Escuela Nacional de Antropología e Historia (ENAH), the Universidad Veracruzana, and the Benemérita Universidad Autónoma de Puebla—have provided visual historians with positions, and they in turn have legitimated these studies through their production, as well as their direction of many MA and PhD degrees in History that focused on photography.[71] Recently, the ENAH opened up an MA and PhD in Social History and Image, the first such program that has been created, at least in the Western Hemisphere, to permit students to utilize vernacular photographs as a source of history.[72]

In 2015, Mexican photohistorian Rebeca Monroy estimated that there were some twenty-five researchers dedicated to studying photography, and that "around 150 books have been published in recent years."[73] Two years later, Monroy documented 116 *licenciatura*, master, and doctorate theses on photohistory that were produced in the period from 1990 to 2019, the great majority after the turn of the century.[74] Journals such as *Alquimia* and *Luna Córnea* have provided spaces to publish and have been recognized as being among the world's most solid publications in photographic history.[75] Further, longstanding seminars, both informal and institutional, have been carried out almost continually since around 1985. Hence, historians—and photographers themselves—have constructed an unusual receptivity to the rigorous analysis of photography. And, although the government has had its own reasons for subsidizing *historias gráficas*, the extraordinary number of important studies related to the photography of the Mexican Revolution that appeared in relation to the Centennial celebration of 2010 and that were stimulated in part by official subsidies, as well as the possibility of publishing, indicates that Mexican historians have known how to use official financing for their own purposes.[76]

PHOTOGRAPHIC DOCUMENTS FOR ENVISIONING THE PAST

What might happen if we were to use photographs as documents of social pasts that could stimulate and guide research as well as provide clues we could follow in doing our photohistories? The first thing that strikes one about photographs is the ease with which they are made as compared to other images. Hundreds of photographs can be taken in the space of minutes without much forethought because something can always be salvaged in image selection and cropping. A product of mechanical reproduction, photography's singular capability to include details that the photographer may have had no intention of documenting leaves historians with the possibility of discovering things that were invisible to the imagemaker.

This capacity for the unintentional inclusion of details is a significant factor in contemplating photography's contribution to social histories. Consider, for example, the picture by one of the Hermanos Mayo of preparations for a feminist march in Mexico City during the 1980 protest against the officialist and reactionary Mother's Day celebration.[77] (See Figure 10.) As a working photojournalist (and member of a collective who maintained control of their negatives in order to later sell prints to other buyers), Mayo was there to cover the march in its entirety. Painting posters and preparing banners were among the preliminary activities that make important background material for reporting on this event (as well as contributing to the collective's archive). In the middle of this image a young man stands, wearing a Boston College t-shirt. Dressing in clothes—shirts, sweat suits, jackets, caps, sweaters, and so forth—covered with the logos of US colleges and professional sports teams is so common in Mexico that people do not notice it. However, despite their ubiquity (or better, because of it), these emblems are largely invisible to Mexicans; they are too banal, too mundane. On many occasions, I have shown the Mayo photograph to Mexican audiences and posed this question: "You are historians a century from now. What can you find in this photograph that is an important artifact about Mexico in the twentieth century?" They rarely see the Boston Col-

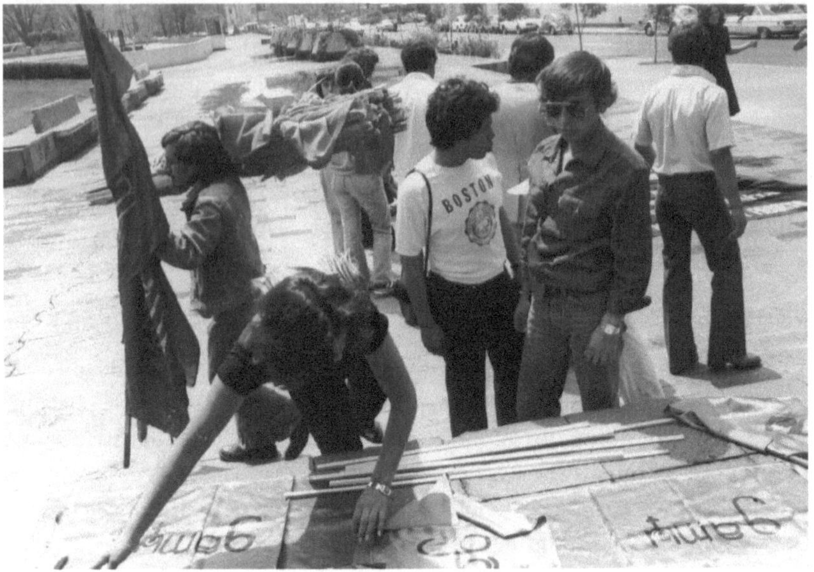

FIGURE 10. Hermanos Mayo. Preparations for a protest march against Mother's Day, 8 May 1980. Fondo Hermanos Mayo, Concentrated Section, Manifestación de mujeres, Archivo General de la Nación.

lege t-shirt, and Mayo probably didn't either; it may well be a case of the "unintentional incorporation" that photography's mechanical reproduction produces. Its very invisibility is ominous, for it is an eloquent statement on cultural neocolonialism and a symptom of the "Americanization" of Mexico.

As a newly arrived foreigner with sensitivity to cultural colonialism, I was immediately struck by items of clothing featuring US logos. When I began working in television during 1981, I observed the ubiquity of such dress in the highlands of Jalisco, and mentioned it to members of the crew; they saw nothing unusual about it and could not understand my interest. Shortly thereafter, I photographed a woman in Coyoacán wearing a Dallas Cowboys t-shirt; it proclaimed that she was in some way that team's "property." This is perhaps the most popular US football organization in Mexico, to judge by the paraphernalia seen on the streets. Hence, the image serves as an acute example of how cultural neocolonialism is played out, because it continues to be publicized as "America's team" on the NFL networks. (See Figure 11.) I remarked on this phenomenon to Paul Vanderwood, and he carried out a highly informal and very short "survey," alluding to the different NFL logos on shirts Mexicans were wearing in the different businesses he visited: "Your team is doing very well," "Your team is not so hot this year," "What do you think of your team's chances this year?" He said that

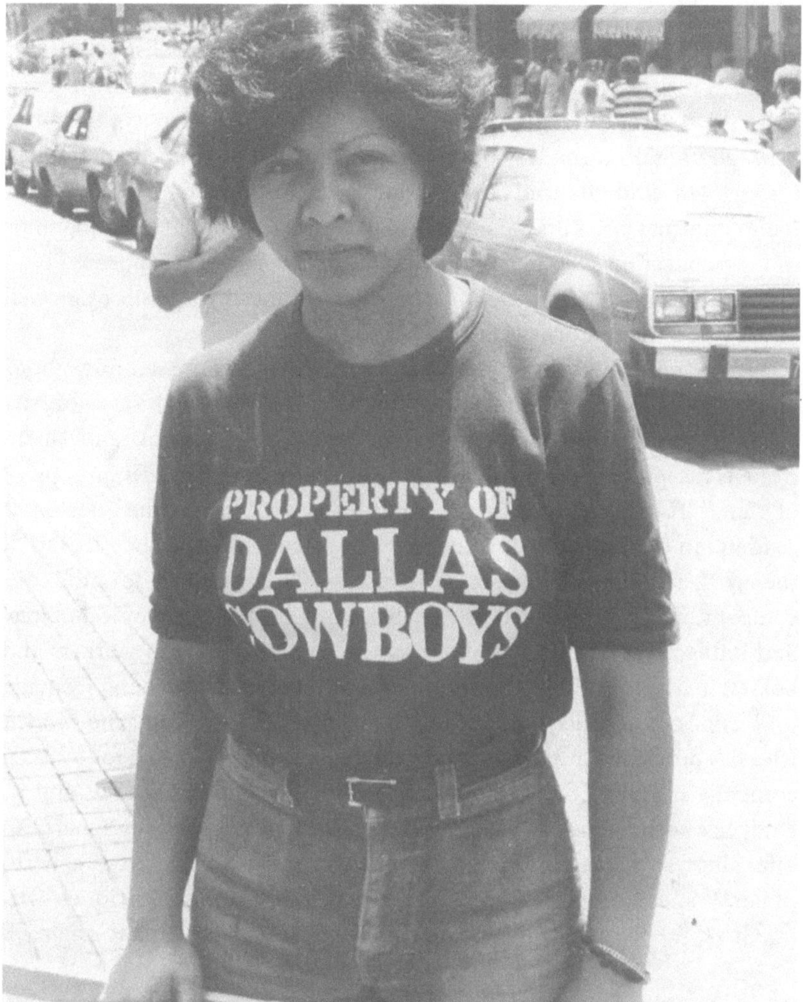

FIGURE 11. John Mraz. Woman with a Dallas Cowboys t-shirt, Coyoacán, Mexico City, 1982. Collection of John Mraz.

most Mexicans had no idea what he was talking about.[78] Although there is a following of NFL football in Mexico, the quantity of apparel seems disproportionate to any real interest in the teams, other than perhaps the Dallas Cowboys.

Dense technical images, photographs would seem to offer unlimited possibilities in developing visual social histories, for pictures can be gleaned from a wealth of sources. One of the richest founts is photojournalism, and the archives of collectives such as the Casasola dynasty, the Hermanos Mayo, and Díaz, Delgado y García contain among them some seven or eight million negatives.[79] The usefulness of photojournalist collections varies in relation to the information that accompanies the archival negatives, the state of cataloguing, and the degree to which access is enhanced through digitalization. It is unfortunate that, even in the best catalogued (though still undigitalized) archive, the Hermanos Mayo, the data is limited to minimal notes on the negative envelopes. Locating the photographs in the publications where they originally and subsequently appeared is an arduous task, but such research can open up interesting questions, as well as provide useful information.

Other genres of photography are also important. For example, photographs taken for political purposes can be useful. This is the case of Ana Victoria Jiménez, who photographed the Mexican neo-feminist movement from its inception in the 1970s, registering that process from a feminist point of view.[80] The images in the archive of Guillermo Treviño, the Puebla railroad union militant who documented labor struggles from the 1920s until the 1970s, are vital in telling workers' history. On the other side of the coin, company archives can also be invaluable sources for histories of technology and industry, as well as documenting the relations between workers and bosses; in Mexico, "there are no real in-depth studies of photography made for business enterprises," according to historian Thelma Camacho Morfín, who has published important works on the imagery produced for tobacco company El Buen Tono.[81] Studio photography is another source, and its study has been relatively well developed in Mexico.[82] Finally, foreigners can offer alternative insights, such as the pictures of Desiré Charnay, Teoberto Maler, François Aubert, C. B. Waite, Winfield Scott, Alfred Briquet, Otis M. Gove, F. E. North, and William Henry Jackson, among many others.[83]

FAMILY PHOTOGRAPHY

An important visual source for historians is family photograph albums; these can be invaluable for studying the past, above all if interviews are carried out in relation to the pictures, as was the case of the series mentioned above, *Veracruz: Imágenes de su historia*.[84] The photographing of families in studios began almost from the camera's invention, but once George Eastman invented the Kodak camera in 1888 the mode of producing familial representations fell increasingly into the hands of the members of the household itself. In one of his early research projects, Pierre Bourdieu documented the centrality of family photography within this medium, affirming that,

> More than two thirds of photographers are seasonal conformists who take photographs either at family festivities or social gatherings, or during the summer holidays. . . . Photographic practice only exists and subsists for most of the time by virtue of its family function or rather by the function conferred upon it by the family group, namely that of solemnizing and immortalizing the high points of family life, in short, of reinforcing the integration of the family group by reasserting the sense that it has both of itself and of its unity. . . . There are few activities which are so stereotyped and less abandoned to the anarchy of individual intentions.[85]

Bourdieu has clearly outlined the limitations of family photography. We may be tempted to think that family images offer a great variety of representations that embalm daily life, domestic contexts, and those miniscule bits of the phenomenal world that make photographs such an important source of social history. Nonetheless, snapshots do not usually document mundane activities such as the family watching television, seated at their computers, working in the kitchen, or cleaning the bathroom. Instead, they are generally taken when the family is engaged in exceptional gatherings.

Embedded in the fundamental rites of family life, photography is a chronicler as well as a central activity of these rituals; moreover, it solemnizes them. Family photography is commonly stereotyped and conventional, because it represents people in the roles to which they have been socially assigned—the mother, the husband, the aunt from Morelia—rather than capturing their individuality. It is also often idealizing of the institution, as most images capture smiles and hugs rather than the fights over the dinner table, the latent resentments, the sibling rivalries, or the generational incomprehension that are also part of family reunions. Practitioners of family photography adhere unconsciously and insistently to long-established codes of posing, in which only good and socially approved behavior is photographed. Later, another process of selection occurs in which those images chosen to enter into the album must conform to the desired attitudes. Far from opening the doors onto domestic realities, the varied filters are designed to safeguard family secrets and protect what Sontag described as "that claustrophobic unit, the nuclear family" from public scrutiny.[86]

Do the preceding observations mean that family photographs are not useful for historians? There is no doubt that they can offer wonderful opportunities if we know how to interrogate them. As technical images, they conserve fundamental aspects of material life and social relations, perhaps often without that being the intention of the photographer. For example, they "provide information about the layouts of rooms, the styles of furniture, the size of houses, the menus at picnics."[87] Moreover, family photographs are the domestic document that predominates, particularly among workers and *campesinos*, who have left few written texts such as diaries, letters, or memoirs. Hence, they offer the possibility of telling the story of the "other half," those often hidden or silenced or made invisible. They can be important tools of resistance for subaltern peoples, for as sociologist Stuart Hall argued, "it is only through the way we represent and imagine ourselves that we come to know how we are constituted and who we are."[88]

Family photographs can provide crucial testimonies for the study of immigrant groups. Photohistorian Kevin Coleman analyzed the images made by Palestinians who had moved to Honduras, asserting that, "These family photographic collections reveal how this ethnic group navigated the social and cultural journey between their homeland in the Levant and their hostland in the Americas."[89] According to other scholars of emigrants, family photographs of Ukrainians in Argentina are expressive of developing a new identity, in documenting the "two basic processes at work in the immigrant group experience: assimilation and integration versus differentiation and a tightening of ethnic boundaries."[90]

Although I have never carried out a research project that focused on family photographs, I have often employed them in my documentary films. I had explored this idea by incorporating home movie footage in the 1973 Super 8mm film, *Cracks in the Wall: America/the Fifties*.[91] However, I only began to utilize family photographs in my videotape *Made on Rails: A History of the Mexican Railroad Workers*.[92] I used a great variety of images in this work, relying on national archives such as the Casasola and Hermanos Mayo holdings in the Fototeca Nacional and the Archivo General de la Nación respectively, private collections of the Directors of the Workers' Administration (1938–40), and the Communist leader Guillermo Treviño, as well as the guild shields preserved in the Sindicato de Trabajadores Ferrocarrileros de la República Mexicana. However, I felt that a history of railroad workers needed to decentralized, and so included a microhistory of Oriental, an isolated town in the desert of Puebla State. By conducting an almost door-to-door search, we were able to turn up images that were crucial for telling the town's political history—such as its founding in 1917—as well as being socially significant. For example, a photo of young boys posed on the fronts of trains was shown during a sequence where an informant described how every male family member works for the railroad, "All of us who live here work for the railroad. You work for the railroad or you leave, because there is no other way to make a living."[93] (See Figure 12.) Photo-

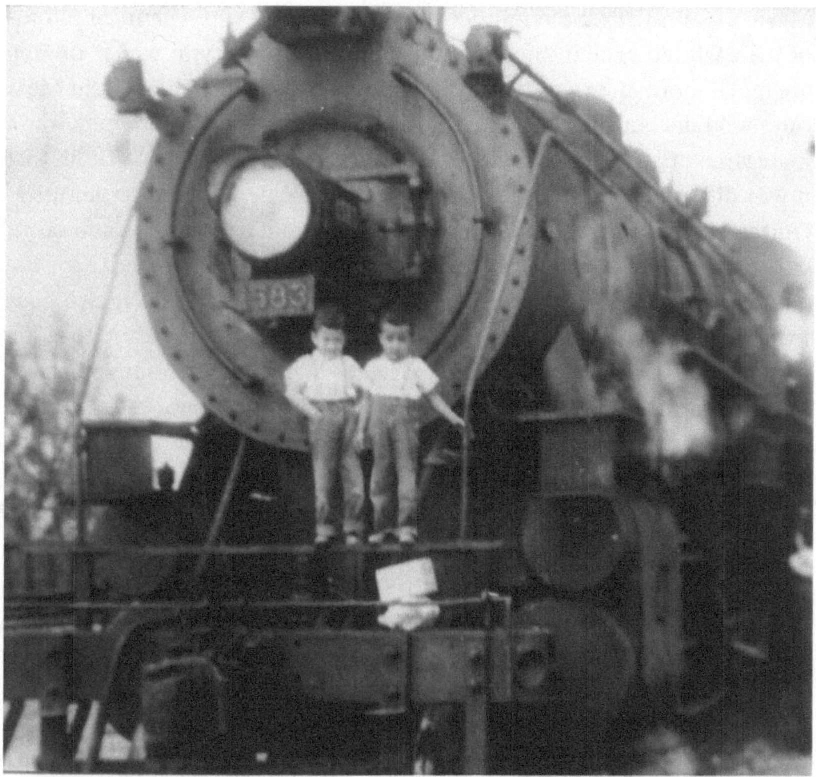

FIGURE 12. Unknown. Boys on train, Oriental, Puebla, ca. 1950. Collection of John Mraz.

graphic absence can be as telling as presence: here, the absence of girls in the family photos taken around the trains is revealing of gender relations.

The use of family photo albums in Oriental was a critical element in presenting a history from below; to observe that a "people's history" of Oriental could only have been told through such family images is to belabor the obvious. Unfortunately, our very limited budget allowed for only one day of shooting in Oriental, so we were not able to carry out interviews with the owners. Doing history with modern media often requires us to work within the particular restraints that the project imposes. In this case, the object was to make a videotape, rather than carry out an oral family history research that would appear in book form, so the albums were quickly copied in 35 mm film for slides, without considering the importance of establishing either the owners or the subjects.

The question to which our attention ought now to be drawn is how to apply the generalized methodologies for studying family photography to

Mexico, again with the reminder that I am dealing with chemical photos of the past, rather than the more recent digital imagery in which women are much more incorporated as photographers.[94] On which days did Mexican men take out their cameras? Bourdieu found that photography was a masculine privilege in France, and there can be little reason to think that it was different in Mexico. When did Mexican men pose their families? One can imagine that some significant dates would be birthdays and saints' days, Christmas, Easter week, the first communion, and the party for the *quinceañera* (the girl who turns fifteen). Where did they decide to pose them: in which parts of the house, in front of which structures, and together with which objects? How were they dressed? What were the "familial gazes" found in Mexican photography? One scholar observed that, "Every culture and historical moment can identify its own 'familial gaze' . . . [that] situates human subjects in the ideology, the mythology, of the family as institution and projects a screen of familial myths between camera and subject."[95] For example, in Mexico many people are named after saints; their "saint's day" is celebrated equally as their birthday. Finally, what differences can be observed between photos made by *campesino* families, families of workers, of the middle-class, and of the wealthy?

I believe that one of the most important issues is to examine the representation of the hyper-machismo that so dominates public and private life in Mexico. It seems clear to me that the fundamental familial structure is that of a patriarchy that profoundly affects all spheres of Mexican life, with the result of producing impunity for anyone in power, as well as the incapacity to make rigorous critiques. Such patriarchy is embodied in the great father as president, or director, or judge, or policeman, none of whom can be criticized or questioned. What are constitutive elements of this pattern, and how is that represented by a photography in which the patriarch was usually absent, because he was taking the photos?

It is obvious that delving into the profundities of family photography in Mexico will require extensive research. Finding and getting access to the photos is only the first step. Interviews with family members will be fundamental; they are the primary audience for these images and bring a wealth of knowledge and memories to viewing them; they hold the keys to their contents and contexts that will make them intelligible. Using photographs to assist oral history interviews can be a pivotal strategy. In his classic study, visual anthropologist John Collier found that doing interviews with photographs enabled him to extend the process greatly, or at least as long as new photographs appeared, while interviewing informants without photos led to them ending much more rapidly and with significantly less information.[96] Talking about the photographs also sharpened memories and reduced stress.

One excellent study of a particular variety of Mexican family photography was carried out by Patricia Massé, who is a researcher in the Fototeca Nacional. In 1981, a cardboard box of 378 glass plate negatives was donated to the Fototeca, accompanied by a minimum of information.[97] Twenty-two years later, Massé timidly proposed the study of this collection for her doctoral thesis, fearing that I would find such a project fanciful, as nothing whatsoever was known about these images. Instead, I strongly encouraged her to take on this study, because photographs often arrive at archives in such a state. Hence, this project offered the opportunity to carry out a double task: historicizing a group of images and developing a model on how to incorporate them in a photographic archive.

In the ten years that it took to elaborate her thesis, Massé established that the man behind these images was a Porfirian entrepreneur, Juan Antonio Azurmendi, married to Dolores de Teresa, the daughter of one of the most influential and powerful men in Porfirian Mexico, Nicolás de Teresa. Azurmendi was greatly drawn to the photographic medium, but it is not clear whether he himself took any of the images, which were evidently made by at least two different cameras. The photographs document the construction of his mansion, which included—as Massé discovered—the incorporation of many Masonic symbols in the house and the grounds; that he was a Mason is one of the few real facts we know about this individual. There are a number of more domestic images: Azurmendi and his family; the servants; even one in which another photographer appears. Azurmendi attempted to capture movement within a shot, and he also experimented in pushing genre conventions to their limits. Massé argues that the playful picture in which he appears with his wife and daughters is characteristic of the photographic challenges Azurmendi carried out, in this case producing an "anti-portrait" that subverts the conventional uses of portraiture through a comedy that unmasks its ideology.[98] (See Figure 13.)

Personal memories must be linked to the larger history. Here, it may be fruitful to develop comparative research into other visual forms whose subjects are family life, such as movies, television shows (in Mexico, the hugely popular *telenovelas*), radio programs, illustrated magazines, and advertisements. There can be little doubt of the relationship between the psychological structures created by the various forms of modern visual culture and family photography. If researchers can develop the instruments to effectively interrogate domestic snapshots, it will offer an important visual document to construct a people's history of Mexico. Moreover, the incorpora-

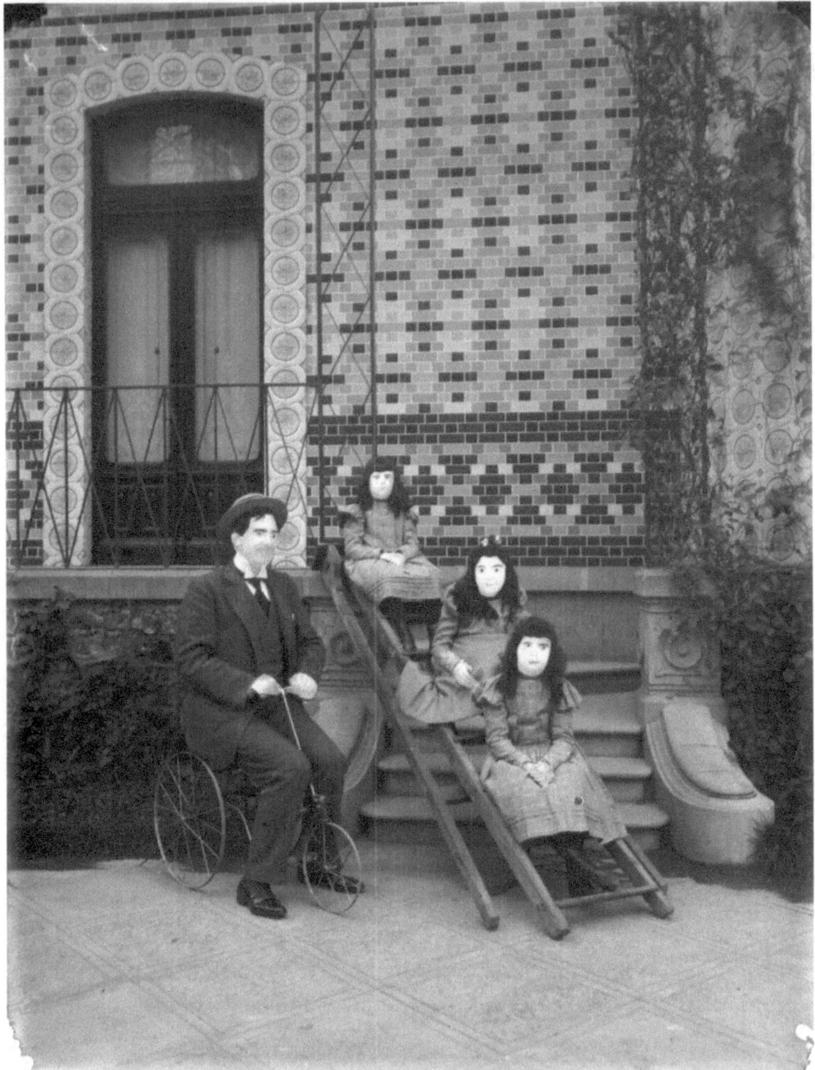

FIGURE 13. Juan Antonio Azurmendi (intellectual author). Juan Antonio Azurmendi, his wife, Dolores de Teresa, and daughters, Gloria and Victoria, posing with masks, Mexico City, ca. 1900. Inv. # 366401, Fondo Juan Azurmendi, SINAFO-Fototeca Nacional del INAH, Secretaría de Cultura.

tion of these new materials makes a notable contribution to moving beyond the current dependence on public archives such as the Fototeca Nacional and the Archivo General de la Nación, where the lack of information seriously limits their holdings as sources of social research. In sum, family photography—what Bourdieu called "the domestic manufacture of domestic emblems"—offers fascinating opportunities for those who know how to research and employ it.[99]

REVEALING THE UNDERSIDE OF HISTORY

What elements from the past are preserved by photographs? First of all, there is the mere presence of people who are often excluded from written texts. As Azoulay observed,

> Even when these traces express cultural and social hierarchies that organize the power relations between photographer, camera, and photographed person, they never simply echo such relations nor do they necessarily reflect the point of view of the most powerful figure present in the arena at the time the photograph was captured. This characteristic differentiates the photograph from all other forms of documentation that we know.[100]

To return to Fontcuberta's allegation that photos lie, we should remember that Simone de Beauvoir described omission as "the most insidious form of lying."[101] Hence, although they are usually buried under the proclamations of male governing bodies, workers, women, and children are present in photographs to be reclaimed for history. At times, these images can provide important "clues" that we could follow to open up research possibilities about things that have not yet been discovered in written documents. Women participated actively in the Mexican Revolution and, though little has been written about that, they appear constantly in photographs. In fact, photographic images have in fact been the primary stimulus for research on female Zapatista officers. For example, we know little about Salgadista-Zaptista-Maderista colonel Amparo Salgado other than the few details that have resulted from interviews carried out as a result of having unearthed her picture (see Chapter 5). We still know nothing whatsoever about other women commanders such as Colonel Carmen Robles, "La Costeña," who was linked to the Zapatista-Maderista army in 1911 and appears in at least three extant photos, one of which was mistakenly identified as being of "La Negra Angustias" in the Fototeca Nacional.[102] (See Figure 14.) Another such figure who served in those same forces, Colonel Esperanza Echevarría, is equally absent from written sources, but both of these pictures are important clues to follow in order to uncover women's role in the uprising.

The same could be said of photographs that demonstrate that child labor continued in Mexico despite the fact that it was forbidden by Article 123 of the 1917 Constitution, which "constituted the most enlightened statement

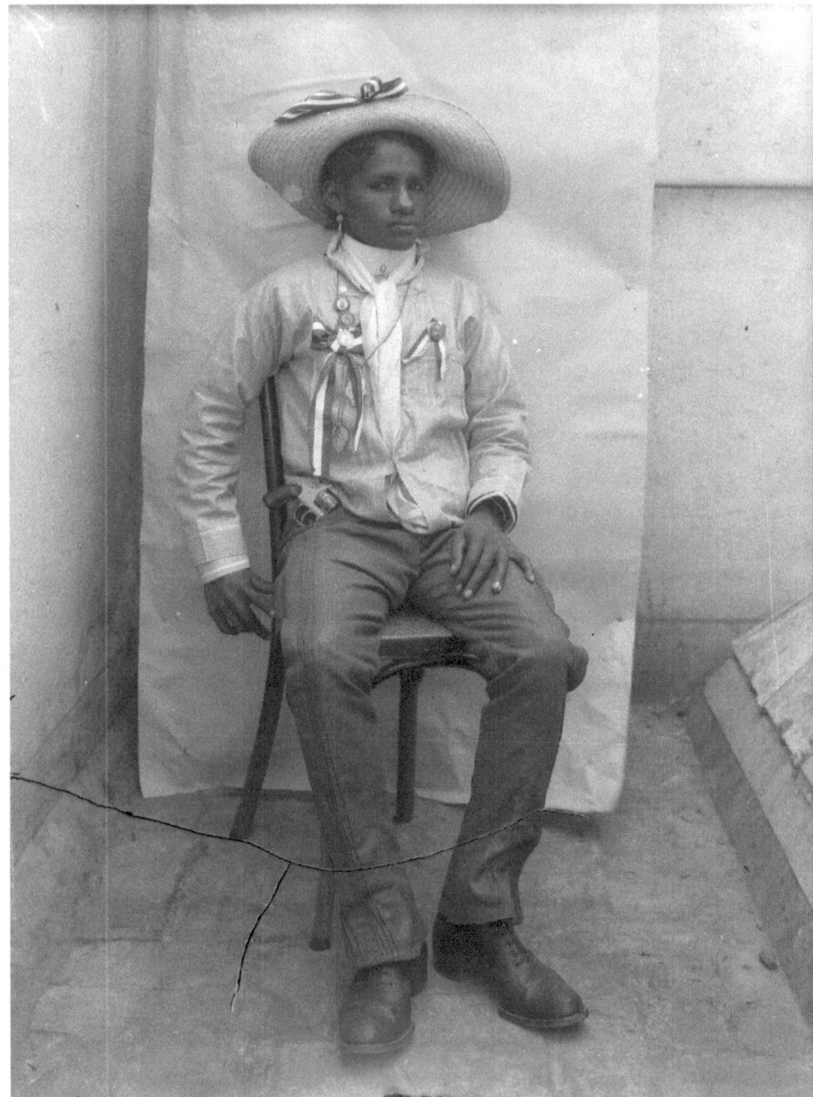

FIGURE 14. Unknown. Carmen Robles (La Costeña), ca. 1915. Inv. # 186387, Fondo Casasola, SINAFO-Fototeca Nacional del INAH, Secretaría de Cultura.

of labor protective principles in the world to that date."[103] (See Figure 15.) The girl in the picture was one of sixteen minors that worked in La Central match company in December of 1919. During that year Juan de Beraza, described as an *inspector ayudante* for the Secretary of Industry, Commerce and Labor, carried out some fifty inspections of working conditions in factories that made cigarettes, cardboard, perfumes, dolls, toys, and a wide

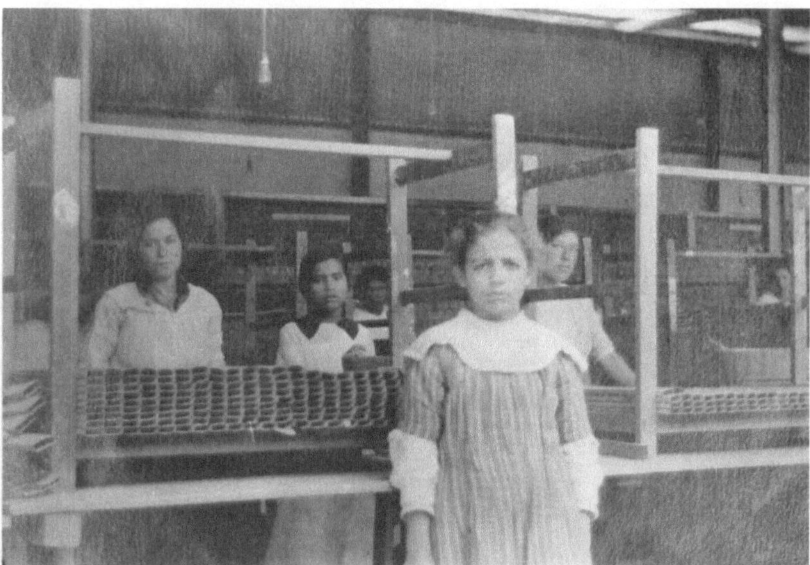

FIGURE 15. Juan de Beraza (intellectual author). Girl working in the match factory "La Central," Mexico City, 30 December 1919. Departamento del Trabajo, caja 163, expediente 12, Archivo General de la Nación.

range of clothing, including the Corsetería Francesa. In eight of the workplaces he visited in Mexico City he was probably the author of small format photographs, perhaps with a Kodak Brownie; in most cases he took one or two pictures.[104] The photos were essentially to denounce child labor, for children were supposed to be in school, and businesses were forbidden to hire illiterates, a point de Beraza made repeatedly in his reports. He seems to have widely investigated violations of the constitutional mandates, at times making suggestions for workers' health and comfort.[105] The images are generally quite poor, so perhaps de Beraza took a better photographer along when he went to investigate the women who worked in eleven small retail mills for the Compañía Mexicana Molinera de Nixtamal, selling the ground corn to make tortillas, and made seven images.[106] He did not accompany any of his thirty-seven reports of 1920 with images, and thereafter he evidently ceased to work for the Secretariat.

Photographs can contribute to social histories in representing material culture and daily life. Here, they can take us into the most mundane aspects of human existence, for images of activities related to eating, drinking, housing, transportation, and disasters can be fundamental in allowing us to reconstruct the everyday lives of people in the past. Photographs also preserve cityscapes and their transformation, as well as landscapes and ecological impact, as perhaps no other medium could. However, in order to take advantage of what these images can offer us, we must develop knowledge of the contexts in which they were originally taken; when the images can be combined with contemporary texts, we are in a position to develop social histories. But, what sort of a history will it be? It may well be based on traces, on indexes, on seemingly insignificant minutiae—Carlo Ginzburg's "unconsidered trifles"—and on the sovereign particularity of photographs.[107] Words are conventional symbols for similarities; they do not possess the dramatically singular experience of a photograph, which brings us face to face with the immediate *this*: this fraction of a second, this particular place, this unique individual or group. Such a history may be very much at home in a world reduced, at best, to aphorisms, as well as publicity slogans and continuous partial attention (CPA).[108]

As the de Beraza research indicated, one place photographs are found together with extensive textual descriptions is the Departamento del Trabajo of the Archivo General de la Nación, where inspectors' reports on, and workers' complaints about, labor and living conditions are sometimes accompanied by images. For example, on December 14, 1919, miners who worked for the Peñoles Mining Company in Mapimí, Durango, wrote to President Venustiano Carranza to complain about their situation. They felt that the "*malditos* (damned) *señores gringos*" treated them very badly, worse than animals, as if they were "slaves."[109] They argued that they were paid very little, that they were fired without cause, and that—in spite of being *hijos de México*—they had no guarantees; they could be fired without cause and were not allowed the right to redress their situation. Miners had died because of medical inattention, but the "gringos" blamed those deaths on the workers' stupidity. Although the company deducted a peso every month from their salary for an Italian doctor, he would do nothing without being paid extra. They were aware of the rights won by the prolonged revolution, but affirmed that the bosses scoffed at Article 123. The miners noted that the Mexican employees were "the hangmen for the damn bourgeoisie," and that the local authorities would do nothing for them because they were paid off by the company. They also lamented their own lack of words to adequately describe their situation, and did not sign the letter because they feared that they would be expelled or shot. Perhaps most importantly, they advised the president that if nothing were done about the situation, "they would be obligated to take the law into their own hands."

Conscious of the fact that Mexican workers retained their arms after nine years of war, and in line with the revolutionary reforms, the Secretary of Industry, Commerce and Labor sent investigators to look into the min-

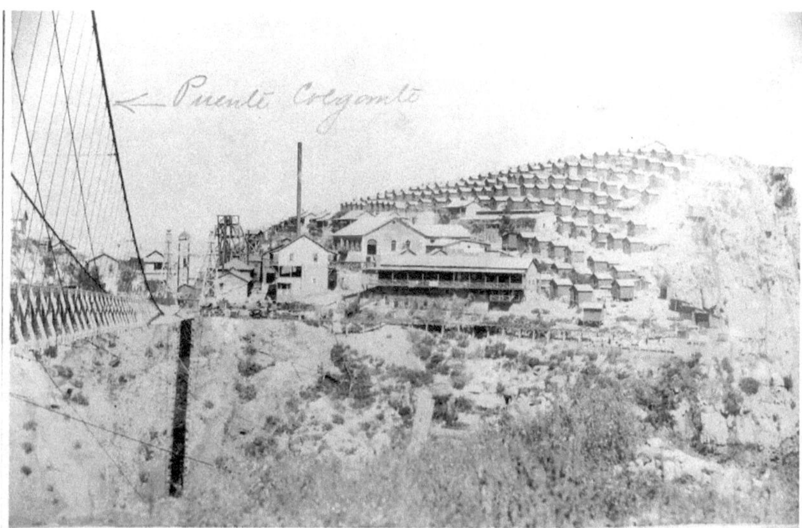

FIGURE 16. Unknown inspector of the Secretaría de Industria, Comercio y Trabajo. Miners' housing, Mapimí, Durango, January 1920. Departamento del Trabajo, caja 220, expediente 4, Archivo General de la Nación.

ers' complaints. They replied in a report on January 18, 1920. The inspectors found a "gloomy ambience" caused by the reduction of salaries by 50 percent while the cost of living was high. They noted that the company was one of the first to return to production after the revolution and had been paying good salaries for eight-hour workdays, as well as double time. However, because many workers were attracted by the decent pay, leaving jobs such as shoemakers and butchers, the company began to reduce wages. Miners were fired if they complained, so they attempted to form a union, but the company was paying both the federal and local authorities to encourage workers to form mutual aid societies, such as those that existed during the *Porfiriato*, rather than combative trade unions. Because laborers were charged for medical costs on the day they began work, a form of debt peonage existed. Boys under sixteen were hired at very low wages and put to work in particularly dangerous areas. The workers' daily life was hard: corn, beans, and sugar were sold in the company store at prices higher than those in Mapimí, and the water had "a disagreeable taste."

The inspectors took photographs of the housing provided by the company, and coupled them with a description of the living conditions. (See Figure 16.) Although the image itself is eloquent, the reports conserved in the Ramo de Trabajo provide us with insight into these people's existence:

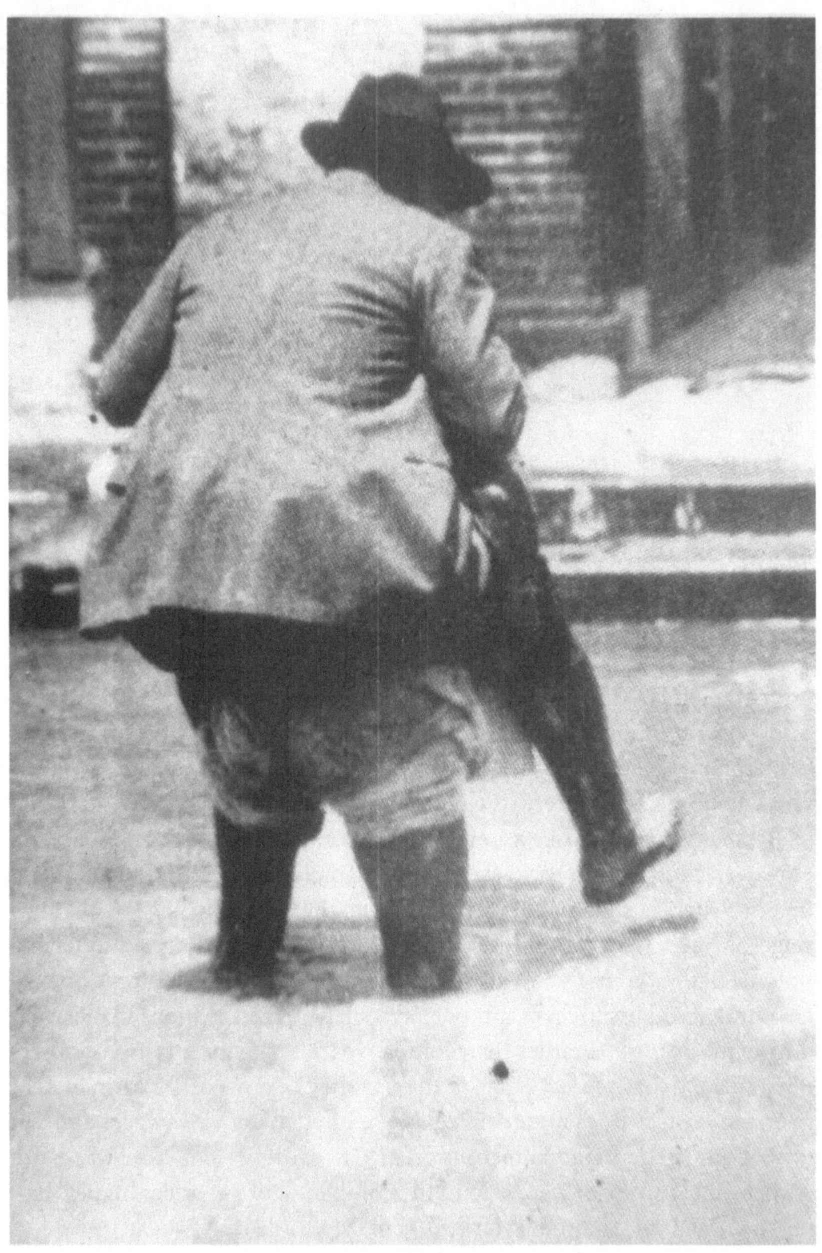

FIGURE 17. Miguel or Ismael Casasola? Wealthy man being carried across the flooded street, Mexico City, ca. 1945. Colección Gustavo Casasola.

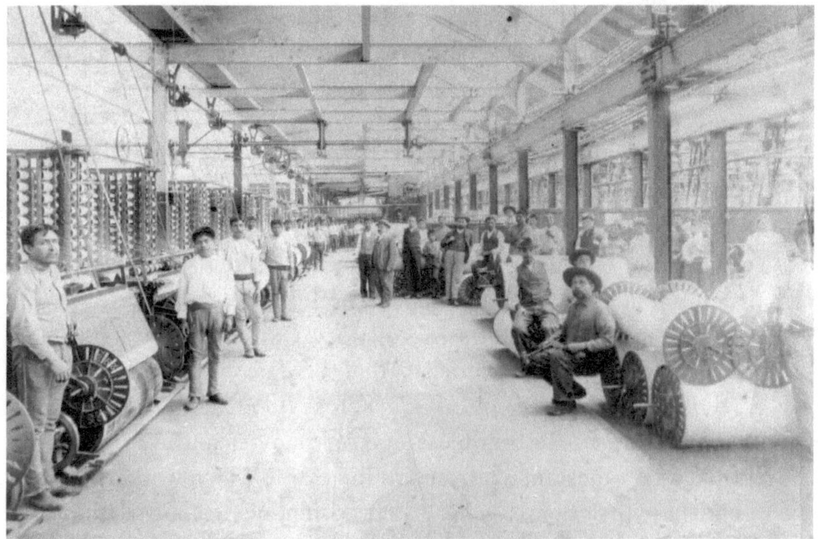

FIGURE 18. Unknown. Textile workers dressed in *charro* pants, Santa Rosa, Veracruz, ca. 1900. Courtesy of Bernardo García Díaz.

> The great majority of the constructions that serve to house the workers and employees are made of wood and covered with roofs of zinc. The workers' habitations are three square meters, consisting of one room without kitchen, bathroom, electricity or water. They are poorly built, and barely fit to house one person, but four or five people usually live in these little huts, and even more when there is an influx of workers. The company has established the custom to place new personnel in these houses, without asking the permission of the inhabitants, so there are usually about four or five people from different families living together. Those families that are not willing to live with people they do not know, and whose customs are different, have begun to construct small stone corrals, such as those used to keep pigs, in which they live, and there are presently many poor families living in such corrals. . . . Wooden bathrooms consist of two large rooms, one for women and another for men. They have been constructed in different parts of the hill, placed in the most dangerous places next to the steepest part of the cliffs, and the slightest carelessness on the part of anyone sitting there could result in their falling down into a great ravine to their death.[110]

Some workers' families lived in primitive caves, and when they were asked if they were content to do so, they answered:

> We prefer them to the company's housing, because when it is cold, there are strong winds on the hill, and many of us have no serapes with which to cover ourselves. So, we freeze in the cold air that blows through the floors and walls of the houses. When it is hot, it is suffocating because the roofs have no ceilings that could lessen the high temperatures within that come from the laminated roofs.

Social relations are also documented in photographs, which can speak articulately about class, race, and gender, both in showing their existence as well as in representing their transformations. Consider, for example, how class relations are illustrated in the fact that some people, the poor, carried others, those better off, on their backs across flooded streets in Mexico City.[111] (See Figure 17.) Testimonies of proletarian demands are evident in the banners of a protest march from around 1911 in which workers reclaim the right to have their Sundays off.[112] Transformations in class relations can be seen in the photo of textile workers in the Santa Rosa (Veracruz) factory who pose next to their machines, garbed in charro pants that were originally designed for riding horseback; their clothing has now been adjusted, as these *campesinos* mutate into "the country's first generation of modern proletariat."[113] (See Figure 18.) We can also perceive at least one facet of race relations and their transformation: the 1913 Río Blanco (Veracruz) soccer team is clearly composed of Whites, whether foreigners or Mexicans of European origin; the 1938 Río Blanco team is made up entirely of mestizos.[114]

Photography embalms gender relations as well. Hugo Brehme captured two children as they played out the roles assigned them next to the Canal de Ixtacalco: the girl (really) washing clothes, the boy pretending to be a boatman. (See Figure 19.) The importance of titles given to images as they appear in different contexts can be illustrated with this image. When Brehme circulated it as a postcard, he wrote on it "*Los amigos*."[115] However, when the photo was published in an INAH collection of Brehme's work, the editors titled it *Niños indígenas lavando ropa en el canal de Ixtacalco* (Children washing clothes in the Ixtacalco Canal).[116] Such a title certainly registers a lack of gender perspective as well as a clear failure to really look at the image. The children are being formed in their gender roles: the boy is playing at being a *trajinero*, the boatmen who guided punts loaded with produce and other commodities through the Ixtacalco Canal to the center of Mexico City; the girl is washing clothes, already incorporated into adult labor.[117]

Women's rebellion against their subjugation can be seen in a photo of a 1930s protest where they hold a banner that states, "We are on strike

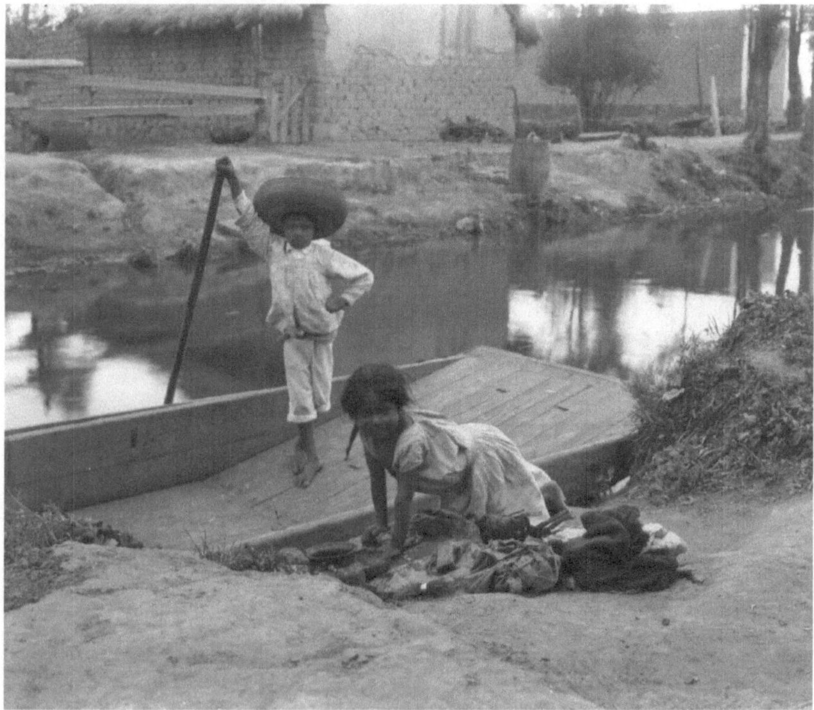

FIGURE 19. Hugo Brehme. *Los amigos* and *Niños indígenas lavando ropa en el canal de Ixtacalco*. Children in the Canal de Ixtacalco, Mexico City, ca. 1920. Inv. # 372055, Colección Hugo Brehme, SINAFO-Fototeca Nacional del INAH, Secretaría de Cultura.

because when we demand a salary raise, they insult us, indicating that we should become prostitutes." (See Figure 20.) The continuity of subordination but the changing face of gender relations can be observed in the images of Constantino Sotero, a 1940s studio photographer from Juchitán, Oaxaca. His portraits show males of all ages dressed in modern clothing, often wearing shoes, while the females continue to dress in traditional garb without footwear.[118] The power of photographs to capture the relations of class, race, and gender so central to history is demonstrated in the image by Enrique Díaz of a shoe factory during the 1930s. There, dark-skinned women labor under the gaze of well-dressed White bosses and their visitors. (See Figure 21.)

Photographs can also document particular expressions of mentalities. For instance, we see a couple who went to the railroad yard of tiny Oriental, Puebla, in the 1940s to pose for a happy family photograph (see Figure 3). The village offered no diversions; as the owner of the family album stated, "There's nothing to do here; there's no theatres or restaurants."[119] The cen-

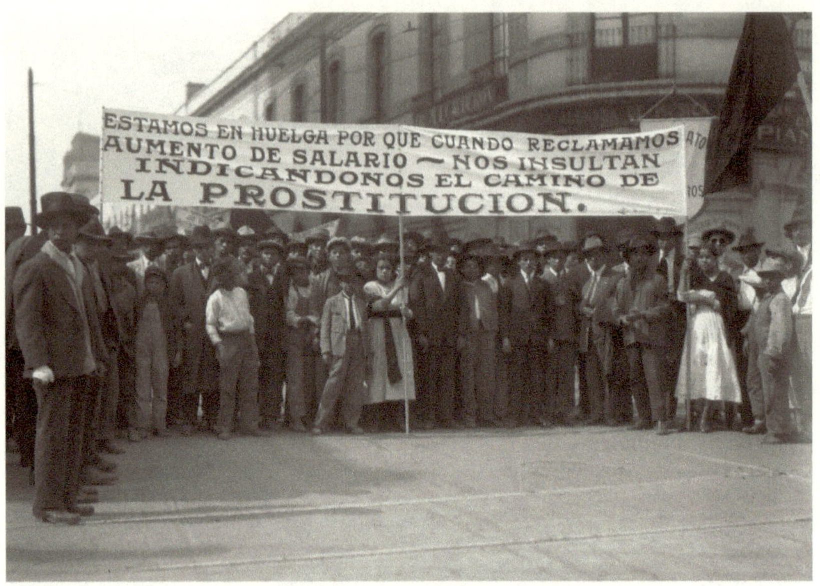

FIGURE 20. Miguel or Ismael Casasola? Women protesting mistreatment, Mexico City, ca. 1935. Inv. # 6350, Fondo Casasola, SINAFO-Fototeca Nacional del INAH, Secretaría de Cultura.

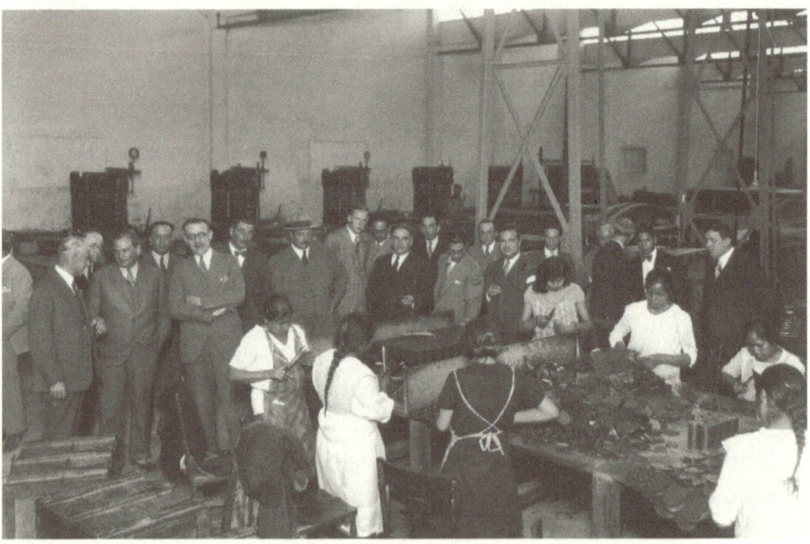

FIGURE 21. Enrique Díaz? Executives, visitors, and women workers in a shoe factory, Mexico City, ca. 1930. Fondo Díaz, Delgado y García, Caja 27/4, Archivo General de la Nación.

trality of the railroad in their lives is demonstrated in their choice of a "studio backdrop." The desire to own a home of one's own is yet another aspect of mentalities that can be represented in a photograph. An image from a family album documents a group of men, women, and children standing on the vacant lot that will (hopefully) soon hold their house; the writing on the picture speaks to their aspirations: "El Sr. Juan Ramos con sus familiares y amigo, en la parte posterior del terreno donde se construirá la casa habitación de su propiedad, Santa Rosa, Veracruz, 20 de diciembre de 1931" (Juan Ramos with family and a friend, on the back part of his land where he will construct a house for himself).[120]

Despite their uses in depicting mentalities, it is crucial to insist that using photographs to document them is completely different from arguing for psychological readings of them. Mentalities are long-term, deeply ingrained socio-cultural patterns; psychology, at least as it appears in photographs, is an immediate emotional state: sadness, joy, disappointment, and chagrin. One of the great temptations of historians who utilize photographs in their work is what I would describe as "psychologism," an error that makes psychological judgments from "evident" expressions of sentiment—for example, deducing depression from a non-smiling face. A classic example of this is Michael Lesy's *Wisconsin Death Trip*, in which the historian juxtaposed photographs of deadly serious people in Wisconsin around 1900 with state reports, news items, and stories of epidemics, suicides, homicides, insanities, bankruptcies, arson, early deaths, and ghosts, to conclude: "If a man didn't kill himself or if a woman didn't murder her own children, the countryside [offered] two varieties of psychic identity. . . . The character type of genteel success now described as obsessive-compulsive, and the character type of failure now called paranoid."[121] Historian Robert Levine also fell into this temptation with his description of the reaction of the Brazilian underclass on being photographed: "Some lower-class men and women stared at the camera listlessly; others appear to be carefree. Whites, who were usually European immigrants, and blacks, likely slaves or ex-slaves, showed similar degrees of weariness, but whites usually wore shoes and were better dressed."[122]

Contrast this use of photography with that of García Díaz's method: he provides us with a 1907 school picture of a class of young boys and their teacher, and alludes to the latter's stiffness: "The professor's rigidity is not just a pose for the school album, this mentor was absolutely convinced that the alphabet letters entered only with blood." (See Figure 22.) Here, however, the photohistorian has not relied on a reading of body language to recreate the disciplinarian atmosphere of schooling a century ago. Rather,

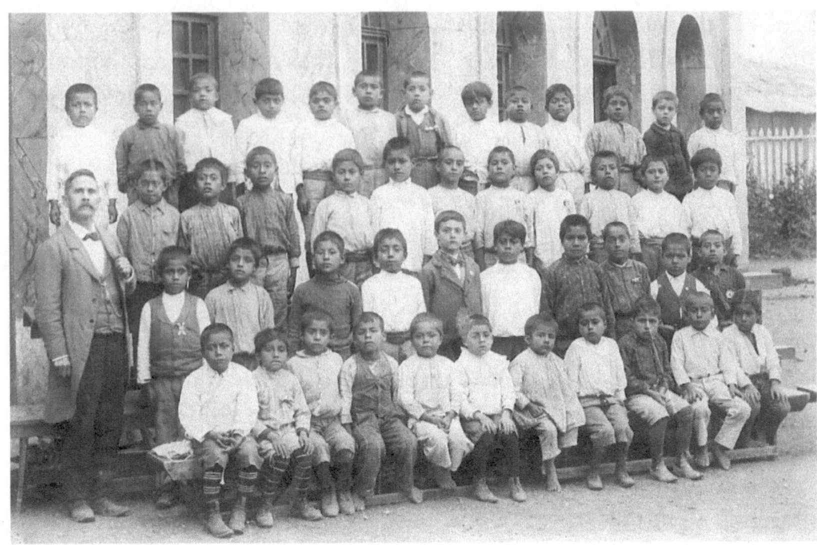

FIGURE 22. Unknown. Municipal school, Santa Rosa, Veracruz, ca. 1907. Family album of Sr. Trinidad Luna. Courtesy of Bernardo García Díaz.

information about the master's penchant for corporal punishment was derived from an interview with one of the boys who appear in the photograph, and from whose family album the picture was copied.[123]

While photographs can be used to study the mentalities of the pictured, the problem with the psychologist approach becomes obvious if we consider exposure times. When films and lenses were slow, people did not look happy because they could not hold a smile for the length of time required; it became a blur.[124] Thus, they necessarily had to maintain a straight face, a result of posing's ordeals, as well as of the conventions that developed for being photographed. Today, however, exposure times are usually in the range of from 1/250th to 1/60th of a second. Obviously, no one could seriously propose to make a psychological analysis based on such a tiny fraction of time, although the 1914 photographs of Zapatistas in Sanborn's Restaurant lure us to do so.[125] In one photo, they are almost incarnations of the image that many urban residents had of them: scarred, violent men who appear ready to cut your throat for the pleasure of it. In the other, they look like harmless *campesinos*, a bit disoriented by finding themselves in an unfamiliar situation. Neither of these readings offers us the "truth" about the Zapatistas; what they do is more important: they evidence the fact that these men occupied a space that had formerly been denied them.

Popular culture and leisure activities are also preserved in photographs. Examples are offered by the image of Zapatistas riding under the banner

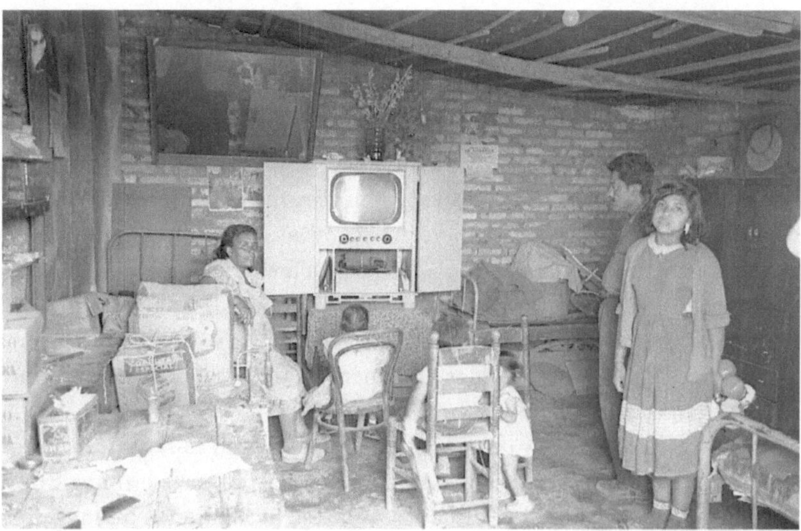

FIGURE 23. Hermanos Mayo. Television/record player set in a poor home, Mexico City, January 1957. Fondo Mayo, Chronological Section, 10837, Archivo General de la Nación.

of the Virgin of Guadalupe as they entered Mexico City in 1914, and the photograph of them visiting the Basílica de Guadalupe during their occupation, with tiny cards of the saint stuck in their sombreros, evidence of her importance for that movement and her ubiquity in Mexican history.[126] Other instances of popular culture embalmed in photographs are those of the Judas dolls, a constant of Mexican life around Easter and still sold on many street corners when I arrived in 1981, though now scarce. Facets of this aspect can be seen as well in photographs such as those made of miners that show them reading *fotonovelas*—another cultural form that is disappearing with the introduction of social media—before entering the mine, as well as surrounded by blond, pale pinups in their communal spaces (which could be analyzed as an expression of sexual taste).[127] In the 1950s, television became as big a part of life in Mexico as in much of the rest of the world, replacing the illustrated magazines by taking advertising away from them. In one Mayo photo we see a television and high-fidelity record player in a poor Mexican house in January of 1957, where multiple beds occupy the room where the apparatus has been placed. (See Figure 23.) The lines of chairs indicate that seats were probably sold for a small sum to the neighbors, and that money was then used to pay the installments on the set.

Up to this point I have been talking about photos that exist, although we want to be clear about the fact that surviving photos are probably around 3 percent of all the images that have been made.[128] We can see how that affects photographic research by considering the analysis that Patricia Massé carried out about the photographic proclivities of Juan Antonio Azurmendi, which is based on the 378 negatives that were donated to the Fototeca Nacional. We don't know why these negatives were preserved, perhaps because they were of such importance to the family or, thinking that they were insignificant, the family left them behind when they moved to Europe. We also would not want to forget that there are many acts of extraordinary importance that are fundamental to social life, only a few of which are pictured or conserved for research. A great majority are not photographed—although with today's technology almost anything is possible. We have only begun to see such significant recordings documenting the systematic persecution of Blacks and Latinos by the US police.

What of the acts that were not photographed, such as rape during the Mexican Revolution and other wars? As Azoulay observed in her study of the Israeli occupation of Palestine, "I looked at thousands of images of horror . . . famine, disease, epidemics, terror attacks, houses torn down, butchered bodies, bombings, torture, mass death, and poverty. . . . [U]ntil I noticed that one image was absent from the various sites—newspapers, photo albums, television programs—in which images of horror are shown: the image of rape."[129]

Photohistorian Nathanial Gardner contests Azoulay's position, affirming that she is simply not looking in the right places. He believes that images of rape do exist, "as any police unit that studies the illicit trade of such images will confirm," but that they are highly taboo.[130] Perhaps part of the reason we do not see them is part and parcel of the machismo that produces rape.

We also need to consider both the biases and the erasures within photo archives. In my study of the photography of the Mexican Revolution, it became clear that the vast majority of the photos held in the Fototeca Nacional had been made by metropolitan photojournalists, because Agustín Víctor Casasola had either taken or acquired them by a variety of means, including rephotographing them from illustrated magazines. The archives of the losing sides, the Zapatistas and Villistas, are largely either lost or were purged. For example, the Zapatista Cruz Sánchez may well have been the most prolific imagemaker for that army, documenting the atrocities carried out in Morelos by the federal and Huertista troops, as well as using photographs to demonstrate the haciendas' expansion as they gobbled up village lands. However, the large archive he formed over the years before, during, and after the revolution has never been discovered, and his surviving images are limited to some twenty or thirty photos. The Cachú Hermanos were Villistas, but there are no images of their leader in either of the two surviving Cachú archives; they were probably discarded as the Constitutionalists began to definitively take control of the country. Company archives can also suffer such amputations. As Coleman remarked about United Fruit Company collection found in the Baker Library of Harvard University, "Although the company made extensive use of photography, we have few images of workers . . . that would permit us to have a greater comprehension of the company's labor relations in Latin America. Almost all those images have remained secret, hidden from generations of workers, researchers, and the general public."[131]

THE SYNTHESIS OF SOCIAL AND CULTURAL HISTORIES

The above survey informs us as to the enormous breadth of possibilities for using photographs to explore past social and material worlds. However, in order to achieve a depth of analysis, we must attempt to examine the photographer's intent, as well as the meanings imposed by the media in which the image is made available.[132] To focus on pictures as acts of representation allows us to understand technical images not only as "transparent" documents of the past, but as constructed discourse as well. At this point, by combining the gaze we directed to study images as if they were transparent with a more informed look derived from our knowledge of the photographer, their moment in history, and what we can assume were the intentions behind the taking of (and publishing) the image, our analysis advances in a way that perhaps can be explained by the metaphor for the manner in which binocular vision provides us with depth. As Bateson asserted, we might consider the fact of having two eyes to be redundant: "What is gained by comparing data collected by one eye with the data collected by the other? Typically, both eyes are aimed at the same region of the surrounding universe, and this might seem to be a wasteful use of the sense organs."[133] However, it is precisely the overlap of the field of vision that provides us with information about depth: "from this new sort of information, the seer adds an extra dimension to seeing." We could employ Bateson's model to argue that overlapping the view of a social historian with that of a cultural approach takes us deeper into the image.

The most famous image created by Nacho López could seem, from a social history standpoint, to objectively document an instance of gender relations in Mexico during the 1950s. (See Figure 24.) However, in order to determine the usefulness of this image as an apparent window onto how men treated women in public spaces in Mexico City during the 1950s, we must approach it from a cultural history perspective, in which we are more interested in

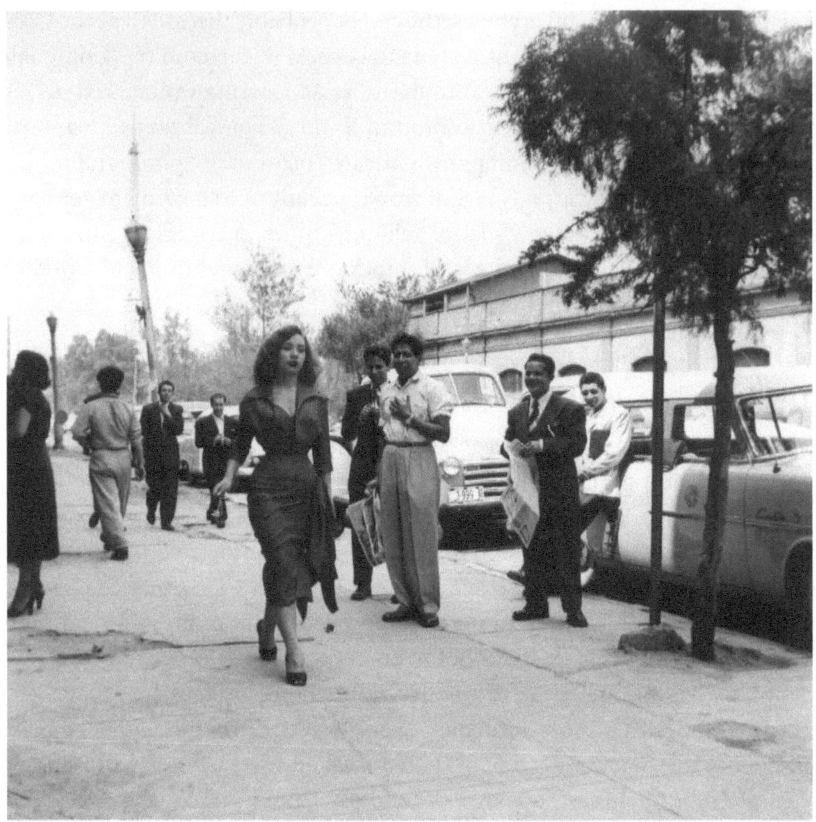

FIGURE 24. Nacho López. Actress Maty Huitrón walking down Balderas Avenue, Mexico City, June 1953. (From the photoessay "Cuando una mujer guapa parte plaza por Madero," *Siempre!*, 27 June 1953.) Inv. # 405608, Fondo Nacho López, SINAFO-Fototeca Nacional del INAH, Secretaría de Cultura. With permission of Martina Guitrón y Porto.

how the photograph represents the *piropo*, and how this representation fits into the larger cultural narrative it enacts. The photograph is a striking—and often reproduced—portrait of Mexican machismo, a defining characteristic of that culture. In fact, I would argue that it is a culture of hyper-machismo, in which male privilege is not only practiced (as it is everywhere), but also celebrated. I was shocked on coming to live in Mexico to discover that close friends, leftist intellectuals who had traveled widely, were vehemently antifeminist and openly espoused *machista* attitudes, and I eventually attributed these vestiges to the visual culture of the 1940s and beyond.[134] López set up the scene by having a voluptuous model and actress, Maty Huitrón, walk by men on the street in order to produce the expected *piropo*. Though Huitrón's role was directed, the men's reactions were nonetheless entirely veridical, an effect provoked by the "catalyst" of Maty.[135]

I believe that the most effective way to analyze a photograph as an individual entity—apart from the contextual meanings imposed in its circulation—is to compare it to a similar image. In order to understand how meanings are generated from without, we reconstruct their contexts of production and circulation; to comprehend how photographic meaning is constructed from within we contrast them to other photos.[136] To discover the formal elements that make López's photograph a celebration of machismo, we compare it to other representations of such male comportment. Taken by López from a slightly low angle (his Rolleiflex camera held at his waist), Huitrón stands out from and above her male admirers, who do not intrude into her space. López gives her a sense of power, despite finding herself in the midst of male harassment, in part by shooting her against an open sky.[137] In Figure 24, I have reproduced the original negative in order to demonstrate the open space around Maty, which is reduced in the cropped reproductions of the magazine and in the book *Yo el ciudadano* but is nonetheless not confining.[138]

Although López was probably unaware of it, Ruth Orkin, a US photographer, had directed a similar image in Italy two years before.[139] Comparing these photos provides insight into the maleness that is so much a part of Latin cultures, for Orkin clearly portrays the oppression that the *piropo* can be for women, trapping her collaborator, Jinx Allen, from a slight high angle against a street crowded with men and looming gray buildings. Thinner and frailer than Huitrón, Allen seems harassed by the men, clutching her purse and folder to her chest and pulling her shawl over her breast as if to protect herself from the gaze of men who lean into her space aggressively, one lewdly grabbing his crotch (in López's image, a Mexican holds his hand to his heart). Further, Italian men block Allen's path; in order to continue her stroll, she will have to step off the sidewalk into the street, where she will still have to dodge further male obstacles as well as motorcycles and other vehicles.[140] We might argue that Orkin's incisive portrayal of this ritual is due to being a woman, although a powerful, spontaneous photograph was later taken by the Catalonian photojournalist Xavier Miserachs of a woman forced from the sidewalk by one of her "admirers."[141]

The fact that both the Orkin and López photographs were directed indicates clearly the message that each wished to convey. This permits us to perceive that López's seemingly transparent document was in fact a highly codified representation that applauds machismo at the level of both content and form; the magazine reinforced that message through the caption, affirming that she is "indifferent," thus making it a three-fold approbation.[142] Hence, Nacho's photo tells us about how López's vision, and that of his milieu, resulted in this particular image of gender relations in Mexico. As I have argued in the Introduction, we do photohistory not only as a way of knowing the past but of understanding how this media forges the future by offering models of behavior and perception. Mexican men learn to see *piropos* and other such male harassment in a positive sense. In contrast, Orkin and Allen worked together to produce an articulate critique of such behavior. The information about López's and Orkin's point of view that resulted from comparing their pictures places them within particular ideological perspectives of patriarchalism and antimachismo, illustrating the need to link the social and cultural realms whenever possible.

Of all the forms in which photographic meaning is constructed, the most determinant is that generated by words. Because photographs are ambiguous, polysemic, and semantically weak, they can be made to say whatever the context dictates, almost always through the accompanying texts. Hence, at times the meanings imposed by texts may contradict that which the photographers (presumably) wished to express. A photograph that offers an example of how the media is capable of fundamentally transforming meaning is perhaps the most powerful of the five million negatives produced by the Hermanos Mayo. (See Figure 25.) The image is of a mother crying over the body of her dead son, Luis Morales, a leftist student at the Instituto Politécnico Nacional who attempted to participate in the May Day march of 1952.

Perhaps President Miguel Alemán (1946–1952) was looking to generate public demonstration of support for his perennial illusion of reelection, for May Day 1952 was quite different than preceding years. Alemán promoted his nationalist agenda: "In place of the red-and-black banners the workers would be carrying the national flag, and rather than proclaiming the universal solidarity of the working class, they would render homage to President Miguel Alemán for his laborist policies."[143] Moreover, the May Day march that passed through the Zócalo, and beneath the presidential balcony of the Palacio Nacional, was strictly limited to the government-controlled unions, above all the Confederación de Trabajadores Mexicanos (CTM), which was the largest Mexican grouping of unions and a pillar of PRI rule. The obsequiousness of the CTM and other officialist unions on that day were demonstrated in the description provided by the government's newspaper, *El Nacional*, which referred to the "rapturous cheers for the democratic gestures of the 'First Worker of Mexico,' President Miguel Alemán."[144] The march of independent workers was led in part by the muralist David Alfaro Siqueiros, and they were attacked by the fascist *Dorados* and their police minions, who killed Morales and three other workers.[145]

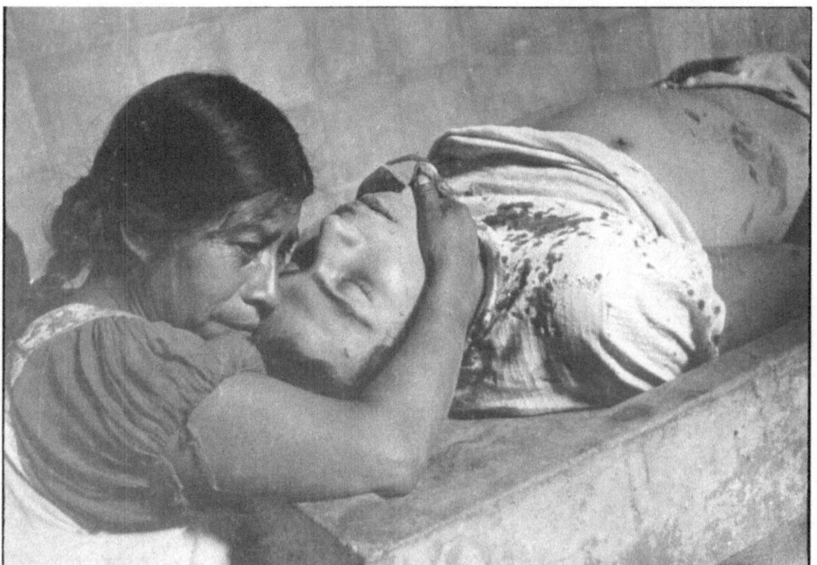

FIGURE 25. Julio Mayo. Mother grieving for her son Luis Morales, dissident worker killed in May Day battle, Mexico City, 1 May 1952. Fondo Mayo, Chronological Section, 3959, Archivo General de la Nación.

The photograph so impressed Siqueiros that he reproduced it in a mural commissioned by the Asociación Nacional de Actores (ANDA) for the Teatro Jorge Negrete. (See Figure 26.) Siqueiros worked directly from Julio Mayo's photo of the mother and son, as I determined upon seeing the image blocked out with masking tape in the Sala de Arte Público Siqueiros when Alfonso Morales was curating an exhibit there.[146] The muralist believed that "photography is an indispensable resource for painting," arguing that "the modern painter who does not take advantage of the documentary input of cinematography and photography is like a doctor opposed to radiography."[147] The mural's fate provides insight into the political culture of Mexico in the 1950s and 1960s. Siqueiros began to paint it in 1958, but before it was finished, ANDA's secretary general, Rodolfo Echeverría (later the director of the Mexican Instituto of Cinematography during the presidency of his brother Luis Echeverría) had the mural walled over. In 1966, ANDA's new secretary general Jorge Fernández had the mural uncovered and asked Siqueiros to finish it, which he did in 1968. However, the mural's odyssey did not end there because in December of that year ultraconservative groups that had been permitted free rein by the government to attack protestors demanding democracy broke into the Theater and damaged the mural, which was later restored.

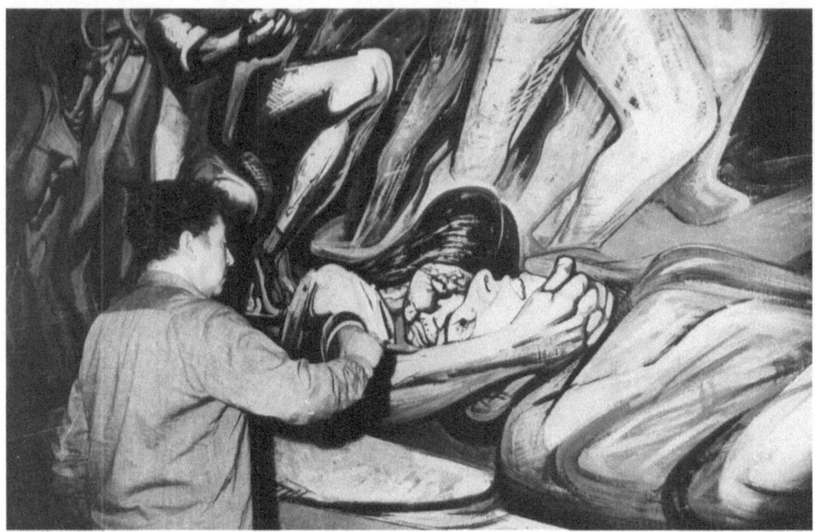

FIGURE 26. Hermanos Mayo. David Alfaro Siqueiros painting the Mayo photo into a mural, *El teatro en México*, Teatro Jorge Negrete, Mexico City, April 1959. Fondo Mayo, Chronological Section, 13428, Archivo General de la Nación.

Although the Mayo photograph is searing, it never appeared in *Mañana*'s coverage of the event. Instead, more ambiguous photographs taken of the street battle by the Mayos were published, such as that of a beating given undercover policeman Carlos Salazar Puebla "who had participated in the armed aggression and assassination of the independent column (PCM-POCM [Partido Comunista Mexicano-Partido Obrero Campesino Mexicano])" in the march.[148] (See Figure 27.) Even members of the officialist unions were incensed by the cowardly killing of protestors, which included two workers affiliated with the CTM. Captured at the entrance to the Bellas Artes building in which the killers had taken refuge, Salazar Puebla was badly beaten. However, he was rescued by the intervention of Siqueiros and Diego Rivera, who turned him over to workers of the officialist CTM and CROC (Confederación Revolucionaria de Obreros y Campesinos). They then walked him from Bellas Artes to the Zócalo, where they presented him in front of the presidential balcony, shouting, "Here is your assassin, *cabrón* [asshole]."[149]

The magazine fundamentally transformed the meaning of this photograph on publishing it. The caption purposefully misidentified Salazar Puebla as a "Communist gunman" (*pistolero comunista*) receiving his due from the workers. Rather than an example of how even officialist syndicalists had been appalled by the government's illegal attack upon and murder of

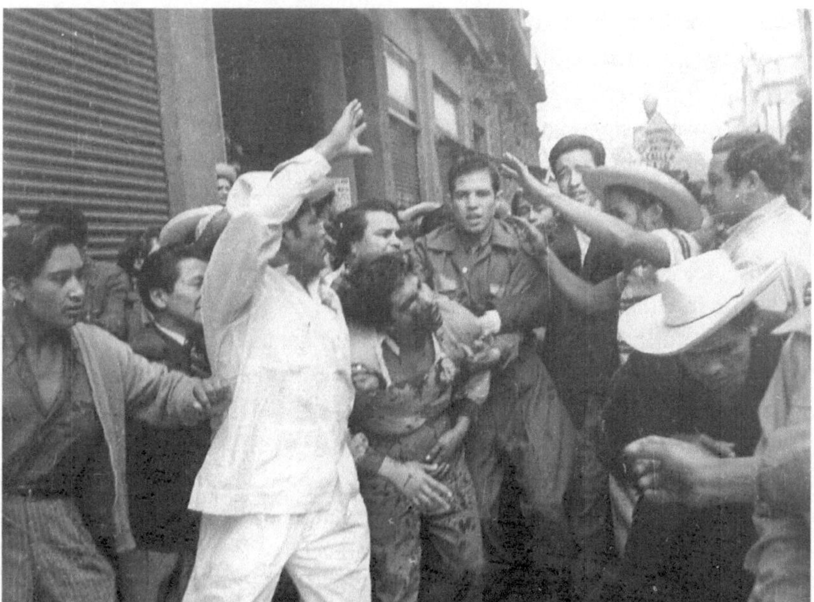

FIGURE 27. Hermanos Mayo. Carlos Salazar Puebla, undercover policeman and *Dorado*, is taken to the Zócalo by members of the CTM-CROC, Mexico City, 1 May 1952. Fondo Mayo, Chronological Section, 3959, Archivo General de la Nación.

dissidents, this photograph was turned into an object lesson. The text that accompanied it determined its meaning and is a wonderful example of the illustrated magazines' participation in maintaining the party dictatorship:

> A group of senseless anti-patriotic provocateurs attempted to lessen the force of the Mexican workers' formidable and vigorous unity with the Government of the Republic presided over by Miguel Alemán, causing fratricidal violence in a battle with the May Day parade marchers in front of Bellas Artes. This photograph of tremendous drama reveals the instant in which one of the communist *pistoleros* is detained by the inflamed multitude. The workers' serene and measured comportment kept the street battle from becoming a bloody tragedy, without precedent, without name.[150]

The magazine's problem with the photograph of the grieving mother was that its meaning could not be transformed at that moment, because it was too powerful and spoke too much for itself; hence, it could not be published in the reportage on May Day 1952. However, with the passage of time, the photograph could be recontextualized; thus tamed, it appeared in a 1955 photoessay titled "13 instantáneas" that pretended to present "the most journalistic photos of the Hermanos Mayo, taken, one each year, from 1943 to 1955."[151] There, the image was ripped out of its original matrix with a cynicism that relied on the ambiguity of even the most potent photographs. It was assigned a fabricated significance that transformed a historical instance of the struggle against the government's control of unions into a timeless and recurrent phenomenon of daily life. It was essentially converted into a *nota roja*, a very popular genre of Mexican media that focuses on the ugly side of the "news"—murders, suicides, accidents, and other tragedies in which blood flows—representing Mexico as a country of mutilators and mutilated: "Who is she? Who is he? Their simple names, from the *pueblos*, are condensed in this brief eloquence: mother and son. The mother destroyed by pain, the son felled by death. The scene: the *Cruz Verde* some day in 1950. Any day in which drama can occur. The moment Julio Mayo etched cannot be more moving."[152]

The case of Julio's image makes it clear that analyzing the itinerancy, the multiple contexts in which photographs travel, is a key factor in historicizing them. As photography scholar Fred Ritchin has observed,

> Photographic observation is given too much credit for clarity, and instead often argues for multiple, overlapping states of being—not only physical, but also cultural and political. . . . In photography's case ambiguity's collapse is usually aided—and often inappropriately forced—by captions that attempt to resolve the uncertainty. . . . The caption is made to constrain the photography into a single state rather than open it up for amplification. If a photograph is said to be worth a thousand words, very few of those words generally come to mind after a caption tells the reader what the photo is supposed to be about.[153]

In Mexico, images are circulated and recirculated, adding ever more complex levels of significance. Nonetheless, all these itinerant images only acquire their meanings upon being anchored to the particular and specific contexts that create their connotations. This can be seen in the reiterated appearances of the Mexican Revolution's icons over time and in different places: at political gatherings and on banners both officialist and dissident; in the pages of picture histories, newspapers, illustrated magazines, books, comics, and broadsheets, national as well as international; on the walls of government buildings, banks, and restaurants; on t-shirts, coffee mugs, postcards, and calendars; on television and in the movies; in murals painted during the postrevolutionary effervescence as well as more recently; and in today's postmodern world of Internet, in news blogs, as well as advertisements to promote karaoke music, the US gun culture, the Costa Alegre Travel Agency, rock groups, rental agencies, and cigars; among many other appearances.[154] These icons are as a stone thrown in a pond; the initial splash is one occurrence and the ripples represent their subsequent appearances. As Azoulay has argued, "I seek to differentiate between the *event of photography* and the *photographed event* that the photographer seeks to capture in his frame. . . . The event of photography is never over."[155]

It is also crucial to note that photographs can *make* history. It appears that German scholars have been addressing this issue since the 1980s, arguing that photos not only reflect the period in which they were made but are capable of shaping it, "which is what often makes it difficult to categorically distinguish between history and image history."[156] In Latin America, one of the most powerful examples is offered by photohistorian Cora Gamarnik, who carried out a reconstruction of the effects of photographs taken on April 2, 1982, when Argentine troops disembarked to take command of the Islas Malvinas (Falkland Islands).[157] The military dictatorship had been generally successful in carrying out a "dirty war" against unarmed civilians since 1976, and their arrogance was such that they felt emboldened to take on the United Kingdom over these islands that have long been a dispute between these countries. They sent a "false Iwo Jima" reconstruction (staged in Buenos Aires) to the national press, but did not realize that an independent photojournalist, Rafael Wollman, was present in the islands to do a photoessay of the *National Geographic* type. Immediately recognizing the importance of the moment, Wollman took photos of British soldiers raising their hands in surrender and being forced to lie on the ground. He was able to return to Buenos Aires with the images, which then circulated throughout the world, "proving" the decadence of the British Empire. In the face of such international humiliation, the British government dispatched a naval task force, and easily defeated the Argentine troops in seventy-four days. The defeat led to the downfall of the military dictatorship.

CRITICAL POSITIONS

Combining histories *of* photography and *with* photography offers new ways of studying the past. Historians have employed them for many years as illustrations, something to make texts more palatable. However, they have been hesitant to incorporate them in a serious way, perhaps in large part because they have lacked the research tools that would allow them to do so. Nonetheless, I believe that they have been trained in exactly the discipline that can provide them with the instruments to interrogate the material and social content in images, as well as to link their production and meanings to functions within specific situations. If historians fail to engage with our hyper-visual world, I am concerned that photographic study will be defined in the humanities, by work in art history or cultural and literary studies, the two fields that dominate the area today. Every discipline must incorporate image analysis; it is a sine qua non in today's universities. Nonetheless, the methods of art historians, literary scholars, and historians are so different from one another that it is important each area develop their own ways to include this media. If the only models offered for doing photohistories are those provided by colleagues from art or literature, I fear historians will be discouraged because they will find that most art history approaches are largely irrelevant to exploring vernacular photography, and that they are little prepared for the speculative mire of literature studies.

I open the next chapter by addressing the issue of art history and photographic study, so I will here close by reflecting on the utility for photohistorians of the approaches developed by scholars in cultural and/or literary studies. It is vital to note that migrants from literature have made great contributions. For example, Mike Weaver and Annie Hammond transformed the journal *History of Photography* from what was an "antiquarian/hobbyist" publication into a dynamic journal that opened its pages to a wide range of vernacular imagery as well as to that produced in areas beyond Europe and the US.[158] Over the ten-year period (1991–2000) of their editorship there were few if any articles that did not directly engage in historicizing photographs. Nor were there publications that employed literary theory, despite or because of the fact that Weaver, coming from American studies, was well acquainted with it. However, that has changed under the succeeding editors, and Hammond noted recently that the publication had "become entrenched" in theoretical approaches to the detriment of both art and photographic history; my own experience with the journal confirmed this observation.[159]

Stimulated by postmodern literary theory, some US and British academics seem to believe that it is obligatory to explicitly address it in analyzing photographs. My impression that this influence has come to dominate the study of photos is enhanced by glance at my bookshelf, where at least half of the works in English on photography are from literary scholars. This has not been the case in Mexico, where the more significant scholarship has largely ignored that trend. This generalized disregard may be an expression of what I have argued is the centrality of the visual in Mexican culture.[160] Rather than continuing to clean our glasses by refining our theoretical approaches, we put them on to explore the photos we have in front of us with methods that arise, to some extent, from the visual materials themselves.[161] It may also be the result of the fact that historians have come to the fore of photographic study in Mexico, with a different relation to theory, using it to open up new questions and research possibilities that can then be explored. For historians, theory is a scaffolding useful to construct a work; once it is complete, it should be removed to better appreciate that which one has built. To apply theory as if it were a grid that must be directly referred to is an example of what Flusser called "textolatry"—idolatry of the text.[162] As Nichols so succinctly put it in writing about documentary film, "My goal is not to import a theory. . . . Films do not answer to theory, but theory must answer to film—if it is to be more than idle speculation."[163]

Demanding that theory somehow form a core of a study can so distort a reading that reviewers completely miss the point of a book. For example, my work on the Mexican Revolution was critiqued by one reviewer because a central concern was to establish the photos' authors.[164] She asserted that the book displayed an ignorance of the "theoretically oriented commentators" who had pointed out how "scholars of photography have attempted to negotiate the medium's status as a legitimate object of study by borrowing auteurist principles from art history." However, my efforts to establish who had made the revolution's pictures had nothing whatsoever to do with "auteurist principles," but with determining the allegiances of the photographers with the warring factions, a subject that had not been addressed in the historiography of that imagery, nor in the photography of any revolution.

In considering the worth of a text, photohistorians expect to learn from a deep knowledge of the subject upon which they can build, as well as open up new research areas, rather than disentangle a theoretical exegesis. Too often the latter produces work that is over-theorized and under-researched. We can find this problem in even the greatest work of photo theory produced by a Postmodern literary theorist, *Camera Lucida*. There, Barthes comments on a photograph by Koen Wessing, a Dutch image-maker whose work was crucial in documenting the revolutions in Central America. Barthes describes what, for him, is an image of little intrinsic interest: "The (photographic) banality of a rebellion in Nicaragua: a ruined street, two helmeted soldiers on patrol; behind them, two nuns."[165] The image did not interest Barthes, but it did provide fuel for a theoretical reflection: "I understood at once that its existence (its 'adventure') derived from the co-presence of two discontinuous elements, heterogeneous in that they did not belong to the same world . . . : the soldiers and the nuns." Had Barthes informed himself even superficially over the rebellions in that area he would have known that, while the Catholic church has generally been a pillar of right-wing rule in Latin America, Christian base communities were crucial in supporting the Central American struggles. Far from being heterogeneous or discontinuous elements, the nuns and soldiers were captured by Wessing as a commentary on the transformed relation of the church to revolutionary struggle.

A particularly flagrant example is provided by a volume (and its review) on Latin American photography produced by a recognized academic in literary studies—an author or editor of more than forty books—in which he affirmed that "perhaps the earliest photographic images we now have of Latin American women are those of prostitutes," made in Mexico around 1900.[166] Under any circumstances, such ignorance would be striking, but it is a bizarre assertion today, when information about and images of daguerreotypes of Latin American women made in the 1840s are immediately available on Internet. Further, the fact that he decided prostitutes were the first to be photographed feeds into the imperial vision of Latin America as a "brothel." A review of this work by a theoretically inclined colleague is revealing of the excessive importunity to address this aspect. The reviewer was evidently unaware of the author's unfamiliarity with photography, because that which he found important to prioritize was the idea that "readers at a high level of expertise might wish for a more thorough discussion of the theoretical bases . . . the theoretical assumptions. . . . The complex theoretical concepts."[167]

I am conscious of the liberty I have felt to explore alternative narrative forms, thanks in part to postmodern critiques such as White's pioneering work *Metahistory*. In fact, the very fashion in which I have chosen to write this book is a product of the self-reflexivity espoused by such approaches. So I have no doubt that the age we are living in requires new ways of thinking, and Frederic Jameson has identified one of the most important issues, arguing that a main feature of postmodernism is "the transformation of reality into images."[168] I understand that each colleague will bring to the task the training they have received, but I remain unsure about the methodological stretch of applying literary analysis to photographs. From the perspective my experience has given me, the dominance of this academic fashion represents a boulder in the path of photographic study in the US and Europe. The concentration on theory seems to lead away from research and into an unintelligible swamp of jargon. Literary scholar Terry Eagleton's take on this fad is hilarious:

> To write in this way as a *literary* academic, someone who is actually paid for having among other things a certain flair and feel for language, is rather like being a myopic optician or a grossly obese ballet dancer. . . . You can be difficult without being obscure. Difficulty is a matter of content, whereas obscurity is a question of how to present that content. . . . There is something particularly scandalous about *radical* cultural theory being so willfully obscure.[169]

Such obscurantism might not be entirely innocent; it may serve as another elitist instrument to exclude those who do not have the time or the money to invest in understanding what is being said in such an obtuse fashion. It is difficult for me to believe that this tendency still continues to exert such a force more than twenty years after the intentionally nonsensical article by physicist Alan Sokal ripped the mask off its pretensions with a deliberately senseless argument that parodied postmodern orthodoxy. There, he asserted (among other absurdities) that it was a Western dogma to believe "that there exists an external world, whose properties are independent of any individual human being and indeed of humanity as a whole."[170] The essay was accepted by *Social Text*, the outstanding journal for postmodern thought and "it was published in a special issue . . . devoted to rebutting the criticisms levelled against postmodernism and social constructivism by several distinguished scientists."[171] On the day it was published in *Social Text*, another article by Sokal appeared in *Lingua Franca* disclosing that he had intentionally written a text that "any competent physicist or mathematician (or undergraduate physics or math major) would realize is a spoof."[172] As Sokal noted in the revelation that he had carried out a hoax, "*Social Text*'s acceptance of my article exemplifies the intellectual arrogance of Theory—postmodern literary theory, that is—carried to its logical extreme. . . . Incomprehensibility becomes a virtue."[173]

My critique has focused on that scholarship that has largely attempted to apply literary methods to photography, not postmodern theory per se. In fact, postmodern photography theorists such as Alan Sekula, Martha Rosler, and Victor Burgin have been of great importance to the development of photohistory, in displacing art photography from its discursive dominance and establishing the importance of vernacular photography. Moreover, they engage directly with imagery, carry out research, and write clearly. One author has targeted these pioneers, asserting that they "viewed photography as a generally nasty business—the photograph is a prison, the act of looking a crime."[174] While her observations open up a new perspective on them, I believe that many of the writers she so assails have developed a critique of particular uses of photographs and have made their position clear in raising the issue of "victim photography," a consideration of great importance to picturing neocolonial societies with exaggerated disparities of wealth. Sekula, Rosler, Sally Stein, and Abigail Solomon-Godeau all address a critical issue on questioning to what extent photos of the downtrodden might be said to constitute "a double act of subjugation: first, in the social world that has produced its victims; second, in the regime of the image, produced within and for the system that engenders the conditions it then represents."[175]

CONCLUSION

If at one point a struggle existed between audiovisual and written discourses, it is over: we can see who won in a glance at this hyper-audiovisual world addicted to modern media. Because photographs float, and can be made to mean almost anything, contextualization and comparison are the royal road to interrogating them. It is only upon their insertion in the concrete contexts in which they were made, and those in which they circulate, that they have meaning. Historians are contextualists by instinct and training, so I urge them to bring their disciplinary framework, their interest in research, and their capacity to express themselves in lucid language to the study of photographs. We have to make this new history ours, doing away with the undisciplined picture histories and coffee table books that have dominated the use of photographs and bringing the same seriousness to their use as we do with words. Only in this way will we find what is really new about this form of talking about and looking at the past.

CHAPTER 3

Historical Photographs

Genres, Functions, Methods, and Power

Although photography generates works that can be called art . . . photography is not, to begin with, an art form at all. Like language, it is a medium in which works of art (among other things) are made. Out of language, one can make scientific discourse, bureaucratic memoranda, love letters, grocery lists, and Balzac's Paris. Out of photography, one can make passport pictures, weather photographs, pornographic pictures, X-rays, wedding pictures, and Atget's Paris. **Susan Sontag**

For many years, I assumed that the history of photography was a sub-genre of history of art. I have come to believe that this is a common misconception in an age still dominated, in academia, by what Flusser describes as one of "writing thinking" rather than "image thinking."[1] As he explained, with the invention of linear writing and its dissemination by the printing press, "texts get out of hand, and the images—as 'art'—are expelled from everyday life." He believes that "photography was invented to bring pictures back into everyday life."[2]

My perception that photography belonged to art history stemmed from the overarching intellectual and market structure created by museums, galleries, dealers, collectors, investors, and speculators, as well as by art history departments; as Solomon-Godeau observed, "art history . . . and the history of photography differs from all other self-contained histories of cultural production (e.g., musicology, architectural history, literary studies, etc.) in that the object of study exists also as a commodity in a market system."[3] Hence, this art historian affirmed, "that an art history of photography is generally confounded with a history of photography tout court is the inevitable consequence of how and why, and in the service of what interests and investments (in all senses) the boundless domain of photography is discursively organized."[4] I now think that photographic art history is a genre of history of photography, but with the particularity of being "one whose genealogy derives from art and aesthetic discourse."[5]

The date when I ceased to think that art history was the defining discipline of photographic study is etched clearly in my mind. In 2003, I was a member of a doctoral committee for a thesis defense on the US image-maker Winfield Scott, who worked in Mexico between the years 1888–1924.[6] The student's studies had been undertaken in the department of historia del arte, because there was nowhere else one could get an advanced degree with a history of photography within the UNAM. The thesis was extraordinary: Scott was formerly little more than a rumor among photohistorians, in large part because his sometime partner C. B. Waite had erased Scott's identifying numbers and replaced them with his own. The research was impeccable, and included investigations in thirty Mexican and fourteen US archives. The student's hypothesis was clearly established and supported: that Scott was an important example of the presence of US photographers connected to US commercial interests in Mexico, alongside figures such as William Henry Jackson and Waite.

Mexican universities have a tradition of giving theses an honorable mention if deserved. After the student had left the room, the jury decided first that she had passed, and then we deliberated on whether she was to be given honors. When questioned, I said that there was no doubt in my mind that she deserved the highest ranking. On the heels of my vote, a colleague from historia del arte firmly disagreed, "*De ninguna manera*" (No way), arguing that the student did not prove the esthetic value of the photographs. I was stunned, and then I started laughing as I replied that the photos have no esthetic value. They were made, usually commissioned, to sell real estate and tourism, as well as attract US investment.

All of a sudden, as we say in Mexico, *Me cayó el viente*—I finally got it.[7] I realized in a flash that the history of photography could not be a subgenre of art history, because the methodologies of that discipline were not applicable to the vast majority of photographs. Photography is a medium before it is an art form, and artistic photography is simply one of the manifold photographic genres. However, as Azoulay argues, "Until the 1990s, the reciprocal relations between art and photography were dominated by a single template whereby the paradigm of art, with its attendant rules, was seen as the dominant—indeed the host—paradigm."[8] This situation was a result of the path followed in legitimizing photography as an art form that was worthy of being exhibited in museums and galleries, as well as becoming a discipline in university curriculums. According to one curator,

"Throughout the first half of the twentieth century, photographic education in the United States was largely centered on development of the medium as a vocational pursuit, and photography courses were typically offered in high schools, polytechnic institutions, community colleges, and trade schools."[9]

Until it began to acquire a monetary value as art, photography was rejected by museums, galleries, and art history programs. Moreover, the study of its history and impact on our daily lives was (and largely still is) completely neglected by universities. One problem in teaching photography was the lack of resources available. A solution was provided by Beaumont Newhall and Nathan Lyons in 1964, who developed a set of 250 slides based on Newhall's 1937 exhibit at the Museum of Modern Art in New York, and his catalogue that was subsequently revised as a book, *The History of Photography*.[10] These slides were distributed widely and shared by museums and universities around the world, canonizing US and European art photographers to such an extent that one of the first recognized photohistorians, Helmut Gernsheim, stated in 1977 that, "I don't think there are any major photographers to be discovered."[11]

Fortunately, studies in Latin America photography have gone far beyond the US-Eurocentrism displayed by Gernsheim, but the art paradigm has shown itself to have serious political ramifications as well as epistemological limitations. For years, art scholars and some curators of Latin American photography have done their best to devalue the importance of this medium as an index of the phenomenal world, to deny the importance of the political and social in our imagery, to uncritically laud and promote "apolitical" photographic "art," and to avoid any discussion of how imperialism and neocolonialism have shaped photographic expression in these latitudes. Since the 1990s, there has been a reaction against what one curator described as "a very simple model" of documentary photography, referring to the landmark First Colloquium of Latin American Photography (1978), *Hecho en Latinoamérica*, which he argued blocked "promising artistic ventures."[12]

More recently, a Mexican art historian continued in this same vein: "At thirty-two years since the colloquium, contemporary photography has distanced itself definitively from a documentary use focused on the political and social to instead explore its symbolic discursiveness and its condition as a medium."[13] It is difficult to know what she means by "contemporary photography," for the medium itself has certainly not distanced itself from its documentary uses, which continue to make it important in the sciences, to cite only one example. I believe that what her statement reflects is exactly what Solomon-Godeau and Azoulay are describing: the tendency of art historians to collapse the medium into the constraints typical of those who work in this particular genre. Moreover, the idea that any expressive form is transformed "definitively" is nonsense.

When we contemplate the enormous variety of photographs—for example, in the large Mexican repositories—it is obvious that only a small percentage were made by avowed artists. As mentioned in Chapter 2, Bourdieu estimated that the majority of photographers are those that record their family's rites. Because digital technology has placed cameras in the hands of (almost) everyone, and photos can circulate infinitely throughout the Internet, we can assume that the percentage of family and friends' photography is significantly higher today. Given this situation we could generously estimate that art photography arguably comprises some five percent.

What are we to do with the other ninety-five percent? What sorts of methodologies are we going to utilize for what we might describe as "genres": photojournalism; family photography; imperial, neocolonizing, decolonizing and subaltern photography; portraits; revolutionary and postrevolutionary photography; Indianist and indigenous photography; photography of and by workers as well as photography produced by companies; politically committed photography; landscapes and cityscapes; scientific photography; social scientific photography done by visual anthropologists and sociologists; photography made by the security forces; advertising photography; pornography; fashion photography; organizational photography; architectural and industrial photography; photography of nature; street photography; postcards?[14] Some of these genres, for example landscapes and portraits, are derived from art history approaches, but the vast majority are specific to photography; moreover, Martha Sandweiss' study on photographing panoramas of the US West provides an example of how little photographic analysis owes to art history, even with traditional genres.[15] The list will be very long, and I believe that as we define the different photographic genres, each will require a particular methodology with which to analyze it.

I am here utilizing the concept of genre as a heuristic device, in order to begin to differentiate between types of photography and work toward the development of a methodology. The sort of photo that we think we are going to see is fundamental in creating the meaning that is perceived. As a literary scholar has argued,

> [The reader] entertains the notion that "this is a certain type of meaning," and his notion of the meaning as a whole grounds and helps determine his

> understanding of details. This fact reveals itself whenever a misunderstanding is suddenly recognized. After all, how could it have been recognized unless the interpreter's expectations had been thwarted? . . . Oh! You've been talking about a book all the time. I thought it was about a restaurant.[16]

Photographic genres are established by a number of factors: by whom they were taken, the historical and geographical context in which they were made, the objects pictured, the esthetic conventions employed, and the uses for which they were intended as well as those to which they are put. Obviously, there are a number of greatly varying elements that function to differentiate photographic genres, but this problem can also be seen in literary genres, which have a much longer history. As Tzetvan Todorov remarked:

> The song is contrasted with the poem by phonetic traits; the sonnet differs from the ballad in its phonology; tragedy is opposed to comedy by thematic elements; the suspense narrative differs from the classic detective novel by the fitting together of its plot; finally, the autobiography is distinguished from the novel in that the author claims to recount facts rather than construct fictions.[17]

Of course, it is crucial to understand that the assignation of genre is only useful if we recognize its subjectivity: "If we believe that [classifications] are constitutive rather than arbitrary and heuristic, then we have made a serious mistake and have also set up a barrier to valid interpretation."[18] There will always be an overlapping of genres, and photographs can belong to different genres depending upon the analysis being carried out.

I have encountered few texts dedicated to recognizing and distinguishing between photographic genres, and fewer that examine the various functions photographs and photographers carry out.[19] The idea that this method could provide a means of historicizing photographs grew out of my studies on Latin American photojournalism. My participation in the polemics produced by the misunderstandings between photojournalists that were generated by the Mexican Sexta Bienal de Fotoperiodismo of 2004 were crucial, but the first inkling I had about the different functions of photojournalists came as a result of an invitation by Eleazar López Zamora, founding director of INAH's Fototeca Nacional. Around 1988, Eleazar asked me to write a book about one of the archives in the Fototeca. He proposed three different possibilities. One was to continue in the line of labor history that I had been working in since coming to Mexico. Eleazar thought I could find some topic related to analyzing the representation of workers in the Casasola Archive. Doing a sort of ethnohistory of the women workers in Mexico City *nixtamal* (corn meal) mills in December of 1919 had left me fascinated by the idea of using photographs to develop vignettes of working class life.[20] However, that had been possible because of the extensive reports from an inspector for the Secretaría de Industria, Comercio y Trabajo that accompanied the photos in the Departamento de Trabajo of the AGN. Such a tightly packaged bundle of graphic and textual information did not exist in relation to the Casasola Archive. I could have approached the study of that collection from the standpoint of a historian, using photographs in terms of the ways their transparency offered the opportunity to do social history with photographs, but the obstacles seemed great.

The other two projects Eleazar had in mind would lead me in a very different direction, that of history of photography. Studying either Tina Modotti or Nacho López would mean that my focus would fall more on the photographers themselves—the visions, intentions, and encodings of Modotti and López—and less on what social details can be gleaned. Invited by curator Reinhard Schultz, I had participated in the first exhibit dedicated solely to Modotti's work, which opened in Berlin in 1989 and continues to travel around Europe.[21] I wrote an essay for the catalogue of that exhibit and then published it in Mexico.[22] However, despite the fact that the INAH archive has the world's largest collection of Modotti negatives, I decided not to continue to work on her, knowing that a number of studies were going to appear on her life and photography over the next few years.

I felt that a work coming out of the Fototeca Nacional should advance the study of Mexican photography through a rigorous analysis of a photographer well-known within the country but essentially unheard of outside it, introducing him or her to a broader public. Prior to the invitation of Eleazar in 1988, I had been researching the Hermanos Mayo, with whose archive I had become familiar while at CEHSMO, before it was purchased by the AGN. I mounted an exhibit on them in 1984, *Trabajo y trabajadores en México, 1940–1960, vistos por los Hermanos Mayo*, the same year I carried out extensive interviews with Julio and Faustino Mayo; in 1988 I published what would be the first of my studies on them.[23] My interest in photojournalism had been stimulated by that background, but I thought of Nacho López as more of an artist than a photojournalist, and told Eleazar that I would prefer to work on the Hermanos Mayo.

Over many *comidas* (the big midday meal in Mexico), *sobremesas* (the long discussions that occur during and after eating), and bottles of tequila, Eleazar made it clear that the invitation was to work on a Fototeca archive.[24] He also convinced me to undertake the study of Nacho López, in large part because of the respect I had for Eleazar's knowledge and judgment. Once I had decided to work on López's photojournalism, Eleazar paid me a year's salary in exchange for giving courses to the rapidly expanding workforce in the Fototeca Nacional, which had received funding to carry out the digitalization and cataloguing of the holdings. I gave one course on the history of Mexican photojournalism and then another on Nacho López. As any teacher will not be surprised to hear, I learned an enormous amount from preparing the classes, and I developed the basic structure for my book on Nacho. The attention that continues to be given López's work in Mexico demonstrates Eleazar's prescience in this case and many others.[25]

From the very beginning, I limited my focus to his work as a photojournalist, for a variety of reasons. I find press photography vastly more interesting than art photography. Photojournalists have to work within a context that constrains their opportunities to express themselves: the politico-socioeconomic position of their employer, the number of events they have to cover, and limited material they are given. The possibilities to develop their own subjects and themes are also limited by the fact that their negatives (prior to digitalization) almost always remained in the storerooms of the media that contracted their work; there, uncatalogued in what are known as morgues, they serve no purpose and are eventually destroyed. Hence, photojournalism embodies that Sartrean dialectic of doing something with what is being done to you. Situated between your own esthetic and social interests (for which one chooses to work in photography), and the demands of the employing media, one is placed in a Batesonian "double bind." Despite the stress of such a seemingly unresolvable circumstance, Bateson remarked that, "If this pathology can be warded off or resisted, the total experience may promote *creativity*."[26] Photojournalist Rodrigo Moya met this potentially schizophrenic situation head-on with his concept of the "double camera": "Almost from the very beginning, I accepted that I had two cameras in my mind: one to comply with the news required by my employer, and the other to capture what I began to understand with a clarity and profundity that we learn from reality and a rebel's consciousness."[27]

Photojournalism has a fundamental relationship to what we loosely call documentary photography. I believe that what is really new about photography is its indexical capacity, hence all photographs are documentary (with a tiny number of exceptions irrelevant to historians). News photography is the one of the highest expressions of such indexicality, linking the "truth-value" of the medium to the presumed activity of actually covering events and situations. This genre offers the opportunity to bring together the two poles of photography: the informative and the expressive. To the degree that this relation tilts toward the informative, the image tends to remain a document, which is what succeeds in traditional photojournalism. To the degree that it leans toward the expressive, it can be turned into a decontextualized symbol. The best photojournalism is made when the expressive and the informative coincide to create an image that provides information about an event but which, at the same time, is incarnated with an esthetic force that enables it to transcend its immediate context, transforming its particularity into a representation of larger, more general truths. As documentary filmmaker Michael Chanan argued, "It works in a double register: where the universal takes the form of the particular and the particular is liable to be read as a universal."[28] That which appears has been found rather than created, but the esthetic power with which it is shown fuses the event and the expression into a whole.

Whatever the differences be between the diverse forms of photojournalism, they have a common background: the belief that the image-maker had no effect on that which he or she has photographed. Documentary credibility is based upon this tenet, and its language is structured within "codes of objectivity" that hide the effect caused by the presence of the photojournalist.[29] Directed photojournalism utilizes this credibility, taking advantage of the new and original status of the photograph as an authentic index of the phenomenal world. This is the "metaphysic" of modern photography, and I suspect that which problematizes photojournalism is not so much a question of ethics as of metaphysics. We find ourselves before beliefs so deep in relation to documentary photography and photojournalism that they seem to be eternal truths, whereas in fact they are relatively recent. According to art historian Gretchen Garner, the paradigm of photography as a "spontaneous witness" was constructed in the decade of the 1930s.[30] In this paradigm, photography has been undertaken by the majority of modern professionals as an act open to chance, and rarely with the intention of direction. The invention of the small and portable 35mm camera led to the creation of an esthetic in which the most important factor was paying attention to what was going on around one, being receptive to contingency, and committing oneself to revelation. This resulted in an "authenticity without intervention," based on the belief that falsification was unacceptable within this convention.

Notwithstanding the direction present in many of the greatest images, photojournalism has a particular relationship to "reality." Though a discussion of what constitutes reality is beyond the scope of this essay, let it suffice to say that there is a real world independent of our perception of it. Though our way of seeing is mediated by a priori constructs—"I'll see it when I believe it"—we are most aware of that otherness when we bump into it, trip over it, or it falls on top of us. Photojournalism deals with reality in at least two senses. On one hand, there is a requisite interaction with the social world; on the wall of his room in the collective's office, Julio Mayo had taped up the following text: "We photographers are the infantry of journalism, because we always march in the front line. We have to go to the news; they can't tell us about it."[31] On the other hand, because photojournalistic images are indexes as well as icons, they offer evidence of presence. As indexes, photographs are traces of material reality, deposited on film or in the computer as a result of the collaboration of mind, eye, and camera: the real key to photojournalism is having the sharpness of vision to discover, and the technical capacities to capture, the phenomena of the world. If it is an art, it is—at least in the classical ideal of photojournalism—an art that attempts to find, rather than to create, the juxtaposition of the socially and formally significant.

I envisioned the book on Nacho López to be constructed in a series of concentric circles through which to eventually focus down on his work. Hence, it was essential to know the history of Mexico in the 1940s and 1950s, a little-studied period. Within that wider circle, it was vital to construct an analysis of the Mexican press in those decades from a limited bibliography. Then, I needed to develop an in-depth knowledge of the illustrated magazines, and the work of their photojournalists so as to be able to compare them to López. I would also be contrasting López's expressive capacity and socio-political commitment to photojournalists whose work I was coming to know, among them the Hermanos Mayo, Héctor García, and Enrique Bordes Mangel. Finally, I would reach the nub of the topic: Nacho López's photojournalism, as well as his writings about it (largely produced in the 1970s). He published in the illustrated press for a relatively short period of time, 1950 to 1960, limiting the number of magazines I would need to consult. Nonetheless, there were no studies on the Mexican illustrated magazines, and few on the press in general. I was to work my way, page by page, through twenty-five years of the weeklies *Hoy*, *Mañana*, and *Siempre!*[32] I could not rely on the magazines' tables of contents, because I was also interested in discovering how López's photography had been used outside of his photoessays, often without being credited to him. Further, I needed the experience of close contact with the magazines, and the opportunity to make my own indexes of their contents.

The literature on photojournalists and illustrated magazines in the US and Europe was just beginning to open up comparative possibilities, as well as issues and questions.[33] At the same time, I was becoming acquainted with the work of Sekula, Stein, Solomon-Godeau, and Rosler, theorists who were exploring ways to analyze documentary photography and photojournalism, as well as being among the first modern scholars to turn the discursive gaze away from art photography.[34] Prior to reading these studies, I had cut my teeth on works that were essential in redefining photography's space in academic analysis and that continue to be fundamental in its study, such as those by Benjamin, Sontag, Barthes, and Berger.[35]

At that moment, the reigning model of Mexican photo books on individual authors was to select a bunch of images around certain themes, assure good reproduction, and write an introduction lauding the artistic contribution of the imagemaker (or have a well-known intellectual compose one). I was determined to develop a methodology that would permit me to analyze López's work as a photojournalist. Hence, although López was largely considered to be among the elite of Mexican imagemakers, my training as a historian required me to determine in just which ways López was an exceptional photojournalist, and that could only be accomplished by first constructing a backdrop of "ordinary" photojournalism. López only worked in illustrated magazines, so I restricted my research to the publications *Hoy*, *Mañana*, and *Siempre!* I had identified these periodicals as the most important of that medium in the period from 1936 to 1960, an era that marked the rise and demise of the illustrated magazines as a center of mass media, including those in which López participated the most. I then invented the strategy of creating an interface between López's intentions and those of the magazines, by comparing the photographs he made (and saved) with those published.[36] I also analyzed the ways they were cropped, in what sizes, and on which pages they appear, as well as the texts that accompany them. I decided not to include López's work done for the Instituto Nacional Indigenista, fearing that the question of Indianist photography required a familiarity with that genre and that issue in Mexican history that I did not possess in that moment.

Almost immediately upon entering the project, I became disillusioned and disoriented. This is not an uncommon experience among photohistorians because in many cases the images have had a prior popular circulation in coffee-table books—for example, the oft-reprinted images from the Casasola Archive—that have created an aura of "author" for individuals who were entrepreneurs as much as photographers. Before recent studies on the Casasolas, the discovery that the Casasola pictures had been taken by some five hundred photographers left many scholars in the past baffled as to how to approach those photos.[37] In the case of López, I had assumed that he was a graphic reporter dedicated to covering newsworthy events, as was made explicit in one of the few books then available on his work, *Nacho López, fotorreportero de los años cincuenta*.[38]

Eleazar had told me that López was a critical leftist (part of his pitch to sell me on Nacho), so I expected to find marvelous images of social struggles and street battles. I knew that the López archive contained some 250 photos of the 1958–59 strikes, so went to the Fototeca Nacional in Pachuca with much anticipation. I was sorely disappointed to discover that the photos López had chosen to conserve did not measure up to what I had seen by the Mayo, García, Moya, and Bordes Mangel. Another rude awakening was learning that Nacho had not made a single image of the 1968 student movement; as he wrote in a letter, he "suffered a severe blow to [his] conscience" (*sufrí un golpe severo en la conciencia*) for not having participated in that struggle.[39] So, what was López if not the press photographer I expected him to be?

The first problem I faced with the López project was determining what photojournalism is. To define it in the easiest way, we could say that it is constituted by images made for periodical publications. Nevertheless, although it seems to be a relatively easy genre to define, in fact it poses real difficulties. At one extreme we find a photographer working in a daily newspaper such as *Ovaciones*, for example, who must cover five assignments a day, for which he was given a roll of twenty-five exposures (pre-digital), and directed to take, in the oft-repeated phrase of Mexican photojournalists, "Five photos in each order; not one more, not one less." At another extreme of photojournalism we find Sebastião Salgado, who can dedicate himself to projects for six or more years (though he publishes selections of his photos in media such as the *New York Times* during that period); in one documented instance, he shot nearly six hundred images a day.[40]

The field of photojournalism is wide and varied, but one basic consideration is the publication for which it is made, the use to which it is to be put. Flusser argues, "The apparent 'objectivity' of technical images is merely a function of the purposes their meaning serves."[41] Photojournalism is a genre in which objectivity is particularly prized, fusing the camera's mechanical reproduction with the stated ideals of at least the most decent of the press. Nonetheless, there is an extraordinary variety of functions in this genre. A press photographer who takes photos for daily newspapers is tied to the necessity of providing information encapsulated in one image. Photojournalists who publish in magazines are further from immediate events; their photos many times form part of reportages with greater profundity and multiple images because of the need to construct a narrative. The Argentine photojournalist and editor Eduardo Longoni described the differences between the two media. He noted that the images selected by the heads of the different sections of a daily newspaper tended to "include a photo simply because they liked it, or because it was vertical or horizontal, and they often 'assassinated,' cropped, an image on a whim."[42] Longoni contrasted that to the importance given the esthetic element in magazines: "In magazines the process is the inverse of the dailies: first they design the photo layout, in order to see the visual rhythm of the reportage, and then they see what spaces are left for the text, because in reality this type of publication is very visual. The first thing people do with magazines of general interest is to leaf through and see the images."[43]

In general terms, I believe there are two key considerations that help us understand the differences between the diverse types of photographers who work in the mass media. The first is the question of authorial control, which is manifested in different ways during the three stages of production: the "conception," the "realization," and the "edition." In other words: To what degree is the photographer the source of the original conception for the article? What control does he or she have over the photographic act? What power does he or she have in relation to the edition of the article? And, the all-important question: What control does the photographer retain over their negatives; that is to say, to what extent can photojournalists be said to be carrying out projects of interest to them, as well as covering the events they have been assigned (as with Moya's "double camera")?

Related to the question of authorial control is the degree of direction assumed by the imagemaker during the photographic act. An example of minimal direction would be that of a situation in which a photographer simply covered an occurrence over which he or she would appear to have had no influence. At the other pole are photoessays for which a photographer has created "events," either by constructing the scene or by composing the essay from their archive. Between these two extremes we find inexhaustible variations of spontaneous and directed photography.

We could construct a heuristic hierarchy in order to delineate the differences between the various groupings, bearing in mind that I am here describing *functions* and not *persons*, because photojournalists change their roles according to the concrete situations in which they find themselves. Such an order would analyze the gamut from those with less control to those with more autonomy, in the following order: press photographer, photojournalist, photoessayist, and documentalist (rather than documentary) photographer. Hence, the Hermanos Mayo functioned as press photographers when they worked for daily newspapers, as photojournalists when they composed their magazine articles, and as documen-

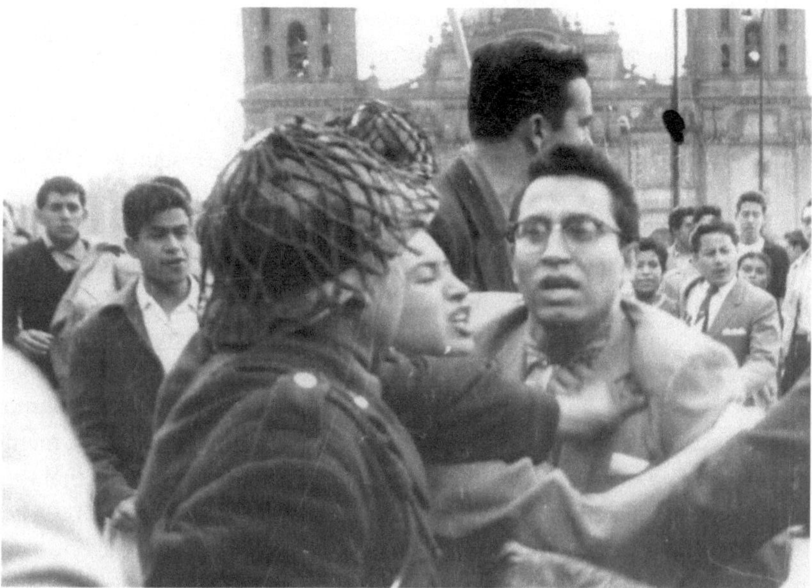

FIGURE 28. Hermanos Mayo. Striking teachers battle with police, Zócalo, Mexico City, 6 September 1958. Fondo Mayo, Chronological Section no. 12754, Archivo General de la Nación.

talist photographers when they took pictures in the street while going to or coming from assignments. The Mayo do not appear to have constructed photoessays, which was the bailiwick of López, who also was a documentalist. This hierarchy does not assign values to the different roles, but instead uses these categories as a way of indicating the great variety of ways in which photographers function within newspapers and magazines, and which of these functions we must take into consideration in analyzing them.

According to this schema, press photographers work in daily newspapers, and have little to say about the conception of a story, because it is most probable that they have been assigned to cover events, as in the Mayo photo of the battle between teachers and police in the Zócalo during the 1958 strikes. (See Figure 28.) Their degree of authorship is determined by the occurrence itself, by the amount of film they have been given (or bring themselves, as with the Mayos), by the pressure of time imposed by other assignments they have that same day, and by the limitations set for publication that have been established in their workplace and that they have more or less internalized as self-censorship. They have no say in the edition of their imagery. In Mexico (and elsewhere), the great majority of photographers in periodical publications have functioned as press photographers.

In a book produced by the Associated Press, *The News Photographer's Bible*, AP photojournalist Ed Reinke provided a classical formulation of how press photographers are expected to work: "As for photojournalism, and I emphasize the word journalism, we make photographs from the circumstances we are given and we don't try to alter those circumstances."[44] Those who earn their living covering "hard news" have very specific opinions about what constitutes the ethics of their guild, as came to float in the controversy that took place around the awards of the 2004 Sexta Bienal de Fotoperiodismo in Mexico City. The Bienal's jury awarded a major prize to the Cuban-born photographer Giorgio Viera (Jorge López Viera), for a reportage, "Mexicalzingo, comunidad en rebeldía," that contained one image, *Alma en la azotea* (Soul on the rooftop), that was a posed re-creation of a photo by Chien-Chi Chang, a recognized Taiwanese photojournalist, and a member of the Magnum Agency.[45] Photojournalist Ireri de la Peña wrote that the photo "generated an intense polemic that polarized the guild: for some, the image was plagiarized, and moreover posed, hence false and beyond any professional ethics."[46] Others believed that its expressive force was such that it transcended the idea of whether it was true or false. The argument became so fierce that it resulted in a publication, "Polémica y debate abierto"; a book edited by de la Peña, *Ética, poética y prosaica*; the cancellation of any further bienales of photojournalism; and Viera's relinquishment of the prize. In the "Polémica," the Mexican news photographers who largely work for daily newspapers and were very critical of Viera's image made explicit their ethical position, which I would summarize in the following ways: They argue that the commitment of photojournalists is to capture reality, of which they are simple witnesses, in order to inform with honesty, transparency, and veracity. Because the images they record are irrefutable and lasting, the first version of history, the only thing they should create are documents. Hence, they are not allowed to stage scenes, nor can they pose or recreate them, nor can the original shot be "manipulated" in a darkroom or by Photoshop, because to do so would be to lie and deceive. They see themselves as dedicated to spontaneously discovering the unknown that occurs in a fraction of a second, so it is not acceptable to copy or be inspired by prior photographs.[47] I would argue that the attitudes of the press photographers in this controversy demonstrate a misunderstanding resulting from applying the rules of a particular function with those of the entire genre of photojournalism.

In my model, "photojournalists" are distinguished from "press photographers" by the fact that they are working for magazines. This allows them to dedicate more time to a story, to take and publish more images, and to

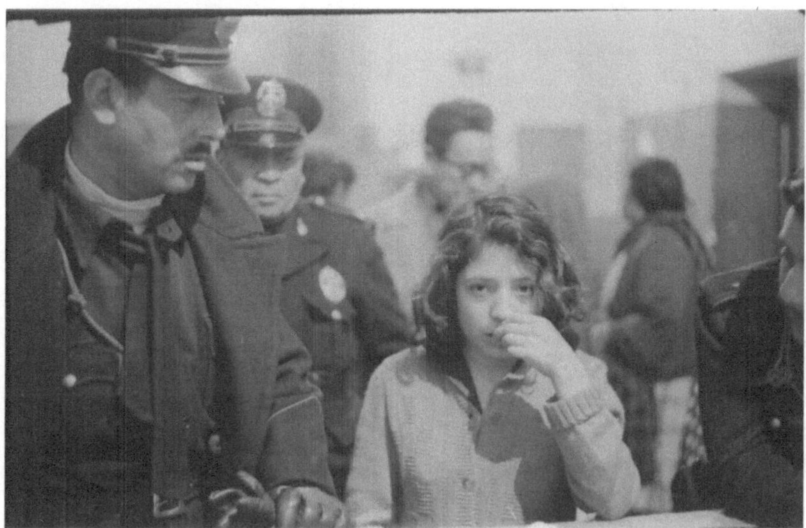

FIGURE 29. Nacho López. Young woman in police station, Mexico City, 1954. Inv. # 405677, Fondo Nacho López, SINAFO-Fototeca Nacional del INAH, Secretaría de Cultura.

construct a narrative. A photographer from the Magnum Agency believes that these categories began to take shape during the 1930s:

> The terminology in photography is almost entirely based on fragile egos. If you were a Fleet Street photographer [British press reporter] in the 1930s, the last thing you ever wanted to do was be confused with someone who did weddings or bar mitzvahs. . . . And in turn, the guy that starts working for *Picture Post* magazine who goes to Africa for three months to do a story on the wind change in Africa is pretty anxious not to be confused with a press photographer, especially because press photographers for the most part [were considered to] have a very limited vocabulary and big ears and wore strange hats with "Press" stuck in the band. So, he was anxious to call himself something different, so he called himself a photojournalist.[48]

Photojournalists would have more control than press photographers over the conceptualization of a project, and may be the originators of the ideas for stories. In the realization stage, they would also have more autonomy, given the fact that their film would be less limited, and the question about what they could or could not publish may have been discussed in an explicit way, into which they could have had some input. The question of whether or not they can (and are allowed to) write the texts is funda-

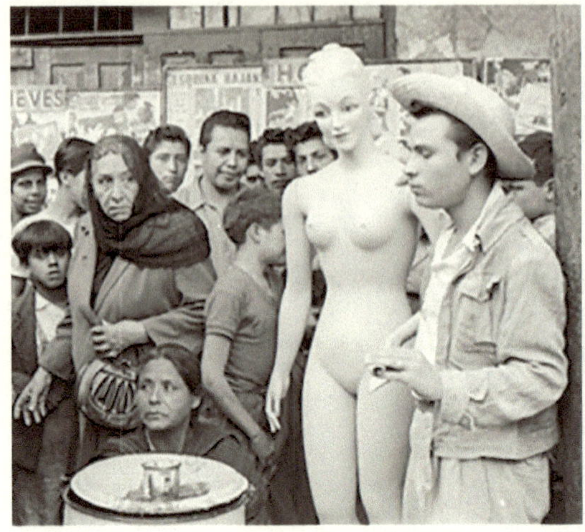

FIGURE 30. Nacho López. Man with mannequin in a group, Mexico City, 1953. Inv. # 405642, Fondo Nacho López, SINAFO-Fototeca Nacional del INAH, Secretaría de Cultura.

mental. López was one of the few Mexican photojournalists that wrote the texts to (some of) his essays, as he did for "Solo los humildes van al infierno" (Only the poor go to hell), when he spent four weeks photographing in the holding cells of Mexico City's police stations.[49] (See Figure 29.) Usually, however, they would probably have little to say about the editing of the story, but their possibilities of intervening would still be greater than would be those of the press photographers. Moreover, as their general function is to relate "human interest features," there is a certain tolerance of staging that would not be permitted in hard news; for example, Eugene Smith was fond of directing his reportages.[50] Almost all directed photojournalist images were made within the category of features, although their credibility is, to a great extent, a result of seepage from the faith generated by hard news imagery.

Distinguishing between a reportage and an essay is fundamental in differentiating a photojournalist from a photoessayist. Reportage involves covering a news event or, at the very least, a "live" event. Thus, in general terms, we could say that reportage has its source in the world, in reality. An essay, on the contrary, tends to originate in the photographer's mind, and in the interest in exploring an idea that existed prior to realizing the photographic act. An essay can be about something "live," but it is distinguished from reportage by the extent to which the photographer's conceptualization has preeminence over the communication of information about an event (as, for example, in Hunter S. Thompson's "gonzo" journalism). Hence, photoessayists would have the greatest degree of authorial control among those photographers who work in periodical publications.

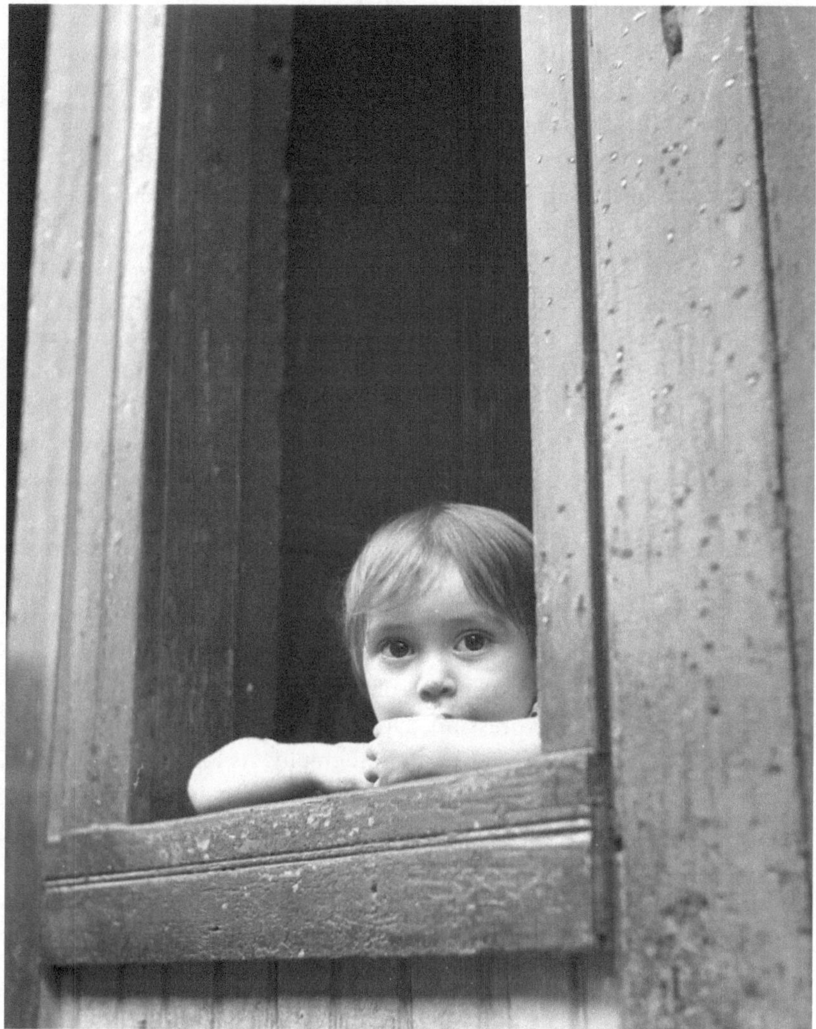

FIGURE 31. Nacho López. Child peering out window, Venezuela, 1948. Inv. # 405763, Fondo Nacho López, SINAFO-Fototeca Nacional del INAH, Secretaría de Cultura.

The photoessay sometimes originates with photojournalists such as López, above all if they can write the texts as well. Because they are looking for ways to express their conceptions, they often attain a greater directorial control over the photographic act, which may include staging scenes that provoke reactions from spectators in the frame, as with the woman who stares at the mannequin that a man hired by López is carrying around in the street. (See Figure 30.) They also compose photoessays from their archives, where the date and place of the photograph is elided. For example,

López's image of a little boy looking out his window was taken in Venezuela during 1948. (See Figure 31.) However, he included it in the photoessay, "Yo también he sido niño bueno" (I've been a good kid too), which ostensibly presented the disappointment of poor Mexican children who will not receive Christmas gifts because of their families' poverty. Although the photoessay was published in the magazine *Mañana* on December 30, 1950, it was described as a *reportaje*, giving the impression that López had encountered these scenes in Mexico during the Christmas season of that year.[51] López was much respected by the editor of the best Mexican illustrated magazines, José Pagés Llergo, for his extraordinary technical and narrative skills. Rodrigo Moya is fond of recounting how Nacho would stroll in to the editor's office and, with enormous confidence and not the slightest hesitation, tell "Pepe" that he had a great idea for a photoessay. Moya was intimidated by the editor, would never have thought to propose a project, and always referred to him as "Señor Director."[52] Nacho wrote about the freedom he had within *Hoy*, *Mañana*, and *Siempre!*, stating, "I was given absolute liberty in the choice of themes and the format of my articles. In *Mañana*, my old friend Esteban Cajiga even [allowed me] to stick my nose into supervising the negatives and the offset impressions."[53]

What I describe as "documentalist photographers" are those who enjoy the greatest liberty of expression. Documentary photography is often loosely defined by opposing it to art photography. As I have argued above, all photographic images are documentary because of their indexical quality. However, the term is usually associated with a canon of socially concerned imagery such that produced in the US by Jacob Riis and Lewis Hine, and in Europe by Magnum's founders, some of whom were connected to the Front Populaire.[54] Here it is important to note that, though all photojournalism is documentary, I am here using the concept of documentalist to describe particular situations, within which a variety of possibilities exist to pursue one's own interests. Mexican photographers who work for institutions are sometimes allowed to test the limits; one example is the National Indigenist Institute (INI), where Nacho López was contracted during and after leaving photojournalism. In the United States the best instance would be the Farm Security Administration, and its photographers such as Walker Evans, Dorothea Lange, Jack Delano, Ben Shahn, Marion Post, and Arthur Rothstein; their images circulated in periodicals and other publications. Evans openly testified to the latitude he experienced: "I was interested, selfishly, in the opportunity it gave me to go around and use the camera. I did anything I pleased, and *ignored* what I was expected to do. If I got an order from anybody saying, 'There's a development out here, go and photograph

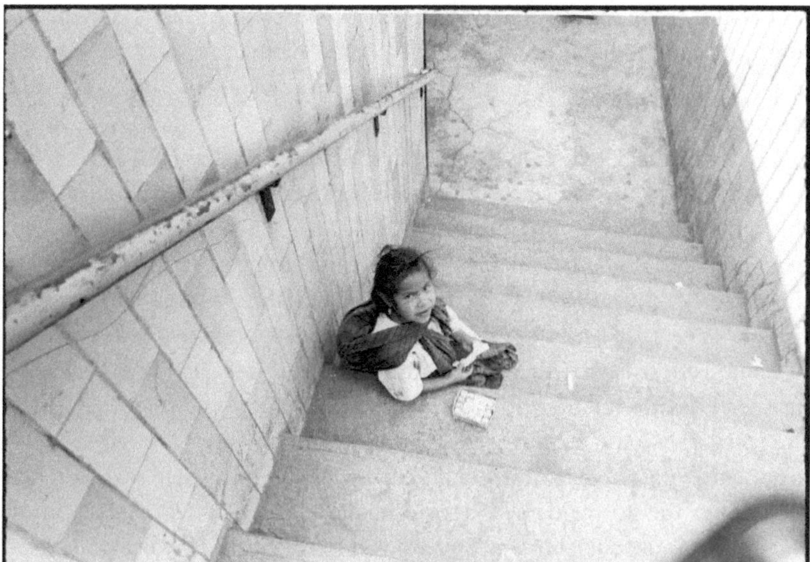

FIGURE 32. Hermanos Mayo. Young girl selling chewing gum on the stairs of an underground passageway, Mexico City, ca. 1960. Fondo Mayo, Imágenes de la Ciudad, Archivo General de la Nación.

it.' I'd tear it up and put it away."[55] Another possibility is to be a freelance photographer who lives from grants, book royalties, and commissions from state governments, banks, or other commercial enterprises, often in conjunction with belonging to an agency.

Finally, we would have to consider those images that photojournalists make on their own initiative, whether while they are working or in their free time; this factor bears an intimate relationship to whether photojournalists conserve and catalogue their negatives. Salgado has often said that his work is closer to documentary photography than to photojournalism, whereas López always insisted that he was a photojournalist. The Mayo were much more photojournalists than documentalists, but a superb example of their work in this function is the picture one Mayo made of a little girl selling chewing gum outside one of the Mexico City underground passageways. (See Figure 32.) We know that this image is unrelated to a work order because it is found in the largest section of the immense Mayo archive where half a million negatives are stored under the category of "Imágenes de la ciudad" (Images of the city). Mayo took the picture on the steps leading to the passageway, probably while going to or coming from a work order. It is a magnificent representation of how Mexican children are ensnared in lives of poverty: the high-angle shot entraps and encloses the girl in the concrete walls—a powerful metaphor for the metropolitan jungle of Mexico City—just as the education she is missing in order to sell gum assures that she will never be able to leave her marginal existence.

It is within the documentalist function that the development of what has become known as "fine art photojournalism" appeared, and I believe that this will be the future of photojournalism. I first encountered the concept in an excellent 1997 essay on Salgado.[56] It could surely be applied to many of the works of Álvarez Bravo, García, and López, as well as what I have called the *Nuevo Fotoperiodismo Mexicano*, a movement that flourished from 1976 to around 2000, largely in Mexico City. The periodicals *Unomásuno* and *La Jornada* permitted photojournalists to develop their own themes, to keep their negatives, and to explore the imagery of daily life. This led to a fine art documentary style within a daily format, a highly unusual situation that resulted in the flowering of a unique realist aesthetic.[57] As digitalization, the Internet, and social media have forced traditional periodicals to adjust or disappear, many Mexican photojournalists have won recognition while working essentially freelance, among them Narciso Contreras and Carlos Cazalis. Considering that the concept seems to have arisen within Brazil, perhaps this is a Latin American sensibility. As the Ecuadorian photojournalist Pablo Corral Vega recently stated,

> I believe Latin American photographers are more willing to navigate freely between fine art and documentary photography. I'm not talking about manipulation of the images, but about a sensibility that allows a subjective vision. I'm convinced that this is the best moment for Latin American photography because photographers are not looking at Europe and the USA for references. The photographers we want to emulate are in our region.[58]

The various research projects I have carried out on Latin American photojournalism have led me to understand the differing functions within that genre and marked the beginning of my idea that the concepts of genres and functions could be applied to the analysis of photographers. I suspect there is a generalized tendency to lump photographers, and especially photojournalists, together as if they have the same aptitudes. I think we need to see them instead with the perspective we bring to thinking about those who write. That is to say, we will surely be disappointed if we expect an economist to be a poet, or a scientist to be a novelist, although they are all writers. Hence, there are photojournalists who have the capacity to catch action in the street, and those whose forte is constructing photoessays; other kinds of photographers are best at studio photography or the many kinds of scientific photography or aerial photography, or any other of the almost infinite photographic genres. For example, Tina Modotti was a photojournalist for *El Machete* during the late 1920s in the sense that she published her images in a periodical. However, she herself recognized her limitations in doing spontaneous street photography: "I know the material found on the streets is rich and wonderful, but my experience is that the way I am accustomed to work, slowly planning my composition, etc. is not suited for such work. By the time I have the composition or the expression right, the picture is gone."[59]

Perhaps the purest example of the classic idea of photojournalism is embodied in the Hermanos Mayo. Their negatives have been preserved in strips, allowing researchers to see the order in which the shots were taken, as well as the number made during any particular work order. I have found that when a Mayo has repeated a shot, the first one is almost invariably the best. They had the eye and the reflexes to capture that confluence of what Henri Cartier-Bresson described as the "decisive moment."[60] Moreover, their compositions in the camera are such that I have rarely cropped one of their photos in my various writings and exhibits on them. In the case of López, I cropped all of his images that I published and found that every one of his photos that appeared in illustrated magazines and books had been cropped as well.

I believe that the method I developed to study photojournalism—that of focusing on the varying functions within genres—can be applied fruitfully to other types of photography. For example, when I was invited to write an essay on portraiture for one of the sumptuous Christmas books produced by Mexican government secretariats, banks, and other industries, I first thought that portraits were an insignificant genre for historians.[61] However, from the very beginning of the project I found them a fascinating source. A daguerreotype of one couple led me to an unexpected insight into genre relations. (See Figure 33.) Louis Daguerre's invention arrived in Veracruz during December 1839, shortly after its public presentation in France. Daguerreotypes were the first popular form of photography, but they were prohibitively expensive for more than 95 percent of the population; moreover, they could not be reproduced, because they had no negative.[62] It would appear that the majority of Mexican daguerreotypes were portraits, almost always of the wealthy, elegantly dressed and settled into poses that they could hold for "between ten and fifteen minutes in the best of cases."[63] As photohistorian Robert Levine observed, "The sitting process was uncomfortable and tedious: slow lenses permitted no movement

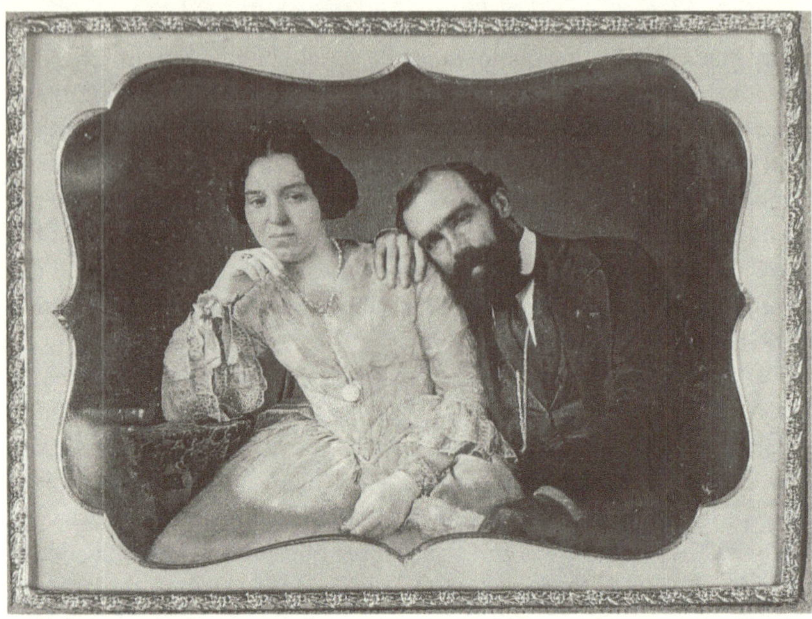

FIGURE 33. Unknown. Couple posing for a daguerreotype, Mexico City, ca. 1845. Museo de Arte Moderno, Instituto Nacional de Bellas Artes y Literatura.

at all; heads had to be held fast by metal clamps."[64] This nerve-racking and lengthy process was described by a woman who posed for the British photographer Julia Margaret Cameron, whose cameras required exposure times of between three and ten minutes:

> Mrs. Cameron put a crown on my head and posed me as the heroic queen. This was somewhat tedious, but not half so bad as the exposure. . . . The exposure began. A minute went over and I felt as if I must scream; another minute, and the sensation was as if my eyes were coming out of my head; a third, and the back of my neck appeared to be afflicted with palsy; a fourth, and the crown, which was too large, began to slip down my forehead.[65]

When we apply our knowledge about how tedious, tense, and frankly painful it was to pose for a daguerreotype, we understand the significance of the fact that the woman has to bear not only her weight, but that of the man as well for what must have seemed like an eternity. Though I am no fan of reading psychological states into photographs, it is tempting to contrast her grimace with his calm visage.

Thanks to having accepted the invitation to research and write on a subject about which I was as ignorant as I was uninterested, I was able to conclude my study of portraiture with the knowledge that it is a genre within which we find a number of different functions. Portraits serve as a living presence and memento mori of our ancestors and our immediate families and friends. They are used to identify criminals. They have been employed to register prostitutes, who turned the identification process around by grasping it as an opportunity to project their own identities.[66] Portraits have been utilized extensively to make political propaganda by placing before the masses the faces of the powerful, both those in power and those battling for it. They also showed how successful and modern people ought to look and provide archetypes of how to be Mexican, in part by rescuing ancient forms of work. Portraits can denounce injustices and inequalities, show a society in transformation, and preserve the visages and vestiges of vanishing ethnicities. They also reflect the metamorphoses of esthetic style. Portraits capture an enormous variety of reactions among the portrayed. Those who are posing within their official role, as president, military officers, or Great Men generally do not return the gaze, rather they look off at a forty-five-degree angle, as if addressing themselves to history itself. Others pose as they have seen modeled by the elite, or as they have been instructed, though there are also individuals who use the situation to compose the image of themselves that they wish to project, as well as others who seem to resist the act itself. Portraits have opened a world unto itself, and onto very different realities.

CONCLUSION

In the following chapters I will attempt to implement this strategy developed from my studies of photojournalism by analyzing a variety of genres. I work from the supposition that photographic representation is almost always—and more so in the case of subaltern groups—a question of power: some photograph, others are photographed; some see, others are seen; some are subjects, others are objects; that is, paraphrasing Octavio Paz, some are the *chingones*, others the *chingados*.[67] The photographic act is never neutral or innocent; rather, it manifests its anchorage in the power relations that can be found within the image, if we know how to look for them. In the following chapter I explore the imbrication of imperial, neocolonializing, and decolonializing photography with the picturing of Amerindians. I will then consider the different forms that leftist, worker, laborist, feminist and decolonizing photography has taken. The task is complex, but the objective is to look for ways historians can begin to sort out this enormous body of documents so as to teach us how to incorporate photographs rigorously into our discipline.

CHAPTER 4

Indianist Imagery

Imperial, Neocolonizing, and Decolonizing Photography

It is hard to escape the impression that sixteenth-century Europeans . . . all too often saw what they expected to see. . . . But, how to convey this fact of difference, the uniqueness of America, to those who had not seen it? The problem of description reduced writers and chroniclers to despair. **J. H. Eliot**

During 1977 and 1978 I lived with my Native American friend Robert Chacanaca in an apartment at UCSC through which passed many Amerindians in the University of California system, including students, faculty, and administrators. Some stayed with us for a time, others came to gatherings in which issues around Native peoples were discussed, and many came for the frequent parties we held. I was struck by the way their reverence for nature, their generosity, and their lack of interest in material belongings differed from the dominant pattern of US culture. I also learned how greatly they disliked being photographed by tourists. Because of that experience, I have largely avoided working on imagery of indigenous peoples, except to play the devil's advocate in asserting that Indianist photographers are, in the main, imperial hunters involved in a sublimated, predatory, and intrusive pillage of people whose reaction to photography is sometimes expressed in avoidance and outright refusal to cooperate.[1] Here, it is fundamental to differentiate between indigenous and Indianist photography: the former is made *by* Amerindians, the latter is made *of* them by people from other ethnicities who have often been foreign interlopers, although Mexicans related to the official ideology of *Indigenismo* have also pictured natives.[2] In this chapter, I have limited myself to analyzing Indianist photography, leaving aside the images produced by indigenous peoples.

Photographing the surviving pre-Hispanic cultures of Mexico has a long, complex, and constantly changing history, in which pictures have served multiple purposes, and I will here utilize the method of placing photos within genres and then carrying out an examination of their historical functions to explore Indianist imagery (which could be considered part of the broader genre of picturing the subaltern).[3] During the nineteenth and twentieth centuries, European and US imagemakers, colonial administrators, soldiers, travelers, and scientific researchers took photographs of "natives" all over the world, which "were presented and read as proof of the justice of the imperial division of the world. The division between those who organised and rationalised and surveyed, and those who were surveyed."[4] In general, imperial photography presents the spaces in which colonial rule will be imposed as having been "empty" and unoccupied, uncultivated and exotic areas that will be explored, just as the picturesque and primitive aborigines will be civilized and put to work.[5] The apparent absence of industry conveys the visual ideology that asserts only colonialism will be capable of putting to good use a natural abundance that the original inhabitants have failed to adequately exploit, although they will be implicitly present to serve as labor for the imperial power (see Figure 48 in Chapter 4). The pertinence of analyzing imperial surveillance today, as well as its decolonizing antithesis, can be seen in the waves of immigrants moving from the destroyed colonial economies of tropical southern hemispheres to the cold but prosperous imperial areas.

One might be tempted to think that photographs have somehow preserved a paradise lost, an ancient, bucolic, and communal possibility for living. Roger Bartra makes short work of that inducement; for him they embalm something very different: "They are testimony of one of the greatest cultural catastrophes in the history of the universe: the devastation of pre-Hispanic societies, the global destruction of their cultures and the annihilation of their populations."[6] There are sixty-eight surviving indigenous languages in Mexico, so we must take into account the great variety between the pueblos themselves, the profound transformations that have continually occurred over the last five hundred years, and the multiformity of the esthetics through which they have been photographed.

FOREIGN PHOTOGRAPHERS AND THE AMERINDIANS

It would appear that foreigners were the first to turn their photographic gaze upon Mexico's indigenous cultures. Such traveler-photographers were usually funded by their governments and should be seen as part of the broader process of imperialism and neocolonization, providing intelligence about unknown areas of the world. They brought with them the Positivist system of classifying and categorizing human beings into a three-fold hierarchical system of "savagery, barbarism, and civilization," a practice inaugurated in 1767 by "the father of modern sociology," Adam Ferguson, and espoused by the famous ethnographer Lewis H. Morgan in his studies of the Iroquois Indians in the US.[7]

The Yucatan peninsula was evidently the initial "contact zone" between Mexican Indians and photography.[8] In 1841, Baron Emanuel von Friedricsthal, the secretary of the Austrian legation in Mexico, made daguerreotypes of Chichén Itzá and Uxmal.[9] Either his funding was limited or he decided to profit from his situation, for he effectively became the first known professional photographer in Mexico, advertising his studio and establishing prices, hours, and the type of clothing that ought to be worn. Around the same time, US president Martin Van Buren commissioned John L. Stephens as a special ambassador to the Federal Republic of Central America. Stephens and the English artist and explorer Frederick Catherwood had documented Mayan ruins in Palenque, Quiriguá, and Uxmal during their 1839–40 incursion, and when they returned to Yucatan in 1841, they brought a daguerreotype camera along. Unfortunately, the technology fell far short of the quality of Catherwood's lithographic reproductions: "Mr. Catherwood began taking views: but the results were not sufficiently perfect to suit his ideas."[10] Nonetheless, Catherwood's excellent lithographs were based on daguerreotypes as well as the method he had developed with a camera lucida. Thanks to the visual "indexes" Catherwood made, he was able to capture—in Eliot's felicitous phrase—"the uniqueness of America," and convey it to those who had not seen it. Hence, he avoided the errors of Frédéric de Waldeck, who had added elephants to his lithographs of Palenque made in the 1830s.

Catherwood's visual "indexes" supported Stephens' contention, derived from direct observation, that the current inhabitants were direct descendants of those who constructed Mayan civilization.[11] Hence, they were a powerful decolonizing message in opposing the racist speculations of Friedricsthal and among the White ruling class in Yucatán and learned European circles that these creations must have resulted from an incursion from the other hemisphere, whether Egyptian, Hebrew, Roman, Norse, Chinese, or any of the other cultures named as the builders of the Mayan ruins.[12] However, the findings of Stephens and Catherwood were not definitive in changing the colonizing mind, as is demonstrated in the writings of Pierre Gourou, who held the chair of Tropical Studies in the prestigious

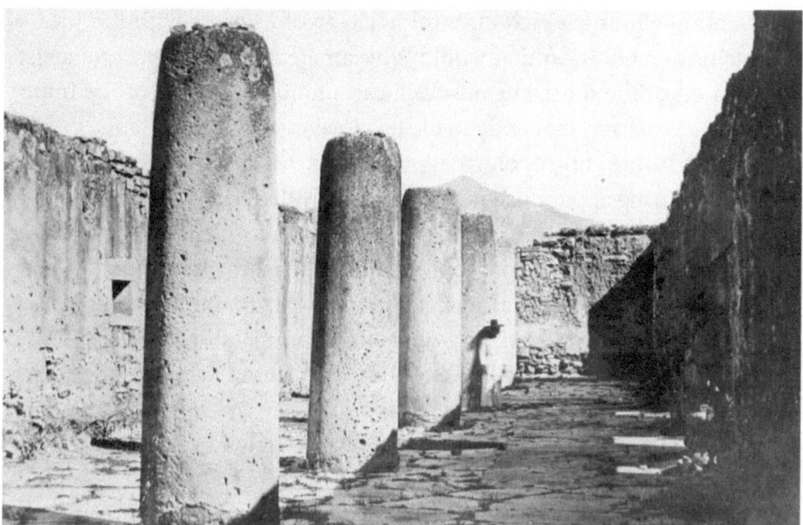

FIGURE 34. Desiré Charnay. Mitla, Oaxaca, 1870. Inv. # 426320. SINAFO-Fototeca Nacional del INAH, Secretaría de Cultura.

Collège de France from 1947 to 1970. More than a hundred years after it was clear that the Mayans had in fact created an extraordinary autochthonous culture, Gourou (according to Aimé Césaire), "expressed the fundamental thesis, biased and unacceptable, that there has never been a great tropical civilization, that great civilizations have existed only in temperate climates, that in every tropical country the germ of civilization comes, and can only come, from some other place outside the tropics."[13]

The intellectual and artistic forerunner of French imperialism in Mexico, Desiré Charnay was commissioned by the Ministère de l'Education to spend the years 1857 to 1861 there. When Charnay returned to Paris in 1861, he immediately presented Napoleon III with a photographic album of his travels documenting the ancient Mesoamerican ruins. This was eventually published as *Cités et ruines américaines* in 1862–63, an "expensive work that was welcomed with rapturous critical acclaim in London (1862) and Paris (1863)."[14] He returned with the invading army in 1864, accompanied by a large expedition organized by the French Scientific Commission on Mexico, whose motto was, "Our scholars are . . . going to march once more in the tracks of our soldiers," a reference to the groups of relic-hungry scientists who had accompanied Napoleon I in Egypt.[15]

Mexico was made into a scientific object, and the reconstruction of its ancient past was an attempt to "civilize" the country. Among Charnay's official missions was that of providing the Louvre Museum with visual information about the rich cultural heritage of Mexico, with the idea of producing a publication that would "give amateurs, foreigners, and artists a collection of the more curious Mexican monuments, and of the imposing ruins."[16] Charnay evidently made few images of the inhabitants, though he did take "some anthropological pictures of Indians, front and side view, near a measuring apparatus, or others where Indian and European helpers appear to give scale to the monuments."[17] (See Figure 34.) Explicitly addressing the importance of his photography in establishing the autochthonous origins of the ruins, he asked, "Aren't monuments bound to tell us if their founders were our brothers and our contemporaries or if this profound country had a genesis apart?"[18] Photohistorian Rosa Casanova asserts that the images in *Cités et ruines américaines* and Charnay's earlier work, *Álbum fotográfico mexicano* (1858), "became obligatory references for archeological photography around the world."[19]

François Aubert accompanied Maximilian and Carlota in Napoleon III's ill-fated imperial adventure, and his official affiliation is made clear in the fact that his imagery was never circulated or sold, and only became known years later when found in French and Belgian military museums. He focused largely on the members of the royal court, following the Emperor's destiny up to his execution in Querétaro. An urban photographer, he made cityscapes of Mexico City and other metropolises, as well as posing the picturesque popular types embodied in street vendors.[20] However, the "Mexican types" of both Charnay and Aubert were hard-edged photographs of miserable, poverty-stricken individuals, and Navarrete has argued that they may well have been part of "a propaganda campaign by the French government to justify the recent conquest of Mexico and promote a new 'colonization' of the country."[21]

Although Aubert traveled around Mexico, the only time he photographed Amerindians as a cultural entity was when a Kickapoo delegation arrived to ask Maximillian for land in 1864. The Kickapoos had been forced out of their original territory in the Lake Erie forests and settled on a reservation in Kansas.[22] Constantly harassed by White "settler colonialism" bent on their extinction, they decided to leave the US, and had appealed to Benito Juárez to allow them to live in Mexico.[23] However, as Juárez was exiled from power at that moment, they directed their plea to Maximilian. The emperor was much impressed by their request to be granted some of the most uninhabitable lands in Coahuila State, and wrote his brother that he had received "a commission of authentic savage pagan Indians from the far northern border, true figures out of [James Fenimore] Cooper in the authentic sense of the word."[24] He directed Aubert to photograph them, and

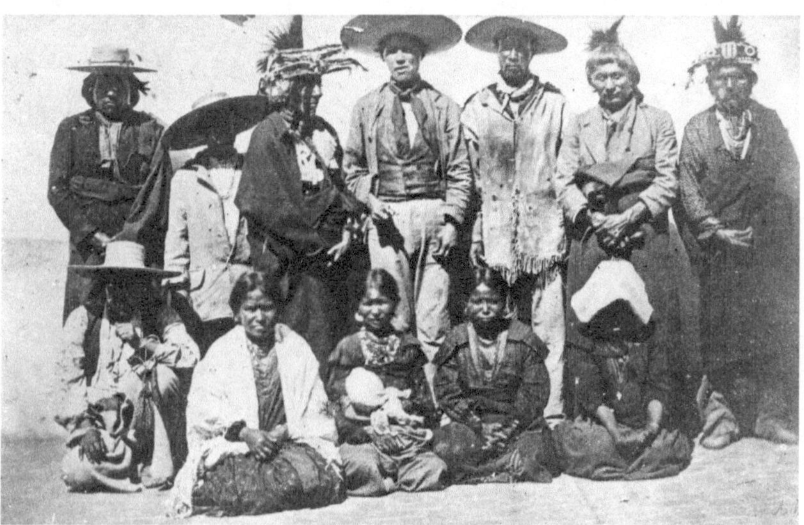

FIGURE 35. François Aubert. Kikapoos, Mexico City, 1864. Center for Southwest Research, University of New Mexico.

the realism of his esthetic captured the group in their mix of traditional and modern clothing. (See Figure 35.) These photographs served as models for colorful images: a lithograph by Casimiro Castro and a painting by Jean-Adolphe Beaucé of the Kickapoo delegates, in both of which appear only those Indians dressed in traditional robes and headdresses.[25] Once again, photography's indexical capacity provided a more veridical representation than other imagery.

A decorated officer of the Pioneer Corps of Austro-Belgian Volunteers that joined Maximilian's forces, Teoberto Maler remained in Mexico when the invading forces retired. He made himself into an itinerant photographer who lived from taking portraits in modest rural towns all over Mexico, representing businesses, and documenting pre-Hispanic ruins.[26] Although Maler had a comfortable nest egg in Austria, he nonetheless had to support himself with his work, and it was not easy to find employment as a foreigner. As one of the leaders of the American colony in Mexico observed in an 1868 letter, "The various ways in which immigrants earn an honest living are truthfully many and sometimes surprising."[27]

Maler had little appreciation for the Spanish heritage or the Mexican mestizo society. Rather, his attraction to the country was based on his empathy with the Native populations, to which he scrupulously referred as the "original peoples" rather than *indios,* a term that carried (and still has) a denigrating connotation:

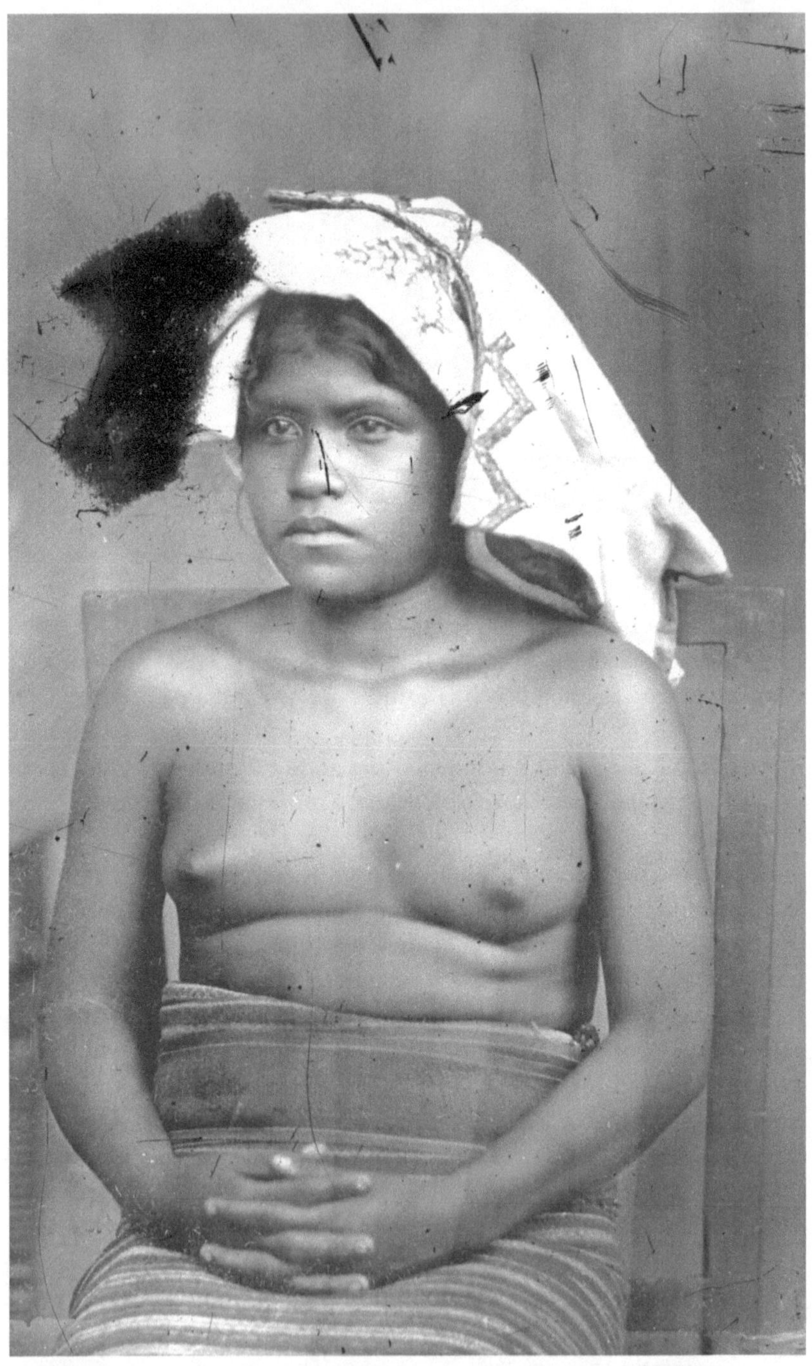

FIGURE 36. Teoberto Maler. Nude Mixteca from the Oaxacan coast, ca. 1875. Inv. # 466926, Colección Teixidor, SINAFO-Fototeca Nacional del INAH, Secretaría de Cultura.

> The original peoples or "*los indígenas*" are the most interesting for me. They are the most solid part of the population in Mexico, upon whose shoulders fall the major part of the work, but they live in extreme ignorance, because the dominant classes tax them but only construct schools for Spanish speakers and will not tolerate schools in the Indian languages.[28]

Maler learned Nahuatl, and clearly understood that the miserable living conditions suffered by the Native races were a product of their exploitation. Moreover, he explicitly celebrated the natives' countrywide attempts to overthrow the White and mestizo ruling classes. Although some photographers had Native Americans as their clients, Maler's may well be the first portraits commissioned by indigenous people in Mexico, and he commented that what "Zapotec women most desire is to have an effigy of themselves."[29]

We do not know all the different forms in which Maler's portraits circulated. Certainly, the general functions of family photography were served among those portrayed and their extended families. Maler also used the portraits for academic lectures he gave in Paris, Berlin, and New York; further, he sold portfolios of his imagery in Oaxaca.[30] He may have done what the German photographer Emilio Herbruger Wheling did in Guatemala, which was to photograph the Native peoples without charging them, in order to "sell copies mostly to foreigners to send back to their countries, which was what the promoter of the portraits wished."[31] Maler was certainly conscious of the need to live from his photography and, on retirement, he supported himself by selling reproductions of the ruins to tourists.[32]

Such economic considerations must be taken into account in viewing his photograph of the semi-nude Mixtecan woman from the Oaxacan coast. (See Figure 36.) Catherine Lutz and Jane Collins have asserted that the magazine *National Geographic* has pictured Native races in very particular ways: "The people of the third and fourth worlds are portrayed as *exotic*; they are *idealized*; they are *naturalized* and taken out of all but a single historical narrative; and they are *sexualized*."[33] Several female nudes can be found in Maler's work, including one woman who appears dressed in traditional Tehuana attire as well as completely nude.[34] Hence, we need to ask whether his pictures entered into the pornography market, given the suspicions that I have expressed about foreign photographers such as C. B. Waite and Winfield Scott, both of whom were accused of trafficking in such imagery.[35]

Maler appears to have had great respect for the Mayans and their civilization, dedicating himself after 1885 to documenting the ruins extensively (financed by Harvard's Peabody Museum beginning in 1897). However, the fact that he was also involved in looting a pre-Hispanic Zapotec tomb in Tehuantepec demonstrates the complexities and contradictions of Indianist photography.[36] Maler had established contact with one of the French founders of ethnography, Ernest Theodore Hamy, who was an expert on the pre-Hispanic past. However, Maler's imagery shows little influence of the "physiognomic and phrenologic enthusiasm" that characterized photographers such as Carl Lumholtz, Frederick Starr, and Leon Diguet.[37]

Little work has been done on the photography of the Frenchman Leon Diguet.[38] As with Charney, Diguet was commissioned by the French Ministry of Education to undertake six scientific missions from 1893 to 1914.[39] His achievements were not limited to photography, for he carried out thoroughgoing investigations of many Mexican resources: shellfish and succulents, orchids and insects, cochineal and oyster cultivation, modern Indians and their ancient ruins. He studied the Huichol language and wrote a book about it in 1911: *Idiome Huichol: Contribution à l'étude des langues mexicaines*, which was published by the *Journal de la Société des Américanistes*. He took the *de rigueur* police-style frontal and profile shots, but he also made portraits, as well as documenting Huichol ceremonies, dwellings, and ritual objects.

Diguet's is essentially a colonialist vision: the Amerindians are simply another product of nature about which knowledge could prove profitable, as well as primitive examples that demonstrate the superiority of Caucasians by comparison. Hence, there is no evidence of rapport with his unsmiling subjects, who appear quite uncomfortable in front of the camera. The inducement Diguet offered the Indians for their consent and participation is unknown. A picture of two Huichol women pressed up against an adobe wall, breasts exposed, offers an example of his perspective and the natives' rather forced resignation to their fate. One of the natives returns the camera's gaze with particular vehemence, as if made to feel somehow ashamed to be photographed in a dress that was perfectly natural to them, or he may have made them disrobe in order to "illustrate anatomical details."[40] Once again, "soft-core pornography," a lá *National Geographic*, raises its head. (See Figure 37.)

Anthropologist Frederick Starr was the most imperial of ethnographic imagemakers, exemplifying academia's role in the neocolonial process. A professor at the University of Chicago for some forty years, he may have been funded by that institution to research in Mexico during the years 1896 to 1899, although the bulk of his financing may have come from trafficking in archeological pieces.[41] He was the intellectual author of pictures made

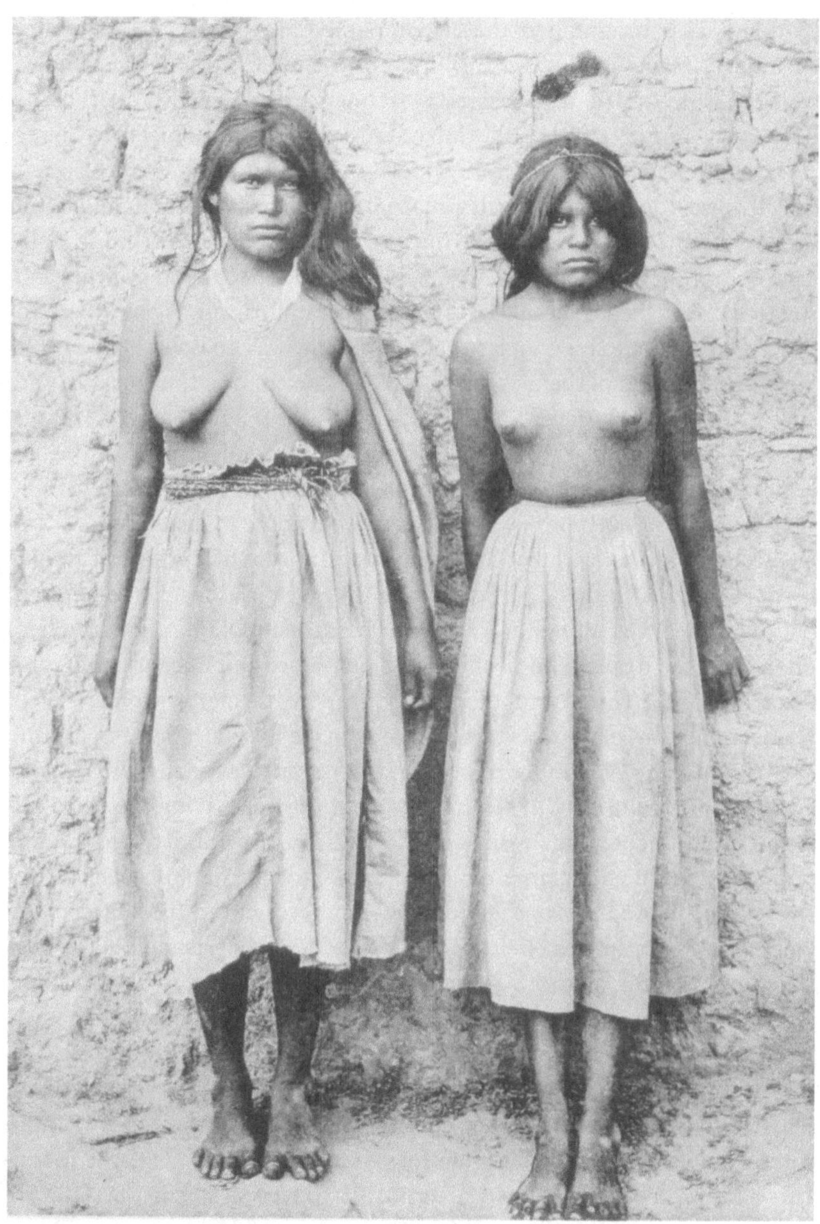

FIGURE 37. Leon Diguet. Huichol women, 1896–1898. Musée du Quai Branly—Jacques Chirac.

by three US photographers that accompanied him on his research trips: Bedros Tatarian, Charles B. Lang, and Louis Grabic. Ethnological studies were (and are) related to the interests that finance them, and were part of the developed countries' rationalization of racism and neocolonial rule. Starr's pictures "were produced to prove a racial theory that today has been scientifically discarded," according to visual anthropologists Deborah Poole and Gabriela Zamorano.[42] One of the most racist and uninformed anthropologists of his time, he compared Mexican indigenous peoples to pygmies and suspected that the Oaxacan Mixes practiced cannibalism. Hence, the arrogance he brought to his contact with the Indians was no doubt responsible for his description of them as distrustful, hostile, ignorant, suspicious, and superstitious. While they may have appeared to be unenlightened in Starr's terms of what sort of knowledge was important, and their beliefs no doubt impressed Starr as being profoundly different from his own, they were right to be wary of Starr's motives, as well as unwelcoming to his presence.

Starr employed the carrot of money as well as the stick of official authority to ensure that Indians participated in his investigations. He sometimes paid volunteers to allow themselves to be measured and photographed, often with the frontal and profile poses employed in police photography. (See Figure 38.) The anthropologist also hired some natives to have their heads molded in plaster casts, which must have been a rather unpleasant experience. However, more important than money were the letters Starr had from Porfirio Díaz to all the pertinent officials giving the unconditional order to cooperate with him; Starr was instructed to go first to the political boss before making contact with the Indians.[43] For photohistorian Jaime Vélez Storey, direct coercion, which also involved the church, was Starr's modus operandi: "It was neither closeness nor friendly interaction nor consensus that permitted him to make his photographs, but the force of governmental and clerical authority."[44]

Women were particularly resistant to his demands, running away or barricading themselves in their houses despite threats to burn them down. Starr callously narrated one episode: "With cries of terror, the poor creatures would start off as fast as their legs would carry them, over the mountain trails, with the whole town government, sixteen strong, in pursuit with yells and screams. It was like nothing but the chase of deer by hounds."[45] His racist and imperialist mentality was later demonstrated when he became a fervent defender of the appallingly cruel and universally condemned colonial policies of Belgian ruler Leopold II—described by Mark Twain as the "king with 10 million murders on his soul"—in the Congo Free State.[46]

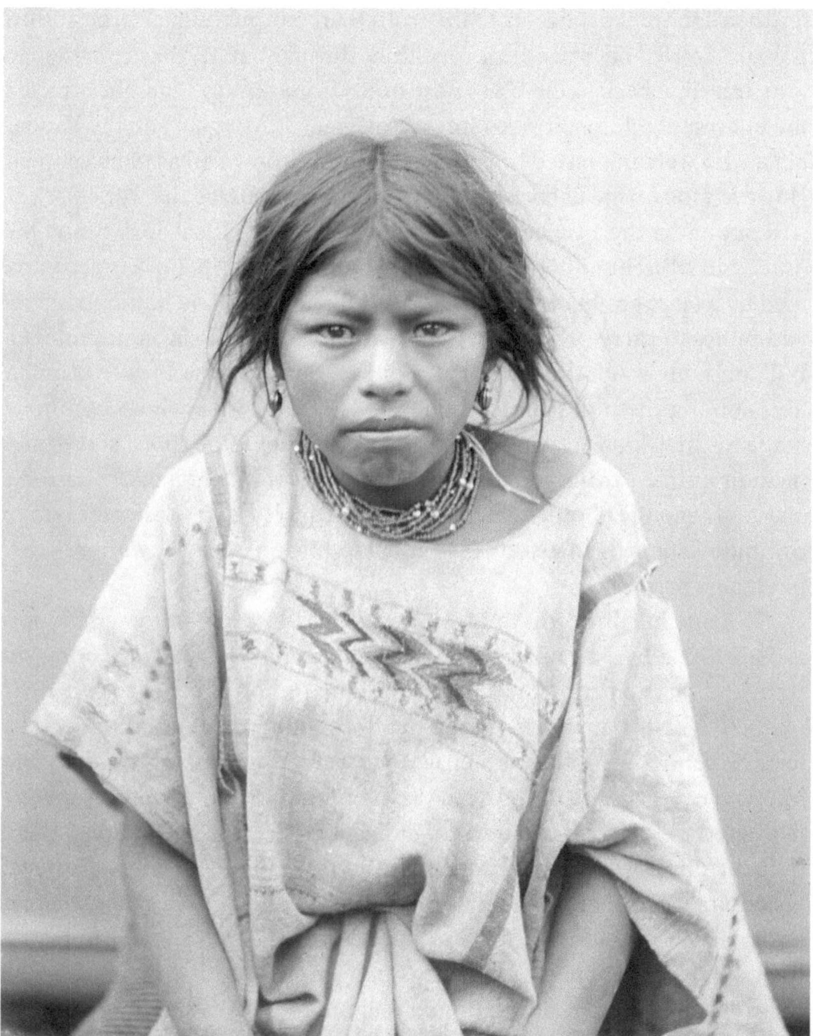

FIGURE 38. Frederick Starr, intellectual author. Triqui girl, Oaxaca, ca. 1900. National Museum of the American Indian, Smithsonian Institution, N16471.

The Norwegian Carl Lumholtz displayed a very different attitude toward Amerindians. Although his appreciation of their cultures was conditioned by the reigning concept of a hierarchical cultural development, he nonetheless understood that it did not necessarily signify underdevelopment: "I felt myself carried back thousands of years into the early stages of human history. Primitive people as they are, they taught me a new philosophy of life, for their ignorance is nearer to the truth than our prejudice."[47] The anthropologist carried out scientific expeditions throughout Mexico from 1890 to 1910, traveling back to the US to raise funds from time to time. He attracted the interest of millionaires Andrew Carnegie, J. P. Morgan, and the Vanderbilts, who were interested in opening up the unknown areas to investment. However, his financial backers remained anonymous, as the work was carried out under the auspices of the American Geographical Society and the American Museum of Natural History. On his first trip, he was accompanied by a large group of thirty men, as well as around one hundred horses and mules to carry provisions; the photographer was Princeton professor William Libbey. On the second expedition, Lumholtz had fewer companions, among them the photographer C. H. Taylor with whom Lumholtz made his first "police style" imagery of front and profile shots, sometimes including a measuring rod. Around May of 1892, Lumholtz dismissed his assistants and the photographer, having "discovered it was easier for him to communicate with and study the Indians while on his own, without other foreigners present."[48]

He made his third trip to Mexico largely by himself—although he was accompanied by a couple of Mexican helpers and Indian translators—to study the Tarahumara, Cora, Tepehuan, Tarasco, and Huichol cultures. His imagery of these groups is among the finest of ethnological photography, for he abandoned anthropometric documentation to focus on daily life. Moreover, he had learned how to take good photographs, and his images registered the different meanings of indigenous clothing decorations. These Indian cultures were largely unknown and resistant to outsiders. However, Lumholtz was able to establish a friendship with a Tarahumara shaman, Rubio, who opened doors for his cameras; he was even allowed to record their sacred ceremonies. Most of his imagery is of Indians posing, some of whom smile, but he also captured them in the acts of hunting, grinding corn, and weaving.

One of his most expressive images documents a Huichol making arrows, which was as much a religious ceremony as it was a practical enterprise. (See Figure 39.) Lumholtz had learned from his time with this culture that "the arrow is the form in which the Huichol most generally embodies his prayer, and it is inseparably connected with his life. When preparing for any event of importance, he makes an arrow, thereby asking favour or protection from the gods."[49] Lumholtz's last Mexican expedition took him to the Sonora desert during 1909 and 1910. He had evidently been commissioned by wealthy patrons to investigate some economic opportunities, but

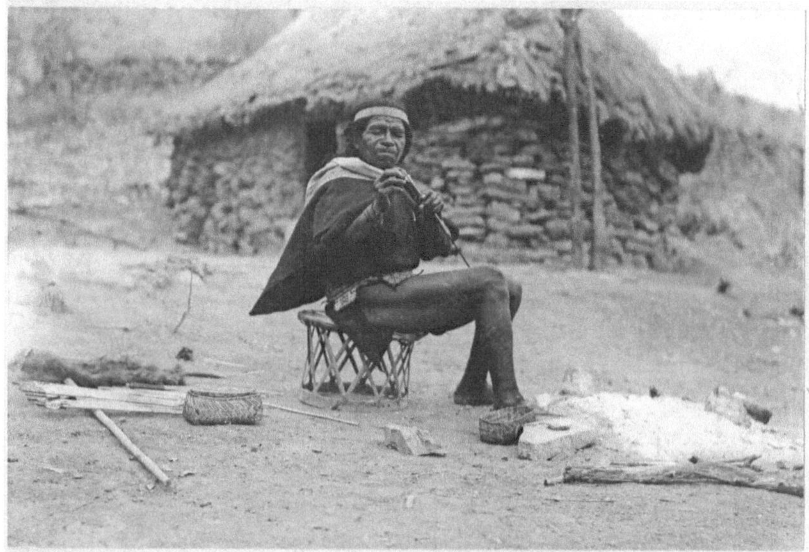

FIGURE 39. Carl Lumholtz. Huichol making arrow, Jalisco, 1895. No. UEMf09972_59_CL, Museum of Cultural History, University of Oslo.

he made few good images because the O'odham tribe in that area objected to his camera and was intensely annoyed by his efforts.

MEXICAN PHOTOGRAPHERS AND THE AMERINDIANS

While foreigners were photographing and measuring and molding Indian heads in plaster casts—providing proof of White superiority as well as linking the current inhabitants to the ancient civilizations—Mexicans were trying to figure out what to do with these populations. As Poole observed, "The Indian was marked simultaneously as both pure and degenerate, noble and servile, and, importantly, as at once incommensurably 'other' and sentimentally 'ours.'"[50] Racism was (and continues to be) ever-present, as can be seen in pronouncements made over 150 years. In 1864, the intellectual Francisco Pimentel asked whether the only solution was to follow the US model, "To kill or to die. . . . Shall we do what the US has done, and cut the throats of all Indians?"[51] Because Amerindians were important to the Mexican economy, he called instead for the breakup of communal landholdings and their subsequent incorporation into the labor force as proletarians. Instead of wiping out the Indians, Pimental believed that European immigration would whiten Mexicans little by little, replacing the "transitional" mestizos; at the same time he felt that the government "should procure that the Indians forget their customs and even their languages, if possible. Only in this way will they . . . form a homogeneous mass with the Whites, a true nation."[52]

In his classic work of 1950, philosopher Luis Villoro described the insistence with which Mexican intellectuals argued that the only salvation for Indians was that of becoming part of the mestiza economic system, but he noted, "such a solution was not inspired by the Indian's own point of view."[53] Villoro recognized the apparent contradiction facing Mexicans: "On one hand the Indian appeared as a stranger; we saw them from afar and were distanced witnesses of their rites and primitive superstitions, of their archaic customs. On the other, they are one of the roots of our most authentic specificity, of our 'Americanism.'"[54] Asserting that the Mesoamerican was one of the few original civilizations created by human beings, anthropologist Guillermo Bonfil emphasized the necessity of allowing the enormous cultural potential of *México profundo*—as his influential work was titled—to flower, recognizing that Mexico was caught between "two civilizing projects, two ideal models of society, and two different possible futures."[55] However, as recently as 2017, the US answer to the Indian problem was articulated by a functionary of the Secretary of Public Education in Puebla State. On his Facebook page he showed an image of Amerindians in traditional dress and used Photoshop to place a Nazi swastika behind them; his message was chillingly explicit: "Let's create a fatherland (*hagamos patria*) and exterminate them; they only live off our taxes without contributing anything. They are bloodsuckers."[56]

We know very little about the production and distribution of images among Amerindians. Photographic studios were scattered throughout Mexico in the nineteenth and early twentieth century: all the large cities had several, and photographers must have opened businesses in many towns as well. The urban studio photographers evidently did not make *indigenista* images, although the firm of Cruces y Campa and other studios did pose city dwellers as "Indian types" during these years.[57] Other photographers from provincial capitals documented Indian groups; Lorenzo Becerril traveled from Puebla to photograph Tehuanas in their natural setting around 1875, and José María Lupercio of Guadalajara made images of Huicholes toward the end of the century, although most are of "types."[58] Nonetheless, there are relatively few Indian types among the existing *tarjetas de visita*, especially when compared to the Negro types found in Brazilian photography collections. The Valleto brothers photographed only the high society of Mexico City, of which they formed part, from 1861 to 1910.[59] There are some five thousand photographs of Amerindians in the Casasola Archive, but the authors of them and the periods in which they were made are unknown.[60] Romualdo García was the most important photographer of Guanajuato, but he evidently made no images of the Native populations in that locale.[61] The Guerra family members were the leading imagemakers of Mérida, Yucatán, but they took no photographs of Native Americans because, as the Director of the Fototeca Pedro Guerra, "Jimmy" Montañez Pérez explained, "Guerra belonged to the bourgeoisie and his photographic studio was a business. If the register didn't ring, there was no photo."[62]

Montañez Pérez has put his finger squarely on the reason Mexican urban photographers probably made very few Indianist images. We might expect photographers in small cities and towns to have taken some pictures, above all because many of them probably traveled to the neighboring villages to make portraits, as did Jesús H. Abitia in the state of Sonora.[63] The Cachú Hermanos also were itinerant photographers, going around Michoacán state with their families to put on theatrical productions, and make studio-style photography in front of the painted backdrops they used for their plays.[64] Sara Castrejón and the Salmerón family set up businesses in the small cities of Teloloapan and Chilapa of Guerrero state. The pattern evident among urban studios also prevailed in small cities and towns: in neither the Abitia nor the Cachú nor the Castrejón nor the Salmerón archives do we find a single image of Amerindians pictured within their own cultural context.[65]

Although individual Mexican studio photographers evidently made few images of Native Americans, the Porfirian government eventually commissioned pictures of the ancient monuments and current inhabitants for international consumption. The Díaz dictatorship had largely disappeared Indians from the national stage, but they were a cornerstone in the Mexican expositions in Paris in 1878 and 1889, the 1892 Exposición Histórico-Americana in Madrid, the Exposición Colombina Mundial in the Peabody Museum at Harvard University in 1893, and the X International Congress of Americanists in 1894 in Stockholm.[66] At the latter meeting, it was decided for the first time that the Americanist congress would be held in the Americas and that it would include scholars from this hemisphere, rather than being a forum for Europeans to present their research on the Americas. In preparing for the exhibits from 1889 on, an extensive photographic project was ordered throughout Mexico, which resulted in the first "ethnographic mapping" of "Indian nations," as they were referred to on the backs of the images.[67] The director of the Museo Nacional incorporated already-existing images, and photographers were hired all over the country to participate in constructing what to this day remains Mexico's "calling card": the pre-Hispanic civilizations.

The list of participating photographers was impressive: Emilio Leal documented Otomís in Guanajuato, Francisco de la Loza portrayed the

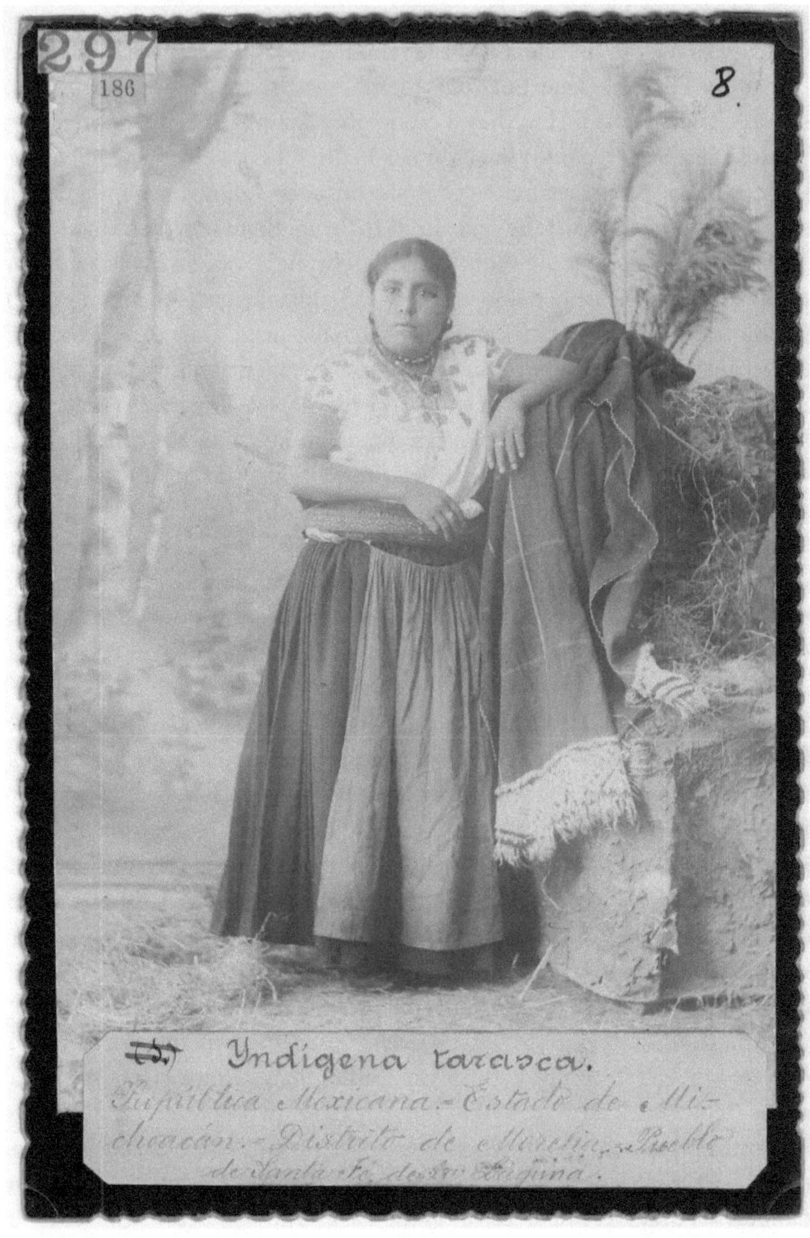

FIGURE 40. Manuel Monge. Purépecha, Morelia, Michoacán, 1892. Inv. # 466870, Fondo Étnico, SINAFO-Fototeca Nacional del INAH, Secretaría de Cultura.

Lacandones in Chiapas, Rafael García registered the daily life of the Totonacas in Veracruz, a Bernal documented the Pápagos of Sonora, Octaviano de la Mora provided archeological views from Jalisco State, and Manuel Monge photographed Purépechas in Uruapan. (See Figure 40.) Foreigners were also recruited for the project: the Belgian Aquiles Gerste photographed the Tarahumaras, the German Antonio W. Rieke was charged with registering the Chiapanecos, and the Frenchmen Desiderio Lagrange and Alfred Laurent made their contribution in respectively picturing Tlaxcaltecan descendants in Nuevo León State and the Seris around Guaymas. The Mexican exhibit was a success, and the images were awarded eleven medals.[68] Two large indigenous nations were not included: the Mayans and the Yaquis, because both were at war with the government in that moment.

INDIGENOUS RESISTANCE AND PHOTOGRAPHY

The Yaquis in the northern state of Sonora had resisted Spanish attempts to colonize them, continuing this same strategy with the Mexican government. In fact, they constructed their own foreign policy, remaining neutral during the independence movement and taking the side of Maximilian during the 1860s. They rose up continually against the impositions of the new nation state, but in the late nineteenth century two events sealed their fate. One was the socio-economic policy of the *Porfiriato* to carry out settlement acts designed to expropriate Indian territories and facilitate the expansion of export-oriented agribusiness, a process that in turn made the natives into workers on the very haciendas and plantations that took over their lands.[69] A series of decrees called for the occupation of "wastelands" (*terrenos baldíos*), which took away the community base of Yaqui resistance. The second was the adoption in 1895 of the Mauser rifle as the weapon of the Mexican army; against such firepower, the Amerindians had little possibility of replying. From around 1900 on, the Porfirian government undertook massive deportations of Yaquis to Yucatán and Oaxaca as a means of accomplishing two ends: ridding northern Mexico of a resistant culture and providing the *hacendados* in the south with slave labor.[70] According to John Kenneth Turner's classic account of that expulsion, Díaz issued "a sweeping order that every Yaqui, wherever found, men, women, and children, should be gathered up by the War Department and deported to Yucatán."[71]

Turner first visited Mexico in 1908, disguised as a wealthy entrepreneur looking to invest in henequen, then a booming export crop to make binder twine for the seemingly limitless demand of the US market. Yucatecan *hacendados* had two advantages over other producers of this

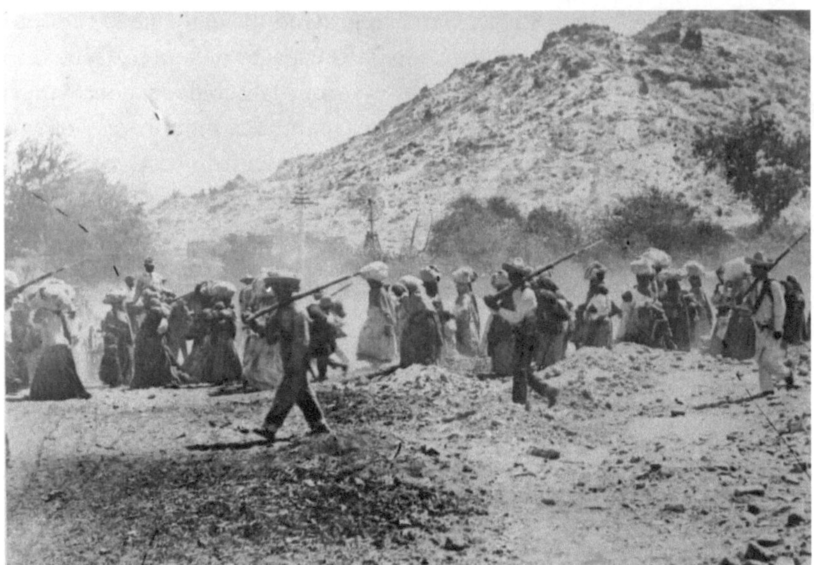

FIGURE 41. John Kenneth Turner (author or intellectual author). *Band of Yaquis on the Exile Road*, Sonora, 1909. Inv. # 34061, SINAFO-Fototeca Nacional del INAH, Secretaría de Cultura.

important commodity: proximity to the US and what amounted to slave labor, which kept costs low. An anti-imperialist and a member of International Workers of the World (IWW), Turner had heard about the atrocious conditions in which many rural laborers lived in Yucatán and Oaxaca, thanks to interviews with Mexican anarchists then jailed in the US. At this moment, "North American corporations controlled Yucatán's economic development," above all the "informal empire" of the International Harvester Company.[72] Facing chronic labor shortages, the Yucatecan planter-oligarchy demanded and was sent thousands of northern Indians, who lived as slaves. They were indebted to the planters for the costs accrued by their forced exodus and could never free themselves from that situation; moreover, the planters owned them and they were sold as part of properties. Turner saw the horrible exploitation to which the Yaquis and Mayos were subject in Yucatán and Oaxaca, but evidently took no photographs to document his findings.

Given the extremes to which the federal government engaged in a genocidal crusade to exterminate the Yaquis, it is clear that it wished to destroy their culture of resistance. From the moment they were captured, the families were broken up and all their property confiscated. They were then piled like animals onto boats, taken to San Blas, and afterward "driven by foot over some of the roughest mountains in Mexico, from San Blas to

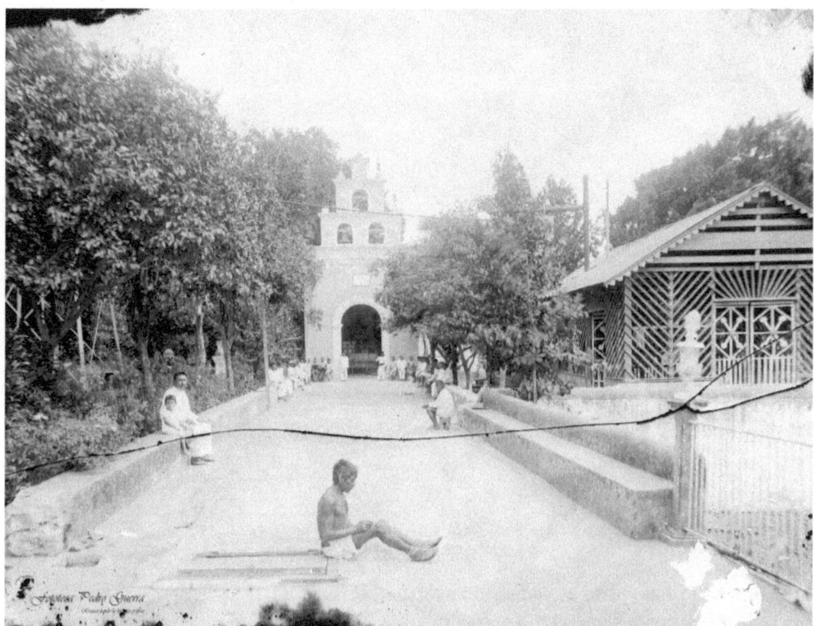

FIGURE 42. Pedro Guerra. Indian worker forced to sit in sun for punishment, Yucatán, ca. 1900. Fototeca Pedro Guerra de la Facultad de Ciencias Antropológicas, Universidad Autónoma de Yucatán.

Tepic, and from Tepic to San Marcos," a journey of fifteen to twenty days.[73] Turner may have photographed part of the journey, documenting a group of women and children held in a bullpen and then marched through the desert hemmed in by soldiers, their few belongings carried on their heads.[74] (See Figure 41.) As one survivor of the death march recounted, "They died on the way like starving cattle. . . . But the cruelest part of the trail was between San Blas and San Marcos. Those women with babies. It was awful! They dropped down in the dust again and again."[75]

On arriving in Yucatán, the assault on their cultural identity continued: they were stripped of all clothing and belongings, which were then burned.[76] To further their alienation, Yaqui women were forced to marry indentured Chinese workers, and workforces were heterogeneous conglomerations that combined Yaquis with Mayans, Asian immigrants, and other *enganchados* (hooked slaves). Photography also served the purposes of the powerful, employed as a form of social control by the *hacendados*: a Yaqui woman told Turner, "They keep our faces on photographs."[77] This was a well-established practice in Mexican photography: prisoners were documented as early as 1854, and Mexico City maids were also required to pay for their identification portraits by an 1871 edict.[78]

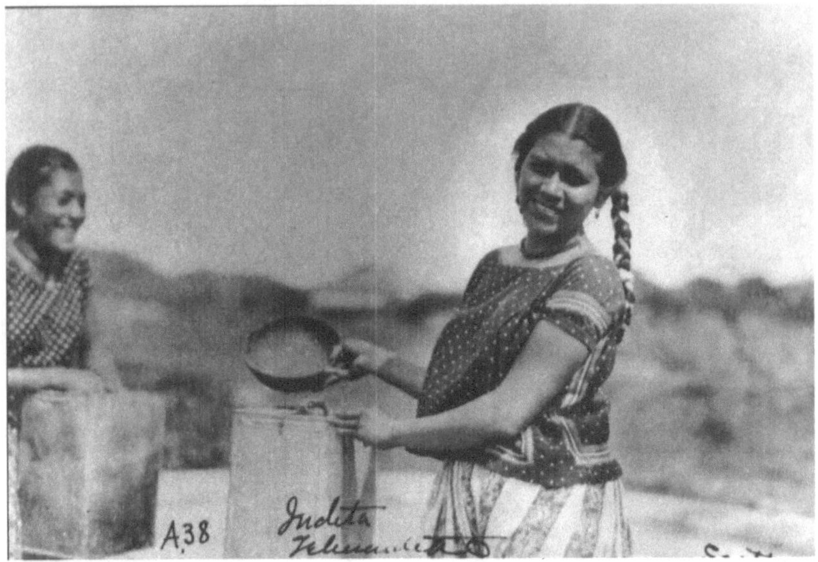

FIGURE 43. Winfield Scott. *Indita*, Tehuantepec, Oaxaca, ca. 1904. Propiedad Artística y Literaria del Archivo General de la Nación.

The demonstration of power may well be the explanation for an otherwise puzzling photograph by Pedro Guerra of an Amerindian worker at a Yucatecan plantation forced to sit under the blazing tropical sun as punishment. (See Figure 42.) As noted above, Guerra was essentially an image-maker for the bourgeoisie, although his archive of some five hundred thousand pictures includes a wide variety of subjects. We can safely discard the notion that the photo was made as a denunciation; rather, it was probably intended as an object lesson, like the highly publicized execution of three *campesinos* in Chalco during 1909.[79] As with other Native populations, the Mayans held very different beliefs than their Spanish and Mexican conquerors: the most important was that land was held in common and village life was organized around cooperative projects. The Mayans were incorporated systematically into forced labor by the Spanish and their Mexican successors and had a long history of resisting both.

When Mexico was invaded by the US in 1847, the Mayans took advantage of the situation and rose in rebellion, acquiring such a following that it eventually became "a struggle between two sovereign powers, Mexico and Chan Santa Cruz, [which represented] a restoration of ancient patterns of village life."[80] The Caste War went on intermittently until 1901, and was "the most sustained and bloody Indian rebellion in the history of Mexico and perhaps of all Latin America."[81] Among the atrocities committed by the planter class was selling captured Mayans into slavery in Cuba.[82] The plantocracy was so terrified of Mayan resistance that they utilized national, state, and private armies and police forces, as well as employing harsh disciplinary measures on their haciendas, as seen in Figure 42.

In the late *Porfiriato*, US photographers with direct commercial interests arrived in Mexico. Gone were the pretensions of ethnological documentation, as Eadweard Muybridge, William Henry Jackson, C. B. Waite, and Winfield Scott came to promote a broad variety of business opportunities usually connected to US enterprises and investors, including steamship lines, railroad companies, mines, rubber plantations, real estate, and tourism, as well as the magazines, books, tourist guides, informational pamphlets, and postcards that publicized such activities.[83] Scott first started photographing while working as a conductor in the Ferrocarril Central Mexicano. This allowed him to travel extensively around the country, focusing on the striking contrast between highly traditional cultures and the rampant modernization brought about and represented by railroads. Both Scott and Waite essentially reproduced the stereotypical colonial view of Mexican Indians that had been established by *costumbrista* lithographs and the studio photography of "Mexican Types."

However, photohistorian Beatriz Malagón argues that Scott tended to go beyond what was required by work orders, establishing rapport with his subjects and always attempting to photograph them in situ, as can be appreciated in his image of a young *Tehuana*.[84] (See Figure 43.) The fact that she (and her friend) are smiling and in the midst of activity breaks with the "typical" portrayal of Native peoples, that is, as "types" rather than individuals. However, the caption on this picture of her goes in the opposite direction, identifying her as a "little Indian girl," whereas on another picture taken of her at the same time, she is named: "Julia."[85]

Although I hesitate to generalize, it appears that Waite had a more distanced relationship with his subjects, sometimes posing them in a studio setting, such as the *Tehuana* woman, who may have been a model dressed up and photographed in his Mexico City studio.[86] (See Figure 44.) Scholars of Mexican photography have asserted that Waite and Scott were instrumental in constructing what would be seen in future generations as a view of "everything that was considered to be distinctively and characteristically Mexican."[87] Their documentation of Amerindians also suggested to foreign investors that they would find an abundant labor force "already so poor that they would be content with just about anything," as asserted

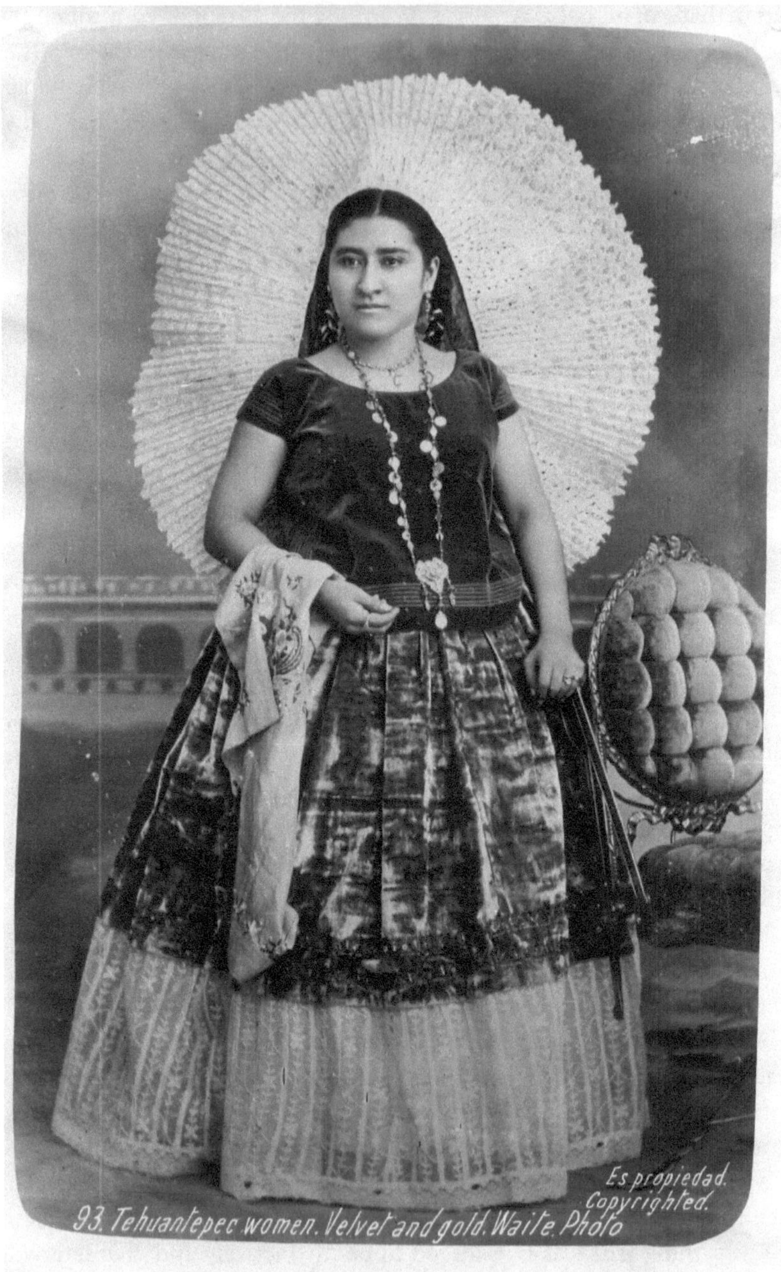

FIGURE 44. Waite. *Tehuantepec women* [?]. *Velvet and Gold*, Mexico City?, ca. 1900. Center for Southwest Research, General Library, University of New Mexico, no. 998-010-0001A.

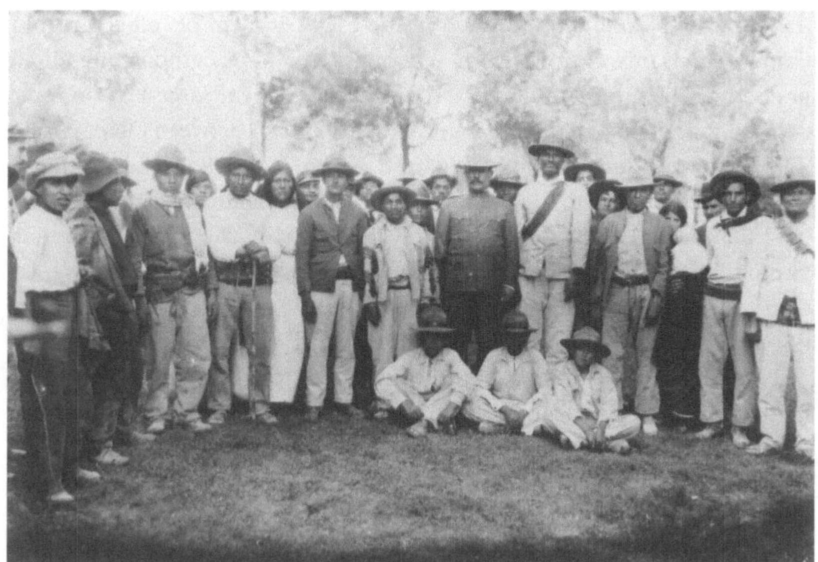

FIGURE 45. Unknown. Álvaro Obregón with a group of Yaqui soldiers, 14 May 1917. Centro de Estudios de la Historia de México, CONDUMEX, XXXI-3, # 47.

by *Modern Mexico*, the magazine that published many of Scott's pictures.[88] Both photographers may well have provided nude and partially dressed images of Amerindian women and children for the pornography market.[89]

Mexican photographers appear to have made few images of Indian nations until they crashed the party and forced themselves onto the stage.[90] Hence, they generally had to make their presence known by subverting the established order of representation whether they were the Mayans who rose up in la Guerra de Castas or the Yaquis who continued to resist on the northern frontier. With the Mexican Revolution, Indian groups entered massively into the anti-Porfirian armies. Yaqui and Mayo Indians appeared with bows and arrows as part of Maderista forces in the northwest as did the Zapatista Nahuas in Guerrero; Chamula giants and dwarfs were photographed with a Maderista governor in Chiapas.[91]

Historian Alan Knight makes a convincing case that the popular agrarian revolt of the Yaqui in the north is the equivalent of the better-known Zapatista uprising in Morelos.[92] Displaying a significant degree of ethnic cohesion, forged over the centuries of battling against the *yori* (Whites), the Yaquis perceived the Maderista uprising as an opportunity to bargain for the return of their lands as the price of their participation. When Madero's government broke those promises, the Yaqui maintained themselves on a war footing, as did the Zapatistas. The long struggle of both the Yaquis and the Zapatistas eventually resulted in the establishment of "official revolutionary agrarianism" in 1914.[93] A year later the Yaquis demonstrated their unending search for autonomy: Urbalejo, leader of the largest Yaqui force, decided to wait out the results of the battles of Celaya between Obregón and Villa before deciding who he would back, although the Yaquis had traditionally been committed to the Villa and José María Maytorena camps. Following Villa's defeat, many Yaquis joined with Obregón, who often appeared in photographs with them, visually linking them to his movement as well as demonstrating through their clothing the degree to which their incorporation in the Constitutionalist army had "civilized" them. (See Figure 45.)

Nonetheless, the Yaquis' battle was always for their *patria chica*, the lands on the Yaqui River, and for an independent existence. A Swedish soldier of fortune felt that the Yaquis had a wider vision of the struggle than did the Amerindians that had been incorporated into the hacienda economy, arguing that the typical peon-soldier "was completely indifferent to anything outside his family, cornfield, nearest village and fiestas."[94] He contrasted that to northern tribes: "The Indian soldiers, who had lived away from the influences of the haciendas, were quite different as they had a broader perspective and interests, such as hunting and fishing, and some had agriculture and trade for their existence. They all made good soldiers." As Knight sums up, "The Yaquis' cultural separateness and lively sense of self-identity distanced them from the national political arena, and made them resistant to the promises, appeals and bargains traded within it; they had (unlike Zapata) been unmoved by the American occupation of Veracruz, and they had not heard of Carranza's 1915 agrarian decree."[95] Their battle for their traditional lands would go on well into the 1920s, until the New Order utilized modern weaponry, including airplanes, as part of their punitive expeditions to terminate Yaqui resistance.

PHOTOGRAPHING AMERINDIANS IN THE POSTREVOLUTION

As the civil war drew to a close in 1917, governmental policies toward the Amerindians underwent a profound transformation. The indigenous peoples were now incorporated as a nationalist symbol within Mexican culture (rather than just for international consumption), and the misery in which many Indians lived was defined as a socio-economic problem that could be solved, instead of a demonstration of their racial inferiority. Nonetheless, with few exceptions, "Indians themselves lacked any shared sentiment of Indianness"; post-revolutionary *indigenismo* was a creation from above and "cannot be attributed to any direct Indian pressure or lobbying."[96]

A key figure in the new orientation was Manuel Gamio, who argued in his influential work *Forjando patria* against the evolutionary racist and hierarchical theories espoused by liberal thinkers that consigned Indians to a primitive dead end: "The Indian has the same aptitudes to progress as does the white."[97] He called for anthropological studies that would establish respect for the Native cultures, paving the way for the eventual "fusion" of Indians and mestizos by involving the former into the capitalist project: "we do not intend to incorporate the Indian by suddenly 'Europeanizing him'; on the contrary, we will 'Indianize ourselves' a bit."[98]

Several governmental agencies embodied the pluralist ethos espoused by Gamio: the Dirección de Antropología, established in 1917 with Gamio as the director; the Departamento de Asuntos Indígenas (DAI) and the Instituto Nacional de Antropología e Historia (INAH), founded by President Lázaro Cárdenas in 1936 and 1939 respectively; and the Instituto Nacional Indigenista (INI), which largely replaced the DAI in 1948, and is today known as the Instituto Nacional de los Pueblos Indígenas (INPI).[99] These projects evolved into extraordinary spaces that offered the opportunity to develop systematic esthetic projects for photographing the Indian nations that provided work to outstanding ethnographic imagemakers such as Julio de la Fuente, Alfonso Fabila, Alfonso Muñoz, and Nacho López, among many others.

Julio de la Fuente offers one of the more fascinating stories of politically committed Indianist photography, dedicated to enabling ethnic justice as well as carrying out a "salvage ethnography" of disappearing cultural artifacts. A multifaceted artist and teacher whose work centered on a defense of cultural pluralism and bilingual education, he taught in rural schools in the early 1930s. He also made lithographs and drawings for the free books and manuals provided by the Secretaría de Educación Pública (SEP), and for its magazine, *Simiente* (Seed), the "emblematic publication of the Escuela Socialista."[100] In this same period, de la Fuente and José Mancisidor founded the magazine *ruta*, in which many members of the Partido Comunista Mexicano (PCM) collaborated. Historian John Lear affirms that de la Fuente made woodcut "covers of individual or collective male workers and *campesinos* with powerful bodies in confrontations with bosses and the forces of fascism and imperialism."[101] De la Fuente was a member of LEAR (*Liga de Escritores y Artistas Revolucionarios*—League of revolutionary writers and artists) from its founding to its demise, and collaborated in its publication *Frente a frente* (Face to face).

Throughout his life, de la Fuente focused on developing forms of visual education within the INI and in the Amerindian communities: teaching courses on drawing and the making of lithographs and posters, as well as programing film series in which movies were critically analyzed. He published prolifically, writing about indigenous ceremonies, illnesses common among the Native peoples, rural schools, ethnic relations, nutrition, statistical bias in the national census, the transformation of clothing styles as cultural change, and Native folklore.[102] De la Fuente carried out anthropological research in the Zapotec town of Yalálag, Oaxaca State, over twenty-two months during 1937 to 1941. Among the photographs in his book on that area are those shot in the frontal anthropological style; others represent the "cultural transition" from Indian to mestizo.[103] Another of his books was a co-authored study with the Polish anthropologist Bronislaw Malinowski on the Zapotec market system.[104] A critical study of alcoholism in Chiapas was shelved by the government because of the objections of the monopolists who sold *aguardiente*, and only published three decades later.[105]

De la Fuente began photographing while collaborating on *Frente a frente*, no doubt influenced by the German refugee Enrique Gutmann (Heinrich Gutmann), from whom he acquired his camera.[106] Gutmann was appointed as the director of photography for *Frente a frente* in 1936 and brought about a greater inclusion of that medium, which came to outnumber prints. His position on photography's functions emphasized their social uses but left room for esthetic experimentation: "the revolutionary photographer should seek not only artistic effects or technical tricks, but the social function of photography."[107]

To judge from his images in the Fototeca Nacho López of the INPI, de la Fuente was constrained by anthropological methods that took precedence over his political commitments. The 2,500 photographs are largely informational rather than expressive; they demonstrate the necessity to take pictures containing as much data as possible, in order to provide material for later confirmation and revision by other anthropologists.[108] The archive is composed of landscapes and townscapes, including markets, churches, indigenous dwellings and ceremonies, and pre-Hispanic architecture; standing portraits of women, children, and INAH functionaries; and photos of schools, some taken at a distance including children and their teacher gathered to be photographed.[109] The reception of his images among the photographed provides a window onto how those pictured felt about de la Fuente's work. They criticized the lack of images showing agricultural labor or the elaboration of sandals, but felt his photographs—above all, those that visually preserved traditional clothing such as the *huipil* (a common upper-body garment among Amerindian women in Mesoamerica)—were generally valued as documents of a history that should be recovered and preserved for the community.[110]

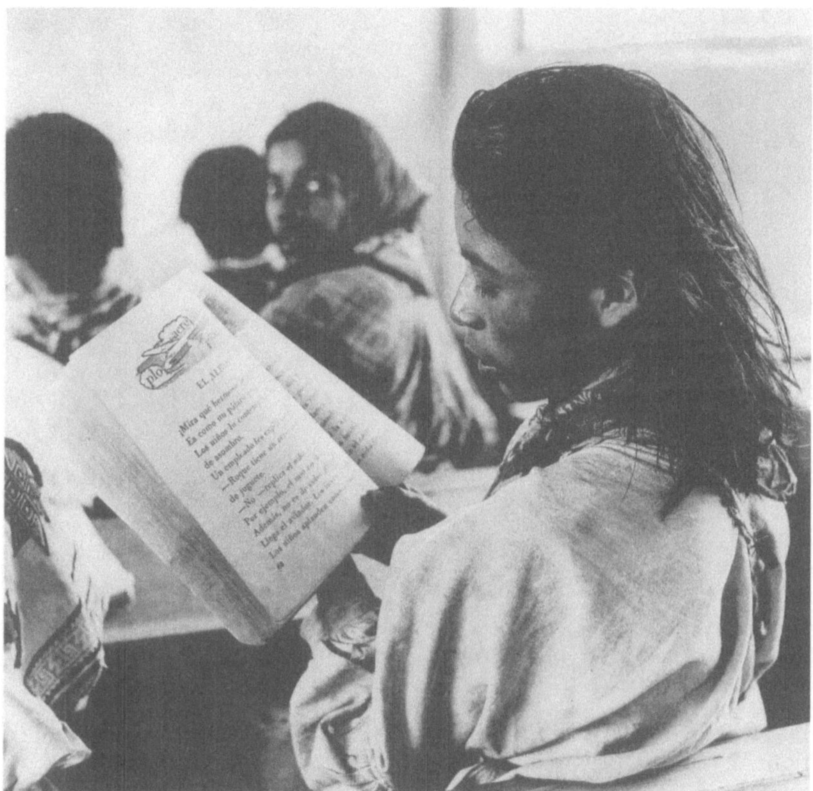

FIGURE 46. Julio de la Fuente. Huichol schoolgirls, Nayarit, ca. 1940. Número de inventario, 202317; Fototeca Nacho López, Instituto Nacional de los Pueblos Indígenas.

One of de la Fuente's photographs offers an intertwined bundle of elements through which he reflects on the relation of Native Americans and the Mexican State. (See Figure 46.) The Huichol girls of Nayarit are dressed in traditional clothing, but the schoolbook one holds is in Spanish. A champion of bilingual education, de la Fuente draws our eyes to the book, both because it is the greatest source of light in the image, and a girl is herself looking at it (and/or displaying it for the photographer). The composition we see is about flying on an airplane, a possibility that is remote for this girl. By focusing on this page, de la Fuente is not only critiquing the imposition of Spanish-language text, but perhaps also its irrelevance to that girl (and the great majority of Mexicans in that moment around 1940).

Learning Spanish is a necessary part of incorporating Amerindians into the nation, a skill that will empower them; however, it also threatens their cultural identity. As one historian has observed, "the predomination of the written word confers an aura of legitimacy to the identity

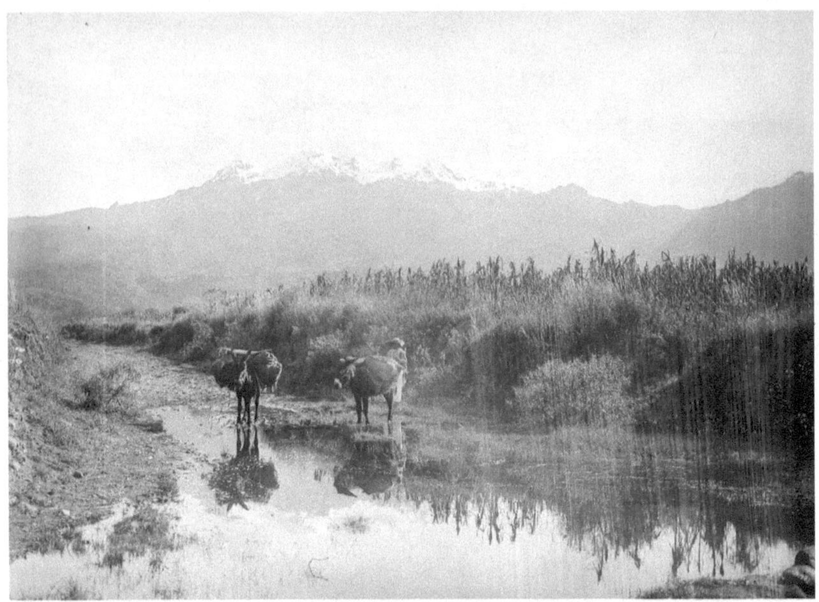

FIGURE 47. Hugo Brehme. *Campesino* and burros posed with the extinct volcano Istaccihuatl behind Puebla, ca. 1930. Inv. # 358656, SINAFO-Fototeca Nacional del INAH, Secretaría de Cultura.

proposals that reaffirm the hierarchies founded on ethno-racial distinctions."[111] The picture's complexity is carried a visual step further by the girl in the background who defiantly returns the camera's gaze, as if commenting on the voyeurism intrinsic to Indianist imagery and insisting that looking is a double-edged sword. We might interpret her challenging stare as expressing that, while Amerindians will learn the mestizo's ways, the Native Americans will always have mestizos as fully under observation as that to which the original peoples are subject. The image as a whole could be said to represent the dialectic of indigenous identities and national incorporation, a method that reflects de la Fuente's ideological perspective. At one point, INAH director Alfonso Caso was interviewing the visual anthropologist for a position, and he asked, "What professional preparation do you have?" De la Fuente answered dryly, "Marxist dialectic."[112]

Photographic artists represented Amerindians, and their work provides us with examples of practices we could describe as imperial, neocolonizing, and decolonizing imagery. A German who emigrated to Mexico in 1906, Hugo Brehme made a living from the wide circulation of photographs made for export. He authored thousands of "artistic postcards," a medium that "produces stereotypes in the manner of the great seabirds producing guano. It is the fertilizer of the colonial vision."[113] He also published two

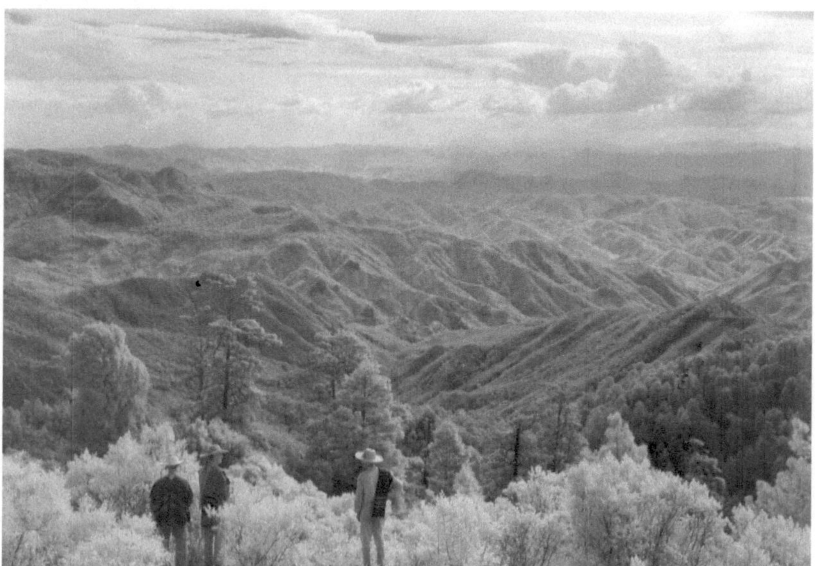

FIGURE 48. Hugo Brehme. Panorama of mil cumbres, Michoacán, ca. 1930. Inv. # 372851, SINAFO-Fototeca Nacional del INAH, Secretaría de Cultura

significant volumes of landscapes, ancient monuments, colonial structures, and "types" that appeared in English, German, French, and Spanish in 1923 through 1925.[114] His images circulated in a slew of books, newspapers, and magazines, among them *National Geographic*, which is now largely understood to function as "a medium that promotes a certain gaze of 'the other' in concordance with the imperial interests of the U.S."[115] His was a classic nineteenth-century style that presented fine-art-inspired images of beautiful, idyllic, and perfectly composed scenes of Amerindians and *campesinos* posing in their picturesque clothing, often near pre-Columbian ruins and colonial churches. In an image made in Puebla state, Brehme created a scene that contains many of the elements that photohistorian James Ryan identified as essential ingredients in imperial photography. (See Figure 47.) Focusing on the much-praised imagery that Samuel Bourne carried out in India, which was informed by the esthetic conventions of the picturesque developed by William Gilpin in the late eighteenth century, Ryan describes those components in the following way: "an expanse of water, with many reflections; wooded banks in the background and foliage in the foreground, allowing for a play of light and shade, and a carefully posed figure to draw the viewer's gaze into the image."[116]

Brehme's technical capacity and esthetic power enabled him to make a powerful picture of the rugged Mexican terrain. (See Figure 48.) However,

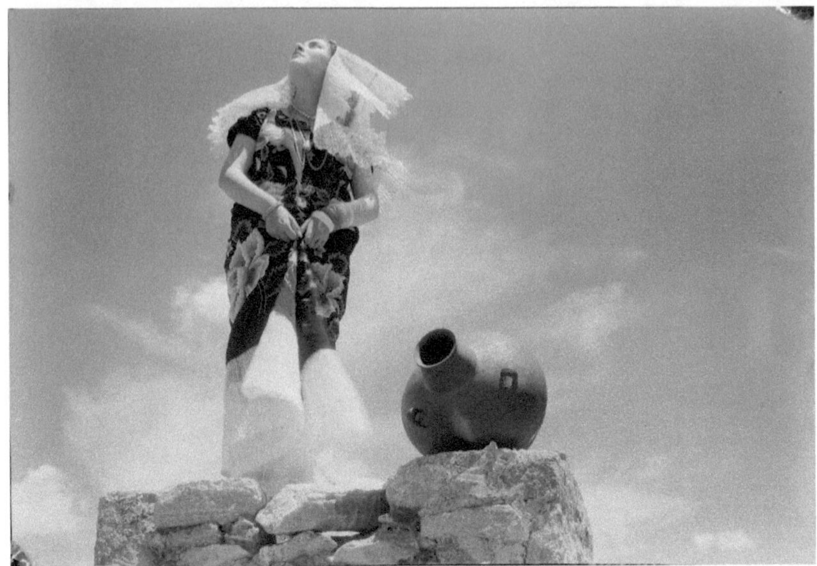

FIGURE 49. Luis Márquez Romay. Mestiza dressed as Amerindian, Mexico City, ca. 1940. Inv. 08.730235, Archivo Fotográfico "Manuel Toussaint" del Instituto de Investigaciones Estéticas de la UNAM.

his imperial vision can here be seen in the representation of an unconquered nature that awaits foreign investments to develop the country. There is no evidence of labor on the part of the *campesinos* in the foreground, who seem content to passively observe. The absence of industry or any evident result of labor conveys the visual ideology that asserts only colonial intervention will be capable of putting to good use a natural abundance that the natives have failed to adequately exploit, although they will be implicitly present to serve as a work force for the colonial power.

Photographic Modernism was introduced in Mexico by Edward Weston in 1923 and represented a sharp break with Pictorialism by emphasizing abstraction, hard focus, sharp angles, and (often, though not always) anti-exoticism. For example, Luis Márquez became the official Mexican folklorist, adopting the new photographic form but filling it with picturesque imagery. This showed that he had internalized the imperial perspective, and his work can thus be considered the neocolonial esthetic equivalent of the economic practices of the comprador class.[117] Working for various governmental agencies, selling postcards, and financed by publications such as *National Geographic*, he traveled extensively around Mexico, photographing and amassing a large collection of Native attire. Despite his acquaintance with a wide variety of Amerindian nations, his photography

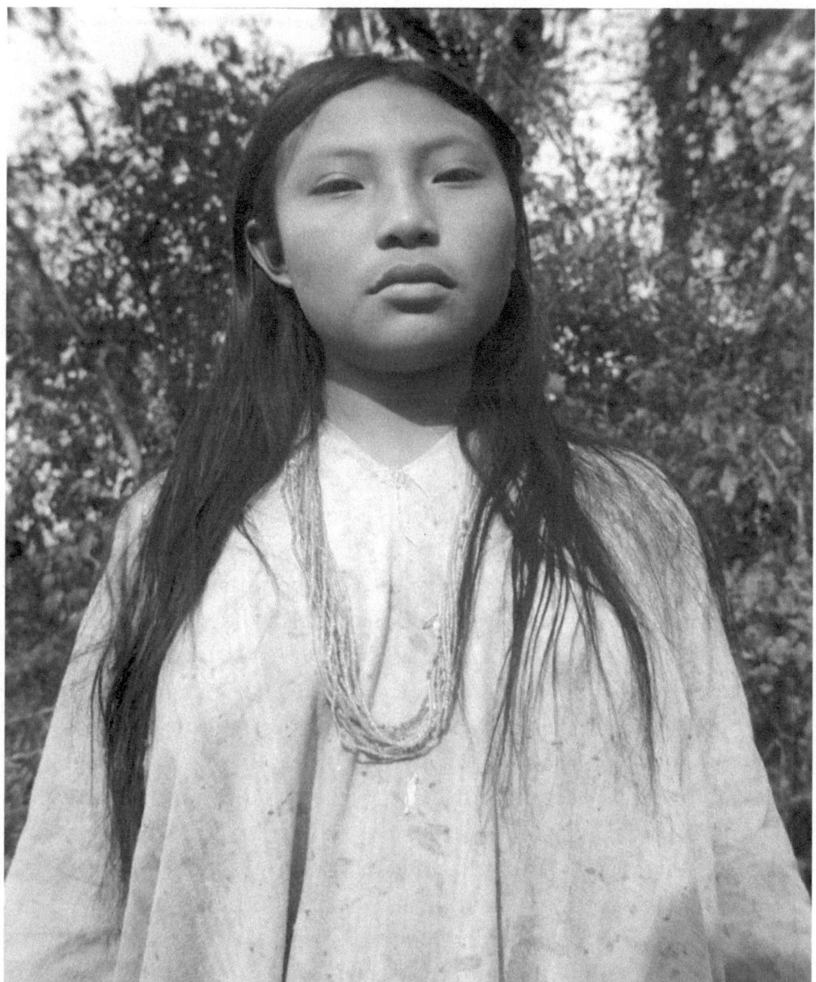

FIGURE 50. Manuel Álvarez Bravo. *Margarita de Bonampak*, Bonampak, Chiapas, 1949. Archivo Manuel Álvarez Bravo, Copyright Colette Urbajtel.

at times homogenizes them because he "took many photographs of non-Indian models dressed up in clothes from his collection," which included almost four thousand items.[118]

Hence, some of Márquez's "Indians"—like those of Edward Curtis in the US—are little more than clothes hangers for folkloric representations.[119] Márquez's is a dramatic esthetic, using a sharp low-angle Modernist shot to silhouette a light-skinned Mexico City mestiza model against the clouds above her, while the foreground is occupied by the decorative clay water pitcher and the stones on which she stands, which presumably represent the ancient past. She maintains the properly stoic, statuesque pose prescribed for Márquez's Native people, gazing off into mythical pre-Colombian yesterdays. (See Figure 49.) The extravagant Tehuana costume she wears reflects Márquez's incessant acquisition of Native attire. Funded by the Mexican government, he began to buy typical Amerindian clothing in the 1920s, but became increasingly interested in the sophisticated dress wore for special celebrations and festivities. By the 1940s, he was actively intervening in the clothing, combining them into outfits that flattened the differences between cultures to create his own colorful and exotic compositions.[120]

The Indianist photography of Manuel Álvarez Bravo is decolonizing in its efforts to force us to see not only the cultural differences manifest in the subject but the common humanity we all share. The image *Margarita de Bonampak* differs greatly from that of Márquez in several aspects. (See Figure 50.) In the first place, she is an Amerindian in her native context, not a Mexico City model. Further, she is identified by name, a strategy that demonstrates she is as fully a person as is the photographer (and the spectators). Moreover, she is not overwhelmed by her dress, rather hers is traditional Mayan clothing, plain and a bit dirty, which allows her face to stand out in all its singularity. The sharp focus on her features essentially erases the natural background that is often used to envelop Indians and *campesinos* in picturesque photography. The low-angle shot empowers her, as does that fact that she returns the camera's gaze. Looking back at the camera is the usual form that resistance takes to visual colonization, and the force she projects reminds us of Frantz Fanon's insistent reminder that "decolonization is always a violent phenomenon."[121] The absolutely unique facial features of Margarita make it impossible to relegate her to a "type"; that is, to suppress her irreducible individuality and emphasize her primitiveness in order to affirm a natural ethnic hierarchy.[122] Álvarez Bravo shows Margarita to be fundamentally different, but as fully human as the representatives from the culture photographing (and viewing) her.

Amerindians were a relatively well-explored theme among the photojournalists who worked in the illustrated magazines, a dominant form of visual culture from the mid-1930s to the mid-1950s. In the great majority of the cases, they served as exotic prototypes of *mexicanidad*, the expected perspective that appealed to the magazines' urban readers. Hence, it appears that there was little critical consciousness in relation to imaging indigenous people during these years. Ismael Casasola's insistent efforts to photograph forbidden ceremonies among the Coras and Kikapus, and in Chichicastenango, Guatemala, was typical of the lack of respect shown indigenous peoples. The magazine's recounting of the dangers Casasola faced served only to buttress the myth of photojournalists as daredevils; that he should never have been there in the first place seems not to have occurred to either the photographer or his editor.[123] There were exceptions: photojournalists Héctor García, Walter Reuter, the Hermanos Mayo, and Lola Álvarez Bravo brought empathy to representing members of the Amerindian nations.

RAPPORT AND PHOTOGRAPHING INDIGENOUS PEOPLES

Nacho López's initiation into photojournalism was also his first photo reportage on Amerindians, "Noche de Muertos," a work for which he both made the images and wrote the text, a rare opportunity for a photojournalist.[124] The natives' rituals were among the keys to illustrating their picturesqueness, and—perhaps stimulated by López's extraordinary accomplishment in illuminating his photos solely by candlelight—*Noche de Muertos* was a favorite theme among photojournalists and photographers during the 1950s.[125] López followed a familiar pattern of photographing the Purépechas from a high angle, entrapping the women and children in their exotic setting. These photos literally embody Sekula's criticism of "the tendency of professional documentary photographers to aim their cameras downward, toward those with little power or prestige."[126] Moreover, the use of this angle is particularly reproachable in light of the fact that he was utilizing a Rolleiflex camera that he held at the level of his waist.[127] Had he been using a 35 mm camera, which is raised to the eye, the angle would have been more understandable. That he chose to photograph from such a high angle indicates that it may have been an expressive decision signifying his perspective toward Native people. A year and a half later, López made his only other excursion into Indianist imagery as a photojournalist, with "Ante el umbral del silencio" (On the threshold of silence).[128] Here, half of the published photos were taken from low angles, empowering the subjects and demonstrating Nacho's capacity to learn from his mistakes.[129]

The transformation of López's Indianist photography that is apparent in these two early articles showed his concern to represent Native people with sensitivity. He could arguably be considered the maestro of this genre in Mexico, not only in terms of his exceptional images, but in his reflections on photographing Amerindians.[130] From the mid-1950s to the end of 1970s he worked at times for the INI, photographing a wide range of *pueblos indígenas*, among them Tzeltales, Tsotziles, Mixes, Coras, Huicholes, Tarahumaras (Rarámuris), and Chontales; his Indianist photography was published in a INI book, *Los pueblos de la bruma y el sol*.[131] In 1978, López contributed an article, "El indio en la fotografía," for a publication celebrating the thirtieth anniversary of INI. There he criticized the cinematographer Gabriel Figueroa, and photographers Luis Márquez, Guillermo Kahlo, Hugo Brehme, and Agustín Jiménez:

> They let themselves be carried away by the picturesque lyricism emanated by the isolated images of Sergei M. Eisenstein and Edward Tissé, director and cinematographer respectively of the film *Thunder over Mexico* (1933). And they searched for particular overtones: the monumentality of landscapes and colonial architecture accentuates the petrified rostrum of the recently bathed Indian, suspended in time and immovable before misfortune. From such clichés were derived the aberrant visions that still persist in tourist postcards.[132]

Thunder over Mexico was one of several films eventually made from the material filmed by Eisenstein and Tissé from 1930 to 1932, and Nacho's is a familiar interpretation of the origins of Amerindian depiction in the classical Mexican film style, embodied in the collaboration of Emilio "El Indio" Fernández and Gabriel Figueroa.[133] However, Eisenstein's portrayal of Indians is certainly more realist than that found among Mexican cineastes. This can be seen, above all, in the use of nonprofessional actors; the director strove to achieve "an absolute realism, without employing 'stars' or professional artists."[134] He was acquainted with Hollywood's stereotypes of pistol-packing *charros* and the Mexican Revolution and wanted to counter that by representing Mexico's fundamental otherness as demonstrated in the Amerindians' ambience of mystery and ancient ruins. Although the material certainly contains elements of the exotic, Eisenstein's projection of the natives is better than the humble "black and brown faced" *inditos* (little Indians) in films such as *María Candelaria* (Fernández, 1943) and *Tizoc* (Rodríguez, 1957).[135] Finally, I believe that Hugo Brehme's photography was a more important influence over Figueroa than was Tissé's cinematography.

To return to López's essay, it is clear that he had come to understand the importance of personal relations and rapport in the photographic act. He identified several photographers—Walter Reuter, Alfonso Muñoz, Hector García, Oscar Menéndez, Graciela Iturbide, and Jesús Sánchez Uribe—as having developed the capacities enumerated below, in a text that distinguished sharply between aggressors and *amigos*:

> The camera can be an instrument of aggression or a connection between friends. In the first instance, the photographer-tourist who arrives at the Indian communities under the weight of his own prejudices, shoots his

> camera as a rifle without any consideration, looking for sensationalism and "magical barbarism" to later show his friends the superficial vision of a "dog's world." These photos are a dime a dozen and are employed by foreign magazines to present us as a sleepy country full of exoticism [as the Mexican magazines often also did].
>
> When the camera is a link of friendship, of legitimate intercommunication, the photographer assumes a great responsibility and a commitment, which implies a critical and analytical position. The photographer arrives at the Indian community equipped with solid information and, after a time, timidly asks the necessary permission to use his camera. He will know to what extent he is accepted or rejected by the family, and will have to use great care not to violate the limits of the most elementary education. He will drink and eat what he is offered, and sleep in any corner. In this way, he will slowly penetrate the culture and the idiosyncrasies of the inhabitants, obtaining a lasting document that will capture people, religion, customs, and traditions, beyond the apparent reality. The possibility of obtaining a picture of national, and finally universal, experiences [is derived] from having observed the delicate and subtle reactions, anticipating the course of tensions and crises.[136]

I have my doubts as to how closely Nacho followed his own prescription for photographing Amerindians and suspect that it is somewhat similar to the relation between his photojournalist imagery done in the 1950s and his 1970s and '80s writings about being a press photographer.[137] Although he included himself among those photographers who have been able to insert themselves within Indian groups, he also admitted, "I have rarely been able to stay for long periods in communities and towns. Because of that, my photographic vision has been limited."[138] He extended the same critique to Manuel Álvarez Bravo, about whom he stated, "he has entered little into the intimate life of the indigenous communities."[139]

Paul Strand had very limited contact with Indians, yet has received accolades for his pictures of Mexican Native peoples. He did not speak Spanish and was always accompanied by a translator and a guide during his short trip in 1933. Evidently preferring not to make personal contact, he sometimes utilized a trick lens that photographed at a right angle to the image he appeared to be taking, for example in the image of the young Purépecha woman and child.[140] He explained his decision in the following way: "When I began to make portraits, especially in Mexico in 1933, the Graflex was perfect with the attachment of a prism for photographing the people without their knowing that they were being photographed — which was absolutely essential because the Mexican Indians don't like to be photographed."[141]

Using a trick lens or hidden camera was a practice relatively acceptable in this period, and photographers such as Ben Shahn, André Kertész, Walker Evans, Helen Levitt, Ilya Ehrenburg, and Lewis Hine (Strand's mentor), among others, employed this deceit. Strand reasoned that such a strategy was acceptable because he did not feel the necessity to establish intimate contact with the Native peoples in order to successfully photograph them. He stated that he abandoned that shibboleth upon coming to Mexico:

> It was always said that you really have to know a place before you start working on it; otherwise you would do something very superficial. Another shibboleth was that you can't make a portrait of a person unless you know that person, and then when you know the person you create the moment or you wait for the moment when they are most alive and most themselves. These shibboleths went out the window.[142]

How are we to understand that three of the photographers who have been most acclaimed for their Indianist imagery spent relatively little time with these groups? I sense that the recognition they have been accorded by intellectuals, artists, critics, and historians is based largely on their following of Western esthetic canons, as well as their reputations within the fine art culture. For example, the Strand photo of the Purépecha woman and child is a typically invasive Indianist image, reminiscent of those that result when tourists stick their cameras in the natives' faces, as are many of the photos of Amerindians and *campesinos* in his book. Nonetheless, all three photographers rejected the exotic inherent in the colonial vision. I have argued that the most significant contribution Álvarez Bravo made to Latin American and Third World photography was his development of an anti-picturesque stance.[143] Strand spoke explicitly of his efforts to approach each Mexican "as a fellow human being, not as a superior example of the white race who found them 'interesting, picturesque and acute.'"[144] López also felt that exotic depiction must be avoided at all costs, arguing that the picturesque "is easy," and he hoped that his photos were "stripped of all folklorism."[145] However, it is also a question of what we find important in their images. In the case of Strand and Álvarez Bravo, little rapport with the photographed is detected. Perhaps, their solution was to capture the very rejection of the outsider's presence as a constitutive element of their otherness.

Developing rapport—that delicate, if difficult to describe, relationship between photographer and photographed—is crucial to moving beyond the representation of nonconcurrence.[146] Sebastião Salgado has often asserted the importance of establishing a connection with his subjects, saying, "an

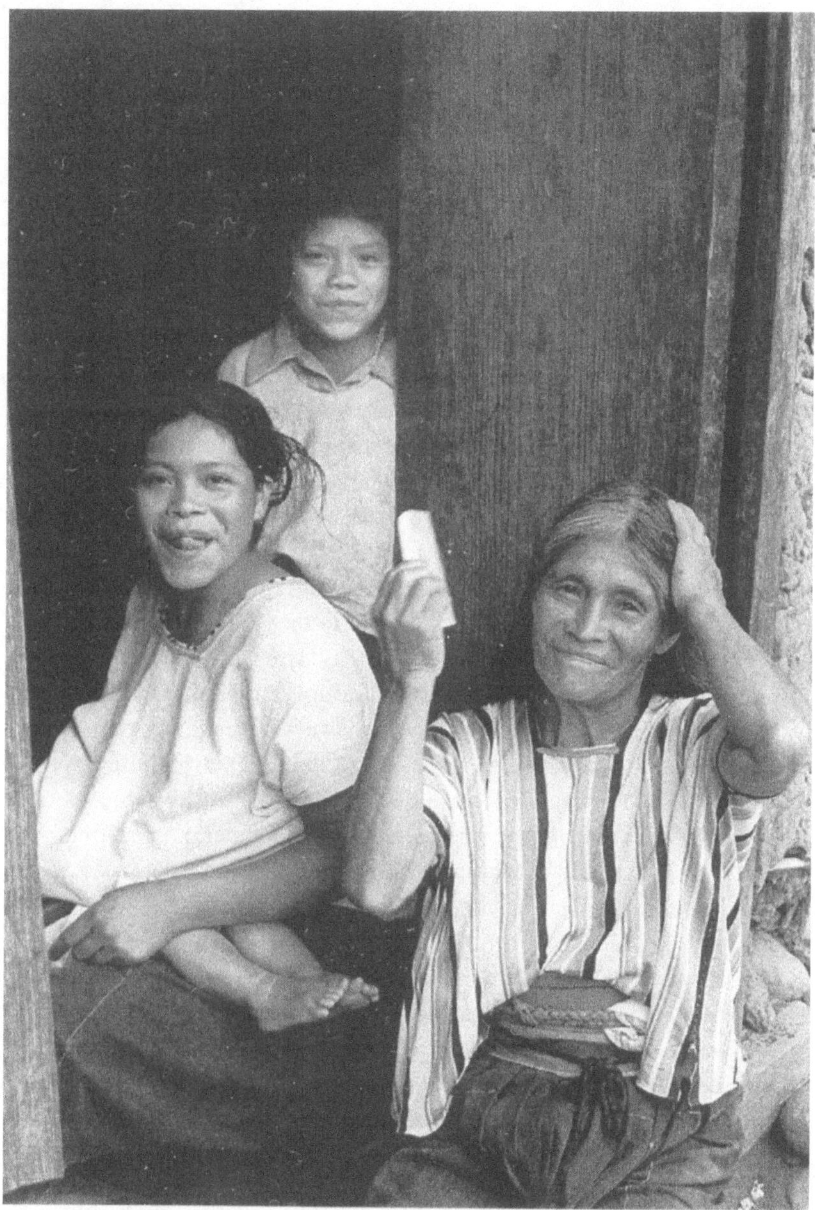

FIGURE 51. Nacho López. Chenalhó, Chiapas, 1979. Fototeca Nacho López, Instituto Nacional de los Pueblos Indígenas.

image is your integration with the person that you photographed at the moment that you work so incredibly together, that your picture is not more . . . than the relation you have with your subject."[147] The personal relations that López had established with the Indians are apparent in their interaction with the photographer, at whom they smile trustingly, as can be seen in his imagery of the women in Chenlhó, Chiapas. (See Figure 51.) Even when Amerindians do not smile at López, they return the camera's gaze, masters of the situation rather than objects of the photographer. It is useful to compare López's interactive approach to the photography produced for the "Concursos de fotografía antropológica," (Contests of Anthropological Photography) over the years 1981 to 1999, of which visual anthropologist Elisa Ramírez Castañeda remarked, "We find no returned gazes in these photographs. . . . Instead of a frank approach, they are spied upon from the side . . . any sign of complicity is absent."[148]

Although López critiqued his own work as not sufficiently informed by longer presences, he seems to have achieved what we might call a "middle" level of integration with his subjects. Photographer Rita Leistner commented on the different forms of relationship that develop with subjects.[149] At the lowest level would be what we know as "street photography," a genre in which photographers try to work without being noticed by their subjects, taking pictures of people who are unaware of the imagemaker's presence.[150] According to Leistner, the point of documentary photography is to get beyond the street and through the "door" into the subjects' lives. The further you get from the street the more you depend on rapport, and the longer you stay in a community the deeper documentary access to the reality of their daily lives will be. As she commented:

> This was especially true with First Nations communities, where the legacy of bad ethics among white photographers was so present that I really wanted to work more slowly and with enormous respect to them. That meant spending weeks in a community before moving from photographing landscapes and architecture to broaching the personal subject of invading someone's privacy by picturing them. Wide shots and reportage benefit from spontaneity. But even much so-called "candid" photography is almost always more successful when the subjects have actually become so accustomed to your being there that they can ignore your presence. It only really appears candid, but in fact the photographer has just become a part of the ordinary interactions of the subjects. . . .
>
> Being a good documentary photographer has more to do with your personality than anything else. People have to be able to feel themselves in front

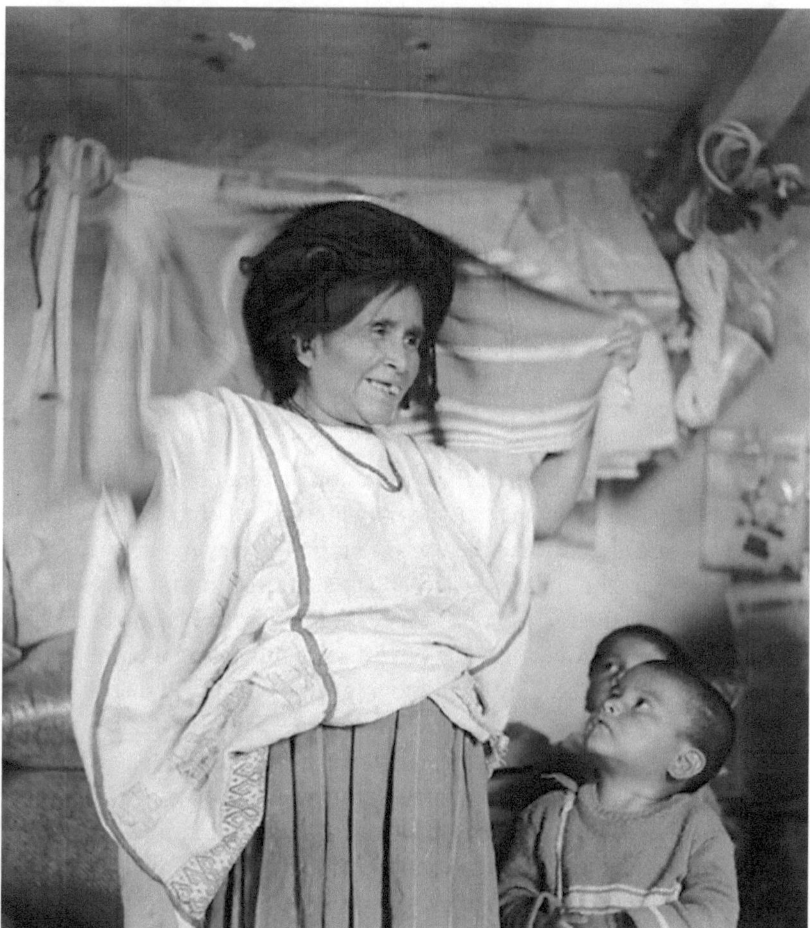

FIGURE 52. Nacho López. Mixe woman (grandmother?) and children, San Juan Cotzocón, Oaxaca, ca. 1970. Inv. # 398934, SINAFO-Fototeca Nacional del INAH, Secretaría de Cultura.

> of your camera. They have to trust that whatever picture you capture of them will be something real. First of all, they need to feel that you yourself are "real." Trust, kindness and respect are paramount and will show in the final picture.[151]

Despite his misgivings about his shortcomings, López's principle aim was finding ways to empower the Amerindian peoples and avoid exoticism. Establishing rapport and utilizing angles to give them force within the image were two important esthetic strategies. Another was infusing images with movement within the frame. Rather than being quiet and resigned, the Indians in some of López's images are active and caught in the second of moving; the snaggletoothed woman (probably a grandmother) in a soiled *huipil* is pictured positively, although she is also aided by her smile and the admiring gazes of the children. (See Figure 52.) Capturing movement within the frame is one of the defining characteristics of modern photojournalism, and López consciously employed it to infuse the image with the grandmother's energy. The first Mexican photographer to employ this strategy was probably Tina Modotti, who evidently moved her camera to make marchers appear to be in motion in her 1926 image, sometimes titled *Campesino March*.[152] Another Mexican photographer, Héctor García, also incorporated movement within the frame, above all in his imagery of the 1968 student movement.[153] If Indianist photography is to be done, the sort of imagery that emphasizes interaction among equals, as well as embodies energy, seems to offer the best option.

At times, López focused on the oppression suffered by Indians in addition to their political activity, an aspect generally missing from Indianist photography until they force themselves onto the stage. As Ramírez Castañeda remarked, "the Indians, as all aborigines, are circumstances of the landscape, never the makers of history."[154] However, López made compelling images of imprisoned Indians, as well as documenting their resistance in political organization. He also photographed them at their daily labors.[155] Identity is not created solely through dress, food, and language; it is also formed by the quotidian tasks we carry out. As a class, Indians are generally agricultural workers engaged in a variety of rural tasks, and Armando Bartra has argued, "Indians have taken over the rural image [whereas] the *campesinos* are the productive face of almost all Indians."[156] The generalized lack in Indianist photography of representations of humor or recreation, fighting or loving has also been commented on.[157] The degree to which López's Indianist photography has been true to his own demands is yet to be determined. What remains clear is that his work provides a wonderful window onto the essential humanity lurking beneath the unique surface of the Native cultures; he has been faithful to his insistence that the most important attribute for a photographer is "to have something to say."[158] He has also given us insight into the infinite forms in which the otherworldliness of Mexico's autochthonous cultures can be represented.

THE NEO-ZAPATISTA REBELLION AND BEYOND

The Neo-Zapatista (EZLN, Ejército Zapatista de Liberación Nacional) uprising that began on January 1, 1994, is a complex indigenous movement that was perhaps the first significant rebellion in the world against neoliberal globalization, in this case in opposition to the signing of the North American Free Trade Agreement (NAFTA).[159] It was also a critique of the capitalist mentality that atomizes society, makes a commodity of nature, and destroys alternative cultures. The leader of the uprising was a former professor at the Universidad Autónoma Metropolitana, Rafael Sebastián Guillén, a mestizo who took the name of subcomandante Marcos (he now calls himself Galeano in honor of a fallen Neo-Zapatista comrade). The immediate response in Mexico was far from positive, and even the leftist newspaper *La Jornada* criticized it. However, Mexican intellectuals such as Carlos Monsivaís, Armando Bartra, Adolfo Gilly, Luis Villoro, Carlos Montemayor, John Holloway, and Herman Bellinghausen played an important role in keeping the government from annihilating the indigenous soldiers (who definitively abandoned armed struggle on January 12, 1994). International writers such as José Saramago, John Berger, Noam Chomsky, and Eduardo Galeano also took a strong proactive stance. The movement is in part a struggle against the speculative practices of finance capitalism, which homogenizes the planet into copies of the "American Way of Life." Local cultures are eliminated by expropriating their lands for multinational corporations and rendering invisible alternative ways of living by making collective labor and respect for the "mother earth" impossible. As subcomandante Moisés argued, "The Chiapas indigenous groups did not exist for the capitalist system, we are not people, we are not even human."[160]

One significant aspect of the EZLN uprising has been the active participation of women. Rebellions in the past (for example, the widespread student movements of 1968) argued that the question of women's equality would have to yield to the necessity of a common front and wait until the triumph of the "revolution." In interviews with Neo-Zapatista women, anthropologist Shannon Speed, herself a Chickasaw, discovered that they felt "it is the opposite, it is through the organization that we begin to struggle, that we begin to become conscious of our rights as women."[161] Comandanta Miriam asserted that, before the rebellion, "They took our lands, our language, our culture. . . . We suffered humiliation, discrimination, marginalization, mistreatment and inequality."[162] Neo-Zapatista women speak of "equilibrium" rather than "gender equality," for the former term is a fundamental aspect of Mesoamerican cosmology.[163] Feminist scholar Silvia Marcos believes that "the Zapatistas are a model and an emblem of how to unite the struggles of women with the struggles of the indigenous peoples."[164]

Photojournalist Angeles Torrejón went to cover the EZLN rebellion shortly after a ceasefire was declared on January 12.[165] She had presented a proposal to her agency, Imagen Latina, to photograph the support base

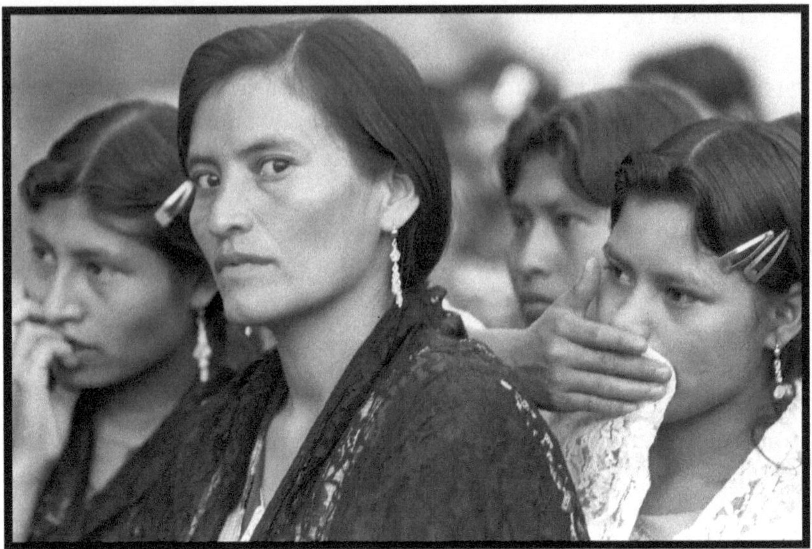

FIGURE 53. Angeles Torreón. *La mirada alzada.* Neo-Zapatista women, Chiapas jungle, 1 May 1994. Courtesy of Angeles Torrejón.

that women provided, feeling that it was important to explore the process of women entering into this uprising.[166] When she arrived in the city of Ocosingo, Chiapas, she found several male photojournalists who were waiting to get permission from the EZLN to enter the jungle; they told her that there was no access. She borrowed a pickup truck and struck out on her own into the jungle. When EZLN soldiers stopped her at the first roadblock, she showed them her project and was allowed to continue. Suddenly, she came upon a large tree trunk that had been laid over the road. She stopped and five or six armed and uniformed women came out of the bush; she was much affected by seeing these tiny indigenous women dressed as soldiers. After reading her project, they lifted the tree, and she was taken to a shack deep in the jungle, where she was interviewed by Captain Irma, who was in charge of that sector: "It seemed incredible to me."

Subcomandante Marcos arrived soon after and said he liked her project of trying to understand how women had left behind their traditional customs to enter directly into the rebellion. When he asked her if she was impressed to meet him, she replied that she was more affected by her contact with the women combatants; he made it clear that she was not to photograph them in uniform without their balaclavas. She stayed for a month, covering training exercises and the May Day celebration. It was at that event she first saw EZLN women dressed in civilian clothes and without masks. She was attracted to an image of four women watching the festivities and took their photo. She had taken two shots before the woman in the foreground turned to look at her after hearing the camera's click. (See Figure 53.) It is an image that the photographer feels embodies the dignity of the Neo-Zapatista women, and she titled it *La mirada alzada* (The raised or uprisen gaze).[167]

Between 1994 and 2000, Torrejón returned to Chiapas and stayed for a month three times a year, almost always in different locations. The Amerindian women initially resisted being photographed, feeling that it "stole their souls." However, inspired by Nacho López's example, Torrejón proceeded very discretely until they came to see the camera as simply an extension of herself. She also brought photos back with her on every stay, and exhibited them hung from clotheslines with clothespins. She believes that the rebellion made a great difference in indigenous women's lives. Before the uprising, marriages were contracted with the *derecho de prenda* (the right of a pledge). This consisted of a boy requesting his father arrange the marriage of a young girl to which he was attracted: the father would give land to the girl's father in exchange for her marriage. This ancient custom was eradicated, one of the examples of local customs being transformed. When Torrejón asked the women if they were not afraid of dying in combat, they replied that it would be a great honor to die fighting in order to get what they deserve in terms of justice, respect, education, food, and health care, and for the *usos y costumbres* (customs) of their culture. Women now enter into all discussions of social life and have no fear to say what they want and do not want. For example, if a man beats his wife, the community decides how he is to be punished. Women believe that they have *pensamiento grande*, the capacity to think in broader terms, and see men as incompetent to understand the larger picture of how to hold society together.

Daily life continues to be very difficult, as it is in all Mexican Amerindian communities; in some there is no electricity, no running water, and no gas with which to cook. When children reach twelve years, it is considered to be a great accomplishment: they say, "*Se me logró*" (I made it), because at that age they are probably not going to die easily from the miserable living conditions. As they have no birth certificates, age is calculated on baptismal documents. When Torrejón asked the women why they didn't use birth control—given the high infant mortality—the women replied that they had been given pills and condoms by the government, but when they ran out, there was no way to buy them in the jungle. The importance that indigenous women have acquired in Mexico because of the Neo-Zapatista movement can be seen in their backing of the nomination of María de Jesús

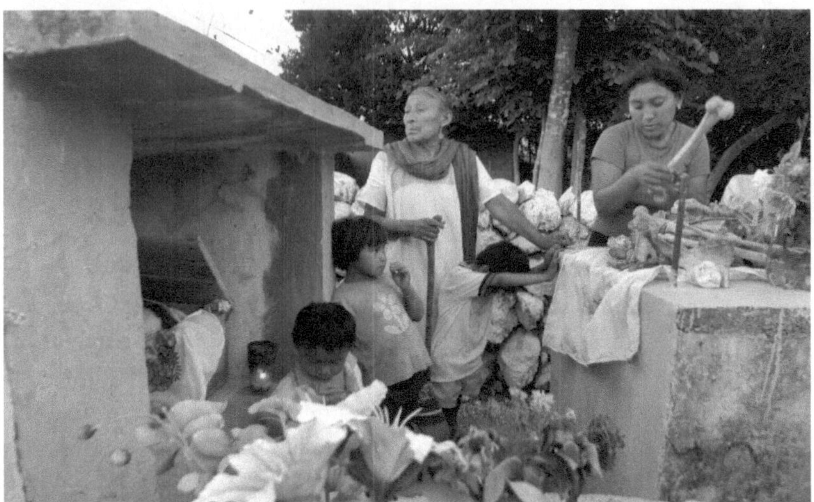

FIGURE 54. Francisco Martín. Mayan family cleaning the bones of deceased relatives on the Day of the Dead, Pomuch, Campeche, November 2006. Courtesy of Francisco Martín.

Patricio Martínez, "Marichuy," an Amerindian from Tuxpan who founded the National Indigenous Congress, for the presidential race of 2018.[168]

Francisco Martin brings a critical eye to the Indianist imagery he has carried out while photographing Mayans over the last fifteen years, financing his project by contributing to different media as a freelance photojournalist. His commitment to photographing today's Amerindians in the Yucatán peninsula derives from his critique of the generalized view of this culture as an archetype from the past. Instead, he focuses on their current daily life, showing the Mayan culture as active and in constant transformation, going beyond the romanticized and ethereal gaze common to much of Indianist photography in order to document "the non-material cultural patrimony that is collectively constructed day by day in the town and cities."[169] Martin renders the vitality of Mayans through both esthetic and ethnographic strategies, as well as his choice of subjects.

Martin's portrayal of Mayan women avoids the "classical" approach that renders them "overdressed" or "underdressed." Rather than portraying *indígenas* posing for the camera with or without picturesque clothing, Martin depicts them caught up in their daily activities. For example, we see them harvesting *chiles habaneros*, bent over in "stoop labor," their tools in one hand while they pick the crop with the other. Their clothing is colorful, but it is integrated in their lives and their work rather than being merely decorative. Images taken during the Day of the Dead also show evidence

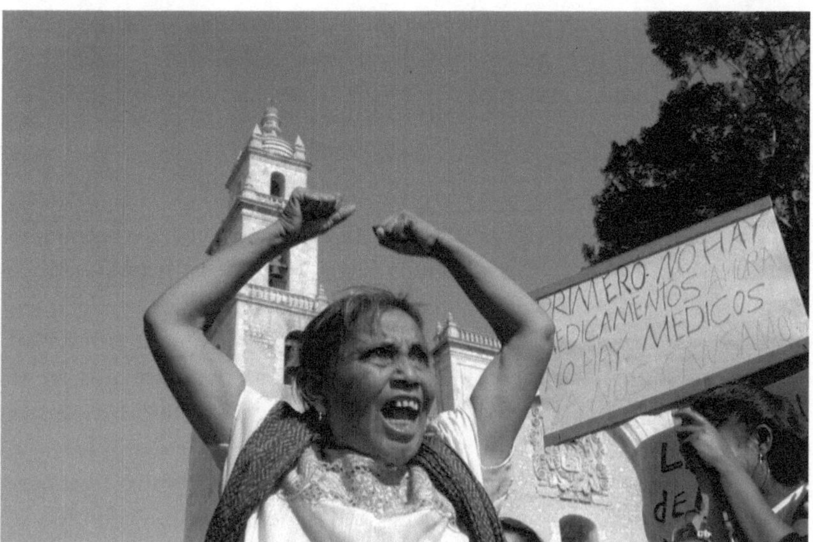

FIGURE 55. Francisco Martín. Mayan woman protesting against lack of medicines and doctors, Plaza Grande, Mérida, Yucatán, 2003. Courtesy of Francisco Martín.

of a multifaceted syncretism. We are provided with a striking photo from Pomuch, Campeche State, of bones being removed from family graves to be cleaned and then returned; three generations participate in this activity: the grandmother is dressed in traditional clothing, but her daughter and grandchildren appear in modern attire. (See Figure 54.) Here, Martin's perspective stands in sharp contrast to many representations of this celebration by foreigners. For example, Sebastião Salgado pictures the Day of the Dead in an opaque, misty tone that creates a veiled and inscrutable image in which a dog dominates the foreground, while the people are lost in the fog behind.[170] Though the presence of a dog in a cemetery may be shocking to imperial sensibilities, there is nothing mysterious about it on All Saints' Day, a time when the families gather to clear the graves of rubbish and reunite with their departed loved ones. Thus, Día de Muertos is essentially the opposite of what Salgado represented in his image, which is clearly made to appeal to the US-European market, and this can be seen by comparing it to the normality of this practice, as captured by Martin.

Martin's vision also differs from the dominant US-European depiction of Amerindians by showing political struggle, as did Nacho López. For example, a low angle shot of an elderly Mayan protesting against the lack of medicines and doctors takes her far beyond the passive representations that are often found in the works of foreign imagemakers.[171] (See Figure 55.)

Here, the woman raises her arms in anger and frustration, while the façade of a church looms over her, a reminder of how Catholicism has served to oppress Amerindians and impose Western values upon them.

CONCLUSION

In sum, the functions of Indianist photography in Mexico have been many and varied. Images of the First Nations have served to testify to the autochthonous origin of great civilizations, as well as to offer proof of racial inferiority. Photos have been testimonies to the cultural distance from Western ways of being, and they can show the fundamental humanity we all share. They have been used as an international calling card for Mexico, as well as to sell tourism and real estate. They have provided "object lessons" to those who do not comply fully in the tasks to which they have been assigned by their White "owners," and to denounce their forced exodus and their enslaving. Photographs of Indian women may well have been used as pornographic material, and demonstrated their resistance to their continued socio-economic and political oppression. They document the transformation wrought by indigenous rebellions such as the Neo-Zapatista uprising. And they have been firmly embedded in imperial, neocolonizing, and decolonizing discourses.

CHAPTER 5

A View from the Left

Worker, Laborist, Decolonizing, and Feminist Imagery

For many of us the final object of our work is to create a world in which working people can make their own life and their own history, rather than have it made for them by others, including academics. **Eric Hobsbawm**

I come from a privileged family. During the Great Depression, my father had gone to the University of Oklahoma and then to its medical school, thanks to his own comfortable background. As a doctor, he had an assured income as well as great latitude in deciding where to live. My parents moved to California in the early 1940s, and they became relatively wealthy over time by buying up land for little money (thanks in part to loans from the extended family) and holding onto it until it became much more valuable. My father acquired the practice of a retiring doctor in Fontana, a town that was then beginning to undergo a fundamental transformation. Sociologist Mike Davis described how Fontana, "an arcadian community of small chicken ranchers and citrus growers living self-sufficiently," was suddenly transmuted into a small city populated basically by the workers employed by the Kaiser Steel Mill, the biggest and only integrated steel complex west of the Rocky Mountains.[1]

The mill opened in 1942 to produce steel for the Pacific Front in World War II. The company did not allow its executives to live in Fontana, and so it became "a gritty blue-collar town, well known to line-haul truckers everywhere, with . . . outlaw motorcycle gangs (the birthplace of the Hell's Angels in 1946), it is the antipode to the sumptuary belts of West Los Angeles or Orange County."[2] As Davis stated, "A loud, brawling mosaic of working-class cultures—Black, Italian, hillbilly, Slovene and Chicano—Fontana has long endured an unsavory reputation."[3] Being the son of the well-off doctor in what was known as the "roughest town in the county," I believe that what Davis refers to as Fontana's "indissoluble toughness of character" rubbed off on me.[4] I grew up surrounded by workers and their families, and eventually ended up laboring in the steel mill after high school, as did many of my classmates, where they would stay until the mill closed in the early 1980s.

For me, the mill was a summer job before I attended UCLA in the fall. Although I was relatively sheltered in the print shop, I experienced an event that left me impressed with how unions functioned as a bulwark for laborers. All workers were issued steel-toed shoes, but since they were clumsy, heavy, and ugly—the footwear furthest from what I considered "cool"—I decided one day to wear tennis shoes. The head of the shop called me in and told me that it was company policy for every worker to wear steel-toed shoes. I assured him I would wear them in the future and left his office. The union's representative immediately approached me to ask about the interaction, and said it would back me if I wanted to make a complaint. I demurred, but was moved by the fact that there was an organization that served as a buffer between the boss and me, should I have need of it. I later worked at a steelyard, tying bundles of rebar, which was a good deal more dangerous, and made me understand the importance of safety equipment.

My family was politically very conservative. In spite of the advantages he enjoyed, my father thought that he was a self-made man and that anybody could become wealthy if they really tried. He was a right-wing Libertarian who hated any governmental interference in his life, above all paying taxes. I cannot remember any real political discussions in our house, even at election times, because it was obvious that the only possibility was the Republican Party. My father ranted constantly against "socialized medicine," of which the example at hand was the Kaiser Health Plan for its workers, and my mother never referred to Eleanor Roosevelt other than as "old horse face." I admired my parents and internalized their conservative position unquestioningly throughout my childhood, adolescence, my first three failed attempts to go to college, and three years in the US Army.

Acquiring a critical consciousness of my own began when I was released from the army in February of 1966 and went to Washington to earn money by working on the construction of the Lower Monumental Dam on the Snake River in the semi-arid region of the southeastern part of the state. An army pal, Ron Babick, came from the nearby Tri-Cities area and had been employed as a laborer on the dam's construction for about a year. We'd maintained contact, and he told me that there was enough demand for workers that he could get me on the job. My friend was high-energy and very conscientious, so his recommendation carried weight. The pay was very good, and the idea of wearing a hardhat splashed with concrete was appealing, probably because of advertising images conjured up by cigarette ads. He took me to the hall of the Laborers' International Union Local 348, and after enrolling in the syndicate, I went to work on the 4 p.m. to midnight shift. The foreman was Ron's friend, so he assigned me to very basic tasks where I was hidden from the higher-ups, until I understood the laborers' various roles. There was no interest and even less patience for neophytes that had to be trained, and should my ignorance be discovered, I would immediately be sent home with the proverbial "pink slip."

The work was hard for me during the first couple of weeks, but I quickly became acclimated. One of the first fears I had to overcome was that of heights, when I was sent up in what was called a gondola, a flat plywood board about 3 × 2 feet with a waist-high thin metal tube that served as a safety railing. The gondola was hauled up from the top of the piers, and my job was to chip off the plastic foam insulation that was applied to keep the freshly poured cement from cracking in the freezing evenings. I was given a long-handled paint chipper and had to push up to get it under the foam to break it off. It required significant force, and every time I shoved it upward the gondola swayed and rocked. I was so high that the men below looked like ants, so it was quite frightening, but any hesitation on my part would have resulted in being fired on the spot; vertigo was not an option.

Workers on the dam were racially separated. The "aristocrats"—electricians, carpenters, and ironworkers—were all White, while the general laborers were a mixed bag of Whites and Latinos. The only Blacks were on the "nozzle" crews, which were composed exclusively of African Americans; they used large vibrator heads connected to fire hoses to settle the freshly poured concrete among the reinforcing steel bars so that there would be no air pockets. I learned about racism and the precarious situation in which even unionized workers live when our foreman decided to declare a wildcat strike, that is, one not fomented by the union leadership but that comes directly from the workers. He was our immediate boss, so we had no choice but to walk off the job. The racial division of labor on the dam site came to the fore when the Black crews refused to participate in the strike, something that provoked much racist resentment among the White and Latino workers. The foreman was fired, but the rest of us were soon able to return to work when the union convinced the company that we had no real choice in the matter. Although I was well paid, I had few doubts about returning to college. You only need one fellow worker telling you to go back to school while waving his mutilated hand in your face—two fingers left as stubs by the sort of accident all too common among laborers—to confirm the idea that a career made possible by education was preferable to such dangers.[5]

WORKERS' HISTORY IN MEXICO

Despite growing up in a workers' town, of personally experiencing the life of a laborer, and of having become a Marxist historian in the 1970s, my entrance into working class history was largely serendipitous. In the period from the mid-1970s to around 1990, labor history underwent a boom in Mexico, impelled by the workers' rebellions against a repressive state apparatus, and the neoliberal policies that were destroying the gains made by unions during the 1930s; it may also have been an expression of Hegel's well-known phrase, "the owl of Minerva spreads its wings only with the falling of the dusk." Pablo González Casanova, an important leftist intellectual and rector of the UNAM (1970–1972), coordinated multiple publications on labor history between 1980 and 1990: the seventeen-volume series *La clase obrera en la historia de México*, and the four-volume series *Historia del movimiento obrero en América Latina*; he also collaborated with Samuel León and Ignacio Marván to produce the five-volume series *El obrero mexicano*.[6]

Many Mexican historians, sociologists, and anthropologists were drawn into the recovery of workers' participation in forming the nation, among them Raúl Trejo Delarbe, Jorge Basurto, Sergio de la Peña, Juan Felipe Leal, Enrique Florescano, Alejandra Moreno Toscano, Arnaldo Córdova, Victoria Novelo, Rocío Guadarrama, Aurora Loyo Brambila, Arturo Anguiano, Mario Camarena, Armando Bartra, and Antonio Alonso. Older Mexican communists who had been instrumental in fomenting leftist movements published their memoirs; the most important was that by Valentín Campa.[7] Feminists also turned toward this issue, with scholars such as Teresita de Barbieri, Nora Lustig, Jenny Cooper, Mary Goldsmith, and Fernanda Navarro contributing to the study of women workers.[8] Latin American exiles participated, including the Brazilian Ciro Cardoso; at least two militant leftist historians worked in CIHMO-UAP: the Haitian Michelle Hector, who directed that center of labor history, and the Argentine Alberto J. Pla. Important publishers such as Siglo XXI, Era, the UNAM, and the UAP were instrumental in making these studies available, including the translation of works by foreigners such as Barry Carr, Marjorie Ruth Clark, Tzvi Medin, Francie Chassen, and Ramón Ruiz. Numerous congresses were organized, photo exhibits were mounted, and institutions were formed to carry out this mission, among them CEHSMO.[9]

HISTORIES FROM THE AGN ARCHIVES

Enrique Suárez Gaona provided me with equipment to copy photos from archives, as well as money to buy them. Throughout my year at CEHSMO, I was working with images in terms of the ways their "transparency" offered the opportunity to do visual social history. For example, my first published article in Mexico was a historical micro-ethnography on women who toiled in eleven tiny *nixtamal* (corn meal) mills in Mexico City during December of 1919; it appeared in CEHSMO's journal, *Historia Obrera.*[10] As has almost always been the case in my work, it began with images. I had discovered seven good pictures of *nixtamaleras* and their workplaces in a box full of dusty photographs that had been torn from their files in the Departamento de Trabajo of the Archivo General de la Nación.

By tracing the photos back to their original registers, I was able to construct a small history about the women's lives from the reports sent by an inspector for the Secretary of Industry, Commerce, and Labor, Juan de Beraza. Either making the images himself or taking along a professional photographer, he conducted interviews with the women and documented the ways they were denied their rights to a decent and legal salary, to the benefits they should have received as nursing mothers, to compensation for work-related injuries, and to protection from sexual harassment. De Beraza argued that they were treated "like slaves," virtual prisoners in the *nixtamal* mills that they practically never left because their bosses insisted that they sleep there to guard the machinery, with neither toilet facilities nor ventilation and only a thin flea-ridden *petate* (mat) between them and the cold, damp, cement floor. The Departamento de Trabajo offered almost no further documentation on such workers in the period from 1909 to 1929, and I could not turn up any other sources that might have given me information about these women. So I was left with what I would call a vignette, a thin slice in images and words of workers' daily lives in one brief moment.

Among other stories I found in the AGN with photographs were those in which foreign oil companies utilized many resources to keep from respecting the progressive labor laws of the 1917 constitution. On October 2, 1924, workers at the Compañía Petrolera Mexicana Holandesa "La Corona" went on strike because the company refused to sign a contract with the Unión de Obreros y Empleados de La Corona, which was linked to the CROM

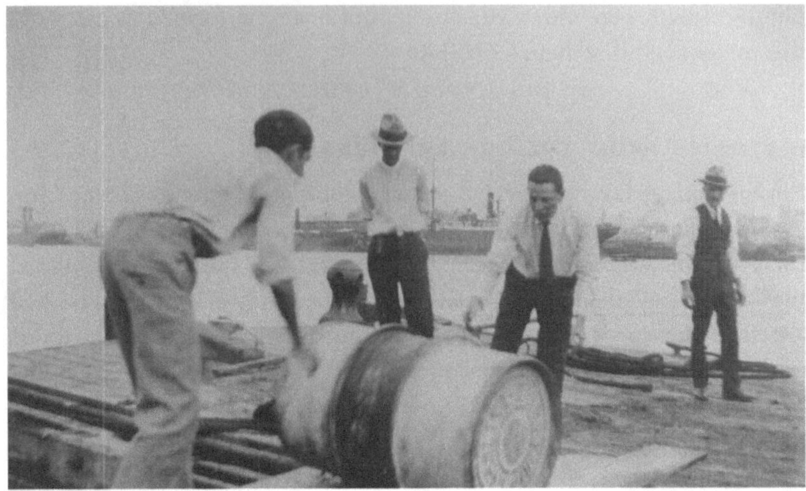

FIGURE 56. Andrés Araujo (author or intellectual author). Office personnel illegally taking the place of striking workers, moving oil drums though still dressed in ties and vests, petroleum camp "El Humo," Pueblo Viejo, Veracruz, 6 December 1924. Departamento del Trabajo, Caja 723, Expediente 16, Archivo General de la Nación.

(Confederación Regional Obrera Mexicana). The strikers took control of the oil plants, and the company asked the federal government to intervene with armed forces. Inspector Andrés Araujo was a conscientious enforcer of the revolutionary legislation protecting the working class, and he warned the Secretariat that the "company pretends to renew work with some of the department heads, which could cause serious consequences."[11]

Araujo drew attention to yet another danger: the company was employing armed *guardias blancas* (company muscle) to stand between the workers and the various labor groups employed as scabs: department heads, office employees, and domestic servants, as well as *chalanes*, the lowest level of common laborers who were probably only hired as strikebreakers and were not members of the union. On October 24, Araujo wrote a letter to the Secretariat, describing how the company had given the workers a letter to sign, in which they had to accept the company's conditions. Although they were threatened with dismissal if they refused, the majority rejected it. Araujo also described the living conditions of the workers: if they became ill or injured and could not work, they were not paid. The so-called houses provided for the workers were constructed of cardboard that was torn and ragged; the habitations had dirt floors, and "the roofs were better in the places that were dedicated to the horses (*caballeriza*)."[12] In November, Araujo informed the Secretariat that the company was using department heads, usually foreigners, to load the ships.

Having sent many telegrams and letters during October and November, the inspector must have decided that photographs would provide a more effective form of evidence to demonstrate the company's noncompliance with the constitutional mandates. On December 9, he sent a message with three images of "the Superintendent and other office personnel doing the work of *peones* (common laborers), a labor very different from that which they carried out before the strike was declared."[13] (See Figure 56.) It is unclear whether Araujo took the photos himself or had them made by a photographer (he does not appear to have included images by himself or a professional in any other files), or whether the workers themselves took them. In any case, he insisted that "the attitude assumed by the office employees has been at the point of causing serious conflict"; for that reason, "before using violent means against the office personnel, the Unión de Obreros y Empleados de La Corona has recurred to the Secretariat in order that justice be attained through legal means."[14] The strike ended when the company signed the contract on December 24, and a month later it began to fire workers because of the production decline in October, November, and December.

WORKER PHOTOGRAPHY

Petroleum workers themselves made images to denounce their situation. Laboring in the oil fields is always dangerous, but it was especially so in the period from 1920 to 1922 for several reasons. The workers were often young *campesinos* who had few of the skills necessary for dealing with modern technology and little experience with industrial rhythms of life. There was much improvisation, and workers were hired by word of mouth, with no written contracts or guarantees. The foremen usually reflected the authoritarianism of the higher-ups, pushing the workers into a "speed-up" mode, especially in this period, when production was at a maximum.[15] Moreover, laborers often did piecework, which encouraged them to finish a job as quickly as possible; as one worker from that period testified, "accidents became more frequent when work was accelerated."[16] Those who labored on the pipelines were particularly exposed, but "no safety equipment was provided, not even the most elemental for hands and feet; everything was very rustic."[17]

Death was common, and the camera offered one method to document injuries caused by explosions. On January 4, 1922, a high-pressure line carrying petroleum burst in the Cerro Azul camp of the Huasteca Petroleum Company, owned by Edward L. Doheny, a US entrepreneur. One worker

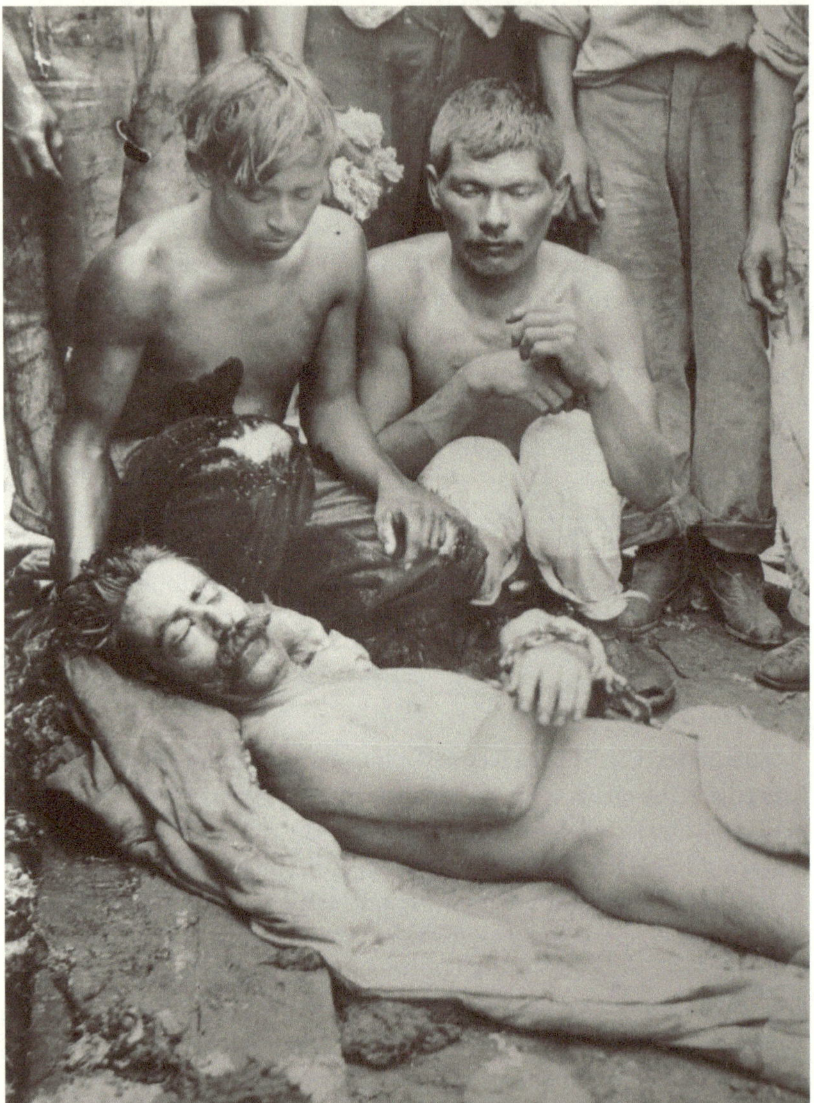

FIGURE 57. Filgenio Vargas and Jorge Miranda. Dead and injured petroleum workers, Tepezintla, Veracruz, 4 January 1922. Departamento del Trabajo, Caja 447, Expediente 3, Archivo General de la Nación.

died from burns inflicted by the explosion, and two were seriously injured. Fellow oil workers Filgenio Vargas and Jorge Miranda took photographs and, as no union protected them, sent them directly to the Secretary of Industry, Commerce and Labor. They explained in the accompanying letter, "since the company did not provide any medical assistance for the victims, we felt the necessity to take their names and some photos in order to take the steps necessary to see if it were possible that they could be provided the medical assistance they lacked."[18] (See Figure 57.) The company may have had minimal medical services, but the medical staff was quite old, something that permitted the owners to save money even though they deducted 2 percent of workers' salaries for this service; the injured were rarely taken to the hospital.[19] However, if the Huasteca Petroleum Company was dilatory in protecting its workers, it showed much alacrity in firing Vargas and Miranda for having taken the photographs and making the complaint.

The oil boom created great housing shortages in cities such as Tampico, Tamaulipas, as well as other deficiencies: water supply, drainage, electricity, transport, and other necessities. In 1900 there were 17,500 inhabitants of that city, but eighteen years later the population had grown to 75,000, and "Tampico and its environs became overcrowded and terribly polluted."[20] Living conditions were sometimes made purposefully difficult, and the camera could then be an important tool in remedying things. The dangers of living in an oil production zone were great, as the risk of explosions was ever-present. In 1917 the Mexican government ordered Pierce Oil Company to relocate its storage tanks away from the populated areas in Tampico.[21] To circumvent the cost of removing and rebuilding their tanks, Pierce rented the land and then attempted to force the workers and their families to move. Given the lack of alternative places to live, they refused. Pierce then built a wooden fence around the land, compelling the inhabitants to enter and leave by crawling under it.

Such callous and inhuman acts were typical of Henry Clay Pierce, an unscrupulous entrepreneur who was described by a fellow oil executive in the following way: "he wouldn't do anything straight, if he could do it in a dirty way."[22] In order to document their situation, a worker, Luis F. Becerril, took a photograph and sent it to the Secretary of Industry, Commerce and Labor along with his complaint in January 1923. (See Figure 58.) When Inspector Araujo came check the situation, the workers and their families told him that they were going to continue struggling to see that justice was done, whether in form of removing the fence or of receiving indemnification for the homes they would lose. The inspector attempted to carry out the conciliatory negotiations that the Secretariat requested. He intended to "make the Pierce Oil Corporation see the irregularity with which they were proceeding," although he also communicated that "the company would avoid any restrictions at their convenience."[23] On February 15, the Secretariat told him to keep them informed about the results, but with that document a curtain is drawn over this human drama, and Becerril, the women,

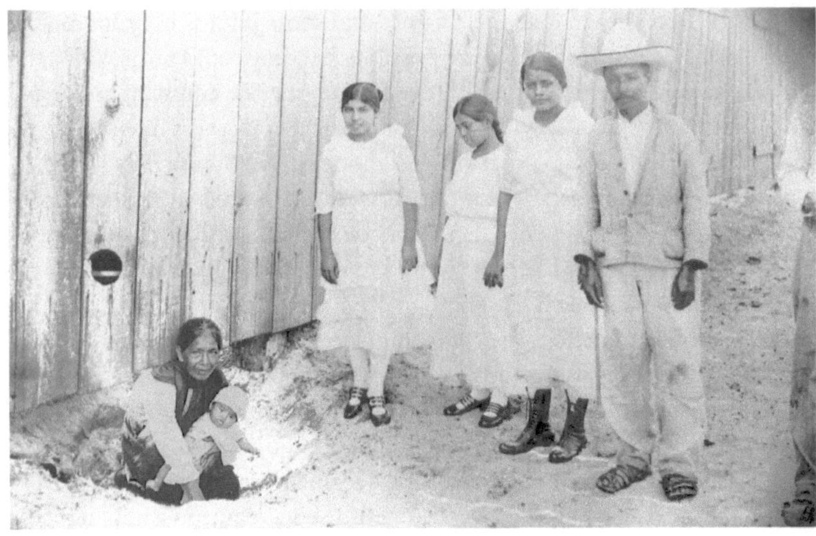

FIGURE 58. Luis F. Becerril. Woman and child going out to the street under a fence, Doña Cecilia, Tampico, Tamaulipas, 1923. Departamento del Trabajo, Caja 653, Expediente 9, Archivo General de la Nación.

her child, and the other petroleum workers posing in the photo disappear from history.

As can be seen in the instances conserved in the AGN, workers in the oil-producing states of Veracruz and Tamaulipas very quickly generated the consciousness to document their oppression through photographs, and it would appear that there was an extended use of the camera among those laborers. García Díaz asserts that images were made on the initiative of the companies prior to 1920, but after that date workers and artisans contracted professional photographers to record their rural outings and excursions, mountaineering, sports teams, schools, food cooperatives, and banks, as well as their orchestras and other musical groups; images of "schools, libraries, sports fields, cinemas, and union buildings tell of a time of labor utopia."[24] One imagemaker who seems to have been important was A. Sierra, who captured the carpenter guilds from the worker towns of Río Blanco, Nogales, and Santa Rosa who had united fraternally "in a country party to express their spirts that had been fatigued in the struggle to earn a living." (See Figure 59.) As García Díaz affirmed, "This development of self-esteem was without doubt one of the most important advances of those years, and contributed to the growing democratization of photography."[25]

The ever-increasing extension of camera use led to creation of family albums that have been a vital source for the imagistic study of work and workers in the important series *Veracruz: Imágenes de su historia*.[26] These

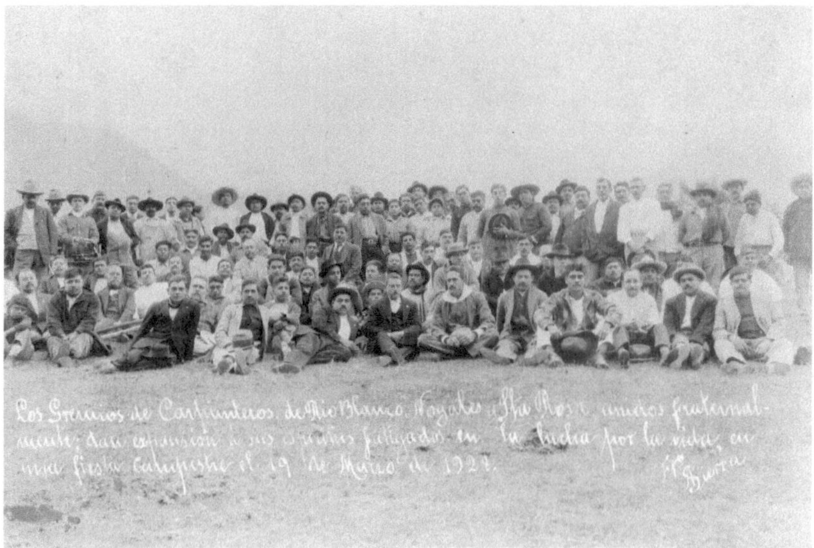

FIGURE 59. Sierra. "The Carpenter Guilds from Río Blanco, Nogales, and Santa Rosa, fraternally united; express their spirits that were fatigued in the struggle to earn a living, in a country party on 19 March 1928," Veracruz. Courtesy of Bernardo García.

volumes and other works by García Díaz are a perfect example of what a trio of photohistorians have described as a wellspring of worker photography: "it is through the mostly unremunerated, unmonetized networks of kin and community that are registered in these vernacular archives that we find traces of what capital forgets and conceals, the unpaid work and care that goes into social reproduction and the maintenance of available, cheap, and vulnerable work forces."[27] However, it is important to note that the photographs workers made, and had taken, generally provide a positive image of them dressed in their "Sunday best." As García Díaz underlines, "What is not captured are the crowded living spaces, the shoeless proletarian children, the premature aging of women submitted to a double day, the violence within the families, alcoholism, the oppression of syndical *caciquismo*, etc."[28]

Another prominent fount of worker photography is union newspapers. Although this issue has been little-explored in Mexico, the periodical founded in 1915 *Pro-paria* (Pro-pariah) was crucial in publishing photographs, largely made by José Mayorga, of protests and social cohesion that demonstrated the force and political capacities of the Orizaban laborers. Mayorga worked for *Pro-paria* from 1920 to 1946; born in Orizaba, Mayorga enjoyed personal relations with the worker families in the textile towns that were fundamental in gaining access to their world. He utilized a

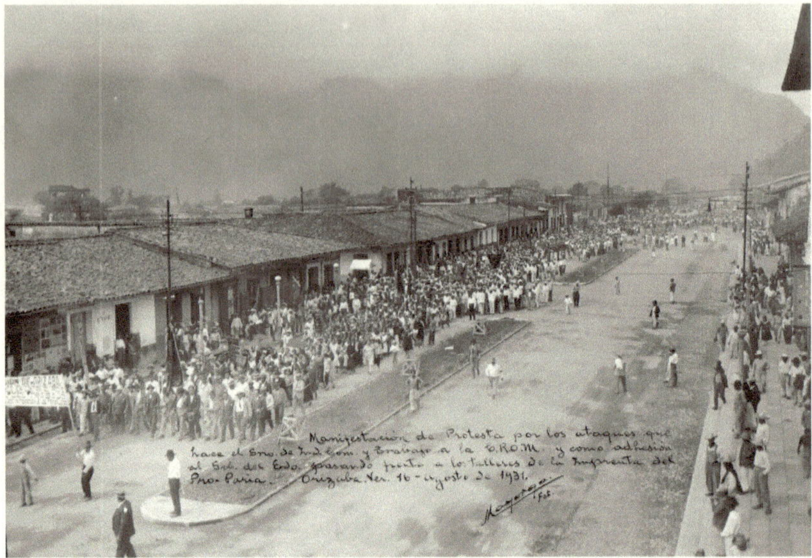

FIGURE 60. José Mayorga. "Demonstration of protest opposed to the attacks made by the Secretaría de Industria, Comercio y Trabajo against the C.R.O.M. and in favor of the Secretary of the State [Veracruz] passing in front of the print shop of *Pro-Paria*. Orizaba, Veracruz, 16 August 1931." Courtesy of Bernardo García.

5 × 7 Kodak camera and artisanal sensitivity inherited from his silversmith father, as well as his dogged capacity to work long hours, to leave an important legacy of labor photography. In a picture that showed union members demonstrating in favor of the local government's support and protesting attacks made by the Secretary of Labor against the CROM, Mayorga chose to photograph from a high angle in order to capture the magnitude of the dissidence. (See Figure 60.) For García Díaz, the workers' media demonstrated an acute visual consciousness:

> From an early moment, they conveyed a detailed iconographic memory of union activities. If before, workers had been objects of photographs, they were now converted into subjects and they were very attentive of being photographed for workers' publications. They clearly understood what propaganda served, and the relevance of the photographic image.[29]

THE ARCHIVE OF A RAILROAD MILITANT

Directing the videotape *Made on Rails* in 1986 brought me into direct contact with Guillermo Treviño, a pivotal figure in organizing the railroad

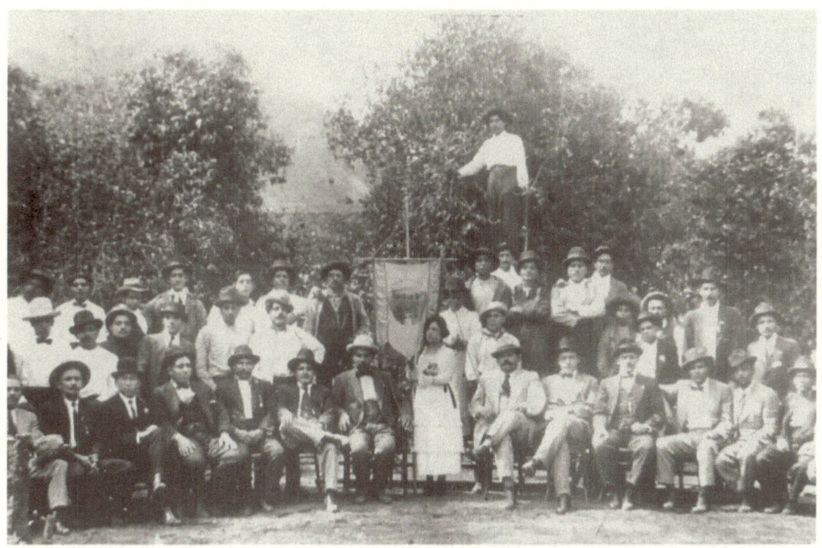

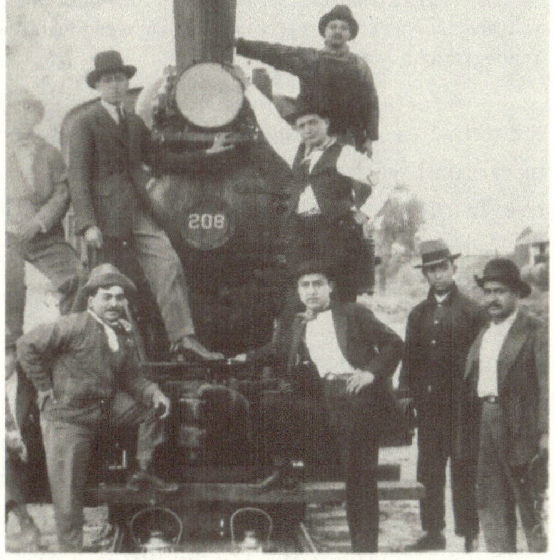

FIGURE 61. (*Above*) Guillermo Treviño. Meeting of the Unión de Conductores, Maquinistas, Garroteros y Fogoneros (engineers, assistant engineers, brakemen, and stokers), Orizaba, Veracruz, 1921. In the center, Herminia Linares, Treviño's wife. Archive of John Mraz.

FIGURE 62.(*Right*) Guillermo Treviño (intellectual author). Treviño (center bottom) posing in front of a train, accompanied by other patio workers, Interoceanic Railway Station, Puebla City, Puebla, 1927. Archive of John Mraz.

unions in Puebla. A participant in a wide range of social struggles from the age of fourteen until his death at eighty-seven, he described himself as a "resolute and committed communist" (*un comunista decidido y entregado*).[30] His photo collection is of particular importance in reconstructing the history of Mexican *ferrocarrileros*, for it is one of the few private worker's archives in which the date and place of the images encountered therein were carefully conserved. Treviño was conscious of the images' use within

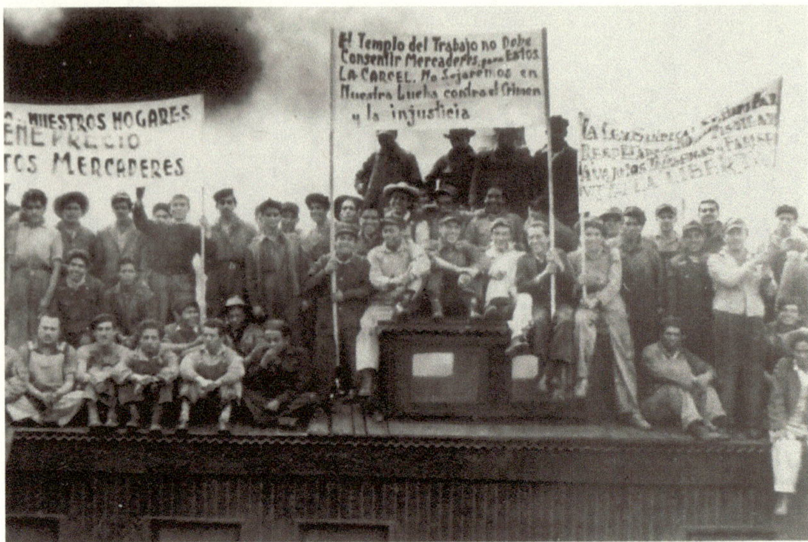

FIGURE 63. Guillermo Treviño. Protest of railroad workers against the government-imposed leaders (*charros*) of their union, the National Railworkers' Syndicate (Sindicato de Trabajadores Ferrocarrileros de la República Mexicana [STFRM]), Mexico City?, 1948. Archive of John Mraz.

the struggles for which they were made, as well as in preserving the culture of railroad workers. Further, it offers a much more militant and combative vision than that found in the archive of the official union, Sindicato de Trabajadores Ferrocarrileros de la República Mexican (STFRM), or the Casasola Archive. This is no doubt related to his family history: his father fought on the Villista side in the revolution and was executed by the Constitutionalists in 1916.

Many elements unique to *ferrocarrileros* are preserved in the Treviño archive. In a photo from 1921, we can see how guilds formed around the different groups of laborers. (See Figure 61.) Treviño's wife, Herminia Linares, stands in the middle of the Unión de Conductores, Maquinistas, Garroteros y Fogoneros (Union of engineers, assistant engineers, brakemen, and stokers). This photo establishes the participation of women, something very important to Treviño, who wrote two plays related to women's struggles.[31] It also reveals the personal support Treviño enjoyed from his family in his political battles, something of great importance given the time he spent away from them due to his political commitments, which also included lengthy prison terms and years of exile. In another photo, from 1925, we can see the unique felt hats that *ferrocarrileros* wore in the first thirty years of the century. (See Figure 62.) This headdress may well have been an impor-

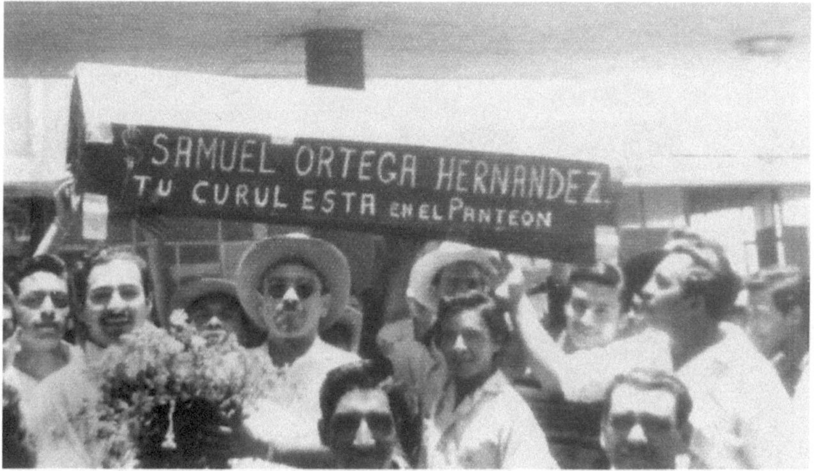

FIGURE 64. Guillermo Treviño? Protest of striking workers carrying a fake coffin with the name of Samuel Ortega, then the leader of the railroad union, Mexico City?, 1958. Archive of John Mraz.

tant element of identity among railroad workers and appears to have been worn largely by those who remained in the stations as dispatchers and telegraphers, as well as those who labored in rail yard operations, which was Treviño's position as a *patiero* (trainyard worker).[32] At the center of the photo stands Treviño, with one leg raised and his left arm akimbo; his affinity for dressing well can be appreciated in the suit, hat, white shirt, and tie slung back over his shoulder.

Catholicism is a significant part of Mexican culture, and Treviño's photo shows how workers incorporated their beliefs into their struggles. The *ferrocarrileros'* slogans on their banners decried the presence of "merchants" in their "temple of work," a reference to Matthew 21:12, "Jesus entered the temple courts and drove out all who were buying and selling there. He overturned the tables of the money changers and the benches of those selling doves."[33] (See Figure 63.) Treviño himself had an ironic take on the patron saint of Mexico: "I know all the police stations in Mexico City except one, that of La Villa, because the Virgin of Guadalupe would not accept me under any condition."[34]

A photograph taken during the important 1958–59 strikes represents what may be a singular form of worker protest that developed in those years. (See Figure 64.) In an image from Treviño's archive, striking *ferrocarrileros* hoist and pose in front of a fake coffin of then secretary general of the STFRM, Samuel Ortega Hernández, who had been installed by the government in 1957. Their writing on the coffin indicated to him that the seat of

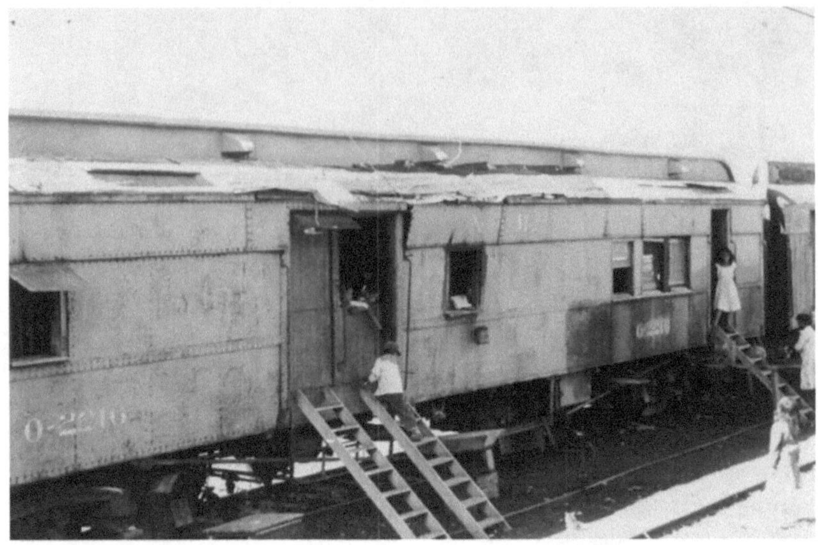

FIGURE 65. Guillermo Treviño. Ruined railroad cars in which the *ferrocarrileros'* families live, Puebla, 1958. Archive of John Mraz.

power he occupied, his *curul*, could be found in the cemetery. It does not appear that this practice had occurred before in Mexican labor struggles, and it would seem to contain a veiled threat that the sellouts will be held accountable and perhaps killed, something also expressed in the many fake "hangings" of such leaders.[35] The act is an assertion that the officialist union head is "dead" to the workers, who will now follow leaders of their own election. The carrying of fake coffins by protesting workers does not seem to have been practiced in other Latin American countries.[36] Empty coffins were carried in the Mexican student movement of 1968 to represent those who had been killed by government repression, and in the years thereafter it has been extended to human rights protests, where families of the disappeared carry coffins to represent their loved ones.

In 1958, Treviño was serving as the secretary-general of the Puebla contingent of the STFRM and decided to use his camera to document the difficult living conditions of railroad workers and their families, capturing them in the ruined train cars that served as their homes. (See Figure 65.) Such imagery was prompted by the *ferrocarrileros'* demand that the government, and the union it controlled, put into practice Article 123 of the 1917 Constitution. In the videotape *Made on Rails*, the well-known Communist *ferrocarrilero* and intellectual Valentín Campa referred precisely to this question, affirming that the strikes of 1958–59 were "the first time in Mexico that workers had forced the government to accept the validity of Section

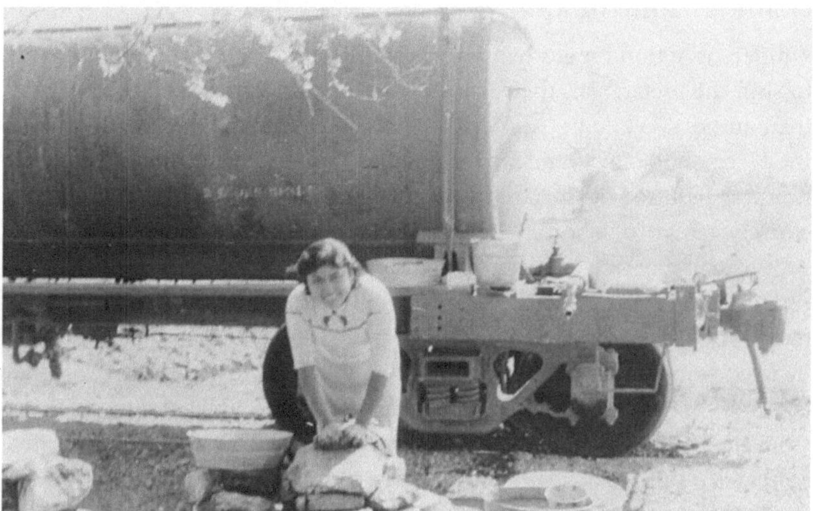

FIGURE 66. Guillermo Treviño. Woman washing clothes next to the railroad track, Puebla, 1958. Archive of John Mraz.

XXII of Article 123, which stated that every company with more than 100 workers had to construct comfortable and sanitary houses for them."[37] The lack of hygienic conditions can be appreciated in the photo of the woman washing clothes next to the tracks. (See Figure 66.) However, the rapport Treviño had with her enabled him to picture her not as a victim, but as a human being in the midst of the most mundane yet necessary activity—almost exclusively carried out by women—smiling back at him and the future viewers of her image.

When I got the position in Puebla, I found myself pulled in different directions. However, the experience of directing *Made on Rails* left me with a clear understanding that I would either have to develop a specific project of my own or remain dependent on my colleagues. I also hesitated about continuing to work toward doing a visual history of Mexican labor because so much of it was a sad tale of officialist unions governed by sold-out millionaire thugs such as Fidel Velázquez, who controlled the umbrella organization of workers, the Confederación de Trabajadores Mexicanos (CTM), almost from the moment of its founding in 1936 to his death in 1997. One possibility was to produce more vignettes of workers' lives such as the *nixtamaleras* or the petroleum workers, but I felt that I was unlikely to find similar cases where the limited information available made it excusable to cut off the research.

LABORIST PHOTOGRAPHY

A different option for studying workers' history through photographs was to shift the focus from their use as "transparent" artifacts to the study of their authors. While in CEHSMO, I had discovered the massive archive of the Hermanos Mayo, and I continued to work on them after that collection was acquired by the Archivo General de la Nación. There could be no clearer example of laborist photographers, as their very name implies: The Brothers of May Day. The most prolific photojournalist collective in the history of Latin America, the five "brothers" took the nom de guerre "Mayo," to denote their commitment to the working class. The agency was formed by five Spaniards who fought on the Republican side in the Spanish Civil War and escaped to Mexico in 1939.[38] In 1984, David Sweet obtained a grant from the University of California Consortium on Mexico and the United States (MEXUS) to have me produce five series of eighty slides each on the modern history of Mexico, made from original negatives of the Hermanos Mayo. I chose to focus on the following themes: daily life, women, images of the US in Mexico, urbanization, and work and workers. My experiences in carrying out this project gave me an idea of the immensity of the Mayo collection. The director of the AGN allowed me to separate the negative strips from the envelopes in which they were filed by the Mayo. This was a unique opportunity because the strips themselves bear no identification, and they become useless if they are left out of the envelopes that bear the information about when and where they were taken, who therein appears, and what is happening, as well as other limited data.

The director gave me two weeks to separate out the strips with negatives I wished to copy and permitted me to bring in a photographic technician to reproduce the selected images. In order to find four hundred negatives in ten days, I had to see the most possible during each visit. I soon discovered that I could only review some two thousand 35 mm negatives a day, a task that left my eyes as red and burning as Mexico City smog at its worst. Using that number as reference, I determined that if a researcher could see two thousand negatives a day, and work every day of the year (including Christmas), it would take roughly seven years to see the Mayo negatives. This method of studying photojournalism is based on comparing the images a photographer takes with those chosen for publication and, as the Mayo worked for more than forty periodicals, it is clear that it will require a team of researchers to rigorously study them as a collective.

In the face of such an overwhelming task, I have focused on specific aspects of Mayo imagery: the braceros and Mexican workers.[39] Their photos of the 1958–59 strikes have been rarely consulted or published after that period. In fact, the state of their negatives demonstrates whose history gets illustrated: their negatives of the 1968 student movement are badly scratched and scarred, while the hundreds of negatives of the 58–59 strikes are in pristine condition. Although they have largely disappeared from view, the 1958–59 strikes were of great importance, above all when seen through the optic of today's neoliberal war on the unions. With forty images from one of the series I curated an exposition, *Trabajo y trabajadores en México, 1940–1960, vistos por los Hermanos Mayo/Work and Workers in Mexico, 1940–1960, Seen by the Hermanos Mayo*, that was exhibited in the UAP and later in several US universities.

I emphasized their commitment to and documenting of workers, arguing in the catalogue and short essays that their oeuvre could be considered workers' photography because, as Julio explained in a 1986 interview, "Ninety-nine percent of our photos are the result of work orders we've received to cover stories."[40] I addressed what I perceived to be their "alienated" labor by citing photohistorian David Levi Strauss, who wrote of the imagery made by Richard Cross and John Hoagland, distinguished US photojournalists killed in El Salvador, "They did not *own* the pictures they made any more than a worker in a munitions factory owns the weapons he makes while employed."[41] While that seemed to me to be a compelling argument at the time, I later came to appreciate the complexity of studying photojournalism as a genre in the fact that the Mayo never received material or equipment from the publications for which they worked, and they never turned in a negative. They owned their negatives and did with them as they pleased, although they rarely had any say about their use in the press.

PERIODICALS AND WORKERS

The Mayo attempted to overcome their vulnerability as photojournalists through various tactics: working in a collective, possessing their own archive, and participating actively in founding and contributing to leftist publications such as the short-lived magazines *Tricolor* and *Más*, as well as the more perdurable newspaper *El Día*.[42] Héctor García was another Mexican press photographer who railed against the officialist bounds created largely through "chains of gold" and "persistent servility" to the president in power; he created a magazine, *Ojo! Una revista que ve*, which appeared once before it was destroyed.[43] Establishing an alternative press was a crucial step because Mexican journalism—prior to the appearance of lasting oppositional periodicals in 1976—largely ignored the working class except when they were engaging in vicious attacks on labor leaders. The illustrated magazines showed factories in which workers were generally absent, while machines and bosses were captured by the cameras. A labor historian has demonstrated the ambivalence of US periodicals in picturing the working class, as well as the enormous number of labor periodicals. She noted that "Images of solidarity, community, or collective, public security rarely appeared in photographic prints as something worth fighting for," and that "women workers rarely appeared as coparticipants."[44]

The problem of how to include the "working man's eye" in the mass media was addressed directly by the international worker photography movement from the mid-1920s up until the outbreak of World War II.[45] This campaign to educate workers to a new way of seeing began in Germany, but it quickly spread to countries such as Holland, Great Britain, Belgium, France, Czechoslovakia, Austria, Japan, and the US.[46] The *Arbeiter-Illustrierte-Zeitung* (*AIZ*, Workers' illustrated magazine) started publishing in 1924, the first periodical to resist the media's dependence on well-established photographic agencies, which "usually lacked images of the magazine's core theme—the working class in all aspects of its everyday life."[47] In the spring of 1926, *AIZ* organized a photo competition and provided guidelines for the contestants—documenting the revolutionary workers' movements, their social and working conditions, their daily life, and modern technology—and concluded, "You must courageously capture the beauty of your own work and workplace, but also the horrors of social misery."[48]

The contest led quickly to the founding of a monthly magazine, *Der Arbeiter-Fotograf* (The worker-photographer), where Franz Höllering explained what the task was: "Learn to see the simple great facts, photograph them plainly and clearly, so that they can't be explained away."[49] As the movement developed, the cultural policies of the Communist International (Comintern), during its turn to the left from 1928 through 1935, attempted to link progressive film and photo groups in the Soviet Union with those in other countries. Its policy of "class against class sought to mobilize and politicize the broadest possible sections of the working class by appealing to them directly as a class, irrespective of the political parties to which they belonged."[50] The slogan of the Dutch Association of Worker Photographers (VAF, Vereenigning van Arbeiders-Fotografen) called for "our own life by our own photographers in our own press."[51] Men and women workers entered the different proletarian clubs, some simply to learn how to photograph; being a member of the Communist Party was not required, and the only stipulation was that they not belong to a bourgeois camera group.

There is no evidence that the documentary photography these associations promoted had any influence in Mexico, although the photomontages by John Heartfield on many of the *AIZ* covers certainly did. The Hermanos Mayo would seem to have been the most likely collective to have had some connection, but both Julio and Faustino denied that any equivalent existed in Spain.[52] Paco was the Mayo who would have been most informed about these movements; unfortunately, he died in 1949. Nonetheless, the creation of these leftist cultural movements did have some consequences, for Cristina Zelich has written of Spanish photography that,

> During this period more than any other, photographs appeared containing a degree of overt or implicit ideology which greatly contributed to the political dialectic: from portrait albums conceived as ethnographic documents . . . to works with a clear and obvious ideological basis (such as those produced by the *Arbeiter Fotografie* in Germany or later by the Film and Photo League in the United States). Finally, photojournalistic activities (cinema newsreels are an example) concerning the Spanish Civil War, for instance, represented simply an institutionalized use of the photographic image as a means of promoting certain currents of public opinion. Following this general spirit, Spanish documentary photography in the era between the World Wars centered on popular themes.[53]

The Mexican photographer who would have had the most direct connection to the photo leagues is Tina Modotti, who was deeply involved with the Comintern's International Red Aid organization in Mexico, and made a photo of Diego Rivera addressing a rally with the group's banner behind him in Tizayuca, Hidalgo, April 4, 1929. She had published a photo on the cover of *AIZ* in 1928 but does not appear to have had any direct relationship with the workers' photography movement until she arrived in Berlin in 1930, when she immediately connected with them through the magazine's editor, Willi Münzenburg. One key member, Eugen Heilig, provided her with a press pass through his agency Unionfoto.[54] Several of her photos were published on the cover of *AIZ* and featured in *Der Arbeiter-Fotograf*; she also mounted a small exhibit in the studio of photographer Lotte Jacobi.[55] However, she was financially strapped and faced technical difficulties because the Graflex camera she had brought with her was out-of-date in Germany, where photographers used more compact cameras that were less conspicuous and bulky. The new equipment held different film, so Modotti had to order Graflex stock from the US, and even the German paper size was distinct.

Modotti's style and training in photography was best suited for portraiture, which was not a feasible option because Berlin was full of established studio photographers. Moreover, she did not like working with the smaller cameras, nor did she feel that she was fit to do news reportage. Her comments on the limitations she felt provide an interesting insight into how even this revolutionary woman was affected by the ways in which gender construction creates roles that deny women the opportunity to empower themselves:

> I still think it [photojournalism] is a man's work in spite that here many women do it; perhaps they can, I am not aggressive enough. Even the type of propaganda picture I began to do in Mexico is already being done here: there is an association of "worker-photographers" (here everybody uses a camera) and the workers themselves make those pictures and have indeed better opportunities than I could ever have, since it is their own life, and problems they photograph. Of course, their results are far from the standard I am struggling to keep up in photography, but their end is reached just the same.[56]

THROUGH PROGRESSIVE EYES

Photography has been a crucial tool of leftist imagemakers in Mexico, with its capacity to render visible contradictions that are disguised by the bourgeois media, to document mass movements against injustice and corruption as well as the repression of this opposition, to critically examine forms of representation that reproduce and validate inequalities, and to testify to the imperialist invasions that maintain the "open veins of Latin America."[57] One would expect no less in a culture that emphasizes the ocular, in which extreme class difference and neocolonialist effects are transparently obvious, though the survival of traditional cultures often circulates as the picturesquely natural face of the country. In 1978, the Consejo Mexicano de Fotografía made explicit the commitment expected of Latin American photographers in the call for participants in the important international exhibit *Hecho en Latinoamérica*: "Photographers . . . face the responsibility to interpret the beauty and conflicts, the triumphs and defeats and aspirations of their peoples (*pueblos*). . . . They refine and affirm their perception expressing the reactions of men before a society in crisis, and, in consequence, attempt to realize an art of commitment and not of evasion."[58]

The Mexican Revolution had brought about fundamental changes in image production and circulation, permitting critical photos to find a place in the larger culture for the first time. During that struggle, the photographers connected to the popular movements—Maderista, Villista, Zapatista, or Constitutionalista—visually expressed a progressive point of view. They were often regional studio photographers who saw the possibility of articulating their commitments and having their work subsidized. The Mexico City studio of Heliodoro J. Gutiérrez was linked to the Maderista movement from its beginning, when Aurelio Escobar went north to cover the rebellion, while Gutiérrez looked for ways to document the resistance in the metropole, making the agency the first revolutionary photographic protagonist.[59] Photojournalist Gerónimo Hernández was a key Maderista imagemaker during the truncated presidency, working for the newspaper that most supported that cause, *Nueva Era*.[60] Another Maderista was Eulalio Robles, a studio photographer from Zacatecas, who sold buttons with Madero's image and then later appears to have served as a spy for the Villista forces attacking the city, providing images of the federal army's geographic distribution, their condition, and the location of their artillery, as well as its characteristics.[61] Pascual Orozco's rebellion against Madero was, in the beginning, similar to the Zapatistas' continued resistance against the northern bourgeoisie.[62] The photographer most engaged with that movement seems to have been Ignacio Medrano Chávez, a studio photographer from Chihuahua City known as *El gran lente*.[63] Amando Salmerón belonged to a family studio in Chilpancingo, Guerrero, and became the photographer of Emiliano Zapata.[64] However, there were other photographers connected to that movement, among them Cruz Sánchez, a professional photographer who was also the municipal president of Yautepec, Morelos.[65] A certain Hernández appears to have been the imagemaker for Domingo Arenas, agrarian revolutionary from the Puebla region.[66] The Cachú brothers, Antonio and Juan, were itinerant photographers from Michocán who performed plays and made portraits; they became the photographers closest to Pancho Villa.[67] As the wealthiest and least progressive force, the Constitutionalists had many imagemakers, including the vast majority of Mexico City's photojournalists. However, a studio photographer from Hermosillo, Sonora, Jesús H. Abitia joined the Maderista movement from the beginning and has been considered "*The* Constitutionalist photographer."[68]

For a studio photographer from Teloloapan, Guerrero, the question of commitment was more complex. The only woman to extensively document the revolution, Sara Castrejón appears to have had an early allegiance to the Maderista-Zapatista forces, particularly those under the command of Jesús Salgado.[69] However, she never left Teloloapan and documented the different armies as they passed through the city. Among her tasks was that

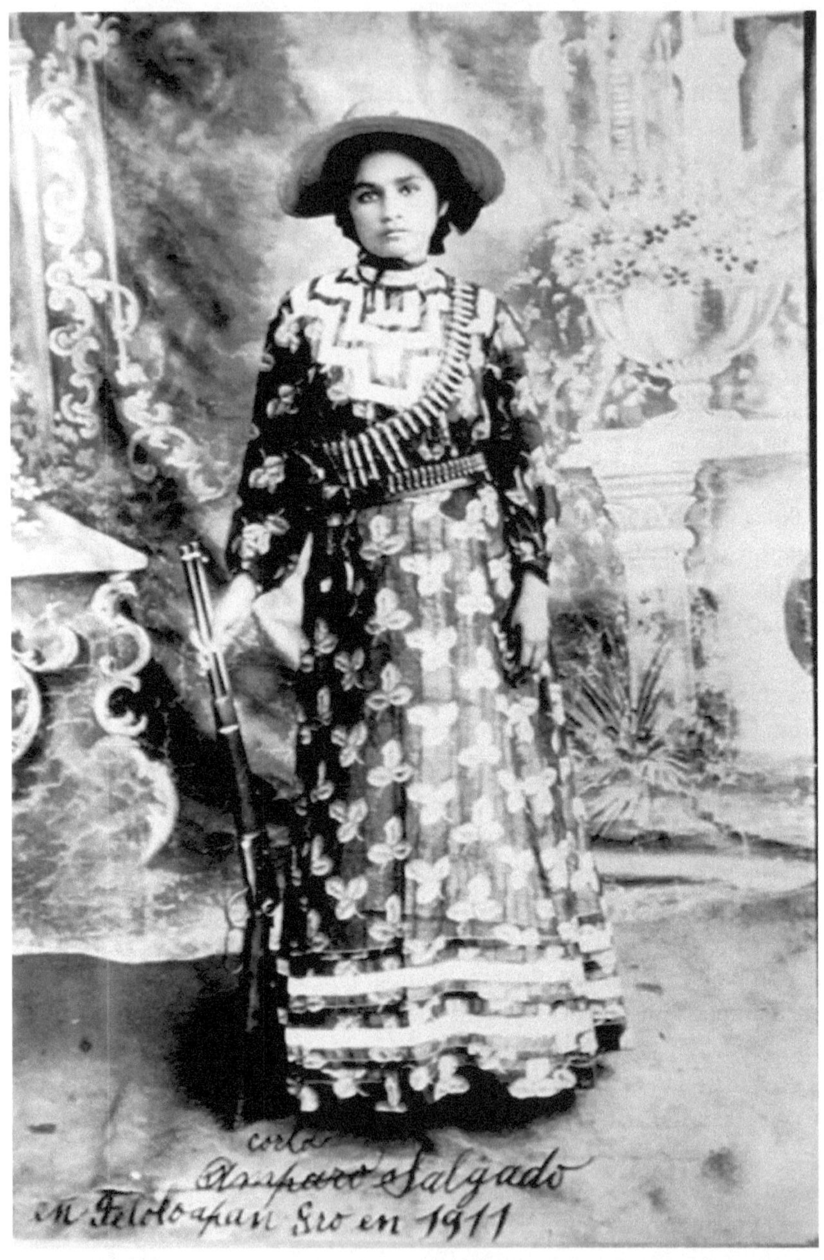

FIGURE 67. Sara Castrejón. Salgadista-Zapatista-Maderista Colonel Amparo Salgado, Teloloapan, Guerrero, April 1911. Courtesy of Consuelo Castrejón.

of photographing young men about to be executed to provide a last image for the families and then documenting the execution as proof for the federal army. Nonetheless, perhaps her greatest commitment was to testify to the participation of women in that struggle. (See Figure 67.) In the photo of the Salgadista colonel Amparo Salgado, the ornate backdrop painted by Sara's sister provides an intriguing play with the floral motifs of her dress. It is noteworthy that Salgado wore this dress (or Sara decided to have her wear it), because it was apparently not the customary way in which the colonel dressed. Rather, she was described as "a crazy woman who ran around with the men, armed, and dressed in pants," a testimony provided by Lucila Figueroa, a highly conservative anti-Zapatista woman from Teloloapan's upper class and a member of the Figueroa clan that would rule Guerrero for many decades.[70]

Was she clothed in a fancy dress, an elegant hat, and highly buffed (perhaps high-heeled) shoes as a strategy to address her gender and how it is usually pictured? If so, the rifle, pistol, and cartridge belts stand in stark juxtaposition to the femininity of her attire, offering an example Barthes' famous "punctum." The colonel was the daughter of the entrepreneur Florencio Salgado, and her decision to join the rebellion marked a severe rupture with her well-off family. She was disinherited, left Guerrero with *agrarista* forces, and died in Michoacán, although the cause of her death is unknown.[71] She participated in the armed struggle, leading both men and women into combat, so the arms that appear in the photo were not simply decoration as was often the case with this performance trope.[72] I believe that Castrejón's gender consciousness—her recognition and hence representation of the active role women were taking in the conflict—led her to make this complex, contestatory image of Amparo, which I consider to be her most powerful photograph of the revolution, but it is not the only one in which women appear.

The key photographer of the postrevolutionary cultural effervescence was Tina Modotti. Her pictures in *El Machete*, the newspaper of the Partido Comunista Mexicano (PCM), matched the powerful woodcut prints and line drawings of Xavier Guerrero, David Alfaro Siqueiros, and José Clemente Orozco. Modotti entered into the periodical in 1924, doing translations from Italian, but it was only in 1927 that she began publishing radical photojournalistic and advertising imagery. One of her images demonstrates the direct connection of her pictures to socialist programs. (See Figure 68.) For me, it also testifies to the inadequacy of non-contextualist speculation about photographic meaning. The figure of a *campesino* family grouped together in front of an adobe wall with a foreground composed of corncobs was, until recently, a

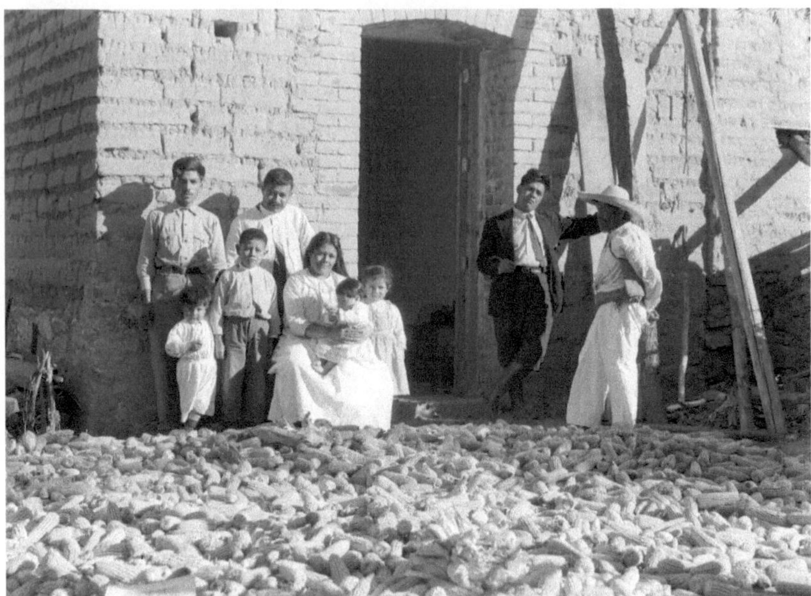

FIGURE 68. Tina Modotti. *The Harvest of the President of the Agrarian Committee of Chiconcuac, with which the Seeds will be Selected for the Next Planting*, Chiconcuac, Mexico State. Inv. # 842259, SINAFO-Fototeca Nacional del INAH, Secretaría de Cultura.

conundrum for photohistorians. In an earlier work, I asked whether the dark doorway that bifurcates the picture, with the family on one side and a man dressed in a Western suit on the other, might be a critical commentary on the "internal colonialism" carried out by *ladinos* in *campesino* communities.[73]

Subsequent research has established that the image is of Miguel Delgado, president of the Chiconcuac's Agrarian Committee, and his family, posing in front of their corn harvest. The man dressed in the suit is probably a teacher in the Escuelas Libres de Agricultura (Free Agricultural Schools) of Mexico founded by Pandurang Khankhoie, a Communist agronomist from India. Further, one of Modotti's still lifes was used as the letterhead symbol of the Escuelas Libres de Agricultura, that of the sickle, cartridge belt, and corncob.[74] As Massé has argued, this composition represented "a conceptual synthesis of three revolutions: the Mexican, the Bolshevik, and the green revolution driven by the pedagogical projects of the Free Agricultural Schools."[75] The presence of Concha Michel—a political activist and folk singer—in a couple of Modotti's photos taken at the Escuela Libre de Agricultura Emiliano Zapata in 1928 also allows us to locate these images, which were formerly identified only as "Woman playing guitar."[76]

The most iconic image of worker repression in Latin America—and certainly one of the most reproduced of images from these latitudes—is

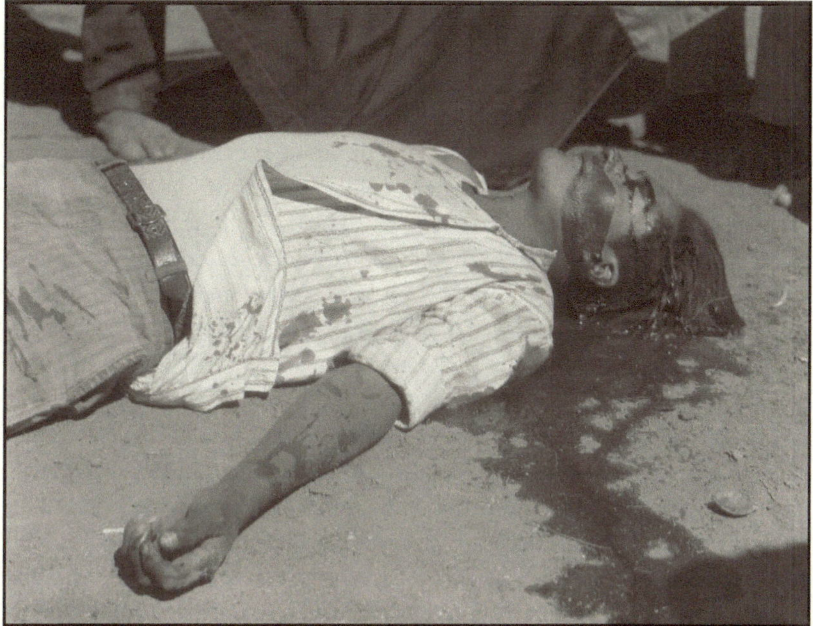

FIGURE 69. Manuel Álvarez Bravo. *Obrero en huelga asesinado* (Striking worker assassinated), Veracruz, 1934. Archivo Manuel Álvarez Bravo, Copyright Colette Urbajtel.

Manuel Álvarez Bravo's *Obrero en huelga, asesinado* (1934; Striking worker, assassinated). (See Figure 69.) Scattered references to his politics address this photo, though it is generally seen as somewhat of an anomaly in his work. Because his images are often displayed in "apolitical" art exhibits, his critical eye is often subsumed in an emphasis on his complex esthetic, sometimes referred to as his "indigenous vision."[77] However, he was a key "participant in the most brilliant period of cultural nationalism" during the 1920s and 1930s.[78] In the first half of the '30s, the artist was particularly engaged in producing photos with a "social content" and has identified similar examples of critical imagery: *Los agachados* (1932 or 1934) and *Trabajadores de fuego* (1935).[79] I would include his decolonizing, antipicturesque pictures from that period that show this progressive vision, such as *Señor de Papantla* (1934) and *Sed pública* (1934), the latter of which the photographer insisted be displayed next to *Obrero* in his books and exhibits.[80]

The "veracity" of *Obrero* depends upon whether the title corresponds to that which we see pictured, a subject that has not yet been researched in depth. One scholar believes that this image is not what it purports to be, but that it was misleadingly identified as an incident of labor struggle to serve a particular purpose: "Manuel Álvarez Bravo's photo did not capture an act of repression but an accident. However, the epoch's turbulence determined its political use."[81] This is an issue of importance that I believe is resolved by the image from the only other negative of that incident that I have published here, in which bare feet are seen next to the pennant, suggesting they belonged to members of a group of sugar cane workers who formed around the body, holding the colors of their union.[82] The photographer's trip to Tehuantepec, where he says the incident occurred, has been well documented in interviews with him. He had acquired a movie camera from Eduard Tissé, Sergei Eisenstein's cinematographer, and was given a thousand feet of film by Carlos Chávez, a pivotal figure in the postrevolutionary culture, both as a composer and director of the National Institute of Bellas Artes.[83]

His new equipment was first put to use in filming what he described as a superficial essay that featured picturesque Tehuantepec and its legendarily beautiful women. While shooting on a tripod, he heard what he thought were fireworks for a fiesta, and grabbed his cameras, both moving and still, to document it. When he arrived on the scene, he discovered that the sounds had been gunfire; a striking sugarmill worker had been killed by a scab: "I had a Graflex, and there were two shots left. I didn't look for an angle. I didn't have any preconceived ideas. I just had an impulse and photographed."[84] Recognizing that he had little film, and limited time—locals urged him to move on quickly because he had no idea what he was getting into—he created an unforgettable icon. It is shot right up next to the man, harshly cropped from the waist up, very low to the ground, and with an expressive angle in which we are drawn into the photo by the extended arm that leads us to the bloodied head and the union banners. This provides an incredible intimacy with him, as if one were related to or attempting to aid him; we are the brother of the fallen comrade.

Álvarez Bravo was looking to send an explicit message about the underpaid and badly treated sugarcane workers, their organized resistance, and "one heroic death . . . not a general statement of violent death."[85] In the beginning he apparently felt that the photo needed no further explanation than the picture itself, but it has been much republished, and at times incorporated into essentialist and reactionary readings linking it to pre-Hispanic "ritual sacrifice," which one scholars argues, provides "An ecstatic indulgence of violence to reinforce the existing social order rather than overturn it."[86] Death is certainly a major theme in the photographer's work, and as he says, "I think the symbols one can find in my photographs essentially refer to life and death."[87] Nonetheless, he made it clear that this image was about a very particular case. The image provides information about the event itself that had been found rather than created—for instance, the feet and background flag testify to the presence of organized labor—but is so esthetically expressive that it transcends that immediate context to become a larger truth about capitalists' willingness to employ the ultimate punishment to conserve their privileges. For that reason, Álvarez Bravo created a title that was designed to make a specific point:

> In a certain moment I made a photo with a very concrete intention. I am referring to *Obrero en huelga, asesinado*. . . . I remember that a journalist alluded to it as "the photo of a dead man with a strand of blood seeping from his mouth." I, evidently, wanted to photograph and express something more than that. In order to pin down my intention, I had to title the photo. Here I see the advantage of the written word: it is more concrete. "Worker" means "worker," and on reading the word "strike" everybody knows what that's about.[88]

If *Obrero* were the photo of a worker killed accidently, this image would lose the power of having fused the informative and the expressive, although the title would articulate to an even greater degree the photographer's critique of capitalism.[89] However, although the photographer's intention is explicit in either case—and from the perspective of cultural history it could be argued that it is irrelevant whether the image is veridical—I believe that whether it is what it purports to be certainly constitutes information important for photohistorians. The fact that he would so explicitly identify the image underlines his commitment, for he had moved toward a realist esthetic, pulled away from his earlier interest in visual poetics by the impact of the world depression. Many Mexican intellectuals and artists were leftist in this period, including Álvarez Bravo who, though he never joined the Mexican Communist Party, was a member of LEAR (Liga de Escritores y Artistas Revolucionarios).

One early appearance of the photo was on the cover of the May Day issue of LEAR's magazine *Frente a frente* (Face to face) in 1936; there, a photomontage was constructed that placed the dead striker beneath the portraits of Adolf Hitler, Benito Mussolini, and Plutarco Elías Calles. (See Figure 70.) Although Álvarez Bravo would later insist that the dead man was a worker, the image was described in the following way in *Frente a frente*: "*Campesino* assassinated by the *hacendado's* private police forces in his struggle for land" (*Campesino asesinado por guardias blancas en la lucha por la tierra*).[90] The photographer participated in that issue, where it was reproduced in a "graphic reportage," "*México es feliz*" (Mexico is happy).

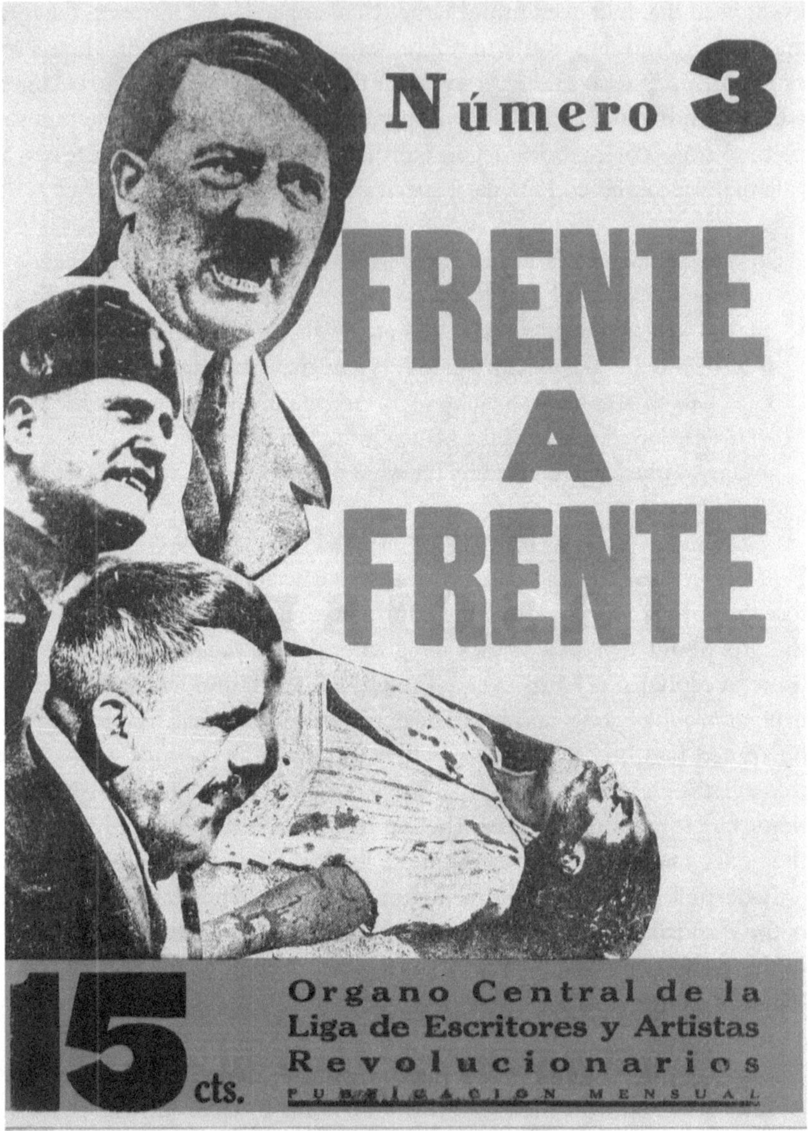

FIGURE 70. Cover of *Frente a frente*, 3 (May 1936). Archive of John Mraz.

Although the title differs from what it would eventually become, there was probably little difference between workers in the sugar fields and the mill. Álvarez Bravo collaborated with Enrique Gutmann (Heinrich Gutmann), a German refugee who continued with leftist activities after arriving in Mexico. Gutmann became the director of photography for *Frente a frente*, and worked with Vicente Lombardo Toledano in *Futuro*, but little else is known about him, other than he apparently was active in México during the period from 1935 to 1941.[91]

Lola Álvarez Bravo (Dolores Martínez de Anda), appears to have been a more active member of LEAR than her husband, Manuel, and one of her photomontages filled a cover of *Frente a frente.* Lola had been born into a wealthy family but on her father's death she was sent to live with a very pious aunt who attempted to make Lola into a "good girl . . . wanting to teach me how to serve tea and such things. I immediately felt a great rebellion."[92] On separating from Manuel in 1934, she determined to make her living as a photographer and joined the magazine *El Maestro Rural*, one of the socialist education projects of Narciso Bassols, a visionary administrator who had been responsible for, among other progressive ventures, bringing Paul Strand down to photograph, as well as make the classic film *Redes.* Mexico had a profound effect on Strand. As photohistorian James Krippner remarked, "He became a full-fledged Marxist in Mexico, and remained a Marxist for the rest of his life."[93] As is to be expected in US art institutions, Strand's political commitment was always downplayed by Aperture, the institution to which he willed many negatives and that has been the principal editor of his published works.

Although she provided countless images for *El Maestro Rural* from all corners of Mexico, Lola's work was often published without credit. Developing a Modernist style that complemented the magazine's leftist perspective, she took close-ups of hands at work, often shot with extreme angles. However, her most radical experimentation was in creating photomontages such as *El sueño de los pobres*, influenced by leftist artists such as John Heartfield and Josep Renau.[94] She had taken photographs of a boy sleeping in a rural market but, for the montage, she dirtied his clothes and body, and then situated him under a bizarre machine that appears ready to bury him with coins or gobble him up and convert him into money. The photomontage was originally created for a 1935 Guadalajara exhibit of revolutionary posters made by women.

Lola had an eye for portraying racial and gender discrimination in Mexico. She was particularly interested in documenting the lives of remote Indian communities such as Yalálog, Oaxaca; her image of a burial there was included in Edward Steichen's famous exhibit *Family of Man* (1955). She affirmed, "My commitment is to care for and conserve the beauty of the race and make the people who cause their misery feel shame when confronted with the Indian's poverty, abandonment, and their slow and terrible death."[95] She incorporated metaphors for the prisons in which Mexican and Indian women find themselves. Her photograph *Por culpas ajenas*

(Through the fault of others), of a blind, seemingly desperate Indian woman in front of iron bars that serve as a synecdoche for her incarceration, is an articulate expression of Lola's perspective. Another of Lola's photos is a poignant rendering of a woman trapped in her domestic duties, *En su propia cárcel* (In her own jail), in which she employs the shadow of bars to create the prison of her daily life.[96] While working as a photojournalist—then an almost exclusively masculine profession—she was harassed by reactionaries such as Enrique Díaz, but the Hermanos Mayo respected her work.

The political consistency of the Hermanos Mayo and Enrique Gutmann stands as an exception to that of other leftist refugees. For example, Walter Reuter had participated in the *Arbeiter Illustrierte Zeitung* and photographed for the Republicans in the Spanish Civil War. However, he stated, "I never made a negative photo of Mexico: never. . . . My reportages were positive; I never criticized, but always supported the positive side of the government and the Mexicans. Because first of all they saved my life."[97] Nonetheless, Reuter took some photos that embody an implicitly critical vision.[98] Other leftist refugees largely abandoned political imagery. Juan Guzmán (Hans Gutmann, 1911–1982) fled Germany and joined the Partido Comunista Español in 1936, but he apparently made no critical imagery in Mexico.[99] Kati Horna considered herself to be "an artistic laborer, linked to the Spanish Civil War by ideological affinity," and she was deeply involved with anarchist publications of the Confederación Nacional de Trabajo.[100] However, it does not appear that she made any truly leftist photography after coming to Mexico, instead focusing largely on making portraits, although she did do some reportage for different Mexican magazines.[101] Mariana Yampolsky was a later immigrant; she came from the US in 1945 and was quickly integrated into the Taller de Gráfica Popular, a leftist organization dedicated to creating political art that had been founded by Leopoldo Méndez, among others. She was joined in the Taller by US artist Elizabeth Catlett in the following year, and both remained in Mexico until their deaths. Yampolsky's socialist sympathies must have fit well into that atmosphere; nonetheless, her photography generally focused on common people, particularly Amerindians, in rural communities.

Mexican photojournalists Nacho López and Héctor García made vital contributions to progressive imagery, but little has been written about another leftist photographer of this generation, Enrique Bordes Mangel.[102] He worked for several critical entities: the magazines *Política* and *Rototemas*, as well as the publications of the electricians' union, *Lux* and *Solidaridad*. He also provided images for *Mañana*, *Siempre*, *El Nacional*, and other periodicals, often working for the Agencia Prensa Latina. He felt

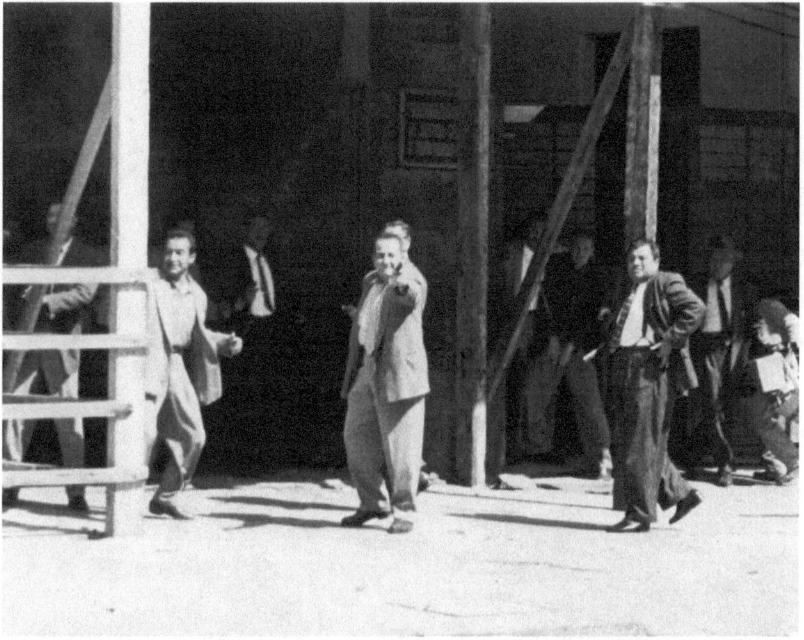

FIGURE 71. Enrique Bordes Mangel. *Mi pelotón de fusilamiento* (My firing squad), plain-clothes policeman points gun at Bordes Mangel, Mexico City, 25 August 1958. Archivo Fotográfico "Manuel Toussaint" del Instituto de Investigaciones Estéticas de la UNAM.

that photojournalism "allows you to show events as they happened," but it should always be carried out "in a committed manner, with honesty and courage, putting myself *on the edge* [*al filo*]."[103] For Bordes Mangel, being a graphic reporter "is one way to confront occurrences and to avoid that others write history at their whim, for which reason it is a practice that should never be abandoned."[104] He retrieved his negatives after their use and maintained his archive of some twenty-two thousand images. However, faced with great economic difficulties caused by a long-term illness, he sold it in 1989 to a Licenciado César Fentanes Méndez who later disappeared; this has been one factor contributing to the absence of studies on his work. While covering the 1958 strikes, he took a photo of judicial police in front of the Procuraduría del Distrito Federal; one of them pointed his pistol at Bordes Mangel and evidently shot at the photojournalist, but Bordes' aim was superior. He named the photo *Mi pelotón de fusilamiento* (My firing squad), perhaps a tribute to his father who had served in the Mexican Revolution, and the photograph circulated widely. (See Figure 71.)

He continued to cover attacks on civil dissidence in the 1960s, as the government sent the police and army against marches in favor of the Cuban

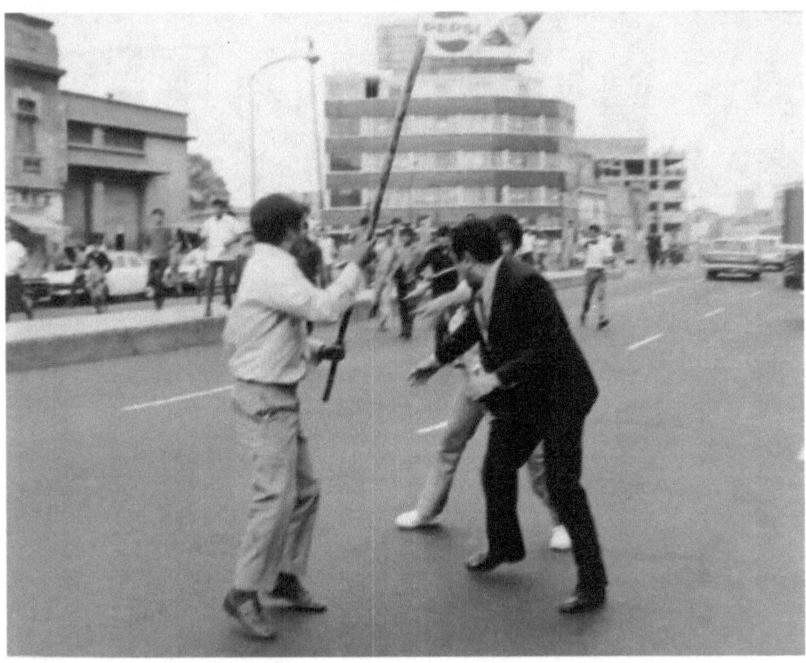

FIGURE 72. Enrique Bordes Mangel. Photojournalist Alfonso Carrillo attacked by *halcones* ("hawks," hired thugs), Mexico City, 10 July 1971. Archivo Fotográfico "Manuel Toussaint" del Instituto de Investigaciones Estéticas de la UNAM.

Revolution as well as those against the Vietnam invasion, the strikes by doctors and nurses in 1965, and the 1968 student movement. On July 10, 1971, he photographed the repression of workers and students carried out by the *halcones* (hawks), thugs financed by President Luis Echevarría when he decided to stifle opposition to his regime.[105] The *halcones* were a paramilitary group that had been well trained and armed with kendo sticks and steel rods as well as rifles and pistols to ensure that social movements such as those that had developed in 1958 and 1968 did not recur. They had specific instructions to destroy the photojournalists' cameras: as Bordes Mangel recounted, "I was struck from behind by a *granadero's* [anti-riot police] rifle butt, and when I tried to go forward toward the march a guy appeared in front of me yelling, 'Get the cameras, get the cameras!' They had been told to break our cameras so that there was no proof."[106]

Many photojournalists and reporters were beaten and kidnapped, and their cameras were destroyed; Bordes Mangel photographed his colleague Alfonso Carrillo being attacked. (See Figure 72.) Having changed his roll before he was assaulted, Bordes Mangel knew he had publishable photos; he gave some to Carrillo, who had been left without images when his camera was destroyed. Bordes Mangel alleges that Carrillo showed little gratitude, "Carrillo asked if I could give him some photos so that he would not have to return empty-handed. . . . He ended up shamelessly crediting them to himself and won a journalism prize with my photos."[107] Soon thereafter Bordes Mangel received death threats for the photos of the *halcones* and spent the decade of 1973 to 1983 in a Canadian exile. When he returned to Mexico, he continued documenting leftist movements such as the rise of the Partido Revolucionario Democrático (PRD) and urban support for the Neo-Zapatista rebellion.

NEOCOLONIALISM AND DECOLONIZATION

The preeminent decolonizing Mexican photojournalist is Rodrigo Moya, who covered US invasions of Panama and the Dominican Republic as well as armed rebellions around Latin America. Hence he is also a bridge to the internationalism practiced by the New Photojournalists, because he is the first Mexican to function as a war correspondent outside of the country.[108] He photographically served leftist causes between 1955 and 1968, beginning his labors in the magazine *Impacto*, for which he made reportages on the strikes of 1958–59. There he developed his concept of the "double camera" he carried in his mind, which I have discussed in Chapter 3. He left the magazine in 1959, unhappy with its refusal to publish critical imagery. Joining the Mexican Communist Party in 1961, he provided images to a variety of Mexican periodicals. While working freelance, he covered marches against the Bay of Pigs invasion as well as those protesting the US intervention in Vietnam. Always outspoken and opinionated, Rodrigo wrote me after having read my book *Looking for Mexico*, in which I asserted that the Hermanos Mayo, Héctor García, and Enrique Bordes Mangel had made the best images of the 1958–1959 strikes. Moya retorted:

> I don't agree. Those you mention often worked beside or behind the police, the *granaderos*, or the secret agents of the Dirección Federal de Seguridad, with whom they were friends [*cuates*]. I, on the other hand, viscerally detested them from a young age. That's why my close relations with the strikers enabled me to take better images in the middle of the battles. The Mayo are upright, though not always, but the others convey the point of view of the repressors; they are on the side of the law, of power, among the soldiers. My work was so good that the magazine negotiated in order not to publish it, and I was only able to recover part of my negatives.[109]

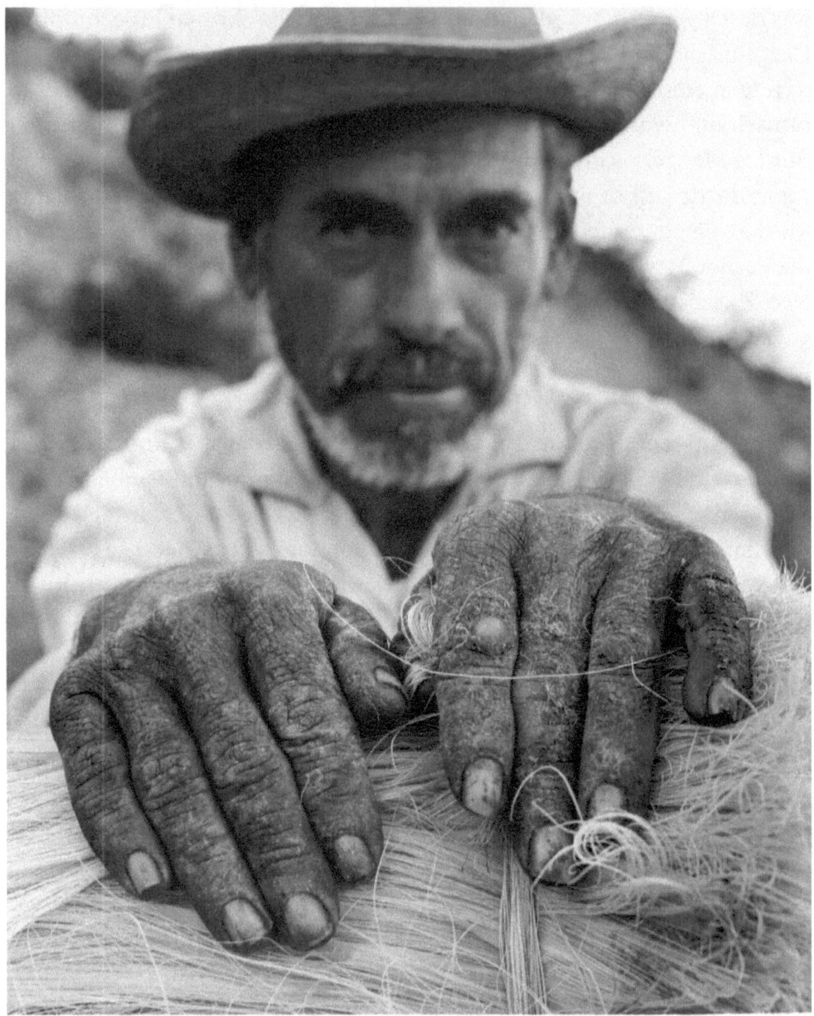

FIGURE 73. Rodrigo Moya. *Ixtelero*, a campesino who extracts fiber from agave plants, northern Mexico, 1966. Courtesy of Rodrigo Moya.

Whether we agree or not with Moya, his position provides food for thought, and there is little question that many of the photos in the Casasola Archive demonstrate that they were taken from the side of the powerful. In 1964, Moya joined the staff of *Sucesos para Todos*, "Bastion of the Mexican and Latin American left, and a forum for their debates."[110] There, one of his photoreportages, "El ixtle es hambre" (The *ixtle* is hunger), focused on the marginalization and extreme poverty of the two million *campesinos* in the northern deserts who work as independent gatherers of *ixtle*, a fibrous plant

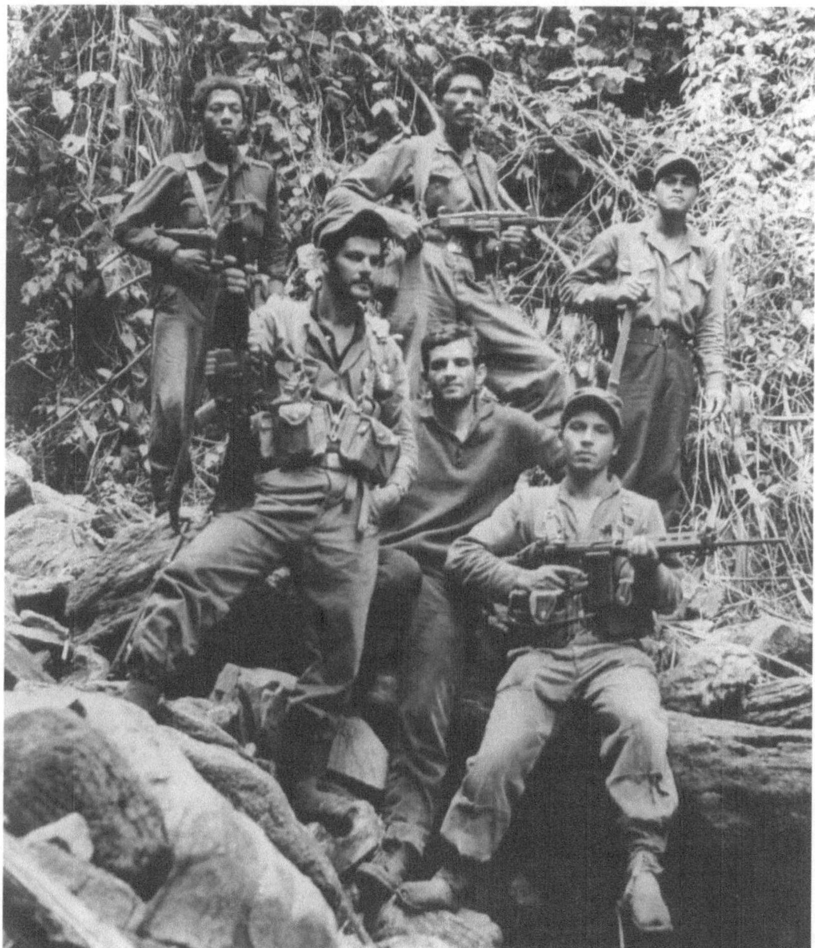

FIGURE 74. Rodrigo Moya. *Guerrilleros en la niebla* (Guerrillas in the fog); Moya with the guerrilla in Sierra Falcón, Venezuela, 1966. Courtesy of Rodrigo Moya.

similar to agave that grows in the wild. Moya collaborated with the journalist Froylán Manjarrez to produce a graphic report of twenty-six pages and more than thirty photos on the misery in which these workers and their families lived, earning around a peso a day, often in coupons redeemable only in the overpriced stores of local merchants, a situation reminiscent of the *Porfiriato*'s company stores. Rodrigo had one *campesino* pose and sharply focused on his hands callused by the tannins which damage the skin as workers separate out the fiber from the plant. (See Figure 73.)

Moya began his odyssey of documenting imperialism and revolution in 1964, traveling to Cuba to cover the transformations wrought as well as make portraits of Che Guevara, and then on to Panamá to denounce the massacre of civilians by US Marines in complicity with the United Fruit Company. A year later he managed to get into the Dominican Republic to cover the US invasion, the only photographer to break the information barrier that had been established. There, he came under fire but was always protected by "the young men who were suicidal dreamers."[111] In 1966, he entered Guatemala, where he and Mario Menéndez, director of *Sucesos*, spent five weeks passing as tourists while they made contact with the guerrillas; they lived with them in the mountains for a week. There, he was forced to photograph the killing of an individual who was accused of collaborating with the army. Although both Moya and the guerrilla leader objected to the summary execution, Menéndez insisted because it would be a scoop for his magazine. Soon thereafter Moya and Menéndez went to Venezuela and linked up with the guerrilla forces of Douglas Bravo and Luben Petkoff; among the photos made by Moya is one in which he appears alongside the rebels. (See Figure 74.) Moya became increasingly disenchanted with Menéndez and his political adventurism. As he explained in one of his "Encromes" (Ensayos-crónicas-memorias), "When Che died I understood that my work was outside of time and place, and I slowly abandoned photography."[112] Rodrigo dedicated himself to other projects and only began to order and make his archive available in the early 1990s, but his imagery and articulate texts have since appeared in several important books and exhibits.[113]

WORKER AND FEMINIST IMAGERY

In recent years, some photographers have come from within progressive projects. Jorge Acevedo Mendoza photographed social movements at his own initiative while working for the INAH. Labor struggles were of particular interest to him because he was much involved in the INAH's union, at one time serving as the Secretary General of that syndicate.[114] He followed the various demonstrations of the Tendencia Democrática within the electrical workers' union (SUTERM, Sindicato Único de Trabajadores Electricistas de la República Mexicana), as well as those who labored in the General Motors plants, participating as both a demonstrator and a witness armed with a camera. His images were published in several magazines but, more importantly, circulated in posters, pamphlets, and labor publications, often without credit.[115] He was a member of the Sindicato Nacional de Trabajadores de la Educación (SNTE), the largest teachers' union in Latin America, because the INAH was then under the Secretariat of Public

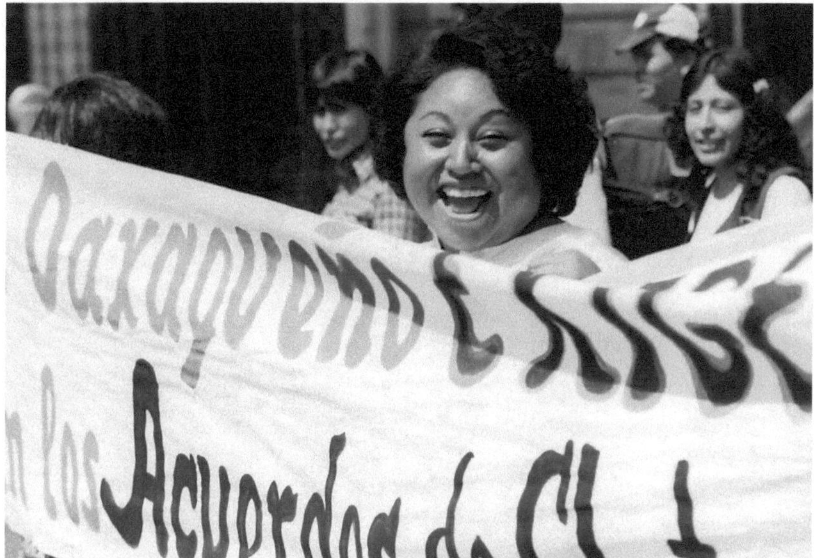

FIGURE 75. Jorge Acevedo Mendoza. Oaxacan teachers protesting in Mexico City, 1980. Courtesy of Jorge Acevedo Mendoza.

Education (SEP). However, he switched his allegiance to the more progressive Coordinadora Nacional de Trabajadores de Educación (CNTE), when it was founded in the poorer southern states during 1979 as a response to the extensive corruption and antidemocractic tendencies of the SNTE. When the combative Oaxacan CNTE teachers came to Mexico City, he captured one of the protestors in a dynamic and powerful shot. (See Figure 75.) He became deeply involved with this union, which continues to battle against the abysmal salaries and harsh working conditions for Mexican teachers, as well as the government repression to which they are periodically subject; in 1986, he moved to Oaxaca in order to work more directly with them. He was employed by the INAH, but—in a similar strategy to Moya's—Acevedo always carried two cameras. One was provided by the INAH and he utilized it to document archeological sites, turning in the negative strips at the end of a shoot. However, he was always alert to photographing social problems and unrest, which he captured with his own camera. Acevedo was also one of the few photographers to document the feminist movement.[116]

Among those imagemakers to cover the neofeminist movement extensively was Ana Victoria Jiménez, who photographed it from its inception in 1970 up until 1990. She documented the 1971 protest at the Monumento a la Madre (the first neofeminist act of resistance, and a site at which such

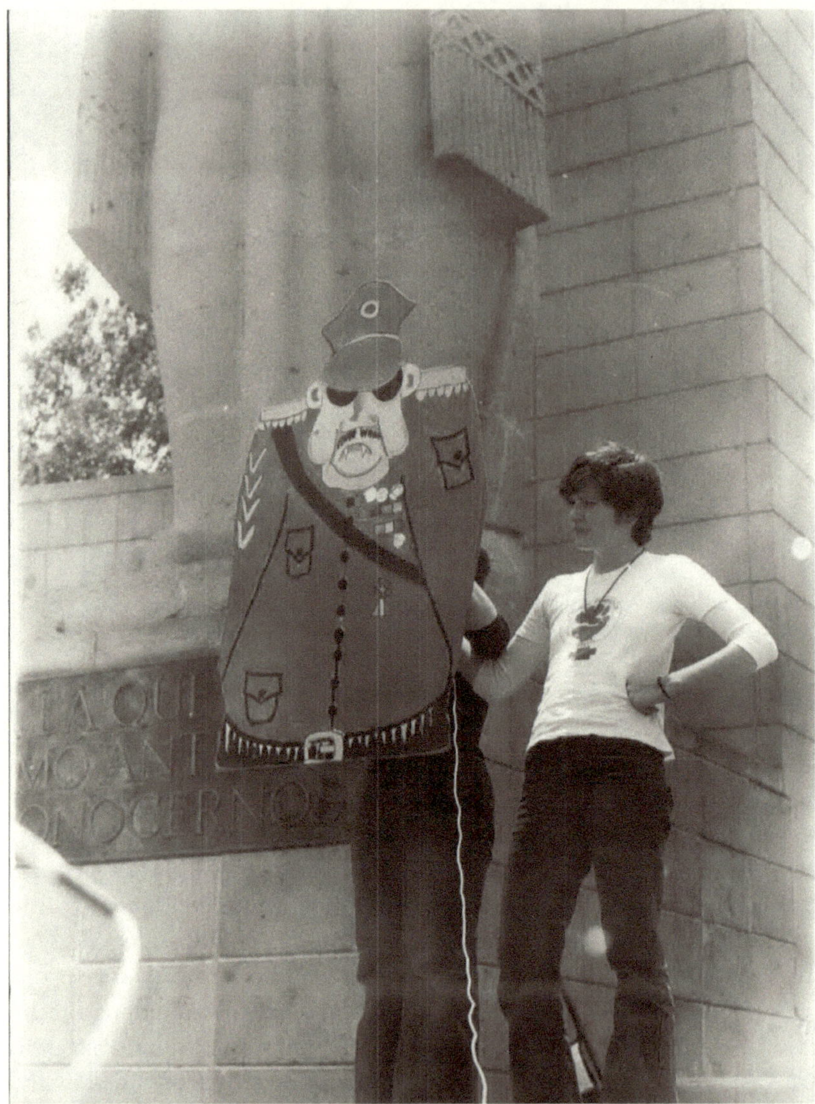

FIGURE 76. Ana Victoria Jiménez. Feminist Indra Olavarrieta in a performance criticizing patriarchal personajes, Monumento a la Madre, Mexico City, 1976. Universidad Iberoamericana.

demonstrations would be constantly repeated), covered the 1979 demand—expressed in front of the Cámara de Diputados—for the legalization of abortion, and pictured the recurring objections to the Miss Universe competition, in addition to photographing theatrical performances and political acts around Mexico City.[117] (See Figure 76.) Few of her photos were published in the mass media, but they were standard fare in Mexican feminist magazines such as *Fem*, *DobleJornada*, *Cihuatl*, and *La Revuelta*, as well as in US feminist publications. Her archive of four thousand documents (photographs, posters, and flyers) was acquired by the Universidad Iberoamericana in 2011. There, an exhibit was organized, *Women and Something More: Reactivating the Archive Ana Victoria Jiménez.* Some of the thematic cores of the exhibit were "From women as objects to dolls in action," which explores the ways the feminist movement makes visible and at the same time questions the stereotypes of gender, as well as their social and cultural effects; "Revolution and rebellion: Artistic strategies," which reactivates and updates the cultural and artistic strategies employed by feminism since the 1970s; and "The diversity of feminist militancy," which highlights the complexity and diversity of the strategies, ideologies, postures, and struggles that enter into play with feminism with respect to gender equality in Mexico.[118]

Although Lucero González began to photograph at an age by which most imagemakers have a well-defined body of work, she has rapidly made up for lost time. She joined the neofeminist movement in 1972, becoming a founding member of La Revuelta soon thereafter, and dedicated herself to that cause.[119] In the early 1980s, as she neared forty, she began to take photographs, and has since provided images to the newspaper *La Jornada* as well as to magazines such as *Debate Feminista*, *Desacatos*, and *Ms.* She also mounted exhibits and produced several calendars. Her principle interests have been in portraiture and nude imagery, rather than documenting street activities. For González, a portrait is a game in which she attempts to bring to the surface the individual's interior she perceives, by capturing a detail such as the movement of a hand or the position in which the portrayed places their legs. She is convinced that the personality of the represented can be found at a point somewhere between what they wish to portray and that which the photographer elaborates. A major focus has been that of "rescuing" women artists and intellectuals from the marginalization to which they are usually consigned. One example is the piercing image of the famous Mexican-English painter Leonora Carrington. (See Figure 77.) A rebel all her long life—though never explicitly feminist—Carrington collaborates with González to produce a powerful rendition of aging feminine beauty.[120] Pictured cuddling one of her favorite cats, a major theme in her work, she is said to have remarked, "People under seventy and over seven are very unreliable if they are not cats."[121]

Although some of her feminist compatriots are surprised by her work with female nudes, González considers that, to a certain point, this move-

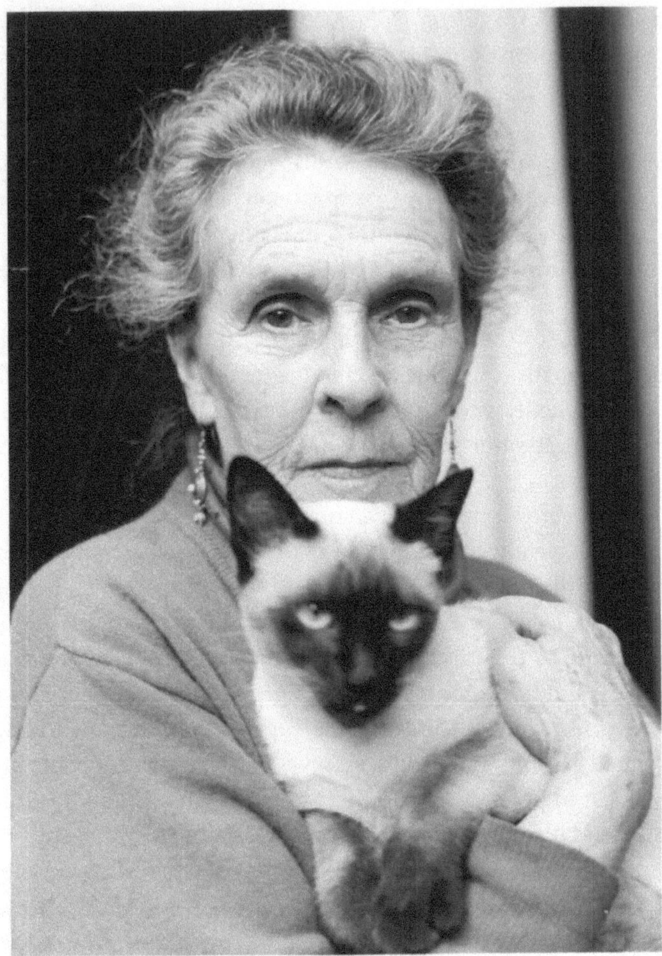

FIGURE 77. Lucero González. Artist Leonora Carrington, Mexico City, 1993. Courtesy of Lucero González.

ment has participated in the generalized repression of women's bodies. She attempts to capture the sensuality and beauty of female shapes of all ages, frequently cutting off the models' heads in order to emphasize the formal aspects, fearing that the force of the visages will interfere with the sculptural qualities she seeks. She has been influenced in this area by the triangular compositions of Imogene Cunningham, which she references through the use of elbows, doubled knees, and the angle between the breasts and body. Other major influences on her work are the Cuban Maria Eugenia Haya

(Marucha), and the Mexicans Lola Alvarez Bravo and Graciela Iturbide. Her focus on reclaiming women's contributions to art led her to establish the bilingual online Museo de Mujeres Artistas Mexicanas (MUMA) in 2008, a project that continues to flourish with the explicit mission of recognizing the value of the art produced by Mexican women during the twentieth and twenty-first centuries.

Rotmi Enciso is the most important lesbian-feminist activist photographer in Mexico. A prolific artist, she has brought her skills to a wide variety of expressive forms including video, painting, theatre, and performance. She has also constructed an important archive to preserve the images and sounds of feminist and lesbian movements, and a wide panorama of women such as sex workers, domestic workers, Amerindians, Afromexicans, mothers of the "disappeared," and those that are in jail. She joined the lesbian-feminist struggle in Mexico City during the early 1980s, and between 1985 and 1989 was a member of the collective Mujeres Urgidas de un Lesbianismo Auténtico (MULA, Women urgently seeking an authentic lesbianism), which focused on sexual liberty for lesbians and women in general.[122] In 1987, she founded the collective Producciones y Milagros: Agrupación Feminista (Productions and miracles: Feminist collective), together with her partner, Ina Riaskov, which is dedicated to documenting feminist, lesbian, and women's movements in Mexico as well as other Latin American countries. Between 1992 and 2003, Enciso published more than thirty works—including photographs, articles, and poems—for the important feminist magazine *Fem*.

Among her extensive publications is the book *Ni santas ni putas sólo mujeres* (Neither saints nor whores just women), which reunited her photographs from 1987 to 2008.[123] This maxim has been a core affirmation of the feminist movement, because women are consigned to one of two roles, either that of the sanctified or of the defiled, the virgin or the mother, a situation that confines them to particular roles. As Francesca Gargallo observed of Enciso, "She is lesbian, heterosexual, indigenous, mestizo, angry, smiling, happy. It is a gesture of the exhausted protestor, the fury against the rape of a young women, the pain of a mother, and the irreverence of students, anarchists, punks [*punketas*], [and of] artists toward the world of masculine respect—a respect that signifies imposition and submission."[124] The figure of the protestor with the sign has become an icon for the Chicana feminist movement, and many activists grew up with it in the bedrooms. They mistakenly believed it had been taken in the 1960s, and Enciso was surprised by both the iconization of her image, and by the mistaken identification.[125] (See Figure 78.)

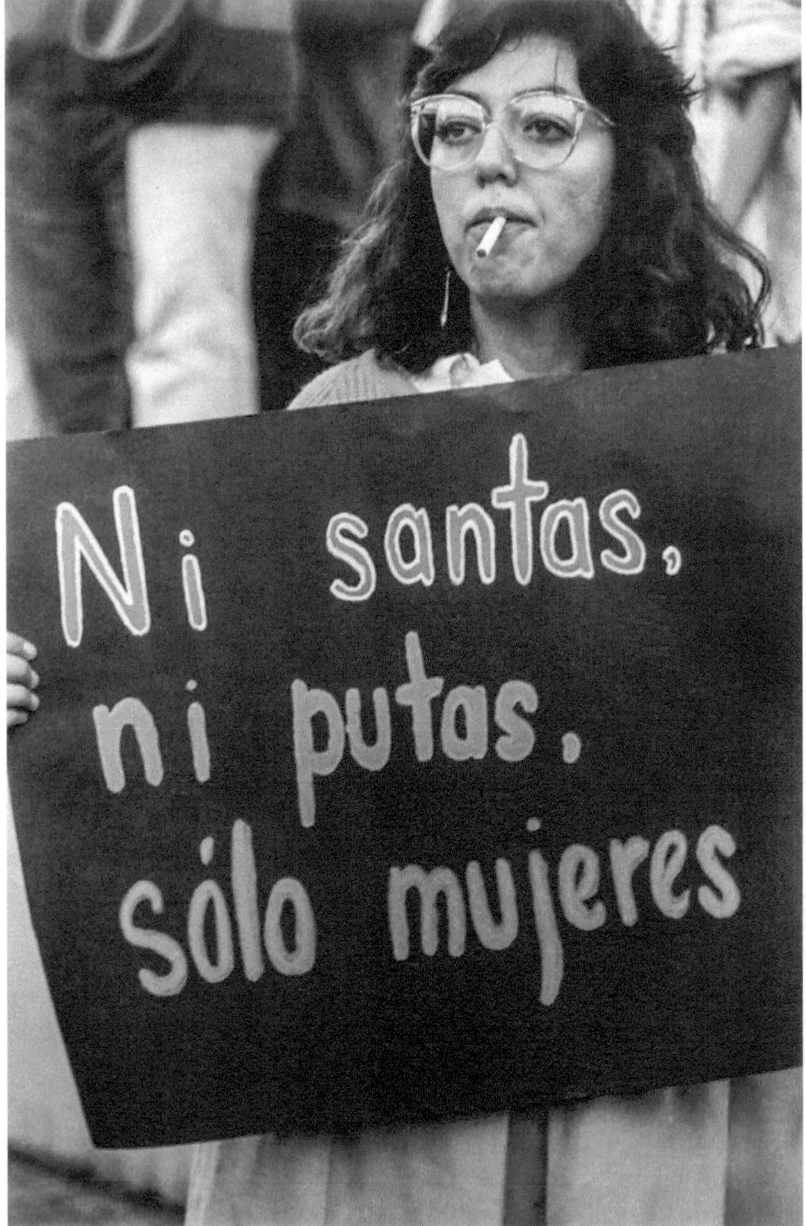

FIGURE 78. Rotmi Enciso. Woman protesting, Mexico City, 8 March 1991. Courtesy of Rotmi Enciso.

Enciso has participated in an incredible range of activities, documenting domestic violence, femicides, protests around the right to abortions and women's health issues, and large feminist and lesbian gatherings such as the Encuentro Feminista Latinoamericano y del Caribe and the Encuentro Lésbico Feminista Latinoamericano y Caribeño. She has also achieved some renown for her portraiture, which includes imagery designed to make visible women's participation in public life, such as of the singers Lila Downs, Betsy Pecanins, and Gloria Trevi, the actors Ofelia Medina and Ana Colchero, the politician Amalia García, the writers Robin Norwood and Isabel Allende, and the critical journalist Lydia Cacho. As she remarked, "I've made a series of photographs of women from various countries in which their strength is what they have in common, that part of them that allows us to forge ahead in spite of discrimination and oppression. That is, we are not victims, rather we confront our situation as a challenge, and in spite of everything, they are playful images."[126] Her efforts to bring prominent women into the foreground notwithstanding, she has also portrayed the life of unexceptional women. "During the many years I worked in *Fem* I dedicated myself to looking for women in everyday life: a woman who goes to the supermarket or who is putting on makeup in the subway with curlers in her hair. I look for women that don't appear on the covers of any magazines."[127]

MEXICO'S NEW PHOTOJOURNALISM

The New Photojournalism of Mexico was a product of the dilatory opening of political spaces after the 1968 Tlatelolco massacre. In 1977, reforms were carried out, largely under the guidance of the respected intellectual Jesús Reyes Heroles, to allow the existence of opposition parties and their access to the mass media. This was done with the intention of controlling them through electoral fraud—something that the PRIAN employed with great success until 2018—as well as to prove to the world that Mexico was a truly democratic system.[128] Among the periodicals that appeared were the magazine *Proceso* (1976) and the newspapers *Unomásuno* (1977) and *La Jornada* (1984), all of which have (or had) a clearly leftist orientation and a photography that reflected "inclusivity."[129] The new media offered space to include what was generally excluded by the traditional Mexican press: the photographers' interest in personal expression and the dissemination of their images beyond the confines of journalism; ordinary people and their daily lives; women and their particular perspective on the world; the political opposition and their struggle against the PRI's monopoly on power; and

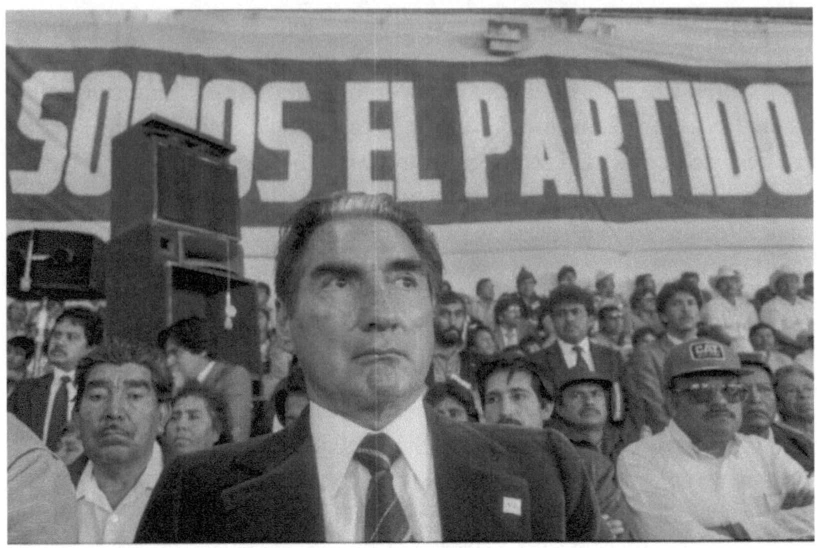

FIGURE 79. Francisco Mata Rosas. Emilio Azcárraga Milmo, director de Televisa, in a meeting of the Partido Revolucionario Institucional (PRI), Querétaro, 1988. Courtesy of Francisco Mata Rosas.

a critique of the glorification of the president and the army as well as the taboo against any criticism of them.

Mexico's New Photojournalists also made images of anticolonial struggles in Latin America, as in the photos Pedro Valtierra took of the Sandinista revolution in Nicaragua.[130] Antonio Turok went to live in Nicaragua after the Sandinista triumph, where he stayed for seven years to document resistance to the US-funded Contra, composed largely of ex-soldiers of the Nicaraguan National Guard who had maintained the dictator Anastasio Somoza Debayle in power through torture and assassination. They raped and killed but were described by US president Ronald Reagan as "Freedom Fighters."[131] Turok later moved to Chiapas, where he was the first photojournalist to cover the Neo-Zapatista uprising, as he captured them entering into San Cristobal de las Casas.[132]

A movement that began in 1976 and ended around 2000, the New Photojournalism reached its expressive zenith between 1984 and 1988. The participants are conscious that every shot expresses their political position, as was made evident in the statement provided for a 1988 exhibit:

> A new generation of image creators now exists that recognizes the ideological, cultural, and symbolic character of their work; who obviously maintain the premise of their duty to inform but without pretending to be a "faithful"

> register of reality. They are conscious that what they transmit is their point of view, opinions, and the position they assume in front of the events they see day after day.[133]

The New Photojournalists used esthetic resources to critique a system that maintained itself in power largely through the mass media that produced *telepresidentes* such as Enrique Peña Nieto (2012–2018). This can be seen in the way that Francisco Mata Rosas employed a wide-angle lens to pillory then owner of Televisa Emilio Azcárraga Milmo in front of a PRI banner that reads, "We are the party." (See Figure 79.) Mata explained that the majority of photojournalists worked in a very discrete manner, but the movement in which he was a significant participant utilized wide-angles lenses (among other tactics) "to deform, to caricature, to get too close, looking for low-angle shots [taken] with wide angle lenses."[134]

Jesús Villaseca Chávez was a participant in the New Photojournalism movement. He was the only imagemaker to extensively cover the Atenco revolt, which represented a conflation of the *campesinos'* attachment to their lands and the history of their resistance to being expelled from them, the participation of women in this struggle, and the rising opposition of impoverished Mexicans to the kleptocracy of their rulers. On October 22, 2001, President Vicente Fox (2000–2006) announced that a new airport for Mexico City would be built on the area held by the *ejidatarios* in the towns of San Salvador Atenco, San Felipe Chimalhuacán, and Texcoco, among others.[135] No negotiations had been held with the *campesinos*, who were being forced off their lands, "leaving behind their only way of surviving: their crops, their fields and their houses, but above all their customs and the culture they had inherited from their Aztec ancestors."[136] They were offered the absurd amount of seven pesos per square meter for the expropriated areas.

During nine months, they vainly attempted to establish a dialogue with the authorities and employed all available legal means. The government argued that the project would provide economic opportunities to their *campesino* "partners," but the position of the Frente de Pueblos en Defensa de la Tierra (FPDT) was firm: "*La tierra no se vende, se ama y se defende*" (Land is not sold, but loved and defended). Atenco became the center of resistance, which included constant marches into Mexico City where—armed with machetes—the militants confronted the police. Outside of the city, they blocked off main highways, burned and decommissioned official transport, and made prisoners of members of the federal forces as well as government bureaucrats, in response to the hundreds of *campesinos*

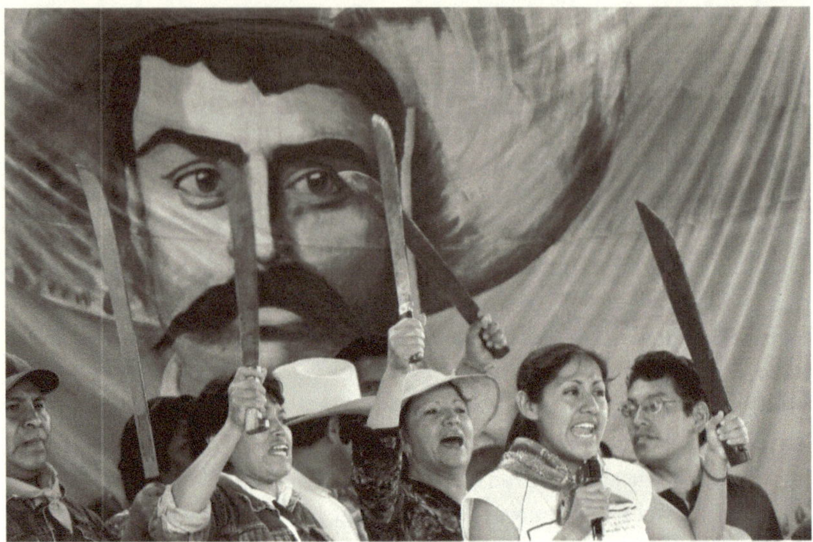

FIGURE 80. Jesús Villaseca. Protest in the municipal palace of Atenco, Mexico State, 2006. Courtesy of Jesús Villaseca.

who had been captured and tortured. The bloody battles resulted in some *campesino* deaths and many wounded on both sides, but on August 1, 2002, the presidential decree was cancelled.

Women played an important role in stopping the airport project. In fact, there were numerous families that broke up over the militancy assumed by women whose husbands felt that they were overstepping patriarchal bounds.[137] In many cases, the women who had taken up machetes divorced those spouses who objected, and then later married *compañeros* they found in the midst of the struggle. (See Figure 80.) The *campesinos'* victory stuck in the craw of the ruling class, which had lost both the monies spent in the battles as well as the enormous sums they expected to receive from the corruption connected to the airport construction.

In May of 2006, the government struck back with a vengeance, using the excuse of a meaningless disagreement over flower vendors. On May 3, 2006, the discussion led to a violent confrontation between *campesinos* and police that ended when the latter fled the scene. On May 4, 2,500 armed federal forces invaded Atenco, attacking everybody they encountered and breaking into houses. Two *campesinos* were killed and two hundred were taken prisoner. Women were raped again and again, as well as penetrated with clubs. The Mexican Supreme Court ruled that there were "grave violations of individual rights," and in 2017 the Interamerican Commission of Human Rights determined that the eleven women who had petitioned to

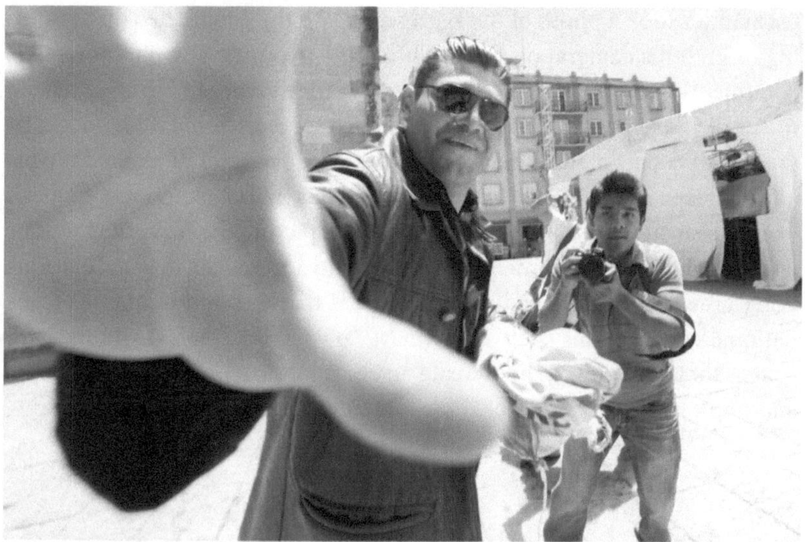

FIGURE 81. Edwin Hernández. *El pago por ser fotoperiodista* (The pay for being a photojournalist); plainclothes policeman attempts to take away Hernández's camera, Oaxaca City, Oaxaca, 2010. Courtesy of Edwin Hernández.

them had suffered severe violence that was "emblematic of the torture and discrimination because of gender."[138]

Another of Villaseca's important contributions to developing critical perspectives is the photography workshops he has been conducting over the past twelve years in El Faro de Oriente (Fábrica de Artes y Oficios de Oriente).[139] The Faro de Oriente was the first to be established, and is an extraordinary space designed to provide a cultural response to the disintegrating social structure of Iztapalapa, the most populous borough in Mexico City. With some two million people crowded into this eastern *alcaldía* characterized by socio-economic marginalization and crime, it has the highest rate of rape and domestic violence in the metropolitan area. More than three thousand students have passed through Villaseca's Talleres de fotografía (courses), and some sixty alumni have positions in the media, a number particularly significant given that Ixtapalapa's young are often denied jobs because they are considered "high risk."[140] Villaseca emphasizes the reconstruction of identity, insisting in "self-empowerment and collectivity" in order to "achieve successful projects."[141]

The seven books that have been produced by the students of the *Talleres* are filled with photos documenting popular protest and dissent. One image that illustrates the power of Villaseca's project is that by Edwin Hernández of a plainclothes policeman that attempted to arrest a protestor in Oaxaca;

Hernández took a photo of the aggression, and the cop turned on him, trying to grab his camera; on finding himself surrounded by photographers documenting his malfeasance, he ran away. (See Figure 81.) The repression of social movements by the police and army receives much attention by the *Talleres's* participants, but they also carry out explorations in daily life in Iztapalapa and around the country—fiestas, family activities, women's work, urban agriculture, portraits—as well as picture the survival of unique cultural traditions, document political graffiti and cover the *nota roja*. One book grew out of the need to defend local markets and denounce transnational corporations such as Walmart, "owners of great wealth that provoke a social inequality, and create an abysmal distance between the rich and poor."[142]

AMBIGUITY AND IRONY

One of the most audacious experiments in exploring the polysemia of photographs was that carried out by Daniela Rossell in Mexico City between 1994 and 2001 in her exhibit and book *Ricas y famosas*.[143] A family member of the ruling plutocracy, Rossell asked her extremely wealthy friends and relatives to pose for her, allowing them to decide where and how to present themselves. The vast majority chose to have themselves portrayed in their homes, which are settings for an opulent ostentation of a staggering material wealth and neocolonial kitsch that appears to have arrived directly from a gilded Las Vegasian world. In flaunting their wealth, they were also emulating US examples, for Mexicans generally tend to be understated and modest, and usually follow the colonial style of hiding their mansions behind high walls. One posed herself in a gold lamé gown, lying beneath a giant golden Buddha with Mexican pesos scattered around on the statue and its base, while a bottle of Moet & Chandon chills in the large pool below. (See Figure 82.) In several portraits the women pose in the midst of preserved wildlife kills—lions, leopards, gazelles, bears, and mountain goats—while the omnipresence of stuffed toy animals participates in creating the same metaphor: these women are just more "trophies." It has been argued that in that sense these portraits are in fact a radical critique of typical feminine representations of the home, above all because of the bold and sexualized ways in which they pose.[144] Further, the question of national identity is never far away, in images of the Virgin of Guadalupe, Emiliano Zapata, and Mexican folk art.[145] It could be claimed that the work offers a neoliberal and *nouveau riche* option of identity—for a very limited part of the population.

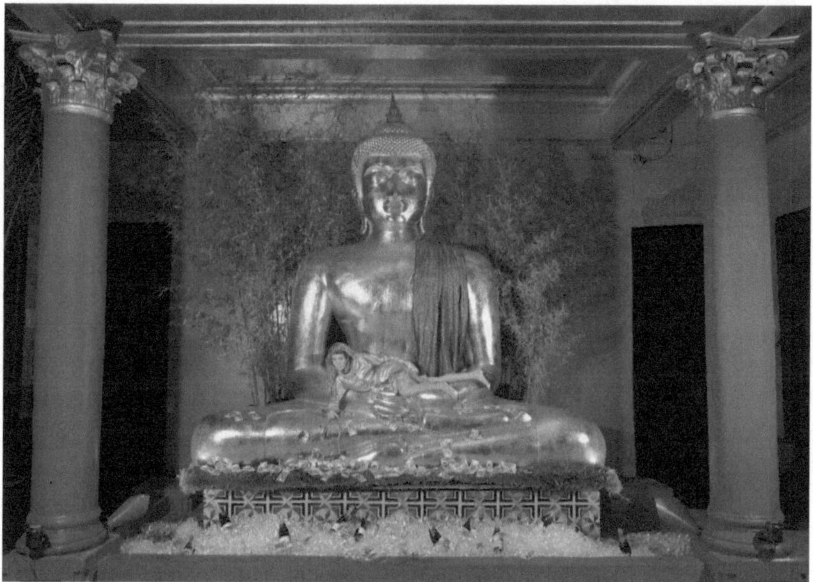

FIGURE 82. Daniela Rossell. Wealthy Mexican woman posing in her house, Mexico City, ca. 1995. Courtesy of Daniela Rossell.

The participants were evidently satisfied with their portrayal, which circulated in exhibits mounted in Mexico City, San Diego, Madrid, New York City, and Berlin. However, scathing articles began to appear that criticized the brandishing of such grandeur in a country in which almost half the population lives in poverty that is largely the product of an enormous corruption at all levels. For example, Juan Villoro argued that the photos are the visual expression of *Priista* cynicism and shamelessness that has been converted into an ideology by statements such as that of Carlos Hank González: "un politico pobre es un pobre politico" (A politician who is poor has been a poor politician).[146] As the critiques multiplied with the publication of the book, the women recognized how they were perceived by the larger population, both in Mexico and the world. They became furious and tried to sue Rossell; when she received death threats, she abandoned the country. As she remarked of her former friends and relatives, "I totally see how ridiculous they are, that's the truth. I would be upset if no one was outraged."[147] One of the most important lessons of this experiment is the importance of context in determining photographic meaning. The women were posing in one context—one totally divorced from the reality in which 99 percent of Mexicans live—but one in which they felt free to express themselves as they did. However, when the photos were placed in the different context of national and international media, where the cumulative effect of the images made itself felt, they were perceived as an ironic critique of corruption and the brandishing of ill-gotten wealth.

AFTER PHOTOGRAPHY

Until the creation of the Internet, leftist photographers were impeded from publishing their images because the mass media of periodicals and television are largely controlled by the wealthy and powerful. However, the almost-unlimited circulation that the Internet and other social media make possible creates a situation in which photography is increasingly a crucial site for the generation of a genuinely critical civil discourse, although it is important to recognize that all the elements of the political spectrum have access to the new social media, including fascists. Latin American Internet sites that post opposition photography appear and disappear with frequency. One important enterprise was Nuestra Mirada, la Red de Fotoperiodistas Iberoamericanos, which was organized by Pablo Corral Vega and Manuel Ortiz Escámez in 2006, and provided a forum until 2010, when it ceased to function except as a Facebook page.[148] In 2010, Corral Vega founded Pictures of the Year LATAM (poylatam.org/en/home-en), which continues to offer a place to publish critical photography and texts, as well as annually hosting "the most prestigious visual journalism contest in Ibero-America," with prizes offered in numerous categories within professional and amateur photography, as well as multi-media productions. Mexican students from Villaseca's Talleres find a home in these Internet sites. One member of Nuestra Mirada is Iván Castaneira; trained in Villaseca's workshops, he focuses on social movements such as protests by the teachers against the police. Another of Villaseca's students from the El Faro workshops, Rosario Servín López, is the editor of Latitudes Press (www.latitudespress.com) another important Internet site, and her activities point to the increasing participation of women.

Pedro Valtierra has been a key component of the New Photojournalism, as well as a pivotal figure in promulgating Mexican and Latin American critical documentary photography and photojournalism; he founded the agency Cuartoscuro in 1986. His magazine, *Cuartoscuro*, has been published for twenty-five years and more than 160 issues have appeared; his website, www.cuartoscuro.com, began in 1997. Among the excellent photographers who collaborate in the Cuartoscuro Agency is Félix Márquez, who lives and works in Veracruz State, one of the most dangerous areas in a country considered by the Committee to Protect Journalists to be "one the deadliest places in the world to work in the media, just behind Iraq and Syria."[149] Although twelve journalists were assassinated during the government of Javier Duarte (2010–2016), Márquez asserts that "the risk is not that something could happen to you physically, the risk is in not informing about what is going on."[150]

The possibilities for a genuine civic discourse will be mediated largely by the struggle between López Obrador's progressive government and the ruling class. Aside from a few bright moments such as the New Photojournalism and some exceptional photographers—López, García, los Mayo, Bordes Mangel, Moya—Mexican journalism has been a story of political subservience and self-censorship. Even today, newspapers such as *Excelsior* "prohibit their photographers to take pictures of the poor and the darker," as Eduardo Miranda recounted.[151] He now works at *Proceso*, a magazine that continues to publish photographs of oppression and resistance, particularly since the New Photojournalist Marco Antonio Cruz took the reins as the director of photography in 2006.[152] Nevertheless, Mexican journalism has rarely strayed from the *pan o palo* (carrot or stick) option offered during the *Porfiriato*, and those who fail to participate in the widespread pattern of corruption often find themselves eliminated by the latter option. Rubén Espinosa Becerril, a photojournalist for *Proceso*, *La Jornada*, and the Cuartoscuro Agency, who was murdered in Mexico City in 2015, is only one of the martyrs in a long line that includes outstanding journalists such as Belisario Dominguez (1863–1913) and Manuel Buendía (1926–1984).

Mexico is currently the most perilous place to practice journalism in the world and, according to the International Federation of Journalists, it "has topped the list of countries with the most journalists killed for four of the past five years."[153] In 2020, the Committee to Protect Journalists reported that Mexicans accounted for a third of all the journalists killed in the world in that year.[154] Some media, both national and international, blame López Obrador for what one writer described as an "unprecedented public hostility towards the media by the president who has frequently used daily press briefings to denigrate independent journalists and activists."[155] This is simply uninformed. Rather, the president has responded to unrelenting attacks by an established press that represents the interests of its wealthy owners and journalists who had accommodated themselves to the bribes (*chayotes*, *embutes*) that provided them with a living wage.[156] The assault against López Obrador by print, television, and radio journalism that were part and parcel of PRIAN corruption, as well as by organic intellectuals of the socio-economic class in power who also enjoyed lavish PRIAN subsidies, is comparable only to that waged by the newspapers and magazines against Francisco I. Madero after the overthrow of Porfirio Díaz.[157] López Obrador has not "denigrated independent journalists and activists," and Mexican journalists have not been killed by "public hostility," but at the hands of the cartels that were allowed to grow and infiltrate all levels of government under the extraordinary corruption of PRIAN rule. These are moments of fundamental transformation in Mexico, and doing critical photography will be as crucial as it will be difficult and dangerous.

CONCLUSION

The leftist photographers of Mexico have carried out a wide variety of functions. The Mexican Revolution offered the opportunity to photographers to commit themselves to the different progressive armies, usually lauding the leaders, but they also served as spies, made a last souvenir for families of those about to be executed, and provided testimony of the executions. In the postrevolution, inspectors from the Secretary of Industry, Commerce, and Labor, as well as workers themselves, used cameras to denounce the abuses to which they were subject, including grave health risks, poor housing, and the company's employment of strike breakers. The workers also documented their solidarity, their organized resistance to the ruling class, and specific elements of their culture, from clothing to fake coffins. They also provided images that attested to the most important worker rebellion in Mexico, the 1958–1959 strikes. Magazines sought to develop a new way of seeing, through the eyes of the working class. Pictures by Tina Modotti were a testimony to the "green revolution," while Lola Álvarez Bravo documented women's oppression. Leftist photojournalists demonstrated the repression of students and workers, including attacks on the press photographers themselves. Decolonizing imagemakers were present to reveal US invasions of Latin America as well as the revolutionary responses, both those of the failed struggles in Venezuela and Guatemala and the success of the Cuban Revolution and Sandinista movement in Nicaragua, until the US undermined the former with economic blockades and destroyed the latter with the Contra. Feminist photographers covered women's struggle for equality as it was expressed in celebrations, protests, and portraits. Progressive photojournalists drew attention to the way in which the mass media, especially television, allied itself with the party dictatorship. And the wealthy themselves were photographed where and how they wished, without understanding that their conspicuous consumption, extreme corruption, and neocolonial taste were pilloried by the camera. Finally, leftist imagemakers entered into the new media provided by the Internet.

Epilogue

"What a Long Strange Trip It's Been."

Without the cold and desolation of winter
There could not be the warmth and splendor of spring.
Calamity has tempered and hardened me,
And turned my mind to steel. **Ho Chi Minh**

We must develop rigorous ways of bringing modern media into our disciplines, utilizing photographs not as mere illustrations but as sources that tell us about things we may have been ignorant of without them, and that provide clues to follow in order to open up new areas of inquiry. We can begin to interrogate the huge photographic archives with which we are faced by placing them in genres, and then understanding how the many varied functions that the photos have served provide them with their meanings. By placing photos in the contexts in which they were made and in which they circulate, we learn how photographic meaning is generated from without. In comparing photographs of similar scenes we can see how meanings are produced from within. We can criticize the representations of the past that we are shown by commercial cinema, unveiling the myths they embody with their present-mindedness and their ignorance of the otherness of societies and cultures from yesterday. We can also learn to make our own cinema, discovering our own esthetic and eschewing the Hollywood model; this is particularly true today with the availability of cheap and lightweight equipment. One important language acquisition theory is the idea that children learn through actively speaking rather than by passively listening; they make mistakes and advance by trial and error. Producing cinema and taking photographs will allow us to become increasingly capable of understanding what these media are telling us.

It is important to reiterate that my focus in this book has been on "modern" media, rather than what I would describe as "postmodern" media—ICT (information and communication technology) that is done through digitalization, the Internet, and new social media. Important works have been published on the use of these new media, particularly those by Roy Rosenzweig, which draw attention to some of the possibilities they create—among them a new kind of interactivity between users and access to previous inaccessible sources—as well as limitations: the fragility of evidence when digital formats become obsolete, making the information unreadable.[1] Photohistorian Martha Sandweiss has applied the same observation to historical photographs, noting that digitalization allows for the preservation of fragile formats, enhancement that reveals details, and widespread accessibility. However, she also emphasizes that finding an image online leaves us in a situation in which "we must still inquire about its original format, the original medium, the notes printed on the back, the pictures that once lay next to it in an album."[2] Whatever its limitations, the Internet is a fundamental tool for a new kind of history:

> Just as the novel, poetry, and the memoir have explored the permutations of memory, so too might the digital photograph evoke a more complex past. Rather than a singular, inarguable reference point that is thought to be truer than human recollection, it can serve as an element in a web of other supporting and contradictory imagery, sounds and texts, a menu of possible interpretations, a malleable dreamscape and memory magnet. In a digital environment a photograph can be easily linked to newspaper headlines of that day, locally or globally, to weather reports, to diaries and appointment books, to photos and texts written by others in one's family or anybody else. Most important, others can also link to it, amplifying and contravening what its initial author claimed it represented, a central tenet of Web 2.0. Holistically, the photograph sprouts electronic roots and branches and is, in turn, entwined by other media.[3]

My own experience with doing research on the Internet had been relatively limited, because I have always been suspicious of the ways the very openness of the media allows for the generation and perpetuation of myths. However, the Internet site of Fotógrafos de la Revolución (fotografosdelarevolucion.blogspot.com) was a fundamental tool for my research on the photography of the Mexican Revolution.[4] More recently, I had that experience confirmed when the cartoonist Gonzalo Rocha asked me to provide a text that would be included in a book of his cartoons that had been published in the magazine *Proceso* since 2000. Every week, he had been given articles to illustrate; when he invited me to participate in the book, I was provided with only the images. As caricatures are necessarily tied to specific historical events and public figures, it was crucial that I inform myself—and the book's readers—exactly what was being depicted in the cartoons. It would have been an endless task to plow through fifteen years of *Proceso*, searching for the published images and the accompanying texts. However, since I recognized most of the references and could ask Gonzalo about those I had forgotten, I was able to do the research online and provide the text that made the images more comprehensible to readers. Our collaboration in going from text to image and then back to text could be considered a "mini-experiment" in doing visual history and provides a felicitous introduction to this period in Mexico, which could no doubt also serve teachers in livening up their classes.[5]

My struggles to do history with modern media within US academia and my decision to move to Mexico have shaped my work. I never expected my life to be what it has been. When I was spending ten years in graduate school, even my wildest fantasies would not have included the possibility of moving to a different country and getting a researcher's job, being sent to Nicaragua to make a videotape with the Sandinistas, or being invited to curate the national photography exhibit of the Centennial of the Mexican Revolution—as well as that on the New Photojournalism—or to write a book about Nacho López, among a myriad of other projects. My career has also given me many opportunities to travel and, perhaps most importantly, to work on the country in which I am living rather than being another "area specialist," a group that is generally looked down on in US academies. During those years at UCSB and UCSC, I imagined that, with luck, I'd get a teaching job at some institution such as Cucamonga Community College and be so loaded down with courses and administrative duties that I would never be able to do what I really wanted.

But if I was luckier than I thought possible, I also proved to be very stubborn. Once I found what I wanted to do with my life, I could never give it up if at all possible. I always emphasize this in talking with students and younger scholars: if you are ever lucky enough to find what you really want to do, hold on to it as if it were more precious than life itself, because you will eventually succeed. When you are laboring in something you love, it isn't work, so you don't hang up your briefcase or camera bag at the end of the day because the "day" never ends for you. You put in a real 24/7, while other people work as little as possible at the alienated labor with which they earn their daily bread, and rightly so.

I was also capable of taking a risk. Perhaps I had internalized the tagline from a 1966 Schlitz beer commercial: "You only go around once in life."[6] Of course, I did have things in my head apart from advertising slogans. In the late 1960s and the 1970s, much experimentation was going on with mind-expanding drugs such as LSD. Aldous Huxley's *The Doors of Perception* set the tone on how you perceive under its effects: "This is how one ought to see, how things really are."[7] I'm sure some people had trips they regretted that led the ever-Puritanical US society to make psychedelic drugs illegal and stop funding for important experiments in 1966. However, since around 2000, scientists have returned to examine these drugs and recent research indicates that it can be a positive life-changing event. Participants in psilocybin experiments have ranked them as one of the most meaningful experiences they have had, which have "reshaped their lives and work in profound and enduring ways."[8]

I believe that it was one of my life-changing experiences. I came to understand that it was a drug not to be taken lightly and above all not with an escapist intention, but with a serious desire to explore oneself in a nonthreatening-environment, preferably in nature, and always with close friends. In 1974, three of my best friends and I hiked back into the spectacular Matilija Canyon, near the city of Ojai, a spiritual site where Jiddu Krishnamurti lived from 1923 to his death in 1986, and where he established his foundation in 1969. We were all men in our early thirties, recently separated from our wives, and at the point of leaving Santa Barbara to go on to other pursuits of which we were largely uncertain. During our trip, I can clearly remember "seeing viscerally" that I only had one life to live, and knowing at the deepest level that I was not going to live it other than doing exactly what I wanted, above all since I had discovered my reason for being here.

This was there in the background to the best decision I've ever made: moving to Mexico. This is so not entirely because I met the love of my life—although the personal and professional ought always to be intimately intertwined—but because I found a place where it was still permitted, even encouraged, to be a human being. Richard Morse was among the first US scholars to suggest that his colleagues might learn something from Latin American cultures. He outlined the usual way that people in the US perceive those south of the border: "Latin America is deceptively recognizable—to novitiate and expert alike—as a poor and slightly disreputable Western cousin."[9] Although he never appeared to understand that this perspective is intrinsically linked to the neocolonialist worldview, he did urge US academics to move beyond the "peon-*pistolero*-busboy image" to ask whether this mirror provided by the hemisphere's other half might show the flaws of the path that Anglo-American society has chosen:

> The North American who looks south wrestles with an insidious doubt. Even in the face of the cruelty, poverty, and tumult of Latin America, he cannot escape the lurking suspicion that it is just barely conceivable that his own civilization may have taken a wrong turn in the sixteenth and seventeenth centuries . . . [when] we were forced to cauterize some of those easy instincts, to abandon some of that immemorial social wisdom, in which the Latin American world abounds. Latin America confronts us with much that we have swept under the rug, with much that might still have been ours. Can it be, can it possibly be, that our several strategies for keeping Latin America at an intellectual and psychic remove were devised so as to obscure this simple fact?[10]

US academia is the reflection of a very ill society. As novelist James Baldwin observed, "White Americans are probably the sickest and certainly the most dangerous people, of any colour, to be found in the world today."[11] In US academia this is played out through a blasé irony and jaded weltschmerz I have often encountered when, as a visiting professor or while giving a lecture, I express the enthusiasm with which I live in Mexico. As novelist and professor David Foster Wallace spelled it out before he paid the highest price by hanging himself at the age of forty-six, "The most frightening prospect . . . becomes leaving oneself open to others' ridicule by betraying passé expressions of value, emotion, or vulnerability."[12] Moreover, the hyper-competitive spirit imbued in US academics, first in graduate school and then among colleagues, creates a dog-eat-dog world that I do not yet find in Mexican universities. Perhaps because we are living in the precariousness of the neocolonial situation, Mexican colleagues seem to feel fortunate just to have a position. Although there are many intrigues and much corruption in our universities, I have not found the attitude that Nobel-prize economist Paul Krugman described in US academia: "I've spent my whole adult life in rarefied academic circles, where everyone has a good income and excellent working conditions. Yet I know many people in that world who are seething with resentment because they aren't at Harvard or Yale, or who actually are at Harvard or Yale but are seething all the same because they haven't received a Nobel Prize."[13]

A discussion I had with a US anthropologist who I had aided in getting a position in my university, demonstrates the fundamental difference of worldview. The institute's director had organized an event on the patio of an exquisite colonial building to celebrate his re-election. The entire institute was there, eating a delicious *comida*, drinking well-chosen wines and other alcoholic and nonalcoholic beverages, and listening to live music played by a most accomplished trio. Both academics and workers attended, so it served to promote mutual bonding, which was important because we researchers usually saw little of one another since we were often in archives or writing in our houses. I had listened, *ad infinitum*, to the anthropologist's complaining about the way things were done in Mexico—he'd been there some fifteen years without ever really integrating into the society or adapting himself to its norms—so I could not help but call his attention to the incredible moment we were living. His response—never underestimate the Puritanism of a US leftist!—was "We don't spend public monies on crap such as this." "No," I thought, "you spend it on bombing people who cannot defend themselves into the stone age and destroying villages in order to save them."[14] He was, I believe, an embodiment of what Morse meant when he referred to the fact that "for many of our Latin Americanists the intensive study of their subject kindles their subconscious hostility to it."[15]

LIVING IN MEXICO

Being an immigrant is never easy, and I describe myself as a "voluntary exile," as the lack of academic positions in the US certainly was part of my decision.[16] In my case, the fact that I worked in a field disparaged by history departments and was a Marxist would certainly have made academic employment even more unlikely. However difficult the situation that those who chose to leave encounter, they nonetheless have an opportunity to shape their experience—some more, many others much less—into forms of their choosing. The word *exile* itself has apparently only come into widespread use since around 1939; prior to that date it would appear that *emigration* or *uprooted* (*desterrado*) were the more common terms.[17] One of the major problems I have experienced in Mexico is dealing with the moral reaction that automatically surges forth at the violation of social norms I internalized as a gringo: you don't show up late nor promise things you have no intention of doing; you don't drive through red lights nor play music so loud that it is distorted and prohibits conversation.[18] I feel a moral outrage, and my problem is adjusting to a different way of seeing the world rather than allowing my indignation to determine my reactions. However, despite whatever inconveniences or slight aggressions I have experienced in Mexico, I would not even begin to compare them to what Latin Americans suffer in the US. Instead, I have always tried to appreciate the liberties

I have had as an exile from my native land and from history departments that believe that there is only one way to practice that discipline.

It is clear that we are living in a world in which ecological disasters and their accompanying social catastrophes will expel more and more people from where they were born and raised. Flusser, who fled Czechoslovakia in 1939, asserted that it was crucial to view exile as a positive situation, and a "breeding ground for creative activity. . . . We, the uncounted millions of emigrants (whether we are guest workers, expellees, or intellectuals traveling from one seminar to another), do not recognize ourselves as outsiders, but rather as pioneers of the future."[19] His perspective enabled him to perceive the limitations imposed by the reigning prejudices and habits of nationalism: "I recognized what makes patriotism (whether local or national) so devastating: it anoints the human ties that bind and neglects the ties that we accept freely; it privileges family ties to elective affinities, the real or imagined biological relations to those of friendship and love."[20]

Flusser argued convincingly that the expelled must exercise their creative possibilities to "change oneself and others as well" and hence "should be considered role models whose examples we follow in case we are sufficiently daring."[21] Nevertheless, as was the case with Morse, he failed to learn to see through Brazilian eyes despite his more than thirty years of living in that country. His belief in the possibility of constructing the utopian "dialogic, telematic societies" of the future seems to be based upon the continual neocolonial subjugation of the Third World: "I can project scenarios to undermine my expectations for a telematic society—a nuclear war, for example, or a third-world revolt. . . . But such scenarios do not describe catastrophes: they describe things that are predictable and that therefore can, at least theoretically, be avoided."[22] In other words, the dominant imperial powers will create their utopias in direct proportion to ways the neocolonial areas remain dystopias.

Living under the imperial boot, for a great many Latin Americans daily life is a catastrophe. Noam Chomsky finds this situation to be scandalous: "With its resources, Latin America ought to be a rich continent, [but instead suffers from] terrible poverty and extreme inequality, some of the worst in the world."[23] Working and living in Mexico has given me a front-row seat to see how imperialism has affected this area. Many Latin Americanist academics in the US and Europe honestly believe that the US has an interest in fomenting true democracy, but the empire's real concern is maintaining control of the continent. As Chomsky has acutely pointed out in *On Power and Ideology*, US foreign policy has a "maximum objective and a minimum objective."[24] The former is to overthrow any government that threatens their control, as it did with democratically elected presidents Jacobo Arbenz (Guatemala, 1954) and Salvador Allende (Chile, 1973). If that proves impossible, then the "virus" must be contained by using client states—Bolsonaro's Brazil would be the most recent example, mercenaries such as the Contra that terrorized Nicaraguans, and sanctions that create situations in which military dictatorships flourish—as in the cases of Cuba, Nicaragua, and Venezuela—to make sure they cannot serve as a useful example to other Latin American states.

It may come as a surprise for English-language readers to hear that many Mexicans with whom I spoke expressed little sympathy for the victims of the 9/11 attacks in 2001. Instead, the responses demonstrated the profoundly different ways the US is seen from inside and outside. Although one or another of the middle-class neighbors with whom I have a nodding acquaintance expressed horror that the attack had occurred, the vast majority of Mexican friends, both leftists and conservatives, felt that the US got what it had earned. If it was going to go around the world bombing countries and indiscriminately killing civilians, the very least they could expect was a reaction that would finally touch them on their home soil. Further, the fact that Allende's government had been overthrown on September 9, 1973, largely through CIA intervention, created an ironic coincidence that was widely commented on. The result of 9/11 in the US was to heighten the paranoia of a population indoctrinated into being terrified of life; in Chile it meant the installation of a military dictatorship that jailed eighty thousand, tortured tens of thousands, and killed around four thousand people over seventeen years.[25]

Many Chileans fled to Mexico, among them photohistorian Ariel Arnal, who has described the pain of leaving behind family and friends to experience the "multiple personalities of a schizophrenic" in constructing a new identity, the "double life" lived as a Mexican outside of, and as a Chilean within, the immigrant circles who maintain antiquated customs such as drinking tea at 11 a.m.[26] As he recounts, the exile finds him or herself in front of "the temptations of San Antonio in their particular Mexican version, the vibrant Mexico, lover of life, of colors, of smells, and of flavors that become a sin of identity to which one must never yield." For Arnal, an exile will always remain in that condition but, "there are as many exiles as there are exiled, and each can live their personal exile, reinventing what they have been and constructing what they wish to be."[27]

The Chilean case offers an interesting insight into the different political stances of Mexico and the US. In broad terms, Mexico seems generally to have opened their borders to leftist immigrants. The exiles from the Spanish Civil War entered in large numbers, as did many Guatemalan refugees after the CIA and the United Fruit Company collaborated with the Guatemalan military to overthrow Arbenz. US cultural dissidents also found a refuge from the repression carried out under the McCarthyism that dominated the Cold War mentality of the 1950s and early 1960s, and South American intellectuals and artists were welcomed during the "dirty wars" in Argentina, Chile, Brazil, and Uruguay in the 1970s and 1980s. The US, on the other hand, seems to have been much more welcoming of right-wing immigrants: the Cubans who have been a steady stream since the triumph of the revolution in 1959, and the Vietnamese who fled when the US lost that war in 1975.

In Mexico, refugees from the Spanish Civil War fundamentally transformed Mexican culture with an influx of intellectuals, artists, scientists, philosophers, poets, bakers, industrialists, financiers, doctors, and workers of all kinds. They were intimately connected to the creation of El Colegio de México, and founded important publishing houses such as Grijalbo and Joaquín Moritz. Their children have become one of the bedrocks of cultural life. Although the contributions of US exiles during the Cold War are in no way comparable to the effect of those from Spain, it has been argued that they developed a critical transnationalist perspective that challenged the US government's projection of "American exceptionalism" as a beacon of freedom. African American émigrés were particularly important in revealing "the racialized imposition of colonialism worldwide."[28]

The Mexican government also opened the door for South American refugees, providing them with "homes and work for a determined period, as well as recognizing their university titles without the paperwork that would normally be required."[29] Moreover, tourism from Chile was suspended to protect the exiles, preventing the Pinochet government from sending agents to assassinate expelled leaders as they did when they killed Orlando Letelier in Washington, DC, in 1976. As Arnal said, "For the Mexican government, caring for the exiled Chileans was a question of honor, a consequence of the close cultural and affective relationship with Allende's government."[30] This was also in line with the Estrada Doctrine formulated in 1930, which called for nonintervention, the peaceful resolution of disputes, and the self-determination of all nations.[31] In a sense, it was a rejection of the Monroe Doctrine, which seems to be employed as a tool to allow the US to "police" Latin America; in the early 2000s, the PRIAN administrations drew ever closer to the US and turned away from a Latin Americanist solidarity. However, under the "Third-Worldism" of President Luis Echeverría (1970–76), Argentines, Chileans, Brazilians, and Uruguayans flooded into Mexican universities, above all the Universidad Autónoma Metropolitana, founded in 1974. They, and the children of those who chose to remain, have made a substantial contribution to intellectual life in Mexico.

While I was in the Harry Ransom Research Center I got to chatting with a visiting fellow from a US university who was amazed to hear that I had moved to Mexico and chosen to stay there; her last words to me were, "you're very brave." I hadn't really thought of it that way; I felt I was very lucky, and at times I whimsically say that you have two choices: you can either be scared or bored; I prefer the former.[32] There is an extraordinary beauty to everyday life in Mexico: the folk arts, the colonial buildings, the exquisitely handpainted *talavera* plates and dishes made in Puebla upon which we eat. There is also a feeling of living in the midst of historical density due, above all, to the presence of so many ancient civilizations. If you climb to the top of a pyramid in Dzibanché, Quintana Roo, a zone that is extremely flat, you will see dozens of "hills" covered with dense jungle growth all around you; these are in fact archeological sites that have yet to be uncovered. The riotous colors and neatly arranged piles of fruit and chiles in the *mercados* are accompanied by a quality of human interaction that often seems lacking in the "developed" world; your relationship with your vendor is vital to informing you about which fruit, vegetables, or fish is the best on that day. This carries over into academia. If you run across a friend at a Mexican university, you are expected to stop and talk; should you really be in a hurry you will probably excuse your haste by arranging a future meeting. In US colleges, the rules are different: you have to look busy. If you encounter someone, they will probably glance at their watch, tell you that they are in a rush, but that they will be free for a nineteen-minute lunch in a couple of weeks. Of course, I am exaggerating for effect, and my observations may not go beyond purely personal experiences.

It all depends upon the eyes with which one is seeing. When I drove down to Mexico City from California in the early 1960s and again in the early 1970s, I remember being awed by the green mountains that suddenly shoot up into billowing cloud masses made silver by the tropical sun. Paul Strand viewed the hills as "sinister": "Even the mountains are different. They're supposed to be part of the same mountains, but they don't look the same. And they don't have the same kind of character. They have a different feeling, more sinister than the Rocky Mountains."[33] The extremes with which Mexico is perceived can be appreciated in the character of Kate in D. H. Lawrence's *The Plumed Serpent*. At one point in the novel, she is repelled by the "under-drift of squalor and heavy reptile-like evil," and "those black, inhuman eyes." But a hundred pages later her point of view has been transformed: "Yet here, and here alone, it seemed to her, life burned with a deep, new fire. The rest of life, as she knew it, seemed wan, bleached and sterile. The pallid wanes and weariness of her world! And here, the dark ruddy figures in the glare of a torch, like the centre of the everlasting fire, surely this was a new kindling of mankind."[34]

Dealing with such a dissimilar culture can be difficult because what we might call the "pragmatics of human communication" differ significantly between Mexicans and people from the US.[35] For example, it has taken me years to understand what is meant when a Mexican says, "*Sí, como no*." This phrase is as untranslatable as some of Cantinflas' monologues, and can mean anything from "No way" to "Of course we'll do that. That's a great idea."[36] I sense that this is attributable to the personalist style of Mexican culture. For example, when meeting about a possible project, the communication is not only about that, but about the relationship of the individuals involved. According to Bateson, human interaction operates at many contrasting levels of abstraction, from the simple denotative level to the metacommunicative level; in the latter mode, "the subject of discourse is the relationship between the speakers."[37] The nonverbal contextualization that takes place in a conversation is part of the "analogic communications by which [are] defined the nature of the relationships rather than making denotative statements about objects."[38] As I have argued, the photography of Manuel Álvarez Bravo "is a highly Mexican esthetic: ironic, subtle, understated, and cryptic."[39] These are the very qualities of a culture that can make it difficult for a Southern Californian such as myself to understand the country in which I have chosen to live.

Sometimes I wonder if I shouldn't have made more cinema, but when I saw my best work, *Magí Murià*, projected on a big screen in the Filmoteca de Catalunya (more than twenty years after I directed it), I realized that it was better to have dedicated myself to writing and curating photo exhibits. Moreover, making cinema requires such intense investments of time and energy at the preproduction level—including the never-ending search for money—that it was difficult to dedicate myself to that, as well as turn down offers to curate exhibits, participate in collective works, and travel. Eli and I had the fortune to receive and be able to accept numerous invitations to be visiting professors in exciting cities and university towns.[40] Living for lengthy times in different places gave us the opportunity to make new acquaintances and sometimes develop lasting friendships, search out the best restaurants and music venues, discover bookstores, museums, and galleries, and know a bit about what daily life was like in those locales, as well as have access to top-flight libraries in several countries to carry out both primary and secondary research in our respective areas. This allows for a very different experience than tourism or even academic activities such as attending conferences; the latter can be fun as well but they are more about meeting up with old friends and networking, which allows little time to really know the place to which you have gone.

My decisions to do what I loved and to live in Mexico are part of my broader conviction that life is to be enjoyed. This has fit in well with what I believe is the overriding ethos of this country's culture: that family and friends come before work, above all before alienated labor. Of course, as any US employer knows, Mexicans certainly know how to work when they have to. Chef Anthony Bourdain championed the labor of Mexicans in the US food industry while pointing out the hypocrisy of the claim that they steal jobs: "In two decades as a chef and employer, I never had ONE American kid walk in my door and apply for a dishwashing job, a porter's position—or even a job as a prep cook. Mexicans do much of the work in this country that Americans, provably, simply won't do."[41] Bourdain called Mexican food "one of the most exciting cuisines on the planet . . . older even than the great cuisines of Europe."[42] And food historian Jeff Pilcher pointed to the historical importance that particular food items have acquired: "chiles now form part of the national identity, captured in the popular Mexican refrain: '*Yo soy como el chile verde, picante pero sabroso*' (I'm like green chile, hot but tasty)."[43]

COOKING PASTA POBLANA

One of the delights of being in Mexico comes from year-round access to fresh fruits and vegetables with which I can create incredibly varied and complex meals for long *sobremesas* that can extend a three o'clock *comida* well into a late evening *cena*. I love cooking and learned to make pasta poblana, one of my favorite dishes, in a Mexican penitentiary. I wasn't incarcerated, but often visited a friend, Miguel, who served a six-month term for possession of marijuana. A university professor of philosophy, Miguel liked to smoke *mota* and, in Mexico, middle-class consumers usually buy it in large quantities of about a half pound. Because he had the connection, and it was cheap, Miguel shared generously among his friends, until one couple got busted. The police took the husband away, leaving the wife at home with the children. She feared her husband might spill the beans, so she called Miguel to warn him to get rid of anything he was holding, but the consummate man-about-town was at the movies (this was before cell phones). The husband talked, and the police went to arrest Miguel, but found him gone, and went home to sleep. When he got back around midnight, the wife finally got through, advising him that her husband had pos-

sibly snitched. Miguel didn't have much around the house, or so he thought until he began to clean up the different stas
hes that had accumulated throughout the years. When he finished, he had filled up a small suitcase with ten pounds of illegal vegetable garbage: mostly seeds and stems. Now, however, it was late, and he was too tired to climb back down the three floors to the street in order to throw it away. In wonderful symmetry to the policemen who went on back home and gave him a chance to clean up, Miguel returned the favor by sleeping until the officers knocked on the door at 8 a.m.

Mexican jails evidently have a bad reputation, but—as is the case around the world—the experience is mediated by the prisoner's class and ethnicity. Coming from a wealthy family, Miguel seemed relatively content, passing the time playing tennis and reading. As are all inmates, he was allowed one conjugal visit a week and earned a second by teaching a class to other prisoners on the literature written around jails. The favorite son of a doting mother, he never had to eat prisonhouse fare. Convicts are allowed to receive food from outside, so Miguel's mom put the maid to work cooking up all sorts of meals that could be eaten without reheating or easily warmed up in a microwave. We used to get together with Miguel and other visiting friends around a long table on Saturdays or Sundays, and this dish was served by his mother so often that I finally had to ask for the recipe. I make it incessantly and nobody seems to tire of it. The chile poblanos are usually not all that *picantes* or *picosos*, words that really have no translation to English. In the US they say "spicy" or "hot" but chiles are not a spice and hot is a degree of temperature, not *picor*.

Ingredients

6–8 medium size poblano chiles
350 ml. sour cream
3 Tbsp butter
500 grams pasta: spaghetti, macaroni, etc.
1 Tbsp dry chicken bouillon
500 grams cheese, shredded

Directions

Roast the poblano chiles slowly over the gas burners (if you have an electric stove, place them in the oven under the top burners and turn on the broiler), turning them as they blacken. When the surface is black, and before the chile's meat is consumed by the flames, put them in plastic bags for fifteen minutes. Take the chiles out of the bags and clean off the burned skin, washing them as little as possible under running water. This is best done with gloves, either of the rubber kitchen variety or surgical (which permit more dexterity). Handling chiles without gloves can leave the fingers "contaminated," causing a sharp pain if you should happen to put one in an eye or on any other sensitive part of the body. When the chiles are essentially clean of the blackened skin, put one half in the blender with the cream and the chicken bouillon and liquefy. Cut the other half of the chiles into strips and fry them in butter for a bit.

Boil the pasta and rinse to cool. Put a layer of pasta in the bottom of a rectangular baking dish. Place the fried chiles in a layer on top of the pasta and cover the chiles with another layer of pasta. Pour the creamed poblanos over the pasta and make sure it saturates completely. Cover with shredded cheese and bake in a preheated oven at 350° for about forty minutes. When the cheese has acquired the color you prefer, remove and eat (or let it sit and eat it later in your cell).

Notes

INTRODUCTION

Epigraph. St. Aubyn, *Mother's Milk*, Kindle edition, location 353.

1. Flusser, *Towards a Philosophy of Photography*, 5.
2. I have identified modern visual culture as that produced by technical images and sounds; its defining characteristics are credibility, mass dissemination, and the creation of celebrity culture. See Mraz, *Looking for Mexico*, 3.
3. Gómez-Popescu, "Towards a History through Photography," 7.
4. Elkins, *Visual Studies*, 8. Elkins includes "Art History, English, Women' Studies, Comparative Literature, Art Education, Sociology, Philosophy, Visual Communication, and Television, Film, and Media Studies." Elkins' discussion of Mexican programs is uninformed.
5. Azoulay, *Civil Imagination*, 83. Azoulay discusses the growth of programs to study what she calls "(non)canonical photography" in, "international relations, politics, human rights programs, media studies, sociology and anthropology." The fact that Linda Gordon's work on Dorothea Lange won the Bancroft Prize in 2010 as the best book in American history is promising, although the biographical form was much easier for historians to digest (Gordon, *Dorothea Lange*).
6. For this estimate, see Jowett, "The Concept of History in American Produced Films," 799.
7. White, "Historiography and Historiophoty," 1193.
8. Barthes, *Camera Lucida*, 4.
9. The novelist L. P. Hartley coined the phrase, "The past is a foreign country; they do things differently there" (*The Go-Between*, 1). For a fascinating exploration of the otherness of the past, see Laslett, *The World We Have Lost*.

10. Begiebing et al., "Interchange," 581.
11. Worth, "The Uses of Film in Education and Communication," 273, 283. A play is being made here on the famous statement of Marshall McLuhan, "The medium is the message" (7), in *Understanding Media*, a pioneering text of 1964 that informed many of the explorations in visuality.
12. Berger, *Ways of Seeing*, 7.
13. Arnheim, *Visual Thinking*, v.
14. Sontag, *On Photography*.
15. Becker, *The Heavenly City of the Eighteen-Century Philosophers*, 5. Becker modestly credits the reappearance of this concept to Alfred North Whitehead.
16. Kant, *Prolegomena to Any Future Metaphysics*, 68–69.
17. Harding, *Whose Science? Whose Knowledge?*, 119.
18. Burke, *What Is Cultural History?*, 116.
19. Burke, *Eyewitnessing*, 138–39.
20. Burke, *Eyewitnessing*, 159–68.
21. See Eugenides, *The Marriage Plot*, for an intelligent and entertaining account of how the short life span of individuals created drama in eighteenth and nineteenth century novels because one had little hope for marrying more than once in a lifetime.
22. Gregory Bateson, personal conversation, 1976.
23. Guldi and Armitage, *The History Manifesto*, 2.
24. Paul, "Visual History," 1–2.
25. Flusser, "Photography and History," in *Vilém Flusser: Writings*, 131.
26. Flusser, *Into the Universe of Technical Images*, 51.
27. See a little-noticed book, Reiche, *Sexuality and Class Struggle*.
28. Roth, "Photographic Ambivalence and Historical Consciousness," 94.
29. Ayala, "John Mraz y la alfabetización visual."
30. Berger, "Appearances" (1982) in *Understanding a Photograph*, 69.
31. Anderson, *The Origins of Postmodernity*, 32.
32. Interview with José Mugica, "No compras con monedas sino con tiempo de vida: Mujica," Jan. 9, 2013, teleSUR tv, https://www.youtube.com/watch?v=DhuHKFYV1m8.
33. Chomsky, *Power Systems*, 35–36.
34. Herr, *Dispatches*, 223.
35. See Jurgenson, *The Social Photo*.
36. Sontag, *Regarding the Pain of Others*, 84–85. See also Silverman, "'Pics or It Didn't Happen.'"
37. For an exhaustive overview of the historical contexts of "ocularcentrism," see Jay, *Downcast Eyes*.
38. Lydon, *Eye Contact*, 24–25. Italics in the original.
39. Rosenstone, *Visions of the Past* and *History on Film/Film on History*; Rosenstone, ed., *Revisioning History*.

40. The source of this slogan offers a fascinating insight into US culture. Dan Weiden, the founder of the Weiden+Kennedy ad agency, credits his inspiration to the last words of Gary Gilmore, a murderer executed in Utah in 1977: "Let's do it." He first pitched the motto at an agency meeting in 1988; see Peters, "The Birth of 'Just Do It' and Other Magic Words." However, what was probably the best-known book of the US rebellions in the 1960s was Jerry Rubin's *Do It*. Is it possible that an advertising executive found it more acceptable to attribute his slogan to a spree killer than to someone who wanted to create a more humane society, or is this just another example of the short memory span in contemporary culture?
41. When I entered the university in 1981, it was named Universidad Autónoma de Puebla (UAP). That was changed to Benemérita Universidad Autónoma de Puebla (BUAP) in 1987.
42. Mignolo, *The Darker Side of Western Modernity*, xvi.
43. Campbell, *Mexican Memoir*.
44. The Partido de la Revolución Institucional (PRI) ruled from 1920 to 2000 (under various names). In 2000, the right-wing Partido de Acción Nacional (PAN) won the presidency, which it held until 2012, when the PRI returned to power. Because the two parties essentially represent the ruling plutocracy, I believe they are usefully described as the PRIAN.
45. Hobsbawm, *Interesting Times*; Rosenstone, *Adventures of a Postmodern Historian*; Morse, *New World Soundings*.
46. Costa Lima, *The Dark Side of Reason*, 152. I thank Ignacio Bajter for this reference.

CHAPTER 1

Epigraph. Conrad, *Heart of Darkness*, 24.

1. Leyda, *Films Beget Films*, 9.
2. See my critiques of Mexican picture histories in Mraz, *Looking for México*, 72–76, 192–200, and 226–35. See longer versions in Mraz, "Picturing Mexico's Past," "Representing the Mexican Revolution," and, in its most complete version, "Visualizar el pasado mexicano."
3. The term *visual history* is also complicated by the resemblance to visual anthropology, a highly developed discipline in which anthropologists take photos; historians, on the other hand, work almost exclusively with already-existing images.
4. Lyons and Plunkett, eds. *Multimedia Histories*.
5. At any rate, I prefer *cinehistory* to *historiophoty*, which is what Hayden White offered as a "relatively adequate" way of characterizing "the representation of history and our thought about it in visual images and filmic discourse" ("Historiography and Historiophoty," 1193). White's formulation seems unneces-

sarily complicated, and while it may be useful for talking about history done with and of photographs, it is inadequate in talking about history done with and of media that employ audio components, such as film, video, and digital productions, in a word, *cinehistory*.

6. Leyda, *Films Beget Films*, 9.
7. Leyda, *Films Beget Films*, 23, 41.
8. See the much-reprinted article by the Cuban cineaste, Julio García Espinosa, "For an Imperfect Cinema," first published in 1969.
9. Bluem, *Documentary in American Television*, 148.
10. Henderson, "*The Civil War*," 2.
11. See, for example, Toplin, ed., *Ken Burns's* The Civil War. In my opinion, Burns is not a historian, but an "official chronicler" for the neoliberal and imperial corporations that fund his expensive productions, such as the Ford Foundation, General Motors, the Rockefeller Brothers Fund, and David H. Koch, as well as the US government Public Broadcasting System, where they are shown.
12. Baker, Kaufman, and Mraz, *Coming Apart*.
13. Mraz, Nelson, and Tracy, *Cracks in the Wall*.
14. Nichols, *Speaking Truths with Film*, 132–33.
15. Kracauer, cited in Leyda, *Films Beget Films*, 45.
16. In 1972, Patrick Griffin made a twenty-five-minute 16 mm short on World War I, *Goodbye Billy: America Goes to War*, with R. C. Raack and William Malloch.
17. Mraz and Tracy, "Classroom Production of an Historical Film Essay."
18. Chiles and Mraz, "The Historical Film Essay," 184. Because everything in the Western Hemisphere is American, I no longer employ that word to describe anything from the US; see Mraz, *Looking for Mexico*, 251, note 1.
19. Richter, "Der Filmessay," cited in Leyda, *Films Beget Films*, 31.
20. Sartorius, *Mexico about 1850*, 55, 118.
21. See Elkins, *Visual Studies*, where he asserts that the "ease" with which some projects have been carried out has resulted in "anthologies and books that are more celebratory than reflective and it has given rise to a growing literature of undistinguished cultural criticism," viii.
22. White, *Metahistory*, ix.
23. Griffith, "The Isla Vista War."
24. Interview with Womack in Marho, *Visions of History*, 255.
25. See Chavarría, *José Carlos Mariátegui and the Rise of Modern Peru*. He left academia and founded the magazine *Hispanic Business*.
26. Pedro Castillo, personal communication, 2016.
27. Burns, *Latin American Cinema*, Cortés, Campbell, and Curl, *A Filmic Approach to the Study of Historical Dilemmas*.
28. The Tillich quote is widely cited, though I have not been able to find the original source. However, as one of his former students stated, "I can attest that he invited students to leave questions on the podium and he would invari-

ably open the lecture by responding to them, often in a way that startled the student by revealing what a profound question he or she had asked" (Bunge, "From Hume to Tillich"). On my teaching method, see Mraz, "Light and Sound."

29. Mraz, "*Lucía*: History and Film in Revolutionary Cuba."
30. Bob Dylan, "Absolutely Sweet Marie," *Blond on Blond*, 1966.
31. Conversations with David Sweet, UCSC, 1976–1980.
32. Halliday, ed., *Sirk on Sirk*, 40.
33. Mraz, "Film and History in Revolutionary Cuba." For a synthesis of the study on *Lucía* in my dissertation, see Mraz, "*Lucía*: Visual Style and Historical Portrayal."
34. Mraz, "*Memories of Underdevelopment*." I have never published a visual analysis of this work, though I did do so with a later study of Cuban films on slavery, "Recasting Cuban Slavery."
35. Mraz, "The Revolution Is History."
36. Haley, *Roots*; *Roots*.
37. See McElroy, "Administrative Bloat on Campus: Academia Shrinks, Students Suffer." In 1976, I served as the student representative on the UCSC Building Committee. The campus is set in a lovely sequoia forest, and new constructions are much deliberated. A new large building was being proposed in the middle of one of the protected areas, so I inquired into the intended use. When I was told that it would serve to house administration, I replied that administrators would reproduce like rabbits to fill up any space they were provided. As all the other members were administrators, my observation was not enthusiastically received.
38. Steve Zamora, personal conversation, 2013.
39. Enrique Suárez Gaona, personal conversation, 1982.
40. Mraz, "De la fotografía histórica."
41. Jacoby, *The Last Intellectuals*.
42. See Gilly's response to being rejected by the SNI in 1986, Gilly, "Citas en los pies, ideas en la cabeza."
43. Holloway's works *Change the World without Taking Power* and *Crack Capitalism* have been translated into eleven languages, with Spanish editions published in Argentina, Chile, Mexico, Peru, Venezuela, and Spain.
44. Mitchell also wrote the best book on Flamenco music, *Flamenco Deep Song* (1994).
45. Alfred Gell, cited in Mitchell, *Intoxicated Identities*, 58.
46. Mitchell, *Intoxicated Identities*, 58–59.
47. Television interview, Televisa, 21 September 2017.
48. Moreno, "Guillermo Del Toro on How He Balances the Dark with the Good."
49. Breton, "Recuerdo de México."
50. Lomnitz, *Death and the Idea of Mexico*, 20.
51. Wolf, *Sons of the Shaking Earth*, ix.

52. Padden, *The Hummingbird and the Hawk*, 74.
53. See the comparative percentages in McCaa, "El poblamiento de México," 44. Demographic historian Agustín Grajales estimates the population decline at between 70 percent and 85 percent (personal communication, 2018).
54. Gibson, *The Aztecs under Spanish Rule*, 409. Native Americans may have a genetic disposition to alcoholism and the diseases related to this problem.
55. Cockcroft, *Mexico*, 64.
56. Enzenberger, *Anarchy's Brief Summer*, 2.
57. See McCaa, "Missing Millions." See also Mraz, "War Is Hazardous for Your Health," 894.
58. Lomintz, *Death and the Idea of Mexico*, 43.
59. Roger Bartra, *La jaula de la melancolía*, 76.
60. Lomnitz, *Death and the Idea of Mexico*, 405.
61. Pansters, "La Santa Muerte," 8.
62. See a partial list of some sixty popular terms in Lomnitz, *Death and the Idea of Mexico*, 26.
63. Lockwood, *Castro's Cuba, Cuba's Fidel*, xvi.
64. Dianne Walta Hart, "Communication," 302.
65. I mention the international distribution of this work because many times one is confronted by juries (for funding, festivals, and awards) made up of cineastes whose work has never been accepted by a film distribution company. This is as if one were credited with having a published book and therefore being knowledgeable about a subject, based solely on a manuscript that has not been accepted by a press. The International Movie Database (IMDb) will not list cinema that has not in distribution and has now become an arbiter of a production's "publication."
66. My contretemps in Nicaragua did not disillusion me with the possibilities of revolutionary transformation, as was the case with Michael Johns, who describes himself as a radish, "red on the outside but white on the inside" (*The Education of a Radical*, 74). Johns seems willfully ignorant of the destruction of Sandinista revolution by the US-funded mercenaries, the Contras.
67. Edgar Bravo, Managua, July, 1986.
68. Vanderwood, review of *Innovating Nicaragua* and *Made on Rails*, 48. The latter received several awards and is also distributed internationally.
69. Nichols, *Representing Reality*, 23, xiv.
70. Kuehl, "T.V. History," 129.
71. Neither the personal relations of Gloria Tirado nor the political position of the UAP served to enable an interview with the leader of the 1958–59 railroad movement, Demetrio Vallejo. Gloria had set up the meeting in Mexico City, but when we arrived to shoot, he became petulant, finally saying that I had a "strange" accent; as I was not a Mexican, he would not participate in the videotape. The very opposite occurred with Guillermo Treviño, with whom I bonded immediately both because of Gloria's intermediation and my own political stance.

72. Gardner, "Oral History and Video in Theory and Practice," 105.
73. Ellwood, "Archivo Nazionale Cinematografico Della Resistenza," 31.
74. Erik Barnouw, *Documentary*, 253–62; Rouch, "Jean Rouch," 137.
75. Mraz, *Made on Rails/Hechos sobre los rieles.*
76. See Luna, "El video aplicado a la memoria de las mujeres latinoamericanas."
77. See Portelli, "The Peculiarities of Oral History."
78. Mraz, *Made on Rails.*
79. Conversation with David Culbert.
80. Bartra i Murià, "Les 'febres de l'or' de Magí Murià."
81. Mraz, *Magí Murià.*
82. Mraz, *Magí Murià.*
83. Mraz, *Magí Murià.*
84. Romaguera i Ramió, *Magí Murià.*
85. Mraz, *Julio Mayo.* I do not ask to be paid to curate photo exhibits, but instead look to create a product that will last long after the exhibit has been taken down. In this case, I requested the funding to do an interview with Julio and make the short documentary.
86. Harlan, "Ken Burns and the Coming Crisis of Academic History," 186.
87. Harlan, 187.
88. O'Connor, personal communication, 1987.
89. Henderson, "*The Civil War*," 10.
90. Metz, *The Imaginary Signifier*, 220.
91. MacCann, *The People's Films*, 37.
92. Erik Barnouw, *Documentary*, 201.
93. Tibbets, "The Incredible Stillness of Being," 126.
94. Mraz, "Santiago Álvarez," 135.
95. Czach, "'At Home,'" 11.
96. Sorlin, *The Film in History*, 4.
97. I have been guest editor in of three journals in three fields (and three different countries): *Mexican Photography*, *Cultura visual en América Latina*, and *Cinema and History in Latin America.*
98. Mraz, "Video and Labor History"; Mraz, "Video e historia obrera en México"; Mraz, "Una storia che corre sui binari."
99. Daniel Walkowitz, letter, 12 December 1991; written comments on manuscript, 1991.
100. For an outrageously funny memoir on academia see Eagleton, *The Gatekeeper.*
101. Walkowitz is listed as a co-director on *The Molders of Troy* (1980), where he occupies the third place behind Jack Ofield (who appears to have been the director) and Barbara Abrash; see the listing on IMDb: https://www.imdb.com/title/tt1129385/reference. He evidently worked on two other films, but they are not in distribution. It would appear that Walkowitz's only article on cinehistory is "Visual History." Abrash and Sternberg, *Historians and Filmmakers.*
102. See "Film Reviews: Introductory Note."

103. Rosenstone, *Adventures of a Postmodern Historian*, 165.
104. Rosenstone, "The Historical Film as Real History," 7. See also Rosenstone's *Visions of the Past*; *History on Film/Film on History*; *Revisioning History*; and the "AHR Forum. History in Images/History in Words."

CHAPTER 2

Epigraph. DeLillo, *Point Omega*, 13.

1. The reference here is to the *noeme* of Roland Barthes: "That-has-been" (*Camera Lucida*, 80).
2. "The deciphering of meaning [...] is taken to be the central task of cultural history" (Hunt, "Introduction," 12).
3. Szarkowski, *Mirrors and Windows*.
4. Arnheim, "The Two Authenticities of the Photographic Medium."
5. Barthes, "The Photographic Message," 17.
6. Kossoy, *Fotografía e historia*, 42–43. Italics in the original.
7. See Batchen, ed., "Vernacular Photographies."
8. I have here published the uncropped version of this photo so that readers can appreciate the way Álvarez Bravo constructed the scene.
9. Jimenéz and Villela, *Los Salmerón*, 14.
10. Arago, "Report" (1839), 18.
11. Poe, "The Daguerreotype" (1840), 38. Italics in the original.
12. See Stasz, "The Early History of Visual Sociology," 119–36.
13. Bayard mounted his scene as a protest against the recognition given to Daguerre as the inventor of photography by the Academy of Sciences, contending fruitlessly that he had been the first to do so; see barbarapvn, "El suicidio montado por Monsieur Hipólito Bayard."
14. Stieglitz, "Pictorial Photography" (1899), 117. For the Kodak motto, see "You Press the Button, We Do the Rest" (Wikipedia, https://en.wikipedia.org/wiki/You_Press_the_Button,_We_Do_the_Rest, last edited 6 November 2020, at 00:54).
15. Benjamin, "Small History of Photography" (1931), 66 (Leslie, trans.); Benjamin, "A Short History of Photography," (1931), 202 (Trachtenberg, trans.). I have combined the translations found in Leslie and Trachtenberg.
16. Ibid.
17. Kracauer, *Theory of Film*, 23, 28.
18. Kracauer, *Theory of Film*, 300–301.
19. See Cassirer, *The Philosophy of the Enlightenment*.
20. Kraucauer, *Theory of Film*, 309. Kracauer anticipated the reaction to his *Theory of Film*. In a letter written before the book's release, he stated, "Of one thing I am sure: it will arouse violent controversies, and the art-minded will, all of them, be against it" (Dagmar Barnouw, "The Shapes of Objectivity," 146).

21. Freund's 1936 thesis in sociology and art was titled "La Photographie en France au XIXe siècle." It was translated into Spanish as *La fotografía y las clases medias en Francia durante el siglo XIX*. Her pathbreaking book *Photography & Society* was originally published in French in 1974. The translation into Spanish, *La fotografía como documento social*, is much better known than the English book.
22. Bazin, *What Is Cinema?*, 13.
23. Peirce proposed that there are three basic kinds of signs: indexes, icons, and symbols; see Peirce, "Logic as Semiotic," 102. Nigel Warburton has intelligently synthesized Pierce's thoughts in the following way: "An index is a sign which represents something else because it is in a relatively direct *causal* relation with that thing. . . . An icon is a sign which represents something because of its resemblance to that thing: if a picture of a cat resembles a cat then it can serve as an iconic sign for the cat. . . . A symbol represents by virtue of a convention: the word 'sky' does not have any intrinsic representational properties—it is only because of a general convention that it stands for what it does" (Emphasis mine; "Varieties of Photographic Representation," 204–5).
24. Barthes, *Camera Lucida*, 80.
25. See Lefebvre, "The Art of Pointing."
26. Brecht, *Brecht on Film and Radio*, 164–65.
27. Fontcuberta, *El beso de Judas*, 15.
28. Williams, *Keywords*, 219.
29. Azoulay, *Civil Imagination*, 223.
30. Berger, "Appearances," [1982], in *Understanding a Photograph*, 65–66.
31. Olin, cited in Kevin Coleman, "Photographs of a Prayer," 462.
32. Brand, Kelly, Kinney, "Digital Retouching."
33. See Schultz, "This Professor Can Tell from the Pixels That Your Photo's Been 'Shopped," and Cruz, "Cómo comprobar la autenticidad de una fotografía digital."
34. Dooms, "A Picture Is Worth 1000 Words . . . But Which Language Does It Speak?" and Silverman, "Three Ways to Spot if an Image Has Been Manipulated." However, modern technology is moving so quickly that it is now possible to dub documentary footage with false voice impersonations; see Solon, "The Future of Fake News."
35. A fine analysis of the imagery produced around the Oaxacan teachers' movement can be found in Nahón, "El fotoperiodismo como testimonio y memoria del movimiento popular en Nochixtlán, Oaxaca, 2016."
36. Aristegui, "CNS dijo que son falsas fotos de policías armados"; and Cruz, "Cómo comprobar la autenticidad de una fotografía digital."
37. Cruz, "Cómo comprobar la autenticidad de una fotografía digital."
38. Cruz, "Cómo comprobar la autenticidad de una fotografía digital."
39. Scruton, "Photography and Representation," 579, 590.

40. Walton, "Transparent Pictures," 251. Italics in the original. I am aware that Walton's argument in relation to art may be invalid, as contributors to the polemic such as Edwin Martin, Donald Brook, and Jonathon Friday indicate. However, I am concerned with the use of photographs in history.
41. Walton, "Looking Again through Photographs," 807.
42. Walton, "Transparent Pictures," 267.
43. Jeffrey, *Photography*, 14. See the photo of Notre Dame and carts on this page.
44. See my discussion of Mexican picture histories in Mraz, *Looking for México*, 72–76, 192–200, and 226–35. See also Mraz, "Picturing Mexico's Past"; "Representing the Mexican Revolution"; and "Visualizar el pasado mexicano."
45. Navarrete, *Fotografiando en América Latina*, 199.
46. Mauad, *Poses y flagrantes*. See the works of Brazilian photohistorians Carlos Sampaio, Annateresa Fabris, Maria Pace Chaivari, Ulpiano Bezerra de Meneses, Vania Carneiro de Carvalho, and Solange Ferraz de Lima. I am grateful to Ana Mauad for this information.
47. Deas, *Historia de Colombia a través de la fotografía*. Sandra Sánchez López assured me that there is nothing comparable to the Mexican photohistories in Colombia (personal communication, 2016).
48. Broquetas, ed., *Fotografía en Uruguay*, volumes I and II.
49. Rivas Rivas, *Historia gráfica de Venezuela*.
50. Gutiérrez, *Fotografía latinoamericana del siglo XIX*.
51. Vallès, *Història Gràfica de la Catalunya Contemporània*. As a community dominated by Spain, Catalans have great interest in conserving their culture, and one element for doing so is picture histories; see the 2015 series *La Barcelona d'ahir*, subsidized by the Catalan government.
52. Vallès, *Història Gràfica de la Catalunya Contemporània*, 9.
53. Vallès, *Història Gràfica de la Catalunya Contemporània*.
54. Martínez Assad, *Memoria y olvido*; Florescano, *Así fue la Revolución Mexicana*; Krauze, *Biografía del poder*; Aguilar Camín et al., *Historia gráfica de México*.
55. Samuels, *Theatres of History*, 321.
56. By Great Men, I refer to leaders who are identified in a photo with a name and surname. This category does not include nameless soldiers, workers, and *campesinos*, both men and women who are not in a leadership capacity. Nor does it include named individuals that are being executed for forgery or desertion during the Mexican Revolution. Thomas Carlyle's most famous work was *On Heroes, Hero-Worship, and the Heroic in History*, published in 1841. He asserted that history can be known only through the biographies of Great Men.
57. One particularly trenchant and oft-mentioned example suffices: that of *The Treasure of the Sierra Madre* (Huston, 1948), when the bandit played by Alfonso Bedoya responds to Humphrey Bogart's demand that he show a badge to prove he is a sheriff: "We don't need no badges. I don't have to show you any stinking badges."

58. Edwards, "Photographs as Strong History?," 321.
59. Delgado, *Veracruz: Imágenes de su historia.* I have discussed this series in greater length in Mraz, "Picturing Mexico's Past," 36–39.
60. Canales, *Romualdo García*; Morales Carrillo, *El gran lente.*
61. Tovalín Ahumada et al., *Joaquín Santamaría.*
62. Jiménez and Villela, *Los Salmerón.*
63. Villela, *Sara Castrejón.*
64. Sigüenza Orozco and Mino Gracia, *Imágenes de un pionero del oficio fotográfico en Tlacolula.*
65. The priest is Ignacio Colmenares, known as el padre Nachito, a veteran *cura* who had been imprisoned during the 1920s as part of the Cristero Rebellion (Fernando Mino, personal communication, 2019).
66. Zamora, *Cholula: Memoria e identidad.* The following description of the book's production and the *fototeca's* founding was provided by José Zamora, personal communication, 2019.
67. The Fototeca Nacional contains a total of around a million images. See Davidson, *Picture Collections*, for a guide (now dated) to more than five hundred photograph archives in Mexico, and *Directorio de archivos, fototecas y centros especializados en fotografía.* A more recent project is the "Observatorio de patrimonio fotográfico mexicano," which can be consulted through the Fotobservatoria website, http://fotobservatorio.mx; this is largely a product of Fernando Osorio's efforts to identify, conserve, and make known Mexican photographic collections.
68. This was a key notion of the New Photojournalists of Mexico, whose work is now being extensively analyzed by scholars and graduate students in several universities. See Mraz, "Mexico: The New Photojournalism."
69. Navarrete, *Fotografiando en América Latina*, 208.
70. Noble, Review of *Photographing the Mexican Revolution.*
71. Researchers in the Instituto Mora have been particularly important in explicitly addressing the issue of establishing methodologies for photographic research; see Aguayo and Roca, eds., *Investigación con imágenes*; Aguayo and Roca, eds., *Imágenes e investigación social*; *Tejedores de imágenes.*
72. Rebeca Monroy Nasr, personal communication, 2019.
73. Monroy Nasr, "Los quehaceres de los fotohistoriadores mexicanos."
74. Monroy Nasr, "El constructo visual desde la fotografía." Some photohistory theses are missing from this list.
75. De los Santos García Felguera, "Las principales revistas," 28.
76. I was asked to give the keynote address at the UNAM congress *Fotohistoria de la Revolución Mexicana.* As I collected the published books to produce an overview, they reached a height of more than two meters. See Mraz, "Fotohistorias de la Revolución Mexicana."
77. Mother's Day was invented by the newspaper *Excelsior* in 1922 as a response to the progressive reforms relating to birth prevention, divorce, and women's

suffrage instituted in Yucatán by Felipe Carrillo Puerto's socialist government. For a history of Mother's Day in Mexico, see Acevedo, *El 10 de mayo.*

78. Paul Vanderwood, personal conversation, 1985.

79. The Casasola Archive is located in the Fototeca Nacional, while those of the Hermanos Mayo and of the agency Díaz, Delgado y García are found in the AGN. On Díaz, see Monroy Nasr, *Fotografía de prensa en México.*

80. Archivo de Ana Victoria Jiménez, Biblioteca Francisco Xavier Clavijero, Universidad Iberoamericana.

81. Camacho Morfín, "Los álbumes de 'El Buen Tono,'" 82. Camacho Morfín has focused more on the *historietas* (comic books) of this important "model" company. Other historians whose work has shown the importance of combing company archives are Kevin Coleman's excellent *A Camera in the Garden of Eden*, on the United Fruit Company; Sekula's classic study of the Dominion Steel and Coal Corporation, "Photography between Labour and Capital"; and Nye's *Image Worlds*, on General Electric.

82. See, among other works, Canales, *Romualdo García*; Massé Zendjas, *Simulacro y elegancia en tarjetas de visita*; Negrete Álvarez, *Valleto Hermanos*; Monsiváis, *Foto Estudio Jiménez*; and Ramírez Sevilla, *Villa Jiménez en la lente de Martiniano Mendoza.*

83. On Briquet, Gove, and North, see Aguayo, *Estampas Ferrocarrileras*; and Ribera Carbó and Aguayo, *Imágenes y ciudad.* Other foreign photographers are discussed in Chapter 4.

84. Here I must emphasize that my comments about the limitations of family photography are made in relation to modern media, chemical photography, rather than today's postmodern digital cameras that permit an almost infinite capacity for recording almost anything, almost all the time.

85. Bourdieu, *Photography*, 19.

86. Sontag, *On Photography*, 9.

87. Julia Hirsch, *Family Photographs*, 47. Of course, as Hirsch notes, "The rooms we see most often in family photographs are the ones in which we receive our guests, the living room and the parlor, but until recently it was seldom the kitchen and never the bedroom" (55–56). I would add, and by no means the bathroom, which could offer vital information.

88. Hall, cited in Washington, "African American Photographs as Political Resistance in a Postmodern Consumer Age," 85.

89. Kevin Coleman, *A Camera in the Garden of Eden*, 18.

90. James and Lobato, "Family Photos, Oral Narratives, and Identity Formation," 30.

91. On using personal film footage and photographs, see Mauad, "Imagens que faltam, imagens que sobram."

92. See my reflections on the production of this videotape, Mraz, "Video and Labor History."

93. *Made on Rails: A History of the Mexican Railroad Workers.*

94. Research in family photography does not appear to have been greatly developed in Mexico, although a recent book has addressed this issue, Vázquez Olvera, *El ropero de las señoritas Sámano Serrato*. Among other useful Latin American studies, see, on Brazil, Leite, *Retratos de família*; on Colombia, Silva, *Álbum de familia*; and on Argentina, Triquell, *Fotografías e historias*.
95. Marianne Hirsch, *Family Frames*, 11.
96. Collier, *Visual Anthropology*, 46–66. While using photos in an interview provides an instrument that stimulates memories, the act of taking photos may itself ironically impair one's personal recollection of the event itself; see Knapton, "Taking Photographs Ruins the Memory, Research Finds."
97. Even the name of the "author" was misspelled as "Arizmendi." The material for this paragraph is largely available in Massé Zendejas, *Juan Antonio Azurmendi*.
98. Massé Zendejas, "Juan Antonio Azurmendi," 261–67. Massé Zendejas, *Juan Antonio Azurmendi*, an earlier published study of Azurmendi's photography, does not include a discussion of this picture.
99. Bourdieu, *Photography*, 28.
100. Azoulay, *Civil Imagination*, 24–25.
101. Simone de Beauvoir, *Tout compte fait*, cited in Tidd, "Telling the Truth in Simone de Beauvoir's Autobiography," 13.
102. Angustias Farrera was a *mulata* from Guerrero who led Zapatista forces. See the 1944 novel by Francisco Rojas González, *La Negra Angustias*, and the 1949 film with the same name by Matilde Landeta; both are analyzed in Eli Bartra, "How Black Is *La Negra Angustias*?"
103. Cumberland, *Mexican Revolution*, 347.
104. He did not take the camera or the photographer on his trips outside Mexico City in 1919.
105. For instance, he called for a tie-making company to place raised wooden planks on the cold cement floor, so that the workers' feet were not chilled and they would not develop rheumatism; Caja 163 Expediente 11, Departamento de Trabajo, Archivo General de la nación.
106. See Chapter 5. I have described this case, and reproduced the photos in Mraz, "'En calidad de esclavas.'" In English, see Mraz, *Photographing the Mexican Revolution*, 227–29, and Mraz, "Some Visual Notes toward a Graphic History of the Mexican Working Class," 66–67.
107. Ginzburg, "Clues," 99.
108. The idea of CPA was coined by Linda Stone in 1998; Wikipedia, s.v. "Continuous partial attention," last modified 20 June 2019, 2:10, https://en.wikipedia.org/wiki/Continuous_partial_attention.
109. Departamento del Trabajo, Caja 220, expediente 4, Archivo General de la Nación.
110. Ibid.
111. Other than a searing depiction of class relations, the photo also provides an insight into the politics of the Casasola series. The caption for the photo stated:

"The abuses of the carriers were terrible, in the middle of the Street they asked for more money or they let them fall" (Casasola, *Seis siglos de historia gráfica de México*, 112).

112. See the photo in Mraz, *Photographing the Mexican Revolution*, 79.
113. García Díaz, *Santa Rosa y Río Blanco*, 53.
114. See the photographs in García Díaz, *Santa Rosa y Río Blanco*, 113, 155, This same phenomenon can be observed in the Chalaco soccer teams of 1912 and 1930 in Peru; see Steve J. Stein, "Visual Images of the Lower Classes in Early Twentieth-Century Peru."
115. Frost, *Timeless Mexico*, photograph 17.
116. Brehme, *Pueblos y paisajes de México*, 77.
117. The canal dried up as a result of drainage projects, and is today the urbanized *delegación* (borough), Iztacalco.
118. See Monsivaís, *Foto Estudio Jiménez*. This would appear to be true of Peru and Bolivia as well; see Antmann, "The Peasant Miners of Morococha," 63.
119. *Made on Rails*.
120. See the photograph in García Díaz, *Santa Rosa y Río Blanco*, 97.
121. Lesy, "Conclusion," *Wisconsin Death Trip*, n.p.
122. Levine, *Images of History*, 49. Levine's is an error of "logical types": being shoeless or badly dressed is a condition of some duration; being weary is an immediate state.
123. Bernardo García Díaz, personal communication, 1990. The historian did not note the source of this information in the text, a practice that would be useful.
124. Lesy anticipates this objection by asserting that Charley Van Schaick, the Wisconsin photographer he analyses, "used plates that permitted half-second exposures." Lesy, "Introduction," *Wisconsin Death Trip*, n.p. However, he does not examine the conventions for posing in a studio at that time.
125. For a comparison of these photographs, see Mraz, *Photographing the Mexican Revolution*, 190.
126. Mraz, *Photographing the Mexican Revolution*, 189.
127. See these photographs in Hernández, *Entre la tierra y el aire*, 62, 43.
128. Juan Carlos Valdéz, director of the Sistema Nacional de Fototecas and the Fototeca Nacional, personal communication, 2000.
129. Azoulay, *The Civil Contract of Photography*, 217.
130. Nathanial Gardner, personal communication, 2018.
131. Kevin Colemen, "Las fotos que no alcanzamos a ver," 150–51.
132. The issue of intent is always problematic in photography. However, in the case I discuss below, the photographing of Maty Huitrón, Nacho López's intent was clearly that of producing the expected catcall from the men in the street. See the lengthy description by López of what he called a strategy of "previsualization" in relation to similar images; Mraz, "What's Documentary about Photography." I further discuss the issue of directing photojournalist imagery in Mraz, "From Robert Capa's 'Dying Republican Soldier' to Political Scandal in Contemporary Mexico."

133. Bateson, *Mind and Nature*, 69.
134. See my discussion of cinematic machismo in Mraz, *Looking for Mexico*, 134–42.
135. This is a familiar strategy of documentary filmmakers such as Jean Rouch and Michael Moore. On directed photojournalism, see Mraz, "What's Documentary about Photography?" None of the men who appear in this photo can be found in any of the other images taken for this project; hence, we can assume that the only "actor" is Maty Huitrón.
136. An interesting exercise of comparing photos is carried out by Whelan, *Double Take*.
137. For a more developed discussion of these photographs, see Mraz, *Nacho López: Mexican Photographer*, 117–21.
138. López, "Cuando una mujer guapa parte plaza por Madero," 24; López, *Nacho Lopez: Yo, el ciudadano*, 57.
139. A short discussion of this photo's history, and a reproduction, can be found in Orkin, *A Photo Journal*, 90. I have discussed the question of whether López had seen the Orkin image in Mraz, *Nacho López*, 119. Unfortunately, I was denied the right to reproduce the photo by Ruth Orkin's daughter, who said, "I continuously turn down requests to use this photo for any connection to sexual harassment, etc." (personal communication, June 18, 2017). The image can be seen on the Ruth Orkin Photo Archive website, at http://www.orkinphoto.com/photographs/american-girl.
140. I thank Dominka Gasiorowski for this observation, which I had failed to notice despite the years I have worked with this image.
141. See this photograph in Miserachs, *Barcelona*, 242–43.
142. López, "Cuando una mujer guapa parte plaza por Madero," 24.
143. Rivera Ortiz, *Columnas contra cordones*, 53.
144. *El Nacional*, 2 May 1952, cited in Nares Ramos, "Siqueiros y los Hermanos Mayo," 34.
145. Called *Dorados* because of their gold shirts, the fascist organization Acción Revolucionaria Mexicanista (ARM) was founded in 1934.
146. Siqueiros probably sent an assistant to the Mayo studio to get a copy. At one hundred years of age, Julio Mayo still complained about the lack of respect shown him by Siqueiros, who paid him nothing for the photo, but "could have at least given me a painting" (personal conversation with Julio Mayo, 2017). By contrast, Mexican photojournalists Nacho López and Héctor García enjoyed close relationships with artists. López participated in collective exhibits of Los Interioristas, a group that included artists such as José Luis Cuevas, Francisco Icaza, and Arnold Belkin; see Goldman, *Contemporary Mexican Painting in a Time of Change*. García was also close to Cuevas and worked directly with Alberto Gironella; see Mraz, *Looking for Mexico*, 191–92. The different treatment meted out to the Mayo may represent yet another *ninguneo* of them within Mexican culture. See my remarks about how the "photographic aristocracy have disdained them as mere photojournalists," Mraz, *Looking for Mexico*, 178.

147. Siqueiros, cited in Goldman, *Contemporary Mexican Painting in a Time of Change*, 41–42. See also González Cruz Manjarrez, *Siqueiros en la mira*.
148. Mario Rivera Ortiz, "Aclaración sobre un pie de foto," a letter to the editor published in *La Jornada*, 1 June 2003, 2. The publication of this photo produced a polemic on the pages of *La Jornada* that lasted until 16 June 2003.
149. Rivera Ortiz, *Columnas contra cordones*, 62.
150. *Mañana*, 10 May 1952, 4A, 10A.
151. "13 instantáneas," *Mañana*, No. 627, 3 September 1955. The magazine presented the photos as if they had been taken in the year to which they were assigned. Nevertheless, its interest in obscuring the real origin of this photo was made clear in its allegation that it was taken in 1950 rather than 1952.
152. I questioned Julio Mayo about the use made of this image. Although he was usually passionate and outspoken, he just shrugged and indicated that this was such a common occurrence for photojournalists as to make commentary unnecessary.
153. Ritchin, *After Photography*, 178.
154. Among the photographs made during the armed struggle that have become icons, I find five to be of particular interest: Emiliano Zapata standing stolidly in charro raiment, a sash across his chest, with a carbine in one hand and the other on a sword; "Adelita-the-soldadera" peering intensely from the train; Francisco Villa galloping toward the camera; Villa lolling in the presidential chair next to Zapata; and Victoriano Huerta hidden in the shadows together with his General Staff. See Mraz, *Photographing the Mexican Revolution*, 233–58.
155. Azoulay, *Civil Imagination*, 21. Italics in the original.
156. Paul, "Visual History," 6. A classic contribution in English to photos as "catalysts" is Goldberg, *The Power of Photography*.
157. Gamarnik, "El fotoperiodismo y la guerra de Malvinas."
158. Annie Hammond, personal communication, August 2019.
159. Annie Hammond, personal communication, July 2019. In 2012, I was asked by the editor Luke Gartlan to be guest editor of an issue on Latin American photography. I invited the best Latin American photohistorians I know to participate, but after three years the texts were rejected (with the exception of mine, which I had retired). The editor simply did not understand what we were doing, but he did publish a poorly researched, though perhaps correctly literary, article on Argentina, which he wanted to include in my issue. The articles I solicited from Latin American photohistorians were eventually published elsewhere in Spanish. See Mraz and Mauad, *Fotografía e historia en América Latina*.
160. See Mraz, *Looking for Mexico*, 2–3.
161. I am referring to Freud's famous aphorism about people who clean their glasses but do not put them on.
162. Flusser, *Towards a Philosophy of Photography*, 9, 12.

163. Nichols, *Representing Reality*, xii, xiv.
164. Noble, Review of *Photographing the Mexican Revolution*.
165. Barthes, *Camera Lucida*, 23.
166. Foster, *Argentine, Mexican, and Guatemalan Photography*, xiv. See my review of this book in the *Journal of Latin American Studies*.
167. Brant, Review of David William Foster, 180.
168. Jameson, *The Cultural Turn*, 20.
169. Eagleton, *After Theory*, 77.
170. On the 1996 Sokal Affair, see *The Sokal Hoax*, 11.
171. Sokal and Bricmont, *Intellectual Imposters*, 2.
172. *The Sokal Hoax*, 50.
173. *The Sokal Hoax*, 52.
174. Linfield, *The Cruel Radiance*, 11.
175. Solomon-Godeau, "Who Is Speaking Thus?," 203–4. See as well Sekula, "Dismantling Modernism, Reinventing Documentary"; Rosler, "In, Around, and Afterthoughts (on Documentary Photography)"; and Stein, "Making Connections."

CHAPTER 3

Epigraph. Sontag, *On Photography*, 148.

1. Flusser, "Photography and History," in *Vilém Flusser*, 126.
2. Flusser, *Vilém Flusser*, 127.
3. Solomon-Godeau, *Photography at the Dock*, 4.
4. Solomon-Godeau, *Photography after Photography*, 79.
5. Solomon-Godeau, *Photography after Photography*, 77.
6. See Malagón Girón, "La fotografía de Winfield Scott." The thesis is available as a book, Malagón Girón, *Winfield Scott*.
7. This Mexican saying, "The 20-cent coin dropped," is a reference to the old telephone booths in which the coin fell when the call was answered. In English the phrase is "the penny dropped."
8. Azoulay, *Civil Imagination*, 86.
9. McDonald, "'A History Making Occasion,'" 33.
10. Newhall, *The History of Photography*.
11. Hill and Cooper, *Dialogue with Photography*, 159.
12. Castro, "Crossover Dreams," 65, 61. Castro's essay is in *Image and Memory*, a book published in association with FotoFest, a large congress and exhibit organized in 1983 in Houston that appeared to be focused in its first years on depoliticizing Latin American photography in reaction to the social documentary photography that was promoted by major exhibits of Latin American photography such as *Hecho en Latinoamérica*. The book produced by FotoFest, *Image and Memory*, so slighted documentary photography that the only Mexican photographer that appears is Flor Garduño, whose pseudo-documentary imagery I have criticized; see Mraz, *Looking for Mexico*, 222–23.

13. González Flores, "Nuevas subjetividades en la fotografía mexicana contemporánea," 250.
14. I have analyzed the various functions of photographs within the genre of portraiture in Mraz, "Retratos fotográficos."
15. Sandweiss, *Print the Legend.*
16. E. D. Hirsch Jr., *Validity in Interpretation*, 72, 71.
17. Todorov, "The Origen of Genres," 162.
18. E. D. Hirsch Jr., *Validity in Interpretation*, 111. See also Derrida, "The Law of Genre," 221; and Todorov, "The Typology of Detective Fiction," 48.
19. See Marzal Felici, *Cómo se lee una fotografía*, 82–87; and Solomon-Godeau, *Photography after Photography*. One book whose title appears promising is hobbled by its art history approach, Picaudé and Arbaïzar, *La confusion de los géneros en fotografía.*
20. Mraz, " 'En calidad de esclavas.' " One of the best examples of vignettes as history is the trilogy of Eduardo Galeano, *Memory of Fire*, 1985–1988.
21. Reinhard Schultz, *Tina Modotti.*
22. Mraz, "Tina Modotti."
23. Mraz, "Los Hermanos Mayo."
24. *Sobremesa* has been identified as the first of "10 of the Best Words in the World (That Don't Translate into English)" (*Guardian*, 27 July 2018, https://www.theguardian.com/world/2018/jul/27/10-of-the-best-words-in-the-world-that-dont-translate-into-english). As the correspondents who collaborated on this article noted, "It is also a sybaritic time; a recognition that there is more to life than working long hours and that few pleasures are greater than sharing a table and then chatting nonsense for a hefty portion of what remains of the day." Much business is carried out during Mexican *sobremesas* alongside the "nonsense."
25. In 2016, López was honored with a large exhibit in Bellas Artes, the most important exhibit space in Mexico, and two large edited academic studies of his photography have recently been published: Rodríguez and Tovalín Ahumada, eds., *Nacho López: Fotógrafo de México* and *Nacho López: Ideas y visualidad.* See also the encyclopedic "Nacho López," a special issue of *Luna Córnea*, (no. 31, 2007) dedicated to his work.
26. Bateson, *Steps to an Ecology of Mind*, 278. Italics in the original.
27. Moya, "Las imágenes prohibidas," 4.
28. Chanan, "The Melancholy of a Political Documentarist," 201.
29. Schwartz, "To Tell the Truth," 13.
30. Garner, *Disappearing Witness.*
31. "Foto Hnos. Mayo," Mexico City, 1982.
32. See my study of the Mexican illustrated magazines in Mraz, "Today, Tomorrow, and Always."
33. For example, Vilches, *Teoría de la imagen periodística*; Fulton, *Eyes of Time*; Curtis, *Mind's Eye, Mind's Truth*; Willumson, *W. Eugene Smith and the Photographic Essay*; Kozol, Life's *America.*

34. Sekula, "Dismantling Modernism, Reinventing Documentary"; Stein, "Making Connections with the Camera"; Solomon-Godeau, "Who Is Speaking Thus?"; Rosler, "In, Around, and Afterthoughts (on Documentary Photography)."
35. Benjamin, "The Work of Art in the Age of Mechanical Reproduction"; Sontag, *On Photography*; Berger, *Ways of Seeing*; Barthes, *Camera Lucida*. Berger's important essays on photography have been collected in *Understanding a Photograph*.
36. Nacho did not conserve his negatives in their original strips, as is common among photojournalists; instead he cut them up and saved some of the negatives in individual envelopes, throwing away those he did not want.
37. The information about the many photographers found in the Casasola Archive was first published in Gutiérrez Ruvalcaba, "A Fresh Look at the Casasola Archive." See the important 2014 work by Escorza Rodríguez, *Agustín Víctor Casasola*. I'm confident a similar observation could be made of the images produced for the Mathew Brady studio.
38. *Nacho López, fotorreportero de los años cincuenta.*
39. Letter to Manuel Berman, 1 August 1980, Archivo Documental Familia López Binnqüist (ADFLB).
40. Saunders, *20th Century Advertising*, 112.
41. Flusser, *Into the Universe of Technical Images*, 49.
42. Del Castillo Troncoso, *Fotografía y memoria*, 164.
43. Del Castillo Troncoso, *Fotografía y memoria*, 190.
44. Horton, *The Associated Press Photojournalism Stylebook*, 51.
45. See Castellanos, "Mentiras en la azotea."
46. De la Peña, *Ética, poética y prosaica*, 9.
47. See "Polémica y debate abierto" and de la Peña, *Ética, Poética y Prosaica*.
48. Fulton, *Eyes of Time*, 188.
49. López, "Solo los humildes van al infierno."
50. See Willumson, *W. Eugene Smith and the Photographic Essay*.
51. López, "Yo también he sido niño bueno . . ."
52. Personal conversations with Rodrigo Moya, 2000–2019.
53. López, *Nacho López: Yo, el ciudadano*, 11.
54. I have argued that the term *documentary* seems to arise and become important in situations of social strife; see Mraz, "El testimonio de los índices."
55. Stott, *Documentary Expression and Thirties America*, 319.
56. Stallabrass, "Sebastião Salgado and Fine Art Photojournalism."
57. See Mraz, "Mexico: The New Photojournalism."
58. Estrin, "Latin American Pictures of the Year."
59. Modotti letter to Weston, 23 May 1930, cited in Hooks, *Tina Modotti*, 210.
60. Cartier-Bresson, "The Decisive Moment."
61. Mraz, "Retratos fotográficos," written for the Fundación BBVA Bancomer.
62. The figure of 95 percent is cited in relation to daguerreotypes in Europe and the US; in Mexico it was probably nearer to 98 percent. See Starl, "A New World of Pictures," 37.

63. Casanova and Debroise, *Sobre la superficie bruñida de un espejo*, 22.
64. Levine, *Images of History*, 14. See the Brazilian emperor, Pedro II, with his head in a clamp, 15.
65. Cited in Malcolm, "The Genius of the Glass House," 10.
66. See my discussion of prostitute photography in Mraz, *Looking for Mexico*, 21–22.
67. See the chapter "The Sons of La Malinche," in Paz, *The Labyrinth of Solitude*.

CHAPTER 4

Epigraph. Eliot, *The Old World and the New*, 21.

1. See Mraz, " 'Querían fotos,' " an extreme critique of photographing Indians inspired by the works of Faris: "Photography, Power and the Southern Nuba," "A Political Primer on Anthropology/Photography," and *Navajo and Photography*.
2. There would seem to be few historical examples of indigenous photography in Mexico, and perhaps the most important publication resulted from a project directed by a Mexican American, Carlota Duarte's *Camaristas*. This book includes the imagery of eight Mayans (four men and four women), of which the best known is Maruch Sántiz Gómez, who has acquired an international reputation as an outstanding photographer. Ángeles Torrejón worked over a span of eight years with the Neo-Zapatista women; she is very critical of Duarte's work, describing her as a "satrap" and a "thief" (Corkovic, "La cultura indígena en la fotografía mexicana de los 90s," 951). Corkovic's study provides an important overview that includes interviews with Mexican indigenous photographers.

   Amerindian media in the Andean region has received much attention, perhaps because of the extraordinary imagery made by Martín Chambi, who was a mestizo with Aymara roots and spoke Quechua fluently. On Chambi, see the text by López Mondéjar, "La magia de Martín Chambi"; and the book by Garay Albújar, *Martín Chambi*. In English, see the issue of *History of Photography* on South America edited by Michele M. Penhall. Recent studies point to a notable development of indigenous media in this region; see Zamorano Villarreal, *Indigenous Media and Political Imaginaries in Contemporary Bolivia*; and Schiwy, *Indianizing Film*.
3. For a comprehensive visual introduction to Indianist photography in Mexico, see Vélez Storey, *El ojo de vidrio*.
4. Berger and Mohr, *Another Way of Telling*, 97. Among useful studies on imperial photography, see Hartmann, Silvester, and Hayes, eds., *The Colonizing Camera*; Behdad and Gartland, eds., *Photography's Orientalism*; Hight and Sampson, eds., *Colonialist Photography*; Ryan, *Picturing Empire*.
5. As recently as 2017, the President of RETV (Spanish radio and television), José Antonio Sánchez, alleged that the Amerindian nations were not conquered or colonized by Spain, but that they were "civilized" (Sánchez, "España no fue colonizadora").

6. Roger Bartra, "Stuffing the Indian Photographically," 238.
7. See Roger Bartra, "Jaime Labastida," 8–9.
8. The concept of "contact zone"—"the space in which peoples geographically and historically separated come into contact with each other"—is Pratt's (*Imperial Eyes*, 6).
9. Casanova, "Un nuevo modo de representar," 196–97.
10. Stephens, *Incidents of Travel in Central America, Chiapas and Yucatan*, 99–100.
11. Taracena Arriola, *De la nostalgia por la memoria a la memoria nostálgica*, 171.
12. Taracena Arriola, *De la nostalgia*, 171. On the longer history of attribution of the Mayan ruins, see Depetris, *El héroe involuntario*.
13. Césaire, *Discourse on Colonialism*, 34. The Martinique intellectual was referring specifically to Gourou's 1947 study *Les pays tropicaux: Principes d'une géographie humaine et économique*. Césaire was an anti-assimilationist, and the first to use the concept of "Negritude," believing that the "Negro heritage was worthy of respect, and that this heritage was not relegated to the past, that its values were values that could still make an important contribution to the world" (76). This stance has a great deal of relevance to the question of Amerindians and their culture in today's world.
14. Heilbrun, "Around the World," 166.
15. Cited in Bueno, *The Pursuit of Ruins*, 24. On the Spanish Pacific Scientific Commission to Latin America accompanied by the photographer, Rafael Castro y Ordoñez, see Navarrete, *Fotografiando en América Latina*, 169.
16. Casanova, "De vistas y retratos," 12.
17. Naggar, "The Fascination for the Other," 44.
18. Naggar, "The Fascination for the Other," 44.
19. Casanova, "De vistas y retratos," 14.
20. For examples of Aubert's imagery, see Aguilar Ochoa, *La fotografía durante el imperio de Maximiliano*.
21. Navarrete, *Fotografiando en América Latina*, 52. In this sense, the Frenchmen's imagery differed sharply from the "types" pictured by Mexican photographers such as Cruces y Campa; see Mraz, *Looking for Mexico*, 24–31.
22. Rodríguez Hernández, " 'Ahora aquí, ahora allá,' " 40.
23. Noam Chomsky defines "settler colonialism" as "by far the worst kind of imperialism, because it gets rid of the native population . . . [it] eliminates them, 'exterminates' them" (*Power Systems*, 4). Juárez eventually granted the Kickapoos the land they sought in 1866, and since that day, they have moved freely between the US and Mexico.
24. Rodríguez Hernández, " 'Ahora aquí, ahora allá,' " 36–37.
25. See Castro's beautiful color lithograph in Monsiváis et al., *Casimiro Castro y su taller*, 95.
26. My reading of Maler is based largely upon the work of Gutiérrez Ruvalcaba, *Teoberto Maler*.

27. Letter of Robert B. Gorsuch, December 1868, cited in Gutiérrez Ruvalcaba, *Teoberto Maler*, 20. On Gorsuch, see Schell, *Integral Outsiders*, 1–3.
28. Maler, "Mémoire sur l'estat de Chiapas" [1885], cited in Gutiérrez Ruvalcaba, *Teoberto Maler*, 75.
29. Gutiérrez Ruvalcaba, *Teoberto Maler*, 31.
30. Ignacio Gutiérrez Ruvalcaba, personal communication, February 2017.
31. Ignacio Solís, cited in Taracena Arriola, "Photography in Guatemala as a Social Document," 16.
32. Naggar and Ritchin, *Mexico through Foreign Eyes*, 299.
33. Lutz and Collins, *Reading* Natural Geographic, 89. Italics in the original.
34. Gutiérrez Ruvalcaba, *Teoberto Maler*, 26, 30.
35. See Mraz, *Looking for Mexico*, 35–36.
36. Gutiérrez Ruvalcaba, *Teoberto Maler*, 28.
37. Gutiérrez Ruvalcaba, *Teoberto Maler*, 34. Sekula, "The Body and the Archive," 355.
38. One poorly printed book of his imagery is Diguet, *Fotografías del Nayar y de California*. The photographs were originally in the Museé de l'Home and are now in Musée du Quai Branly—Jacques Chirac. See a recent study on Diguet's photographs, Rodríguez Luévano, "Tipos de prisioneros mexicanos."
39. Debroise, *Mexican Suite*, 126.
40. See, Darling, "Review: Diguet's Studies of West Mexico," 183.
41. Gabriela Zamorana, personal communication, 20 July 2017.
42. Poole and Zamorano Villarreal, eds., *De frente al perfil*, 10.
43. Starr, *In Indian Mexico*, vii.
44. Vélez Storey, "Alegorías raciales de una mirada distante," 49.
45. Starr, *In Indian Mexico*, 133.
46. Twain, *King Leopold's Soliloquy*, 2.
47. Cited in Broyles et al., *Among Unknown Tribes*, 77.
48. Eek, "Carl Lumholtz and His Photographs," 22.
49. Cited in Broyles et al., *Among Unknown Tribes*, 116.
50. Poole, "An Image of 'Our Indian,' " 39.
51. Pimental, *Memoria sobre las causas*, 144.
52. Pimental, *Memoria sobre las causas*, 139–40.
53. Luis Villoro, *Los grandes momentos del indigenismo en México*, 196.
54. Luis Villoro, *Los grandes momentos*, 209.
55. Bonfil Batalla, *México profundo*, 9.
56. Aristegui, "Publica meme contra voladoras de Papantla." Roberto Carlos Vega Monroy was relieved of his post.
57. Cruces y Campa photographed Kickapoo Indians on one of their trips to Mexico City; they are not the same individuals who appeared in Aubert's photos. See Massé Zendejas, *Simulacro y elegancia en las tarjetas de visita*, 31, 34–36.
58. On Becerril's images, see Debroise, *Mexican Suite*, 146–47; see Lupercio's photos of Huicholes in Villela, "Los Lupercio, fotógrafos jaliscienses."

59. See Negrete Álvarez, *Valleto Hermanos*.
60. See the website of the Fototeca Nacional of INAH, https://sinafo.inah.gob.mx/fototeca-nacional.
61. See Canales, *Romualdo García*.
62. "Jimmy" Eduardo Montañez Pérez, personal communication, February 2017. Pedro Guerra Jordán and his son Pedro Guerra Aguilar did make photos of Mayans in their traditional clothing, usually in the studio and often of women, but they do not appear to have taken many, if any, in Amerindian communities outside of Mérida. See an important introduction to the Guerra archive by Rodríguez and Tovalín Ahumada, eds., *Fotografía artística Guerra*.
63. Mraz, *Photographing the Mexican Revolution*, 195.
64. Joaquín Ríos Martínez, personal communication, February 2017.
65. On the Salmerón family, see Jiménez and Villela, *Los Salmerón*. On Castrejón, see Villela, *Sara Castrejón*, and Mraz, "Sara Castrejón." The Salmerón studio began photographing Amerindians during the 1930s.
66. Rojas Rabiela and Gutiérrez Ruvalcaba, *Catálogo de la Colección de Antropología del Museo Nacional*, 13. In comparison, the Brazilian government had included Amazonian tribes more than ten years before, in the Universal Exposition of Paris in 1867 (Navarrete, *Fotografiando en América Latina*, 84).
67. Rodríguez Hernández, "Miradas sin rendición," 27.
68. See Rodríguez Hernández, "Recobrando la presencia."
69. Gilly, *The Mexican Revolution*, 4.
70. Padilla Ramos, *Los irredentos parias*, 23.
71. Turner, *Barbarous Mexico* [1969], 35.
72. Joseph, *Revolution from Without*, 41. Joseph notes that "Harvester's informal empire in Yucatán (the 'Sisal Hemp trust') takes its place alongside those of the American Sugar Refining Company in Cuba and the Dominican Republic (the 'Sugar trust'), and the United Fruit Company in the Caribbean (the 'Banana trust')" (45).
73. Turner, *Barbarous Mexico* [1969], 38.
74. The bullpen photo can be seen in Turner, *Barbarous Mexico*, 1911, 48. Turner became a photographer perhaps inspired by such critical US imagemakers as Jacob Riis and Lewis Hine. Some of the photos in *Barbarous Mexico* are credited to him, and when he was arrested during the *Decena Trágica* (The Tragic Ten Days, February 9 to February 18, 1913) he was carrying a camera and tripods well as some rolls of film; see Eugenia Meyer, *John Kenneth Turner*, 11, 20. As his visual work is as yet unexplored, it is unclear which images he took of Yaquis, because he refers to comments made by G. G. Lelevier about "a photograph showing a lot of Yaquis hanging from a tree in Sonora" (1969, 32). Such a picture appears in the 1911 edition of *Barbarous Mexico* (148), which may indicate that he used an already-published image. The lack of historians' rigor in employing photographs can be found even among the best: Friedrich Katz included Turner's image of hanged Yaquis, but titled it "Captured Villista

soldiers hanged by Carrancista General Francisco Murguia sometime in 1918" (Katz, *The Life & Times of Pancho Villa*, photo section following page 486).

75. Turner, *Barbarous Mexico* [1969], 41.
76. Padilla Ramos, *Los irredentos parias*, 30.
77. Turner, *Barbarous Mexico* [1969], 24.
78. Casanova, "De vistas y retratos," 9–10.
79. See the story of the Chalco photographs in Mraz, *Looking for Mexico*, 51–53.
80. Reed, *The Caste War of Yucatán*, 156, 220.
81. Joseph, *Revolution from Without*, 22.
82. Negroe Sierra, "Introducción," 26. This work contains eighteen photographs of the Caste War, largely of the occupying forces.
83. I have discussed these photographers at more length in Mraz, *Looking for Mexico*, 32–36. On Muybridge, see Navarrete, *Fotografiando en América Latina*, 149–64. On Jackson, see Gutiérrez Ruvalcaba, *Una mirada estadunidense sobre México*.
84. Malagón Girón, *Winfield Scott*. Malagón's important book proves that Scott made many of the photographs previously attributed to Waite. They can be recognized by the black block that Waite used to cover Scott's identification, and on which he sometimes wrote his own numbers.
85. See the second photo in Debroise, *Fuga mexicana*, 119, where it is mistakenly credited to Homer Scott. Photographed Indians were very rarely identified, so the fact that he wrote her name on the image indicates his respect for her singularity, at least in that picture. I have chosen the other photo for publication in line with the "esthetic imperative" that often governs photohistories, though the internal contradiction between the energy displayed and the exoticizing title is also worthy of note.
86. On Waite, see Montellano, *C. B. Waite, fotógrafo*. Debroise affirms that Waite used actresses (Debroise, *Mexican Suite*, 148).
87. Debroise, *Mexican Suite*, 82,
88. *Modern Mexico*, February 1900, cited in Malagón Girón, *Winfield Scott*, 89. See covers of this magazine with Scott photos on page 233.
89. Malagón Girón also analyzes this aspect, *Winfield Scott*, 107–10.
90. Deborah Dorotinsky argues that—prior to the Neo-Zapatista uprising of 1994—Indians "had until then existed in the photographic register as atemporal, ahistoric beings"; however, it is clear that every Indian rebellion brings them into history and, eventually, photography. See Dorotinsky Alperstein, "La vida de un archivo," 3.
91. See the Yaquis and the Chamulas in Mraz, *Photographing the Mexican Revolution*, 221 and 81, and the Zapatistas in Jiménez and Villela, *Los Salmerón*, 52. In fact, the bow and arrow proved a superior weapon in bush fighting; as Thord-Gray observed, "Without the bow and arrows of the Yaquis and Mayos the revolution of 1913–1914 might never have been carried to a successful conclusion" (*Gringo Rebel*, 71).

92. Knight, *The Mexican Revolution*, vols. 1 and 2.
93. Knight, *The Mexican Revolution*, vol. 2, 185.
94. Thord-Gray, *Gringo Rebel*, 142.
95. Knight, *The Mexican Revolution*, vol. 2, 375.
96. Knight, "Racism, Revolution, and Indigenismo," 75, 82.
97. Gamio, *Forjando patria*, 38.
98. Gamio, *Forjando patria*, 172.
99. For an overview, see Dawson, *Indian and Nation in Revolutionary Mexico*. Another project, "México Indígena," was carried forward in the Instituto de Investigaciones Sociales-UNAM between the years 1939 and 1946; the collection contains 5,700 photographs, most of them made by the Honduran Raúl Estrada Discua; see Dorotinsky Alperstein, "La vida de un archivo."
100. Tatard, "Julio de la Fuente," 44.
101. Lear, *Picturing the Proletariat*, 174.
102. See de la Fuente's bibliography in Aguirre Beltrán et al., *Pensamiento antropológico e indigenista de Julio de la Fuente*, 243–66.
103. De la Fuente, *Yalálog*. See photograph 5 of the "Familia en transición," with the older women wearing traditional clothing, while the men, boys, and younger girls are clad in modern dress. On the photography of de la Fuente, see Petroni, "La representación del indio" and "Fotografiar al indio."
104. Malinowski and de la Fuente, *The Economics of a Market System*.
105. De la Fuente, *Monopolio de aguardiente y alcoholismo en los Altos de Chiapas*.
106. Alberto Beltrán says that de la Fuente got his camera from "Juan Gutman," but he is probably confusing the two German refugees with the name Gutmann. Juan Guzmán (Hans Gutmann) does not arrive in Mexico until 1939. Enrique Gutmann had arrived in Mexico during 1933, with his father Paul Gutmann, a writer. See Pohle, *Das mexikanische Exil*.
107. Gutmann, "Algunas intervenciones en el Congreso de la LEAR," cited in Tatard, "Julio de la Fuente," 44.
108. See, for example, the statement of Margaret Mead: "There were times in the field when I worked without filming and therefore have not been able to subject the material to changing theory, as we were able to do with the Balinese stuff" (Brand, "For God's Sake, Margaret," 24).
109. See de la Fuente's archive in the Fototeca Nacho López, Comisión Nacional para el Desarrollo de los Pueblos Indígenas.
110. Petroni, "La recepción de la imagen."
111. San Miguel, *Crónicas de un embrujo*, 56. Hence the importance of indigenous people acquiring audiovisual knowledge that will challenge the "hegemony" of literacy. See Zamorano Villarreal, *Indigenous Media and Political Imaginaries in Contemporary Bolivia*; and Schiwy, *Indianizing Film*.
112. Beltrán, "Julio de la Fuente," 87.
113. Alloula, *The Colonial Harem*, 4.

114. For the publishing history of these books, see Nungesser Herausgeber, ed., *Hugo Brehme*, 202–3, the best introduction to this photographer.
115. See Brehme's advertisements in English and Spanish in Nungesser Herausgeber, ed., *Hugo Brehme*, 75, 77. On *National Geographic* imagery of Latin America, see Muñoz, *Fotografía imperial, escenarios tropicales*, 20. See also Mraz, *Looking for Mexico*, 76–82.
116. Ryan, *Picturing Empire*, 49.
117. Few studies of note have appeared on Márquez. See Dorotinsky Alperstein, "El imaginario indio de Luis Márquez"; Sánchez Estevez, "Luis Márquez Romay y su obra"; and the special issue of *Alquimia* dedicated to his work, "El imaginario de Luis Márquez" (vol. 10, 2000). He appears to have occupied a variety of governmental positions, largely concerned with representing Mexico in other countries as well as in cinema. I have commented briefly on Márquez in *Looking for Mexico*, 108–10.
118. Dorotinsky Alperstein, "El imaginario indio de Luis Márquez," 11.
119. As Faris commented, Curtis' "Navajo work was completely set up, using not only 'phony' costumes, additions, and poses (all non-Navajo photography of Navajo has some of this) but, indeed, in some cases actual phony Navajo" (*Navajo and Photography*, 108).
120. I thank Ernesto Peñaloza for his observations on Márquez's development.
121. Fanon, *The Wretched of the Earth*, 35. Although the power of the returned gaze is important, Álvarez Bravo had given this strategy another turn of the screw in *El señor de Papantla* (1934) by showing an Amerindian who refuses to dignify the camera by returning its look. I have analyzed this photo in *Nacho López: Mexican Photographer*, 6.
122. See Edwards, "Photographic 'Types,' " 241.
123. See the analysis by Dorotinsky Alperstein, "Ser visto al disparar." See also Antonio Rodríguez, "Ases de la cámara. ¡Aquí están las fotos!, dijo, y se entregó a la policía," *Mañana*, 29 June 1946, 37–41; and Antonio Rodríguez, "30 años de aventuras al servicio del periodismo," *Hoy*, 24 June 1950, 30–37. The article in *Mañana* can be found in a useful compilation of Rodriguez's articles on photojournalism, Monroy Nasr, *Ases de la cámara*, 81–83; unfortunately, the book does not reproduce the photographs.
124. López, "Noche de muertos." See my analysis of López's Indianist photography in Mraz, "Universos: Pueblos indígenas."
125. See the following photoreportages: "La fiesta de los muertos," Text: Ignacio Mendoza Rivera, Photos: Julio Mayo, *Mañana*, 20 November 1954; "Vísperas de muertos," Text: Luis Suárez, Photos: Faustino Mayo, *Mañana* 12 November 1955; "Patzcuaro: Noche de muertos," Text: Raul de la Cruz, Fotos: Casasola, *Hoy*, 3 November 1956; "¿Fiesta o drama en Mixquic?," Text: Luis Suárez, Photos: Julio Mayo, *Mañana*, 16 November 1957. Other photographers also passed through Janitzio in the 1950s: Héctor García photographed there in 1951, see his photo in *Héctor García*, 37; Bernice Kolko covered this theme in 1954, see

her photo in Rodríguez, *Bernice Kolko*, n.p.; and Walter Reuter was there in 1959, see his image in Mraz et al., *Walter Reuter*, 223.

126. Sekula, "Dismantling Modernism, Reinventing Documentary," 865.
127. Interview with Rodrigo Moya, 1999. This is also clear in the size of the negatives.
128. López, "Ante el umbral del silencio."
129. I have analyzed these photoreportages at length in Mraz, *Nacho López: Mexican Photographer*, 65–72.
130. Naming the INI *Fototeca* after López is indicative of the respect in which he is held as an ethnographic photographer; it is also related to the fact that he was placed in charge of organizing that archive in 1976.
131. López began to work for the INI in 1956 and, though he was offered a permanent position, he preferred to dedicate himself to his own projects with INI financing. He collaborated most closely with the institution from 1965 to 1978. See López, *Los pueblos de la bruma y el sol*.
132. López, "El indio en la fotografía," 330.
133. On Fernández and Figueroa, see Mraz, *Looking for Mexico*, 107–18. Other films made with this material include *Time in the Sun* (1940) and *¡Que viva México!* (1979).
134. *El Universal*, 9 December 1930, cited in de la Vega Alfaro, *Del muro a la pantalla*, 17.
135. On Dolores del Río in blackface in *María Candelaria*, see Mraz, *Looking for Mexico*, 146–48. Pedro Infante's visage is noticeably darkened for his title role as an Indian in *Tizoc*; coming from the north, the actor was pale by Mexican standards.
136. López, "El indio en la fotografía," 330–31.
137. On the differences between López's theory and practice, see Mraz, *Nacho López: Mexican Photographer*, 164–69.
138. López, *Los pueblos de la bruma y el sol*, n.p.
139. López, "El indio en la fotografía," 330.
140. See this photo in Krippner, *Paul Strand in Mexico*, 231. The difficulty of obtaining rights to this photo from Aperture and Televisa, as well as the cost, make it impossible to include here.
141. Strand, cited in Krippner, *Paul Strand in Mexico*, 125.
142. Strand, cited in Ware, "Photographs of Mexico, 1940," 109.
143. See Ware, "Photographs of Mexico, 1940," 109, and Mraz, *Looking for Mexico*, 85–91.
144. Strand, cited in Alexander, "Paul Strand as Filmmaker," 151. The word "interesting" is characteristically repeated in works by Western ethno-anthropologists; see Kazuyasu, "Examining Specimens, Evaluating Objects," 56.
145. López, *Los pueblos de la bruma y el sol*, n.p.
146. In Chapter 1 I have asserted that this is probably the primary mediation of videohistory's esthetic.

147. Bloom, "Interview with Sebastião Salgado," 8
148. Ramírez Casteñeda, "Espejismos," 33.
149. Rita Leistner, personal communication, 26 August 2017.
150. Westerbeck and Meyerowitz, *Bystander*, 34.
151. Rita Leistner, personal communication, 25 May 2017. See Leistner's Indianist photography in Clements and Leistner, *The Edward Curtis Project*; and Leistner and Mraz, *Una historia moderna de imágenes descolonizadoras.*
152. See the discussion of Modotti's photo in Folgarait, *Seeing Mexico Photographed*, 59–64.
153. See my discussion of García in Mraz, *Looking for Mexico*, 186–87.
154. Ramírez Castañeda, "Espejismos," 37.
155. López published a book, *Los trabajadores del campo y la ciudad*, for the presidential campaign of Miguel de la Madrid (1982–1986).
156. Armando Bartra, "Sobrevivientes," 62, 65.
157. Ramírez Castañeda, "Espejismos," 51; Roger Bartra, "Stuffing the Indian Photographically," 238.
158. López, "La fotografía: ¿Arte o testimonio?," 19.
159. Ramonet, *Marcos*, 24.
160. For the best recent expression of the Neo-Zapatista position, see *El pensamiento crítico frente a la hidra capitalista*, 77–78. A three-volume work that compiled presentations at the Sixth Commission of the EZLN, it can be found online in many forms and languages; one site is Enlace Zapatista, https://enlacezapatista.ezln.org.mx/2015/07/13/indice-volumen-uno-participaciones-de-la-comision-sexta-del-ezln-en-el-seminario-el-pensamiento-critico-frente-a-la-hidra-capitalista. I am grateful to John Holloway for this reference.
161. Speed, *Rights in Rebellion*, cited in Marcos, "Feminismos ayer y hoy," 11.
162. *El pensamiento crítico frente a la hidra capitalista*, 109.
163. Marcos, "Otro mundo . . . otro camino."
164. Marcos, "Otro mundo . . . otro camino."
165. An analysis of the photography made by Mexicans and foreigners of the EZLN uprising and aftermath would be a formidable task. For a study of the most important photo to come out of the rebellion, see del Castillo Troncoso, *Las mujeres de X'Oyep*. One effort to analyze the EZLN indigenous production is that of González Nolasco, "La representación indígena."
166. Information on Angeles Torrejón is based on an interview I carried out with her on 5 December 2017. See also Corkovic, "La cultura indígena en la fotografía mexicana de los 90s," pp. 932–52. The photojournalism that has been made of the women participants has been studied by Zaragoza Luna, "Las neozapatistas en el fotoperiodismo."
167. See Zaragoza Luna, *Alzando la mirada*.
168. While I applaud this nomination, I am not entirely in agreement with the EZLN's electoral practices: in 2006 they mounted *La otra campaña* that took votes away from Andrés Manuel López Obrador. Marichuy did not register enough signatures to become a candidate.

169. Francisco Martin, personal communication, 21 April 2017.
170. Salgado's photo can be found in *Other Americas* (42–43), a book I have sharply critiqued because it portrays Latin America as an area composed almost exclusively of infelicity, misery, death, enigma, and alienation; see Mraz, "Sebastião Salgado." The best book to date on Salgado is Nair, *A Different Light*.
171. See, for example, Everton, *The Modern Maya*, a work made up largely of usually posed, often smiling, and generally picturesque Mayans.

CHAPTER 5

Epigraph. Hobsbawm, *Workers*, 14.

1. Davis, *City of Quartz*, 376.
2. Davis, 375.
3. Davis, 375.
4. Davis, 375.
5. Actually, four carpenters died at the site while I was there, when their gondola fell. However, I was more impressed by the lopped-off limbs than by the graver dangers, which I repressed because they could have made me quit before going up in the gondola again.
6. González Casanova, ed., *La clase obrera en la historia de México*; González Casanova, ed., *Historia del movimiento obrero en América Latina*; González Casanova, León, and Marván, eds., *El obrero mexicano*.
7. Campa, *Mi testimonio*.
8. See the bibliography by Sánchez Bringas and Torres, *De la casa a la fábrica*.
9. One example of the photographic exhibits focusing on workers was *Obreros somos*, mounted in 1984 at the Museo Nacional de Culturas Populares; see Novelo, *Obreros somos*.
10. Mraz, " 'En calidad de esclavas.' "
11. Araujo, Telegram to the Secretary of Industry, Commerce and Labor, 8 October 1924. Departamento del Trabajo, Caja 723, Expediente 16, Archivo General de la Nación.
12. Araujo, Letter to the Secretary of Industry, Commerce and Labor, 24 October 1924. Departamento del Trabajo, Caja 723, Expediente 16, Archivo General de la Nación.
13. Araujo, Letter to the Secretary of Industry, Commerce and Labor, 9 December 1924. Departamento del Trabajo, Caja 723, Expediente 16, Archivo General de la Nación.
14. Ibid.
15. Alafita Méndez and Gómez Cruz, *Tuxpan*, 119.
16. Alafita Méndez, "Trabajo y condición obrera," 189.
17. Alafita Méndez, "Trabajo y condición obrera," 204.
18. Archivo General de la Nación, Departamento de Trabajo, Caja 447, Expediente 3. On the question of creating a union for the Huasteca workers, see Benítez Juárez, "La organización de los trabajadores petroleros en la huasteca veracru-

zana"; and Rittner, "Testimonios de los trabajadores petroleros." The photos of Vargas and Miranda say "Post Card" on the back, so they must have taken them to be developed and printed by a local producer of that medium.

19. Alafita Méndez, "Trabajo y condición obrera," 204.
20. John Hart, *Empire and Revolution*, 163.
21. It is sometimes referred to as the Waters Pierce Oil Company, but Waters had been bought out in 1878; see Rosas Robles, "Un gallo de pelea," 52. I am grateful to Paul Garner for this information.
22. Rosas Robles, "Un gallo de pelea," 58.
23. Report of Araujo to the Secretaría de Industria, Comercio y Trabajo, 10 February 1923. Departamento del Trabajo, Caja 447, Expediente 3, Archivo General de la Nación.
24. Gómez-Galvarriato, *Industry and Revolution*, 1.
25. García Díaz and Flores Rojas, *Los trabajadores del Valle de Orizaba*, 56. See Sierra photos as well in García Díaz, *Santa Rosa y Río Blanco*.
26. See a more extended discussion of this series in Mraz, "Picturing Mexico's Past," 36–39.
27. Coleman, James, and Sharma, "Photography and Work," 10.
28. García Díaz and Flores Rojas, *Los trabajadores del Valle de Orizaba*, 19. *Caciquismo* here means boss rule.
29. García Díaz and Flores Rojas, *Los trabajadores*, 125.
30. Tirado Villegas, *Quiero morir como nací*, 42. This book is based on many interviews and conversations with Treviño by Gloria Tirado. I am grateful to her for making it available.
31. Tirado Villegas, *Quiero morir como nací*, 47.
32. A Tina Modotti image of a worker wearing a seemingly strange hat and reading *El Machete* has puzzled scholars of that photographer. It appeared on the cover of *El Machete* (17 March 1928), where it was titled "The preferred reading" ("*La lectura preferida*"), and was later published on the cover of the Soviet magazine *International Lighthouse*, 3 January 1932. Thanks to Treviño's archive, we can now identify this worker as a *ferrocarrilero*. In a 1923 advertisement for the store La Gran Sombrería Tardán, boxed hats and baseball-style hats with bills are offered for train laborers who leave the station—engineers and Pullman porters; the felt hat seen in the photo occupies the center of the ad and hence appears to be a more generalized headgear for railroad workers who did not travel; see *Trenes y alambres: Revista de la Sociedad Mexicana de Despachadores y Telegrafistas Ferrocarrileros* 6, no. 8 (September 1923). I am grateful to Gloria Tirado for sharing this advertisement with me.
33. Matt. 12:21 (New International Version).
34. *Made on Rails*. The Basilica of our Lady of Guadalupe is the most important pilgrimage site in Mexico, and millions arrive every year on December 12 to celebrate her in La Villa.

35. Both the fake coffins as well as the hangings can be found in many images by the Hermanos Mayo during the 1958–59 strikes.
36. I thank Cora Gamarnick, John Womack, Kevin Coleman, José Mora, Jim Brennan, Ana Mauad, and Magdalena Broquetas for information about their respective areas of study.
37. *Made on Rails.*
38. See Mraz and Vélez Storey, *Uprooted*; and Mraz, "Foto Hermanos Mayo."
39. See Mraz and Vélez Storey, *Uprooted.*
40. Mraz, "Close-Up," 210.
41. Strauss, "Photography and Propaganda," 33.
42. Faustino asserts that *El Día* was the publication that offered him the most control over his photography. Because of his close relationship to Enrique Ramírez y Ramírez, a powerful journalist and politician, he was allowed to select images for inclusion; however, the captions were composed by other journalists.
43. I am here citing the eminent journalist Francisco Martínez de la Vega. I have written extensively about Mexican photojournalism in Mraz, *Nacho López: Mexican Photographer*; "Today, Tomorrow, and Always"; "Mexico: The New Photojournalism"; and *Looking for Mexico*. On *Ojo!*, see Navarro Castillo, *Héctor García.*
44. Quirke, *Eyes on Labor*, 15.
45. "The Working Man's Eye" is the title of Edwin Hoernle's 1930 article in the magazine *Der Arbeiter-Fotograf* (The worker-photographer); see Ollman, *Camera as Weapon*, 20, 54.
46. The bibliography on this movement is limited. Among the more important works other than Ollman's are "Left Photography between the Wars"; *Creative Camera* 197/198 (1981); Gohl and Evans, "*AIZ*"; and most recently, Klein and Evans, *The Radical Camera.*
47. Gohl and Evans, "*AIZ*," 197.
48. Körner and Stüber, "Germany: Arbeiter-Fotografie," 73.
49. Höllering, cited in Ollman, *Camera as Weapon*, 10.
50. See Dennett, "England," 100.
51. Hogenkamp, "Holland," 84.
52. It would appear that worker photography did not begin in Spain until the early 1930s and was a result of anarchist rather than communist publications; see Antebi Arnó et al., *Gráfica anarquista.*
53. Zelich, "Portraiture, Social Documentation and Photojournalism," 161.
54. Schultz and Hirsch, eds., *Tina Modotti*, 114. See the covers of *AIZ* on which Modotti's photos appeared on page 116. The rarely published image of Diego Rivera at the Red Aid gathering is on page 93; it probably has not been included in the many books on Modotti because it is a poor picture that demonstrates her incapacity for spontaneous street photography.
55. Schultz and Hirsch, eds., *Tina Modotti*, 31.

56. Letter of Modotti to Weston, 23 May 1930, cited in Hooks, *Tina Modotti*, 210. Her closing remarks should be interpreted in light of the fact that she was writing to Weston, who was an esthetic perfectionist.
57. Galeano, *Open Veins of Latin America*, 12.
58. Consejo Mexicano de Fotografía, "Convocatoria, Coloquio Latinoamericano de Fotografía," *Hecho en Latinoamerica*, 7.
59. Guevara Escobar, *Aurelio Escobar*.
60. Escorza Rodríguez, "Gerónimo Hernández."
61. Robledo Martínez, *Episodios fotográficos de la toma de Zacatecas*, 107–8.
62. Michael Meyer, *Mexican Rebel*.
63. Mraz, *Photographing the Mexican Revolution*, 82–84.
64. Jiménez and Villela, *Los Salmerón*.
65. Mraz, *Photographing the Mexican Revolution*, 112–14.
66. Mraz, *Photographing the Mexican Revolution*, 114–15.
67. Mraz, *Photographing the Mexican Revolution*, 179–81.
68. Mraz, *Photographing the Mexican Revolution*, passim.
69. Mraz, "Sara Castrejón."
70. Interview with Lucila Figueroa by Samuel Villela. Figueroa was born in 1910 and so must have received this information second hand.
71. Personal communication from Joaquín Ocampo M., March 2018. I thank Samuel Villela for sharing this message with me.
72. On this visual trope of women adorned with crossed-cartridge belts, see Mraz, *Photographing the Mexican Revolution*, 68–70.
73. Mraz, *Looking for Mexico*, 83.
74. This image was also employed in the letterhead paper of the Confederación Campesina Emiliano Zapata in Puebla during the 1920s and 1930s; see Casanova, "Huellas de una utopía," 63.
75. Massé Zendejas, "Tina Modotti y el agrarismo radical en México," 40.
76. In English, see the work of Jocelyn Olcott on Concha Michel: *Revolutionary Women* and " 'Take Off the Streetwalker's Dress.' "
77. A. D. Coleman, "The Indigenous Vision of Manuel Álvarez Bravo."
78. Monsiváis, *Maravillas que son, sombras que fueron*, 68.
79. García, "Encuentro con el fotógrafo Manuel Álvarez Bravo," 3.
80. Perez, "Dreams—Visions—Metaphors," 14. I have analyzed *Sed pública* in Mraz, *Looking for Mexico*; and *Señor de Papantla* in Mraz, *Nacho López: Mexican Photographer*. My insistence in this imagemaker's rejection of picturesque imagery was strengthened upon learning that he destroyed all of his earlier work in that vein, even one photo that had won a prize in Oaxaca in 1925 (González Flores, "Manuel Álvarez Bravo. Sílabas de luz").
81. Reyes Palma, "La LEAR y su revista de frente cultural," 11.
82. This image has never been published before, and I thank Aurelia Álvarez Urbajtel for her customary generosity in allowing me to include it.

83. He bought the camera with his winnings from the legendary Tolteca contest of 1931; Vera, "Viajes a Tehuantepec," 1.
84. Kaufman, "An Essay of Memories," 11.
85. Picton and Valdivia, "Bravo, Bravo!"
86. Weaver, review of *Revelaciones*, 154. For other mentions of "ritual sacrifice," see Perez, "Dreams—Visions—Metaphors," 14.
87. Hill and Cooper, *Dialogue with Photography*, 184–85.
88. Interview with Manuel Alvarez Bravo in Pacheco, *La luz de México*, 65–66. It is unclear when the photographer decided to add this title, but it was certainly post-1936 for reasons explained later in the chapter.
89. A similar case could be made for Robert Capa's image *Death of a Militiaman*; its power resides in the fact that it is what the title says it is. If it were instead that of a soldier who fell during a training exercise, it would lose that fusion. On the much-discussed Capa photo, see Mraz, "What's Documentary about Photography?"
90. *Frente a Frente*, no. 1 (March 1936), 13.
91. See Rodríguez, "Fotomontaje en México," 8–11.
92. Interview with Lola Álvarez Bravo in Pacheco, *La luz de México*, 46.
93. Krippner, *Paul Strand in Mexico*, 79.
94. The cost of reproducing a photograph by Lola is prohibitive. Furthermore, I do not believe that photographic archives of Mexican imagemakers should leave the country. Hence, I decided not to include this image, which can be seen in Ferrer, *Lola Alvarez Bravo*, 129.
95. Interview with Lola Álvarez Bravo in Pacheco, *La luz de México*, 60.
96. See these photos in Ferrer, *Lola Alvarez Bravo*, 77, 67.
97. Mraz and Vélez Storey, "Walter Reuter," 21.
98. See Mraz, "La lente emigrante de Walter Reuter," 75–76.
99. See Morales Carrillo, *Juan Guzmán*; and González Cruz Manjarrez, "Juan Guzmán en México."
100. González Quintana et al., *Kati Horna*, 10; see Antebi Arnó et al., *Gráfica Anarquista*.
101. See García Krinsky, *Kati Horna*.
102. See Mraz, *Nacho López: Mexican Photographer*; on García, see my limited remarks and reference to the bibliography on him in *Looking for Mexico*, 184–92.
103. Interview, Román Alvarado, "Tiempos de convicción," 10. Italics in the original.
104. Ibid.
105. See González Cruz Manjarrez, "Marcas y presencias."
106. Interview by Octavio Nava, cited in González Cruz Manjarrez, "Marcas y presencias."
107. Interview, Román Alvarado, "Tiempos de convicción," 81–82.
108. del Castillo Troncoso, *Rodrigo Moya*, 115.

109. Rodrigo Moya, personal communication, November 2009. *Cuate* is a Nahuatl word that means "twins," but is employed to signify "very close friends" in Mexico. It would require very extensive research among the archives of García and the Mayo to begin to evaluate Moya's position. To further complicate the situation, Bordes Mangel's archive is unavailable and, as Moya states, many of his own negatives were not returned.
110. Morales Carrillo, "Moya en el oleaje de las fotografías," 29.
111. Moya, personal communication, 17 May 2018.
112. Rodrigo Moya, Encrome "La soledad de la cámara sola," cited in Morales Carrillo, "Moya en el oleaje de las fotografías," 38.
113. In English, see the essay by Arnal, "Photography and Conscience."
114. Personal conversation with Jorge Acevedo Mendoza, 2018.
115. See Acevedo Mendoza, *Historia gráfica.*
116. See Acevedo Mendoza, *Al país de la ilusión.*
117. See the photos of Ana Victoria Jiménez published in Bartra, Fernández Poncela, and Lau, *Feminismo en México: Ayer y hoy*, 49–64.
118. Wikipedia, s.v. "Ana Victoria Jiménez," last modified 18 Dec. 2020, 14:27, https://en.wikipedia.org/wiki/Ana_Victoria_Jiménez.
119. On the collective *La Revuelta*, see Bartra and Revuelta, *La Revuelta.*
120. Chadwick asserts that Carrington was "one of the founders of the Women's Liberation Movement in Mexico in the early 1970s" ("Leonora Carrington," 37). However, she did not participate in any aspect of the neofeminist movement nor in any other political or social movement in Mexico.
121. Carrington, *The Hearing Trumpet*, 9.
122. *Mula* is the Spanish word for mule.
123. Enciso, *Ni santas ni putas sólo mujeres.*
124. Gargallo, "Rotmi Enciso."
125. Rotmi Enciso, personal communication, 17 April 2020.
126. "Rotmi Enciso: Imágenes del feminismo en México."
127. "Rotmi Enciso: Imágenes del feminismo en México."
128. The PRIAN is defined in the Introduction.
129. See Mraz, "The New Photojournalism of Mexico." Recent years have seen a proliferation of theses at the level of licenciaturas, masters, and doctorates on this movement.
130. Valtierra, *Nicaragua.*
131. Turok, *Imágenes de Nicaragua.*
132. Turok, *Chiapas.*
133. Gallery statement, "Diez fotógrafos de prensa," Consejo Mexicano de Fotografía, 13 September 1988.
134. Interview with Mata by Iris Moreno Aldana, in Oseguera Pizaña, "Reivindicaciones del fotoperiodismo mexicano," 46.
135. *Ejidos* are lands on which community members individually farm designated parcels and collectively maintain communal holdings. They were established

under the agrarian reform of the Constitution of 1917, in which haciendas were confiscated and some of the land was distributed to form *ejidos*, which are registered with Mexico's National Agrarian Registry (*Registro Agrario Nacional*). The system of *ejidos* was based on an understanding of the Aztec *calpulli* and became an integral element of the revolutionary transformation because of the Zapatistas' participation in the Mexican Revolution. Luis Cabrera is the intellectual most associated with this idea.

136. Villaseca Chávez, *Atenco rebelde*, 5.
137. Conversation with Jesús Villaseca Chávez, 2018.
138. Wikipedia, s.v. "Disturbios de Atenco de 2006," last modified 2 Oct. 2020, 10:01, https://es.wikipedia.org/wiki/Disturbios_de_Atenco_de_2006.
139. A "faro" is a lighthouse, and the name is here derived from the *F* of Fábrica (factory), the *Ar* of Artes (arts), and the *O* of Oficios (trades). Established in 1998 by the Secretariat of Cultura in Mexico City, there are now five Faros, all located on the city's margins in areas of high crime. Their goal is to bring cultural activities to the inhabitants, and train them in the arts and artisanal activities.
140. Interview with Jesús Villaseca Chávez, July, 2015.
141. Villaseca Chávez, "Prólogo," *¡Ya basta!*, 4.
142. Villaseca Chávez, "Prólogo," *Sucumbe el abasto popular ante la ley del más fuerte*, 3.
143. Rossell, *Ricas y famosas*. Photographing the wealthy in ways that points to their responsibility in creating the enormous social disparities in today's world is becoming an important tool of resistance; see Bausells, "Rogues Gallery."
144. Ratliff, " 'A Woman's Place Is in the Home.' "
145. See Luck, "Conspicuous Consumption and the Performance of Identity."
146. Villoro, "*Ricas, famosas y excesivas*."
147. Thompson, "The Rich, Famous and Aghast." The book cannot be bought in Mexico in either the Spanish or English edition.
148. Nuestra Mirada's Facebook page is at https://www.facebook.com/nuestramirada. Materials from the original site can still be seen at https://web.archive.org/web/20120922055922/http://www.nuestramirada.org.
149. Kahn, "Number of Journalists Killed in Mexico Reaches 'Historical High.' "
150. Franco Migues, "Félix Márquez."
151. Interview with Eduardo Miranda, 2016.
152. See the encyclopedic special issue of *Luna Córnea* dedicated to the art and photography of Cruz, "Marco Antonio Cruz." *Proceso* has become increasingly conservative under the new owners who are linked to the right-wing party PAN (Partido de Acción Nacional).
153. Agren, "Mexican Photojournalist Killed after Taking Photos of Bodies along a Road."
154. Lakhani, "Mexico World's Deadliest Country for Journalists, New Report Finds."

155. Lakhani, "Mexico World's Deadliest."
156. See my analysis of the systematic bribery within the Mexican press, as well as other forms of governmental control in Mraz, "Today, Tomorrow, and Always."
157. Knight described the press offense against Madero in the following way: "in bitter, scurrilous and obscene terms; for the first time in Mexican history, the literate public enjoyed the spectacle not only of a free press, but also of a press mercilessly lampooning the head of state" (*The Mexican Revolution*, vol. 1, 390).

EPILOGUE

Title, Grateful Dead, "Truckin'," *American Beauty*, 1970; epigraph, Ho Chi Minh, "Advice to Oneself."

1. See Rosenzweig, *Clio Wired*; Cohen and Rosenzweig, *Digital History*.
2. Sandweiss, "Image and Artifact," 196.
3. Ritchen, *After Photography*, 59.
4. Guevara created the site in 2008 and, as of October 2020, had received 263,542 visits. Personal communication October 13, 2020.
5. Rocha and Mraz, *La visión de los vendidos*.
6. See "Schlitz Brewing Co.," AdAge Encyclopedia, Sept. 15, 2003, http://adage.com/article/adage-encyclopedia/schlitz-brewing/98868 and "What beer company's slogan," FunTrivia, March 21, 2000, https://www.funtrivia.com/en/World/US-Commercials/Answer15009_F0FDA7.html. Perhaps apocryphally, FunTrivia notes that "As soon as these commercial ceased, Schlitz's sales went FLAT.
7. Huxley, *The Doors of Perception*, 10. Huxley remained a believer in the capacity of LSD, and had himself injected with it as he was dying; see "Aldous Huxley, Dying of Cancer, Left This World Tripping on LSD (1963)," Open Culture, Oct. 15, 2011, http://www.openculture.com/2011/10/aldous_huxleys_lsd_death_trip.html.
8. Pollan, *How to Change Your Mind*, Kindle version, location 682. Pollan is a journalism professor at University of California, Berkeley. He has generally focused on issues relating to food supply, but in this book he conducts an overview of research carried out in experiments with psychedelic drugs. He was influenced to enter into this endeavor, including taking psilocybin, by an article published in *Psychopharmacology*, Griffiths et al, "Psilocybin Can Occasion Mystical-Type Experiences Having Substantial and Sustained Personal Meaning and Spiritual Significance."
9. Morse, *New World Soundings*, 172.
10. Morse, *New World Soundings*, 176–77.
11. Baldwin, cited in Hansen, "Unlearning the Myth of American Innocence."
12. Wallace, *A Supposedly Fun Thing I'll Never Do Again*, 63.
13. Krugman, "The Angry Male White Caucus."
14. The first part of the "thought" I've here reconstructed refers to Curtis LeMay's statement, "My solution to the problem would be to tell [the North Vietnam-

ese Communists] frankly that they've got to draw in their horns and stop their aggression or we're going to bomb them into the Stone Age" (Wikipedia, s.v. "Curtis LeMay," last modified 29 Nov. 2020, 08:51, https://en.wikipedia.org/wiki/Curtis_LeMay). The latter part of it was a quote from a *New York Times* article of 8 February 1968 that became part of the anti-war rhetoric, "It became necessary to destroy the town to save it." The history of it is a bit more complex; see Carter, "Destroying a Quote's History in Order to Save It."

15. Morse, *New World Soundings*, 170.
16. I do not agree with Schreiber, who cites Amy Kaminsky in asserting that voluntary exile is an "oxymoron that masks the cruelly limited choices imposed on the subject," Schreiber, *Cold War Exiles in Mexico*, 222.
17. Fornet, *La coartada perpetua*, 39.
18. See Mraz, "Gringo," where I note the problem of identifying people from the US as *Americans* because everybody in the Western Hemisphere is an American.
19. Flusser, *Vilém Flusser: Writings*, 105, 109, 92.
20. Flusser, 98.
21. Flusser, 108, 92.
22. Flusser, *Into the Universe of Technical Images*, 4, 160. I have been informed that some recently discovered writing of Flusser are anti-imperialist, and I hope to explore this issue in the future.
23. Chomsky, *Power Systems*, 6.
24. Chomsky, *On Power and Ideology*, 48.
25. Wikipedia, s.v. "Augusto Pinochet," last modified 7 Dec. 2020, 11:16, https://en.wikipedia.org/wiki/Augusto_Pinochet.
26. Arnal, "El asqueroso olor de la tortilla," 291–92.
27. Arnal, 298.
28. Schreiber, *Cold War Exiles in Mexico*, xiii. US businesses have always had a foothold in Mexico, and there seems to have been a pattern of intermarriage between the wealthy (Schell, *Integral Outsiders*, xiv). I have no personal experience with people of this class and have generally refrained from establishing close friendships with other US immigrants, even academics and filmmakers, many of whom embody the attitude of the anthropologist I have described above. On the other hand, I am delighted to host my US friends for *comidas* and visits.
29. Arnal, "El asqueroso olor de la tortilla," 289.
30. Arnal, 290.
31. The Estrada Doctrine is so named because it was formulated in 1930 by Genaro Estrada, Mexico's Secretary of Foreign Relations.
32. Living in lockdown for months through the COVID-19 pandemic has shown me that it is possible to be both bored and scared.
33. Strand, cited in Krippner, *Paul Strand in Mexico*, 36.
34. Lawrence, *The Plumed Serpent*, 33, 35, 131.
35. See Watzlawick, Beavin, and Jackson, *Pragmatics of Human Communication*.

36. See my analysis of a Cantinflas monologue in Mraz, *Looking for Mexico*, 124.
37. Bateson, *Steps to an Ecology of Mind*, 178.
38. Watzlawick, Beavin, and Jackson, *Pragmatics of Human Communication*, 63.
39. Mraz, *México en sus imágenes*, 149.
40. We have been visiting professors and researchers in more than seventeen universities in Brazil, Colombia, Great Britain, Japan, Mexico, New Zealand, Spain, Uruguay, and the US.
41. Anthony Bourdain, "Under the Volcano," Tumblr, May 3, 2014, http://anthonybourdain.tumblr.com/post/84641290831/under-the-volcano.
42. Bourdain, "Under the Volcano."
43. Pilcher, *¡Que vivan los tamales!*, 163.

Bibliography

Abrash, Barbara, and Janet Sternberg, eds. *Historians and Filmmakers: Toward Collaboration*. New York: Institute for Research in History, Occasional Paper, No. 2, 1983.

Acevedo Mendoza, Jorge. *Al país de la ilusión*. Oaxaca: Secretaría de la Cultura y las Artes de Oaxaca, 2014.

______. *Historia gráfica: Memoria Fotográfica del Movimiento Popular en México, 1970–1983*. Mexico City: Teoría y Política, 1983.

Acevedo, Marta. *El 10 de mayo*. Mexico City: Martín Casillas Editores, 1982.

Agren, David. "Mexican Photojournalist Killed after Taking Photos of Bodies along a Road." *Guardian*, December 11, 2020. https://www.theguardian.com/world/2020/dec/11/mexico-journalists-killed-jaime-castano-zacarias.

Aguayo, Fernando. *Estampas Ferrocarrileras: Fotografía y grabado, 1860–1890*. Mexico City: Instituto Mora, 2003.

Aguayo, Fernando, and Lourdes Roca, eds. *Imágenes e investigación social*. Mexico City: Instituto Mora, 2005.

______. *Investigación con imágenes: Usos y retos metodológicos*. Mexico City: Instituto Mora, 2012.

Aguilar Camín, Héctor, et al. *Historia gráfica de México*. 10 vols. Mexico City: Editorial Patria-INAH, 1988.

Aguilar Ochoa, Arturo. *La fotografía durante el imperio de Maximiliano*. Mexico City: UNAM, 1996.

Aguirre Beltrán, Gonzalo, et al. *Pensamiento antropológico e indigenista de Julio de la Fuente*. Mexico City: Instituto Nacional Indigenista, 1980.

Alafita Méndez, Leopoldo. "Trabajo y condición obrera en los campamentos petroleros de la Huasteca 1900–1935." *Anuario IV, Universidad Veracruzana* (1986): 169–207.

Alafita Méndez, Leopoldo, and Filiberta Gómez Cruz. *Tuxpan*, vol. 5: *Veracruz: Imágenes de su historia*. Veracruz: Archivo General del Estado de Veracruz, 1991.

"Aldous Huxley, Dying of Cancer, Left This World Tripping on LSD (1963)," Open Culture, Oct. 15, 2011, http://www.openculture.com/2011/10/aldous_huxleys_lsd_death_trip.html.

Alexander, William. "Paul Strand as Filmmaker, 1933–1942." In *Paul Strand: Essays on His Life and Work*, edited by Maren Stange, 148–60. New York: Aperture, 1990.

Alloula, Malek. *The Colonial Harem*, translated by Myrna Godzich and Wlad Godzich. Minneapolis: University of Minnesota Press, 1986.

Anderson, Perry. *The Origins of Postmodernity*. London: Verso, 1998.

Antebi Arnó, Andrés, et al. *Gráfica anarquista. Fotografía i revolució social, 1936–1939*. Barcelona: Ajuntament de Barcelona, 2020.)

Antmann, Fran. "The Peasant Miners of Morococha," photographs by Sebastian Rodríguez. *Aperture* 90 (1983): 61–70.

Arago, Dominique François. "Report" (1839). In *Classic Essays on Photography*, ed. Alan Trachtenberg, 15–25. New Haven: Leete's Island 1980.

Aristegui, Carmen. "CNS dijo que son falsas fotos de policías armados; Xinhua prueba autenticidad con metadatos." Aristeguinoticias, June 19, 2016. http://aristeguinoticias.com/1906/mexico/policia-si-uso-armas-durante-desalojo-en-oaxaca-agencia-muestra-metadatos-fotos.

______. "Publica meme contra voladoras de Papantla . . . y lo mandan a 'a volar.' " Aristegui Noticias, February 19, 2017. https://aristeguinoticias.com/1902/mexico/funcionario-poblano-publica-meme-contra-voladores-de-papantla-y-lo-mandan-a-volar.

Arnal, Ariel. "El asqueroso olor de la tortilla: Sumas y restas en la construcción identitaria del exiliado chileno en México." In *Exilios en el mundo contemporáneo: Vida y destino*, edited by Josep Sánchez Cervelló and Alberto Reig Tapia, 287–301. Mexico City: SIMO Cultura, 2016.

______. "Photography and Conscience." In *Rodrigo Moya: Photography and Conscience*, 1–15. Austin: University of Texas Press, 2015.

Arnheim, Rudolf. "The Two Authenticities of the Photographic Medium." *Journal of Aesthetics and Art Criticism* 51:4 (1993): 537–40.

______. *Visual Thinking*. Berkeley: University of California, 1969.

Ayala, Ana Cristina. "John Mraz y la alfabetización visual." Cerosetenta/070, September 6, 2016. https://cerosetenta.uniandes.edu.co/john-mraz-y-la-alfabetizacion-visual.

Azoulay, Ariella. *The Civil Contract of Photography*. New York: Zone Books, 2008.

______. *Civil Imagination: A Political Ontology of Photography*, translated by Louise Bethlehem. London: Verso, 2012.

Barbarapvn, "El suicidio montado por Monsieur Hipólito Bayard," *Hipertextual*, November 16, 2012. https://hipertextual.com/archivo/2012/11/el-suicidio-montado-de-monsieur-hipolito-bayard.

La Barcelona d'ahir. 8 volumes, Barcelona: Adjuntament de Barcelona, 2015.

Barnouw, Dagmar. "The Shapes of Objectivity: Siegfried Kracauer on Historiography and Photography." In *Rethinking Objectivity*, edited by Allan Megill, 127–50. Durham, NC: Duke University Press, 1994.

Barnouw, Erik. *Documentary: A History of the Non-Fiction Film*. London: Oxford University Press, 1974.

Barthes, Roland. *Camera Lucida: Reflections on Photography*, translated by Richard Howard. New York: Hill and Wang 1981.

______. "The Photographic Message." In *Image/Music/Text*, edited and translated by Stephen Heath. New York: Hill and Wang 1977.

Bartra, Armando, "Sobrevivientes." In *De fotógrafos y de indios*, by Armando Bartra, Alejandra Moreno Toscano, and Elisa Ramírez Castañeda, 61–100. Mexico City: Ediciones Tecolote, 2000.

Bartra, Eli. "How Black is *La Negra Angustias*?" *Third Text* 116 (May 2012): 275–83.

Bartra, Eli, Anna M. Fernández Poncela, and Ana Lau. *Feminismo en México: Ayer y hoy*. Mexico City: UAM, 2002.

Bartra, Eli, and Revuelta. *La Revuelta: Reflexiones, testimonios y reportajes de mujeres en México, 1975–1983*. Mexico City: Martín Casillas Editorial, 1983.

Bartra i Murià, Eli. "Les 'febres de l'or' de Magí Murià, pioner del cinema a Catalunya." *Revista de Catalunya* 80 (1993): 83–99.

Bartra, Roger. "Jaime Labastida: Desconfiemos de la realidad." *Revista de la Universidad de México* 157 (2017): 8–11.

______. *La jaula de la melancolía: Identidad y metamorfosis del mexicano*. Mexico City: Grijalbo, 1987.

______. "Stuffing the Indian Photographically." In "Mexican Photography." Special Issue, *History of Photography* 20:3 (1996): 236–39.

Batchen, Geoffrey, ed. "Vernacular Photographies." Special Issue, *History of Photography* 24:3 (2000): 229–71.

Bateson, Gregory. *Mind and Nature: A Necessary Unity*. New York: E.P. Dutton, 1979.

______. *Steps to an Ecology of Mind*. New York: Ballantine Books, 1972.

Bausells, Marta. "Rogues Gallery: How Photographers Are Targeting the 1%." *Guardian*, March 28, 2016. www.theguardian.com/artanddesign/2016/mar/28/daniel-mayrit-you-havent-seen-their-faces-bankers-photography.

Bazin, André. *What Is Cinema?* Essays selected and translated by Hugh Gray. Berkeley: University of California, 1967.

Becker, Carl. *The Heavenly City of the Eighteen-Century Philosophers*. New Haven: Yale University Press, 1932.

Begiebing, Robert, Joshua Brown, Barbara Franco, David Grubin, Ruth Rosen, and Natasha Trethewey. "Interchange: Genres of History." *Journal of American History* 92, no. 2 (2004): 572–93.

Behdad, Ali, and Luke Gartland, eds. *Photography's Orientalism: New Essays on Colonial Representation*. Los Angeles: Getty Publications, 2013.

Beltrán, Alberto. "Julio de la Fuente, el artista gráfico." In *Pensamiento antropológico e indigenista de Julio de la Fuente*, edited by Gonzalo Aguirre Beltrán, et al., 67–87. Mexico City: Instituto Nacional Indigenista, 1980.

Benitez Juárez, Mirna. "La organización de los trabajadores petroleros en la huasteca veracruzana, 1917–1931." *Anuario V, Universidad Veracruzana* (1987): 13–33.

Benjamin, Walter. "Small History of Photography" (1931). In *On Photography*, edited and translated by Esther Leslie. London: Reaktion Books, 2015.

______. "A Short History of Photography" (1931). In *Classic Essays on Photography*, edited by Alan Trachtenberg, 199–216. New Haven: Leete's Island 1980.

______. "The Work of Art in the Age of Mechanical Reproduction." In *Marxism and Art: Writings in Aesthetics and Criticism*, edited by Berel Lang and Forrest Williams, 281–300. New York: David McKay, 1972.

Berger, John. *Understanding a Photograph*, edited by Geoff Dyer. London: Penguin Books, 2013.

______. *Ways of Seeing*. London: Penguin Books, 1973.

Berger, John, and Jean Mohr, *Another Way of Telling*. New York: Pantheon, 1982.

Bloom, John. "Interview with Sebastião Salgado." *Photo Metro* 9:84 (1990): 4–19.

Bluem, A. William. *Documentary in American Television*. New York: Hastings House, 1965.

Bonfil Batalla, Guillermo. *México profundo: Una civilización negada*. Mexico City: Random House, 2013 [1987].

Bourdieu, Pierre. *Photography: A Middle-Brow Art*, translated by Shaun Whiteside. Cambridge: Polity Press 1990.

Brand, Stewart. "'For God's Sake, Margaret': Conversation with Gregory Bateson and Margaret Mead." *CoEvolutionary Quarterly* 10:21 (1976): 1–24. http://alice.id.tue.nl/references/.

Brand, Stewart, Kevin Kelly, and Jay Kinney. "Digital Retouching: The End of Photography as Evidence of Anything." *Whole Earth Review*, July 1985. http://www.oss.net/dynamaster/file_archive/040324/f98095dd2c6a93a397662cfd97a246e5/WER-INFO-69.pdf.

Brant, Herbert. Review of David William Foster, *Argentine, Mexican, and Guatemalan Photography: Feminist, Queer, and Post-Masculinist Perspectives. Hispania* 99 (2016): 179–81.

Brecht, Bertolt. *Brecht on Film and Radio*, edited and translated by M. Silberman. London: Methuen, 2000.

Brehme, Hugo. *Pueblos y paisajes de México*. Mexico City: INAH, 1992.

Breton, André. "Recuerdo de México," translated by Ramón Cuesta and Ramón García Fernández. *Nueva Época* 59–60 (Nov.-Dec. 2002). https://www.uv.mx/gaceta/Gaceta59-60/59-60/pie/Pie07.htm.

Broyles, Bill, et al. *Among Unknown Tribes: Rediscovering the Photographs of Explorer Carl Lumholtz*. Austin: University of Texas Press, 2014.

Broquetas, Magdalena, ed. *Fotografía en Uruguay: Historia y usos sociales, 1840–1930*. Montevideo: Centro de Fotografía, 2011.

Broquetas, Magdalena, and Mauricio Bruno, eds. *Fotografía en Uruguay: Historia y usos sociales, 1930–1990*. Montevideo: Centro de Fotografía, 2011.

Bueno, Christina. *The Pursuit of Ruins: Archeology, History and the Making of Modern Mexico*. Albuquerque: University of New Mexico Press, 2016.

Bunge, Nancy. "From Hume to Tillich: Teaching Faith and Benevolence." *Philosophy Now*, no. 38 (2002). https://philosophynow.org/issues/38/From_Hume_to_Tillich_Teaching_Faith_and_Benevolence.

Burke, Peter. *Eyewitnessing: The Use of Images as Historical Evidence*. Ithaca: Cornell University Press, 2001.

______. *What Is Cultural History?* 2nd edition. Cambridge: Polity, 2008.

Burns, E. Bradford. *Latin American Cinema: Film and History*. Los Angeles: UCLA, 1975.

Camacho Morfín, Thelma. "Los álbumes de 'El Buen Tono': Fotografía y social catolicismo (México, 1894–1909)." *Boletín Americanista*, año LXV, 2, no. 71 (2015): 77–96.

Campa, Valentín. *Mi testimonio: Experiencias de un comunista mexicano*. Mexico City: Cultura Popular, 1978.

Campbell, Howard. *Mexican Memoir: A Personal Account of Anthropology and Radical Politics in Oaxaca*. Westport: Bergin & Garvey, 2001.

Canales, Claudia. *Romualdo García: Un fotógrafo, una ciudad, una época*. Guanajuato: Gobierno del Estado/INAH, 1980.

Carrington, Leonora. *The Hearing Trumpet*. 1974. Reprint, New York: New York Review Books, 2020.

Carter, Stephen. "Destroying a Quote's History in Order to Save It." Bloomberg, 9 February 2018. http://www.bloomberg.com/view/articles/2018-02-09/destroying-a-quote-s-history-in-order-to-save-it.

Cartier-Bresson. "The Decisive Moment." In *The Mind's Eye: Writings on Photography and Photographers*, 20–43. New York: Aperture, 1999.

Casanova, Rosa. "De vistas y retratos: La construcción de un repertorio fotográfico en México, 1839–1890". In *Imaginarios y fotografía en México, 1839–1970*, edited by Emma Cecilia García Krinsky, 2–57. Mexico City: Lunwerg, 2005.

______. "Huellas de una utopía: Las fotografías políticas de Tina Modotti." In "Tina Modotti, expediente inédito." Special Issue, *Alquimia* 50 (2014): 52–73.

______. "Un nuevo modo de representar: Fotografía en México 1839–1861." In *Hacia otra historia del arte en México*, edited by Esther Acevedo, 191–217. Mexico City: Conaculta, 2001.

Casanova Rosa, and Olivier Debroise. *Sobre la superficie bruñida de un espejo: Fotógrafos del siglo XIX*. Mexico City: Fondo de Cultura Económica, 1989.

Casasola, Gustavo. *Seis siglos de historia gráfica de México*. Mexico City: Editorial Gustavo Casasola, 1989.

Cassirer, Ernst. *The Philosophy of the Enlightenment*. Princeton: Princeton University Press, 1951.

Castellanos, Ulises. "Mentiras en la azotea." Fotoperiodista Ulises Castellanos, November 2015. http://www.ulisescastellanos.com.mx/essays/2015/11/mentiras-en-la-azotea.

Castro, Fernando. "Crossover Dreams: Remarks on Contemporary Latin American Photography." In *Image and Memory: Photography From Latin America, 1866–1994*, edited by Wendy Watriss and Lois Parkinson Zamora, 57–94. Austin: University of Texas Press, 1998.

Césaire, Aimé. *Discourse on Colonialism*, translated by Joan Pinkham. New York: Monthly Review Press, 1972 [1955].

Chadwick, Whitney. "Leonora Carrington: Evolution of a Feminist Consciousness." *Woman's Art Journal* 7:1 (1986): 37–42.

Chanan, Michael. "The Melancholy of a Political Documentarist." *Studies in Documentary Film* 13:3 (2019): 196–213.

Chavarría, Jesús. *José Carlos Mariátegui and the Rise of Modern Peru, 1890–1930*. Albuquerque: University of New Mexico Press, 1979.

Chomsky, Noam. *On Power and Ideology: The Managua Lectures*. Boston: South End Press, 1987.

______. *Power Systems: Conversation with David Barsamian on Global Democratic Uprisings and the New Challenges to US Empire*. London: Penguin Books, 2013.

Clements, Marie, and Rita Leistner, *The Edward Curtis Project: A Modern Picture Story*. Vancouver: Talon, 2010.

Cockcroft, James. *Mexico: Class Formation, Capital Accumulation, and the State*. New York: Monthly Review Press, 1983.

Cohen, Daniel, and Roy Rosenzweig. *Digital History: A Guide to Gathering, Preserving, and Presenting the Past on the Web*. Philadelphia: University of Pennsylvania Press, 2006.

Coleman, A. D. "The Indigenous Vision of Manuel Álvarez Bravo." In *Light Readings: A Photography's Critic's Writings, 1968–1978*, by A. D. Coleman, 221–28. Oxford, UK: Oxford University Press, 1979.

Coleman, Kevin. *A Camera in the Garden of Eden: The Self-Forging of a Banana Republic*. Austin: University of Texas Press, 2016.

______. "Las fotos que no alcanzamos a ver. Soberanías, archivos y la masacre de trabajadores bananeros de 1928 en Colombia." In *Fotografía e historia en América Latina*, edited by John Mraz and Ana María Mauad, 149–74. Montevideo: Centro de Fotografía, 2015.

______. "Photographs of a Prayer: The (Neglected) Visual Archive and Latin American Labor History." *Hispanic American Historical Review* 95:3 (2015): 459–92.

Coleman, Kevin, Daniel James, and Jayeeta Sharma. "Photography and Work." *Radical History Review*, 132 (2018): 1–22.

Collier, John. *Visual Anthropology: Photography as a Research Method.* New York: Holt, Rinehart and Winston, 1967.

Conrad, Joseph. *Heart of Darkness.* Dublin: Roads, 2013 [1899].

Consejo Mexicano de Fotografía. "Convocatora: Coloquio Latinoamericano de Fotografía." In *Hecho en Latinoamerica: Primera muestra de la fotografía latinoamericana contemporánea*, edited by Muestra de la Fotografía Latinoamericana Contemporánea, 7–9. Mexico City: Consejo Mexicano de fotografía, 1978.

Corkovic, Laura Miroslava. "La cultura indígena en la fotografía mexicana de los 90s." Doctoral Thesis, Historia de Arte, Universidad de Salamanca, 2012.

Cortés, Carlos E., Howard Campbell, and Alan Curl. *A Filmic Approach to the Study of Historical Dilemmas.* Riverside: University of California, Riverside, 1976.

Costa Lima, Luiz. *The Dark Side of Reason: Fictionality and Power*, translated by Paulo Henriques Britto. Palo Alto, CA: Stanford University Press, 1992.

Creative Camera 197/198 (London, May/June, 1981): 70–124.

Cruz, Mónica. "Cómo comprobar la autenticidad de una fotografía digital." *El País Verne*, 21 June 2016. http://verne.elpais.com/verne/2016/06/21/mexico/1466467549_467060.html.

Curtis, James. *Mind's Eye, Mind's Truth: FSA Photography Reconsidered.* Philadelphia: Temple University Press, 1989.

Cumberland, Charles C. *Mexican Revolution: The Constitutionalist Years.* Austin: University of Texas Press, 1972.

Czach, Marie. "'At Home': Reconstructing Everyday Life through Photographs and Artifacts." *Afterimage* 5:3 (1977): 10–12.

Darling, J. Andrew. "Review: Diguet's Studies of West Mexico." *Journal of the Southwest* 42:1 (2000): 181–85.

Davidson, Martha, et al. *Picture Collections: Mexico.* London: Metuchen 1988.

Davis, Mike. *City of Quartz: Excavating the Future in Los Angeles.* New York: Vintage Books, 1990.

Dawson, Alexander. *Indian and Nation in Revolutionary Mexico.* Tucson, University of Arizona Press, 2004.

De la Fuente, Julio. *Monopolio de aguardiente y alcoholismo en los Altos de Chiapas: Un estudio "incómodo" de Julio de la Fuente (1954–1955).* Mexico City: Comisión Nacional para el Desarrollo de los Pueblos Indígenas, 2008.

______. *Yalálog: Una villa zapoteca serrana.* Mexico City: Museo Nacional de la Antropología, 1949.

De la Peña, Ireri, ed. *Ética, Poética y Prosaica. Ensayos sobre fotografía documental.* Mexico City: Siglo XXI, 2008.

De la Vega Alfaro, Eduardo. *Del muro a la pantalla: S. M. Eisenstein y arte pictórico mexicano.* Mexico City: IMCINE, 1997.

De los Santos García Felguera, María. "Las principales revistas." In *Historia general de la fotografía*, edited by Marie-Loup Sougez, 25–28. Madrid: Cátedra, 2011.

Deas, Malcolm. *Historia de Colombia a través de la fotografía, 1842–2010*. Bogotá and Madrid: MAPFRE/Banco de la República, 2011.

Debroise, Olivier. *Fuga mexicana. Un recorrido por la fotografía en México*. Mexico City: Consejo Nacional para la Cultura y las Artes, 1994.

______. *Mexican Suite: A History of Photography in Mexico*, translated by Stella de Sá Rego. Austin: University of Texas Press, 2001.

del Castillo Troncoso, Alberto. *Fotografía y memoria: Conversaciones con Eduardo Longoni*. Mexico City: Fondo de Cultura Económica/CONACUT/Instituto Mora, 2017.

______. *Las mujeres de X'Oyep: La historia detrás de la fotografía*. Mexico City: CONACULTA, 2013.

______. *Rodrigo Moya: Una mirada documental*. Mexico City: UNAM, 2011.

Delgado, Ana Laura, ed. *Veracruz: Imágenes de su historia*. 8 vols. Veracruz: Archivo General del Estado de Veracruz, 1989–92.

DeLillo, Don. *Point Omega*. New York: Scribner, 2010.

Dennet, Terry. "England: The (Workers') Film & Photo League." In *Photography/Politics: One*, edited by Half Moon Photography Workshop, 100–117. London: Photography Workshop, 1979.

Depetris, Carolina. *El héroe involuntario: Frédérick de Waldeck y su viaje por Yucatán*. Mexico City: UNAM, 2014.

Derrida, Jacques. "The Law of Genre." *Glyph* 7 (1980): 202–32.

Diguet, Leon. *Fotografías del Nayar y de California, 1893–1900*. Mexico City: Centro de Estudios Mexicanos y Centroamericanos de la Embajada de Francia en México/Instituto Nacional Indigenista, 1991.

Directorio de archivos, fototecas y centros especializados en fotografía. Mexico City: Centro de la Imagen, 2001.

Dooms, Ann. "A Picture Is Worth 1000 Words… But Which Language Does It Speak?" Ingrid Daubechies, *TEDx Brussels: The Territory and the Map*, 8 December 2014. Available at: https://www.youtube.com/watch?v=OPg4wbvCfcM.

Dorotinsky Alperstein, Deborah. "El imaginario indio de Luis Márquez." In "El imaginario de Luis Márquez." Special Issue, *Alquimia* 10 (2000): 7–11.

______. "Ser visto al disparar Ismael Casasola en Guatemala." In "Fondo Casasola: Relecturas." Special Issue, *Alquimia* 25 (2005): PP

______. "'La vida de un archivo': México indígena' y la fotografía etnográfica de los años cuarenta en México." Doctoral Thesis, Historia del Arte, UNAM, 2003.

Duarte, Carlota, ed. *Camaristas: Fotógrafos mayas de Chiapas*. Mexico City: Centro de la Imagen-CIESAS-Casa de las Imágenes, 1998.

Dylan, Bob. "Absolutely Sweet Marie." *Blond on Blond*. New York: Columbia Records, 1966.

Eagleton, Terry. *After Theory*. New York: Basic Books, 2003.

______. *The Gatekeeper: A Memoir*. New York: St. Martin's Press, 2001.

Edwards, Elizabeth. "Photographic 'Types': The Pursuit of Method." *Visual Anthropology* 3 (1990): 235–58.

______. "Photographs as Strong History?" In *Photographic Archives and the Idea of Nation*, edited by Costanza Caraffa and Tiziana Serena, 321–29. Berlin: De Gruyter, 2015.

Eek, Ann Christine. "Carl Lumholtz and His Photographs." In Broyles, Bill, et al., *Among Unknown Tribes: Rediscovering the Photographs of Explorer Carl Lumholtz*, 11–41. Austin: University of Texas Press, 2014.

Elkins, James. *Visual Studies: A Skeptical Introduction*. New York: Routledge, 2003.

Ellwood, David W. "Archivo Nazionale Cinematografico Della Resistenza, Torino—Oral History and Film History: The Use and Misuse of Interviews." In *History and Film: Methodology, Research, Education*, edited by K. R. M. Short and Karsten Fledelius, 21–32. Copenhagen: International Association for Audiovisual Media in Historical Research and Education, 1980.

Eliot, J. H. *The Old World and the New, 1492–1650*. Cambridge: Cambridge University Press, 11970.

Enciso, Rotmi. *Ni santas ni putas sólo mujeres. Imágenes del movimiento feminista en la Ciudad de México*. Mexico City: Instituto de las Mujeres del Distrito Federal and Producciones y Milagros Agrupación Feminista, A. C, 2008.

Enzenberger, Hans Magnus. *Anarchy's Brief Summer: The Life and Death of Buenaventura Durruti*, translated by Mike Mitchell. London: Seagull Books, 2018 [1972].

Escorza Rodríguez, Daniel. *Agustín Víctor Casasola. El fotógrafo y su agencia*. Mexico City: INAH, 2014.

______. "Gerónimo Hernández, un fotógrafo enigmático." *Dimensión Antropológico*, año 16, vol. 7 (2009): 143–68.

Estrin, James. "Latin American Pictures of the Year." Lens (blog), *New York Times*, 1 June 2017. https://nytimes.com/blogs/lens//2017/06/01/latin-american-pictures-of-the-year.

Eugenides, Jeffrey. *The Marriage Plot*. New York: Farrar, Strauss and Giroux, 2011.

Everton, Macduff. *The Modern Maya: Incidents of Travel and Friendship in Yucatán*. Austin: University of Texas Press, 2012.

Fanon, Frantz. *The Wretched of the Earth*, translated by Constance Farrington. New York: Grove Press, 1968.

Faris, James C. *Navajo and Photography: A Critical History of an American People*. Albuquerque: University of New Mexico Press, 1996.

______. "Photography, Power and the Southern Nuba." In *Anthropology and Photography, 1860–1920*, edited by Elizabeth Edwards, 211–17. New Haven: Yale University Press, 1992.

______. "A Political Primer on Anthropology/Photography." In *Anthropology and Photography, 1860–1920*, edited by Elizabeth Edwards, 253–63. New Haven: Yale University Press, 1992.

Ferrer, Elizabeth. *Lola Alvarez Bravo*. New York: Aperture, 2006.
"Film Reviews: Introductory Note." *American Historical Review*, 123:2 (2018): 529.
Florescano, Enrique, ed. *Así fue la Revolución Mexicana*. 8 volumes. Mexico City: Senado de la República-Secretaría de Educació Pública, 1985–86.
Flusser, Vilém. *Into the Universe of Technical Images*, translated by Nancy Ann Roth. Minneapolis: University of Minnesota Press, 2011.
______. *Towards a Philosophy of Photography*, edited by Derek Bennett. Göttingen: European Photography, 1984.
______. *Vilém Flusser: Writings*, edited by Andreas Ströhl, translated by Erik Eisel. Minneapolis: University of Minnesota Press, 2002.
Folgarait, Leonard. *Seeing Mexico Photographed*. New Haven: Yale University Press, 2008.
Fontcuberta, *El beso de Judas: Fotografía y verdad*. Barcelona: Gustavo Gili, 1998.
Fornet, Ambrosio. *La coartada perpetua*. Mexico City: Siglo XXI, 2002.
Foster, David William. *Argentine, Mexican, and Guatemalan Photography: Feminist, Queer, and Post-Masculinist Perspectives*. Austin: University of Texas Press, 2014.
Franco Migues, "Félix Márquez: El riesgo es dejar de publicar." *Testigos Presenciales*, 15 September 2015. http://nuestraaparenterendicion.com/testigospresenciales/felix-marquez.
Freund, Gisèle. *La fotografía como documento social*. Barcelona: Gustavo Gili, 2015 (15th edition).
______. *La fotografía y las clases medias en Francia durante el siglo XIX*. Editorial Losada: Buenos Aires. 1946.
______. "La Photographie en France au XIXe siècle: Essai de sociologie et d'esthétique." Doctoral Thesis, Sorbonne, 1936.
______. *Photography & Society*. Boston: David. R. Godine, 1980 [1974].
Frost, Susan Toomey. *Timeless Mexico. The Photographs of Hugo Brehme*. Austin: University of Texas Press, 2011.
Fulton, Marianne. *Eyes of Time: Photojournalism in America*. Boston: Little, Brown, and Co., 1988.
Galeano, Eduardo. *Memory of Fire*. 3 vols. New York: Pantheon, 1985–1988.
______. *Open Veins of Latin America: Five Centuries of the Pillage of a Continent*. New York: Monthly Review Press, 1973.
Gamarnik, Cora. "El fotoperiodismo y la guerra de Malvinas: Una batalla simbólica." In *Fotografía e historia en América Latina*, edited by John Mraz and Ana Maria Mauad, 225–56. Montevideo: Centro de Fotografía, 2015.
Gamio, Manuel. *Forjando patria (Pro nacionalismo)*. Mexico City: Porrúa Hermanos, 1916.
Garay Albújar, Andrés. *Martín Chambi, por sí mismo*. Piura: Universidad de Piura, 2010.
García, Manuel. "Encuentro con el fotógrafo Manuel Álvarez Bravo." *Sábado*, supplement of *Unomásuno*, 31 January 1998, 3.

García Díaz, Bernardo. *Santa Rosa y Río Blanco*, vol. 2: *Veracruz: Imágenes de su historia*. Veracruz: Archivo General del Estado de Veracruz 1989.

García Díaz, Bernardo, and Hilda Flores Rojas. *Los trabajadores del Valle de Orizaba y la Revolución Mexicana*. Veracruz: Universidad Veracruzana, 2011.

García Espinosa, Julio. "For an Imperfect Cinema," translated by Julianne Burton. *Jump Cut: A Review of Contemporary Media* 20 (1979, 2005): 24–26. https://www.ejumpcut.org/archive/onlinessays/JC20folder/ImperfectCinema.html.

García Krinsky, Emma Cecilia. *Kati Horna: Recuento de una obra*. Mexico City: CENIDIAP-INBA, 1995.

Gardner, Joel. "Oral History and Video in Theory and Practice." *Oral History Review* 12 (1984): 105–11.

Gargallo, Francesca. "Rotmi Enciso: Fotografías del movimiento feminista." *Cuadernos feministas: Convergencia de feminismos de izquierda*, October 22, 2008. http://cuadernosfem.blogspot.com/2008/10/rotmi-enciso-fotografas-del-movimiento.html.

Garner, Gretchen. *Disappearing Witness: Change in Twentieth-Century American Photography*. Baltimore: John Hopkins University Press, 2003.

Gazzaniga, Michael. *The Bisected Brain*. New York: Appleton-Century-Crofts, 1970.

Gibson, Charles. *The Aztecs under Spanish Rule: A History of the Indians of the Valley of Mexico, 1519–1810*. London: Oxford University Press, 1964.

Gilly, Adolfo. "Citas en los pies, ideas en la cabeza." *Nexos* 110 (1987): 11–13.

______. *The Mexican Revolution*, translated by Patrick Camiller. New York: The New Press, 2005.

Ginzburg, Carlo. "Clues: Roots of an Evidential Paradigm." In *Myths, Emblems, Clues*, translated by John and Anne C. Tedeschi, 96–125. London: Hutchinson Radius, 1990.

Gohl, Silvia, and David Evans. "*AIZ*—A Marxist-Leninist Picture Magazine." *Camerawork* (November, 1982): 197–200.

Goldberg, Vicki. *The Power of Photography: How Photographs Changed our Lives*. New York: Abbeville, 1991.

Goldman, Shifra. *Contemporary Mexican Painting in a Time of Change*. Austin: University of Texas Press, 1977.

Gómez-Galvarriato, Aurora. *Industry and Revolution: Social and Economic in the Orizaba Valley, Mexico*. Cambridge: Harvard University Press, 2013.

Gómez-Popescu, Liliana. "Towards a History through Photography: An Introduction." In "Photography and History." Special Issue, *Estudios Interdisciplinarios de América Latina y el Caribe* 26, no. 2 (2015): 7–11.

González Casanova, Pablo, ed. *Historia del movimiento obrero en América Latina*. 4 vols. Mexico City: UNAM/Siglo XXI, 1984–1985.

______. ed. *La clase obrera en la historia de México*. 17 vols. Mexico City: UNAM/Siglo XXI, 1980–1990.

González Casanova, Pablo, Samuel León, and Ignacio Marván, eds. *El obrero mexicano*. 5 vols. Mexico City: UNAM/Siglo XXI, 1984–1986.

González Cruz Manjarrez, Maricela. "Juan Guzmán en México: Fotoperiodismo, modernidad y desarrollismo en algunos de sus reportajes y fotorafías de 1940 a 1960." Master's Thesis, Historia del Arte, UNAM, 2003.

______. "Marcas y presencias: El reportaje de Enrique Bordes Mangel del 10 de junio de 1971." *Imágenes. Revista Electrónica del Instituto de Investigaciones Estéticas*, 16 December 2010. http://www.esteticas.unam.mx/revista_imagenes/anteriores/numerosant.html:

______. *Siqueiros en la mira*. Mexico City: Museo de Arte Moderno, 1996.

González Flores, Laura. "Manuel Álvarez Bravo. Sílabas de luz." Unpublished manuscript, 2013.

______. "Nuevas subjetividades en la fotografía mexicana contemporánea." In *Caminar entre fotones: Formas y estilos de la mirada documental*, edited by Rebeca Monroy Nasr and Alberto del Castillo, 249–66. Mexico City: INAH, 2013.

González Nolasco, Iván. "La representación indígena. Análisis de un film documental neozapatista: 'Oventic, construyendo dignidad (1994–2005)," Master´s Thesis, History, Instituto de Ciencias Sociales y Humanidades-Benemérita Universidad Autónoma de Puebla, 2006.

González Quintana, Antonio, et al. *Kati Horna: Fotografiás de la guerra civil española (1937–1938)*. Salamanca, Ministerio de Cultura, 1992.

Gordon, Linda. *Dorothea Lange: A Life beyond Limits*. New York: Norton, 2009.

Griffith, Winthrop. "The Isla Vista War—Campus Violence in a Class by Itself." *New York Times*, 30 August 1970.

Griffiths, R. R., et al. "Psilocybin Can Occasion Mystical-Type Experiences Having Substantial and Sustained Personal Meaning and Spiritual Significance." *Psychopharmacology* 187:3 (2006): 284–92.

Guevara Escobar, Arturo. *Aurelio Escobar, Fotógrafo: La H. J. Gutiérrez Foto y Francisco I. Madero*. Mexico City: INAH, 2014.

Guildi, Jo, and David Armitage. *The History Manifesto*. Cambridge, UK: Cambridge University Press, 2014.

Gutiérrez, Jorge Luis. *Fotografía latinoamericana del siglo XIX: La historia no contada*. Caracas and Andalusia: Biblioteca Nacional de Venezuela/Universidad Internacional de Andalucía, n.d. (2004?).

Gutiérrez Ruvalcaba, Ignacio. "A Fresh Look at the Casasola Archive." In "Mexican Photography." Special Issue, *History of Photography* 20:3 (1996): 191–95.

______. *Una mirada estadunidense sobre México: William Henry Jackson, empresa fotográfica*. Mexico City: INAH, 2012.

______. *Teoberto Maler: Historia de un fotógrafo vuelto arqueólogo*. Mexico City: INAH, 2008.

Haley, Alex. *Roots: The Saga of an American Family*. New York: Doubleday, 1976.

Halliday, Jon, ed. *Sirk on Sirk: Conversations with Jon Halliday*. New York: Viking Press, 1972.

Hansen, Suzy. "Unlearning the Myth of American Innocence." *Guardian*, 8 August 2017. https://www.theguardian.com/us-news/2017/aug/08/unlearning-the-myth-of-american-innocence.

Harding, Sandra. *Whose Science? Whose Knowledge?: Thinking from Women's Lives*. Ithaca: Carnell University Press, 1991.

Harlan David. "Ken Burns and the Coming Crisis of Academic History." *Rethinking History* 7:2 (2003): 169–92.

Hart, Dianne Walta. "Communication: Some More Real than Others." *Studies in Latin American Popular Culture* 8 (1989): 299–304.

Hart, John. *Empire and Revolution: The Americans in Mexico since the Civil War*. Berkeley: University of California Press, 2002.

Hartley, L. P. *The Go-Between*. London: Hamish Hamilton, 1953.

Hartmann, Wolfram, Jeremy Silvester, and Patricia Hayes, eds. *The Colonizing Camera: Photographs in the Making of Namibian History*. Athens: Ohio University Press, 1998.

Héctor García: Camera Oscura. Veracruz: Gobierno de Veracruz, 1992.

Heilbrun, Françoise. "Around the World: Explorers, Travelers, and Tourists." In *A New History of Photography*, edited by Michel Frizot, 149–73. Cologne: Könemann, 1998.

Henderson, Brian. "*The Civil War*: 'Did It Not Seem Real?' " *Film Quarterly* 44:3 (1991): 3–14.

Hernández, Marco Antonio B. *Entre la tierra y el aire*. Pachuca: Asociación Cultural de Real del Monte y Pachuca, 1988.

Herr, Michael. *Dispatches*. New York: Avon, 1978.

Hight, Eleanor, and Gary Sampson, eds. *Colonialist Photography: Imagining Race and Place*. London: Routledge, 2002.

Hill, Paul, and Thomas Cooper, eds. *Dialogue with Photography*. Manchester: Cornerhouse Publications, 1992.

Hirsch, E. D., Jr. *Validity in Interpretation*. New Haven: Yale University Press, 1967.

Hirsch, Julia. *Family Photographs: Content, Meaning, and Effect*. Oxford: Oxford University Press, 1981.

Hirsch, Marianne. *Family Frames: Photography, Narrative, and Postmemory*. Cambridge: Harvard University Press, 1997.

Ho Chi Minh. "Advice to Oneself." Translated by Ailcen Palmer. In *The Penguin Book of Socialist Verse*, edited by Alan Bold, 149. New York: Penguin Books, 1970.

Hobsbawm, Eric. *Interesting Times: A Twentieth-Century Life*. New York: New Press, 2002.

______. *Workers: Worlds of Labor*. New York: Pantheon, 1984.

Hogenkamp, "Holland: Vereenigning van Arbeiders-Fotografen." In "Left Photography between the Wars." *Photography/Politics: One*. London: Photography Workshop, 1979, 83–87.

Holloway, John. *Change the World without Taking Power: The Meaning of Revolution Today*. London: Pluto Press, 2002.
______. *Crack Capitalism*. London: Pluto Press, 2010.
Hooks, Margaret. *Tina Modotti: Photographer and Revolutionary*. London: Pandora, 1993.
Horton, Brian. *The Associated Press Photojournalism Stylebook: The News Photographer's Bible*. New York: Addison-Wesley, 1990.
Hunt, Lynn. "Introduction: History, Culture, and Text." In *The New Cultural History*, edited by Lynn Hunt, 1–22. Berkeley: University of California Press 1989
Huxley, Aldous. *The Doors of Perception*. New York: Harper and Row, 1954.
"El imaginario de Luis Márquez." Special Number, *Alquimia* 10 (2000).
Jacoby, Russell. *The Last Intellectuals: American Culture in the Age of Academe*. New York: Basic Books, 1987.
James, Daniel, and Mirta Zaida Lobato. "Family Photos, Oral Narratives, and Identity formation: The Ukrainians of Berisso." *Hispanic American Historical Review* 84:1 (2004): 5–36.
Jameson, Frederic. *The Cultural Turn: Selected Writings on the Postmodern, 1983–1998*. London: Verso, 1998.
Jay, Martin. *Downcast Eyes: The Denigration of Vision in Twentieth-Century French Thought*. Berkeley: University of California Press, 1993.
Jeffrey, Ian. *Photography: A Concise History*. London: Thames and Hudson 1981.
Jimenéz, Blanca, and Samuel Villela. *Los Salmerón: Un siglo de fotografía en Guerrero*. Mexico City: INAH, 1998.
Johns, Michael. *The Education of a Radical: An American Revolutionary in Sandinista Nicaragua*. Austin: University of Texas Press, 2012.
Joseph, Gilbert. *Revolution from Without: Yucatán, Mexico, and the United States, 1880–1924*. Durham, NC: Duke University Press, 1988.
Jowett, Garth. "The Concept of History in American Produced Films: An Analysis of the Films Made in the Period 1950–1961." *Journal of Popular Culture* 3, no. 4 (1970): 798–813.
Jurgenson, Nathan. *The Social Photo: On Photography and Social Media*. London: Verso, 2019.
Kahn, Carrie. "Number of Journalists Killed in Mexico Reaches 'Historical High,' Report Says." *Parallels: Many Stories, One World*, 22 December 2017. https://www.npr.org/sections/parallels/2017/12/22/572822696/number-of-journalists-killed-in-mexico-reaches-historical-high-report-says.
Kant, Immanuel. *Prolegomena to Any Future Metaphysics*, edited by Lewis White Beck. Indianapolis: Bobbs-Merrill, 1950.
Katz, Friedrich. *The Life and Times of Pancho Villa*. Palo Alto, Stanford University Press, 1998.
Kaufman, Frederick. "An Essay of Memories: Based on Interviews with Manuel Alvarez Bravo." *Aperture* 147 (1997): 4–13.

Kazuyasu, Ochiai. "Examining Specimens, Evaluating Objects: Early Anthropological Photographic and Western Ethno-Anthropology." *Crossing Cultural Borders: Towards an Ethics of Intercultural Communication, International Symposium* 14 (1999): 49–72.

Klein, Mason, and Catherine Evans. *The Radical Camera: New York's Photo League, 1936–1951*. New York: Jewish Museum, 2011.

Knapton, Sarah. "Taking Photographs Ruins the Memory, Research Finds." *Telegraph*, 10 December 2013. http://www.telegraph.co.uk/news/science/science-news/10507146/Taking-photographs-ruins-the-memory-research-finds.html.

Knight, Alan. *The Mexican Revolution: Porfirians, Liberals and Peasants*, vol. 1. Lincoln: University of Nebraska Press, 1990.

______. *The Mexican Revolution: Counter-revolution and Reconstruction*, vol. 2. Lincoln: University of Nebraska Press, 1990.

______. "Racism, Revolution, and Indigenismo: Mexico, 1910–1940." In *The Idea of Race in Latin America, 1870–1940*, edited by Richard Graham, 71–113. Austin: University of Texas Press, 1990.

Körner, W., and J. Stüber. "Germany: Arbeiter-Fotografie," translated by David Evans and Sylvia Gohl. In *Photography/Politics: One*. London: Photography Workshop, 1979, 73–81.

Kossoy, Boris. *Fotografía e historia*, translated by Paula Sibilia. Buenos Aires: Biblioteca de la Mirada 2001.

Kozol, Wendy. Life's *America: Family and Nation in Postwar Photojournalism*. Philadelphia: Temple University Press, 1994.

Kracauer, Siegfried. *Theory of Film: The Redemption of Physical Reality*. London: Oxford University Press, 1960.

Krauze, Enrique. *Biografía del poder*. 8 vols. Mexico City: Fondo de Cultura Económica, 1987.

Krippner, James. *Paul Strand in Mexico*. New York: Aperture, 2010.

Krugman, Paul. "The Angry Male White Caucus." *New York Times*, 2 October 2018.

Kuehl, Jerry. "T.V. History." *History Workshop* 1, no. 1 (1976): 127–35.

Lakhani, Nina. "Mexico World's Deadliest Country for Journalists, New Report Finds." *Guardian*, December 22, 2020. https://www.theguardian.com/world/2020/dec/22/mexico-journalists-deadly-cpr-press-freedom.

Laslett, Peter. *The World We Have Lost: England before the Industrial Age*. New York: Scribner's, 1965.

Lawrence, D. H. *The Plumed Serpent*. New York: Penguin, 1979 [1926].

Lear, John. *Picturing the Proletariat: Artists and Labor in Revolutionary Mexico, 1908–1940*. Austin: University of Texas Press, 2017.

Lefebvre, Martin. "The Art of Pointing: On Pierce, Indexicality, and Photographic Images." Academia.edu, n.d. http://www.academia.edu/192769/The_Art_of_Pointing._On_Peirce_Indexicality_and_Photographic_Images.

Leite, Mirian Moreira. *Retratos de família: Leitura histórica da fotografía*. São Paulo: Edusp, 1993.

"Left Photography between the Wars." *Photography/Politics: One*. London: Photography Workshop, 1979, 71–117.

Lesy, Michael. *Wisconsin Death Trip*. New York: Pantheon, 1973.

Levine, Robert. *Images of History: Nineteenth and Early Twentieth Century Latin American Photographs as Documents*. Durham, NC: Duke University Press 1989.

Leyda, Jay. *Films Beget Films: A Study of the Compilation Film*. New York: Hill & Wang, 1964.

Linfield, Susie. *The Cruel Radiance: Photography and Political Violence*. Chicago: University of Chicago Press, 2010.

Lockwood, Lee. *Castro's Cuba, Cuba's Fidel*. New York: Vintage, 1969.

Lomnitz, Claudio. *Death and the Idea of Mexico*. Brooklyn: Zone Books, 2005.

López, Nacho. "Ante el umbral del silencio." *Mañana*, 26 May 1952, 28–35.

______. "Cuando una mujer guapa parte plaza por Madero." *Siempre!*, 27 June 1953, 22–25

______. "La fotografía: ¿Arte o testimonio?" *Unomásuno*, 24 March 1979, 19.

______. "El indio en la fotografía." *México indígena*, "Número especial de aniversario: INI 30 años después, revisión crítica" (1978): 328–31.

______. *Nacho López: Yo, el ciudadano*. Mexico City: Fondo de Cultura Económica, 1984.

______. "Noche de muertos." *Mañana*, 23 December 1950, 34–41.

______. *Los pueblos de la bruma y el sol*. Mexico City: Instituto Nacional Indigenista- FONAPAS, 1981.

______. "Solo los humildes van al infierno." *Siempre!*, 19 June 1954, 20–25, 70.

______. *Los trabajadores del campo y la ciudad*. Mexico City: IEPES, 1982.

______. "'Yo también he sido niño bueno . . .': Un reportaje de Nacho López." *Mañana* 383 (30 December 1950): 20–26.

López Mondéjar, Mario. "La magia de Martín Chambi." In *Martín Chambi: 1920–1950*, 7–22. Barcelona: Lunwerg, 1990.

Luck, Elaine. "Conspicuous Consumption and the Performance of Identity in Contemporary Mexico: Daniela Rossell's *Ricas y Famosas*." *Journal of Latin American Cultural Studies* 19:3 (2010): 299–315.

Luna, Lola G. "El video aplicado a la memoria de las mujeres latinoamericanas." *Boletín Americanista* 38 (1988): 141–50.

Lutz, Catherine A., and Jane L. Collins. *Reading* National Geographic. Chicago: University of Chicago Press, 1993.

Lydon, Jane. *Eye Contact: Photographing Indigenous Australians*. Durham, NC: Duke University Press, 2005.

Lyons, James, and John Plunkett, eds. *Multimedia Histories: From the Magic Lantern to the Internet*. Exeter: University of Exeter Press, 2007.

MacCann, Richard Dyer. *The People's Films: A Political History of U.S. Government Motion Pictures*. New York: Hastings House, 1973.

Malagón Girón, Beatriz. "La fotografía de Winfield Scott. Entre la producción comercial y la calidad estética de la fotografía." Doctoral Thesis, Historia del Arte, UNAM, 2003.

______. *Winfield Scott: Retrato de un fotógrafo norteamericano en el porfiriato.* Mexico City: Universidad Autónoma Metropolitana, 2012.

Malcolm, Janet. "The Genius of the Glass House." *New York Review of Books*, 4 February 1999: 10–15.

Malinowski, Bronislaw, and Julio de la Fuente. *The Economics of a Market System: An Essay in Contemporary Ethnographic and Social Change in a Mexican Valley.* New Haven: Yale University Press, 1941.

"Marco Antonio Cruz: Relatos y posicionamientos/1977–2017." Special issue, *Luna Córnea* 36 (2017).

Marcos, Sylvia. "Feminismos ayer y hoy." *Poiésis* 8:13 (2014): 8–29.

______. "Otro mundo . . . otro camino . . ." Presentation, Festival de la Digna Rabia, San Cristobal de las Casas, 4 January 2009.

MARHO: The Radical Historians Organization. *Visions of History: Interviews.* New York: Pantheon Books, 1983.

Martínez Assad, Carlos, ed. *Memoria y olvido: Imágenes de México.* 20 vols. Mexico City: Martín Casillas-SEP, 1982–83.

Marzal Felici, Javier. *Cómo se lee una fotografía: Interpretaciones de la mirada.* Madrid: Cátedra, 2015.

Massé Zendejas, Patricia. *Juan Antonio Azurmendi: Arquitectura doméstica y simbología en sus fotografías (1896–1900).* Mexico City: INAH, 2009.

______. "Juan Antonio Azurmendi: Historiar una colección fotográfica y construir a un autor." Doctoral Thesis, Instituto de Ciencias Sociales y Humanidades- Benemérita Universidad Autónoma de Puebla, 2013.

______. *Simulacro y elegancia en tarjetas de visita. Fotografías de Cruces y Campa.* Mexico City: INAH, 1998.

______. "Tina Modotti y el agrarismo radical en México." In "Tina Modotti, expediente inédito." Special Issue, *Alquimia* 50 (2014): 30–49.

Mauad, Ana Maria. "Imagens que faltam, imagens que sobram: Práticas visuais e cotidiano em regimes de execao 1960–1980." *Estudos Ibero-americanos* 43:2 (2017): 397–413. http://revistaseletronicas.pucrs.br/ojs/index.php/iberoamericana.

______. *Poses e flagrantes: Ensaios sobre história e fotografías.* Niterói: Universidade Federal Fluminense, 2008.

McCaa, Robert. "Missing Millions: The Demographic Costs of the Mexican Revolution." *Mexican Studies/Estudios Mexicanos* 19:2 (2003): 367–400.

______. "El poblamiento de México: De sus orígenes a la Revolución." In *La población de México: Tendencias y perspectivas sociodemográficas hacia el siglo XXI*, edited by José Gómez de León Cruces and Cecilia Rabell Romero, 33–77. Mexico City: Fondo de Cultura Económica, 2002.

McDonald, Jessica S. "'A History Making Occasion': The 1962 Invitational Teaching Conference." *Exposure* 45:2 (2012): 33–43.

McElroy, Wendy. "Administrative Bloat on Campus: Academia Shrinks, Students Suffer." James G. Martin Center for Academic Renewal, June 16, 2017. https://www.jamesgmartin.center/2017/06/administrative-bloat-campus-academia-shrinks-students-suffer.

McLuhan, Marshall. *Understanding Media: The Extensions of Man*. New York: McGraw-Hill, 1964.

Metz, Christian. *The Imaginary Signifier: Psychoanalysis and the Cinema*, translated by Celia Britton, Annwyl Williams, Ben Brewster, and Alfred Guzzetti. Bloomington: Indiana University Press, 1982.

Meyer, Eugenia. *John Kenneth Turner. Periodista de México*. Mexico City: Era, 2005.

Meyer, Michael. *Mexican Rebel: Pascual Orozco and the Mexican Revolution, 1910–1915*. Lincoln: University of Nebraska Press, 1967.

Mignolo, Walter. *The Darker Side of Western Modernity: Global Futures, Decolonial Options*. Durham, NC: Duke University Press, 2011.

Miserachs, Xavier. *Barcelona blance i negre*. Barcelona: Amyà, 1964.

Mitchell, Tim. *Flamenco Deep Song*. New Haven, CT: Yale University Press, 1994.

______. *Intoxicated Identities: Alcohol's Power in Mexican History and Culture*. New York: Routledge, 2004.

Monroy Nasr, Rebeca. *Ases de la cámara: Textos sobre fotografía mexicana*. Mexico City: INAH, 2010.

______. "El constructo visual desde la fotografía." *Historias* 98 (2017): 114–21.

______. *Fotografía de prensa en México. Un acercamiento a la obra de Enrique Díaz, Delgado y García*. Mexico City: Universidad Nacional Autónoma de México, 2001.

______. "Los quehaceres de los fotohistoriadores mexicanos: ¿Eurocentristas, americanistas o nacionalistas?," In "Fotografía, cultura y sociedad en América Latina en el siglo XX. Nuevas perspectivas." Special Issue, *L'Ordinaire des Amériques* 219 (2015). https://orda.revues.org/2287.

Monsiváis, Carlos. *Foto Estudio Jiménez: Sotero Constantino, fotógrafo de Juchitán*. Mexico City: Era, 1983.

______. *Maravillas que son, sombras que fueron: La fotografía en México*. Mexico City: Era/Museo de Estanquillo, 2012.

Monsiváis, Carlos, et al. *Casimiro Castro y su taller*. Mexico City: Fomento Cultural Banamex, 1996.

Montellano, Francisco. *C. B. Waite, Fotógrafo. Una mirada diversa sobre el México de principios del siglo XX*. Mexico City: CONACULTA/Grijalbo, 1994.

Morales Carrillo, Alfonso. *El gran lente*. Mexico City: SEP-INAH-Ediciones Jilguero, 1992.

______. *Juan Guzmán*. Mexico City: Fundación Televisa, 2014.

______. "Moya en el oleaje de las fotografías." In *Rodrigo Moya: Foto insurrecta*. Mexico City: Ediciones El Milagro, 2004.

Moreno, Caroline. "Guillermo Del Toro on How He Balances the Dark with the Good: 'I'm Mexican.'" *Huffpost*, 9 January 2018. http://www.facebook.com/HuffPostMexico/videos/1523501631052783.

Morse, Richard. *New World Soundings: Culture and Ideology in the Americas.* Baltimore: Johns Hopkins University Press, 1989.

Moya, Rodrigo. "Las imágenes prohibidas." ENCROME 4. "Proyecto ENsayo-CRÓnica-MEmoria," Archive of Rodrigo Moya.

Muñoz, Laura. *Fotografía imperial, escenarios tropicales: Las representaciones del Caribe en la revista National Geographic.* Mexico City: Instituto Mora, 2014.

"Nacho López." Special Issue. *Luna Córnea*, no. 31 (2007).

Nacho López, fotorreportero de los años cincuenta. Mexico City: CONACULTA, 1989.

Naggar, Carole "The Fascination for the Other." In *México through Foreign Eyes*, edited by Carole Naggar and Fred Ritchin, 41–53. New York: Norton, 1993.

Naggar, Carole, and Fred Ritchin, eds. *Mexico Through Foreign Eyes.* New York: Norton, 1993.

Nahón, Abraham. "El fotoperiodismo como testimonio y memoria del movimiento popular en Nochixtlán, Oaxaca, 2016." In "Fotografía, violencia política y memorias en América Latina," edited by Natalia Fortuny and Cora Gamarnik, Special Issue, *Clepsidra* 6:11 (2019): 110–24.

Nair, Parvati. *A Different Light: The Photography of Sebastião Salgado.* Durham, NC: Duke University Press, 2011.

Nares Ramos, Citlalli. "Siqueiros y los Hermanos Mayo." *Boletín del Archivo General de la Nación* 1 (6ª época, 2003): 29–43.

Navarrete, José Antonio. *Fotografiando en América Latina: Ensayos de crítica histórica.* Montevideo: Centro de Fotografía, 2017.

Navarro Castillo, Raquel. *Héctor García en* Ojo! *Una revista que ve.* Mexico City: CONACULTA, 2012.

Negrete Álvarez, Claudia. *Valleto Hermanos: Fotógrafos mexicanos de entresiglos.* Mexico City: UNAM, 2006.

Negroe Sierra, Genny. "Introducción." In *Guerra de Castas: Actores postergados*, edited by Genny Negroe Sierra, 11–37. Merida: Unicornio, 1997.

Newhall, Beaumont. *The History of Photography, 1839 to the Present.* New York: Museum of Modern Art, 1937.

Nichols, Bill. *Representing Reality: Issues and Concepts in Documentary.* Bloomington: Indiana University Press, 1991.

_______. *Speaking Truths with Film: Evidence, Ethics, Politics in Documentary.* Berkeley: University of California Press, 2016.

Noble, Andrea. Review of *Photographing the Mexican Revolution: Commitments, Testimonies, Icons. Caa.reviews*, 22 February 2013. http://www.caareviews.org/reviewers/1672.

Novelo, Victoria. *Obreros somos . . . expresiones de la cultura obrera.* Mexico City: Museo Nacional de Culturas Populares, 1984.

Nungesser Herausgeber, Michael, ed. *Hugo Brehme, Fotograf-Fotógrafo: Mexiko zwischen Revoluton und Romantik-México entre revolución y romanticismo.* Berlin: Verlag Willmuth Arenhövel, 2004.

Nye, David E. *Image Worlds: Corporate Identities at General Electric.* Cambridge: MIT Press, 1985.

Olcott, Jocelyn. *Revolutionary Women in Postrevolutionary Mexico.* Durham, NC: Duke University Press, 2005.

______. "'Take Off the Streetwalker's Dress': Concha Michel and the Cultural Politics of Gender in Postrevolutionary Mexico." *Journal of Women's History* 21:3 (2009): 36–59.

Ollman, Leah. *Camera as Weapon: Worker Photography between the Wars.* San Diego: Museum of Photographic Arts, 1991.

Oseguera Pizaña, Isaura. "Reivindicaciones del fotoperiodismo mexicano (1976–2006)." *Luna Córnea* 35 (2014): 28–125.

Orkin, Ruth. *A Photo Journal.* New York: Viking Press 1981.

Pacheco, Cristina. *La luz de México: Entrevistas con pintores y fotógrafos.* Mexico City: Fondo de Cultura Económica, 1996.

Padilla Ramos, Raquel. *Los irredentos parias: Los Yaquis, Madero y Pino Suárez en las elecciones de Yucatán, 1911.* Mexico City: INAH, 2011.

Padden, R. C. *The Hummingbird and the Hawk: Conquest and Sovereignty in the Valley of Mexico, 1503–1541.* New York: Harper & Row, 1970.

Pansters, Wil. "La Santa Muerte: History, Devotion, and Societal Context." In *La Santa Muerte in Mexico: History, Devotion & Society*, edited by Wil Pansters, 1–57. Albuquerque: University of New Mexico Press, 2019.

Paul, Gerhard. "Visual History." Docupedia-Zeitgeschichte, 13 March 2014. http://docupedia.de/zg/Visual_History_(english_version).

Paz, Octavio. *The Labyrinth of Solitude: Life and Thought in Mexico*, translated by Lysander Kemp. New York: Grove Press, 1961.

Peirce, Charles S. "Logic as Semiotic: The Theory of Signs," In *The Philosophy of Peirce*, edited by Justus Buchler, 98–119. London: Routledge and Kegan Paul 1940.

Penhall, Michele M., ed. "South America." Special Issue, *History of Photography* 24:2 (2000): 90–139.

El pensamiento crítico frente a la hidra capitalista: Participación de la Comisión Sexta del EZLN. 3 vols. Mexico: Medios Libres, Alternativos, Autónomos o como se llamen, 2015. Index available at Enlace Zapatista, http://enlacezapatista.ezln.org.mx/2015/07/13/indice-volumen-uno-participaciones-de-la-comision-sexta-del-ezln-en-el-seminario-el-pensamiento-critico-frente-a-la-hidra-capitalista.

Perez, Nissan. "Dreams—Visions—Metaphors." *In Dreams—Visions—Metaphors: The Photographs of Manuel Alvarez Bravo.* Jerusalem: The Israel Museum, 1983.

Peters, Jeremy. "The Birth of 'Just Do It' and Other Magic Words." *New York Times*, 19 August 2009.

Petroni, Mariana da Costa A. "Fotografiar al indio: Un breve estudio sobre la antropología y la fotografía mexicanas." *Dimensión Antropológica* 16:46 (2009): 181–215.

______. "La recepción de la imagen: Una reflexión antropológica sobre la representación del indio en México." *Aisthesis* 46 (2009): 128–50.

______. "La representación del indio en las fotografías del antropólogo e indigenista Julio de la Fuente." *Cultura y Representaciones Sociales* 3:5 (2008): 156–76.

Picaudé, Valérie, and Phillippe Arbaïzar, eds. *La confusión de los géneros en fotografía*. Barcelona: Gustavo Gili, 2004.

Picton, Tom, and Marcos Valdivia. "Bravo, Bravo!" *Camerawork* 3 (1976): 3.

Pilcher, Jeffrey. *¡Que vivan los tamales!: Food and the Making of Mexican Identity*. Albuquerque: University of New Mexico Press, 1998.

Pimental, Francisco. *Memoria sobre las causas que han originado la situación actual de la raza indígena de México y medios para remediarla*. Mexico City: Tipografía Económica, 1903 [1864].

Poe, Edgar Alan. "The Daguerreotype" (1840). In *Classic Essays on Photography*, edited by Alan Trachtenberg, 37–38. New Haven, CT: Leete's Island 1980.

Pohle, Fritz. *Das mexikanische Exil: Ein Beitrag zur Geschichte der politisch-kulturellen Emigration aus Deutschland (1937–1946)*. Stuttgart: Metzler, 1986.

"Polémica y debate abierto," de la Sexta Bienal de Fotoperiodismo, Mexico, 2004. Fotografía—Periodismo—Documentalismo, http://www.fotoperiodismo.org/FORO/files/fotoperiodismo/source/html/bienal_sexta/debate_frameset.htm.

Pollan, Michael. *How to Change Your Mind: What the New Science of Psychedelics Teaches Us about Consciousness, Dying, Addiction, Depression, and Transcendence*. New York: Penguin, 2018.

Poole, Deborah. "An Image of 'Our Indian': Type Photographs and Racial Sentiments in Oaxaca, 1920–1940." *Hispanic American Historical Review* 84: 1 (2004): 37–82.

Poole, Deborah and Gabriela Zamorano Villarreal, eds. *De frente al perfil: Retratos raciales de Frederick Starr*. Michoacán: El Colegio de Michoacán, 2012.

Portelli, Alessandro. "The Peculiarities of Oral History." *History Workshop Journal* 12 (1981): 96–107.

Pratt, Mary Louise. *Imperial Eyes: Travel Writing and Transculturation*. London: Routledge, 1992.

Quirke, Carol. *Eyes on Labor: News Photography and America's Working Class*. Oxford, UK: Oxford University Press, 2012.

Ramírez Castañeda, Elisa. "Espejismos." In Armando Bartra, Alejandra Moreno Toscano, and Elisa Ramírez Castañeda, *De fotógrafos y de indios*, 23–60. Mexico City: Ediciones Tecolote, 2000.

Ramírez Sevilla, Luis. *Villa Jiménez en la lente de Martiniano Mendoza*. Zamora: El Colegio de Michoacán, 2002.

Ramonet, Ignacio. *Marcos: La dignidad rebelde*. Valencia: Ediciones Cybermonde, 2001.

Ratliff, Jaime. " 'A Woman's Place Is in the Home': The Spatial Politics of Daniel Rossell's 'Ricas y Famosas.' " *Artelogie: Recherches sur les artes, le patrimoine el la littérature de l'Amérique Latine* 5 (2013). http://cral.in2p3.fr/artelogie/IMG/article_PDF/article_a253.pdf.

Reed, Nelson. *The Caste War of Yucatán*. Palo Alto: Stanford University Press, 1964.

Reiche, Reimut. *Sexuality and Class Struggle*, translated by Susan Bennett. New York: Praeger, 1970.

Reyes Palma, Francisco. "La LEAR y su revista de frente cultural." In *Frente a Frente 1934–1938*, Edición facsimilar, 5–16. Mexico City: Centro de Estudios del Movimiento Obrero y Socialista, 1994.

Ribera Carbó, Eulalia, and Fernando Aguayo. *Imágenes y ciudad: Orizaba a través de la lente, 1872–1910*. Mexico City: Instituto Mora, 2014.

Ritchin, Fred. *After Photography*. New York: W.W. Norton, 2009.

Rittner, Silvia. "Testimonios de los trabajadores petroleros." *Historia Obrera* 24 (1982): 15–20.

Rivas Rivas, José. *Historia gráfica de Venezuela*. 12 vols. Caracas: Centro Editor, 1972–1988.

Rivera Ortiz, Mario. *Columnas contra cordones: 1º de Mayo de 1952*. Mexico City: Mar y Tierra, 1997.

Robledo Martínez, Jaime. *Episodios fotográficos de la toma de Zacatecas, 1913–1914*. Zacatecas: Fototeca de Zacatecas "Pedro Valtierra," 2014.

Rodríguez, José Antonio. *Bernice Kolko: Fotógrafa/Photographer*. Mexico City: Ediciones del Equilibrista, 1996.

______. "Fotomontaje en México: Razones sociopolíticas." *Antropología* 71 (2003): 2–12.

Rodríguez, José Antonio, and Alberto Tovalín Ahumada, eds. *Fotografía artística Guerra: Yucatán, México*. Mexico City and Mérida: Cámara de Diputados/ Fototeca Pedro Guerra, 2017.

______. *Nacho López: Fotógrafo de México*. Mexico City: Museo del Palacio de Bellas Artes, 2016.

______. *Nacho López: Ideas y visualidad*. Mexico City and Veracruz: INAH/ Universidad Veracruzana/Fondo de Cultura Económica, 2012.

Rodríguez Hernández, Georgina. "'Ahora aquí, ahora allá': Los kikapoos en el Segundo Imperio." Special Issue, "François Aubert en México." *Alquimia* 21 (2004): 35–40.

______. "Miradas sin rendición." *Luna Córnea* 13 (1997): 24–31.

______. "Recobrando la presencia." Special Issue, "Antropología e imagen." *Cuicuilco* 5:13 (1998): 123–44.

Rodríguez Luévano, Álvaro. "Tipos de prisioneros mexicanos. Tablas fotográficas de detenidos de la penitenciaría de Guadalajara en la Colección Etnográfica Mexicana de León Diguet." *Historias*, no. 102 (2019): 44–64.

Rojas Rabiela, Teresa, and Ignacio Gutiérrez Ruvalcaba. *Catálogo de la Colección de Antropología del Museo Nacional*. Mexico City: Secretaría de Cultura/ INAH/CIESAS, 2018.

Romaguera i Ramió, Joaquim. *Magí Murià: Periodista i cineasta*. Lleida: Pagés, 2002.

Román Alvarado, Abe Yillah. "Tiempos de convicción: Estética y fotoperiodismo en Enrique Bordes Mangel." Master's Thesis, Historia del Arte, UNAM, 2008.

Rosas Robles, Alejandro. "Un gallo de pelea: Historia de la compañía petrolera Waters Pierce, 1885–1910." *Relatos e Historias en México* 30 (2011): 50–58.

Rosenstone, Robert. *Adventures of a Postmodern Historian: Living and Writing the Past.* London: Bloomsbury, 2016.

______. "The Historical Film as Real History." *Film Historia* 5:1 (1995): 5–23. Available at: http://revistes.ub.edu/index.php/filmhistoria/article/view/12244.

______. *History on Film/Film on History.* London: Pearson, 2012.

______. *Visions of the Past: The Challenge of Film to Our Idea of History.* Cambridge, MA: Harvard University Press, 1995.

______. ed. "AHR Forum. History in Images/History in Words: Reflections on the possibility of Really Putting History onto Film." *American Historical Review* 93:5 (1988): 1,173–227.

______. ed. *Revisioning History: Film and the Construction of a New Past.* Princeton, NJ: Princeton University Press, 1995.

Rosenzweig, Roy. *Clio Wired: The Future of the Past in the Digital Age.* New York: Columbian University Press, 2011.

Rosler, Martha. "In, Around, and Afterthoughts (on Documentary Photography)." In *The Contest of Meaning: Critical Histories of Photography*, edited by Richard Bolton, 303–41. Cambridge: MIT Press, 1989.

Rossell, Daniela. *Ricas y famosas.* Madrid: Turner, 2002.

Roth, Michael S. "Photographic Ambivalence and Historical Consciousness." *History and Theory* 48, no. 4 (December 2009): 82–94.

"Rotmi Enciso: imágenes del feminismo en México." *Proceso*, 6 August 2008. https://www.proceso.com.mx/200686/rotmi-enciso-imagenes-del-feminismo-en-mexico.

Rouch, Jean. "Jean Rouch." In *Documentary Explorations: 15 Interviews with Film-Makers*, edited by G. Roy Levin, 131–45. Garden City: Doubleday & Co., 1971.

Ryan, James R. *Picturing Empire: Photography and the Visualization of the British Empire.* Chicago: University of Chicago Press, 1997.

Rubin, Jerry. *Do It: Scenarios of the Revolution.* New York: Ballantine Books, 1970.

Salgado, Sebastião. *Other Americas.* New York: Aperture, 1986.CITED ON PAGE 200

Samuels, Rafael. *Theatres of Memory.* London: Verso, 1994.

San Miguel, Pedro L. *Crónicas de un embrujo: Ensayos sobre historia y cultura del Caribe hispano.* San Juan: Ediciones Callejón, 2016.

Sánchez Bringas, Ángeles and Nina Torres. *De la casa a la fábrica: La mujer en el mercado de trabajo.* Mexico City: Universidad Autónoma Metropolitana-Xochimilco, 1987.

Sánchez, José Antonio. "España no fue colonizadora; fue evangelizadora: Presidente de la televisión española." El Mundo, 5 April 2017. https://www.elespectador.com/noticias/el-mundo/espana-nunca-fue-colonizadora-fue-evangelizadora-presidente-de-la-television-espanola-articulo-687967.

Sánchez Estévez, José Luis "Luis Márquez Romay y su obra: Apuntes sobre la búsqueda del nacionalismo cultural en México." Licenciatura Thesis, Centro Universitario de Ciencias Humanas, 1990.

Sandweiss, Martha. "Image and Artifact: The Photograph as Evidence in the Digital Age." *Journal of American History* 94:1 (2007): 193–202.

______. *Print the Legend: Photography and the American West.* New Haven, CT: Yale University Press, 2002.

Sartorius, Carl. *Mexico about 1850.* Stuttgart: Brockhaus, 1961.

Saunders, Dave. *20th Century Advertising.* London: Carlton, 1999.

Schell, William, Jr. *Integral Outsiders: The American Colony in Mexico City, 1876–1911.* Wilmington: Scholarly Resources, 2001.

Schiwy, Freya. *Indianizing Film: Decolonizing, the Andes, and the Question of Technology.* New Brunswick, NJ: Rutgers University Press, 2009.

Schreiber, Rebecca. *Cold War Exiles in Mexico: U.S. Dissidents and the Culture of Critical Resistance.* Minneapolis: University of Minnesota Press, 2008.

Schultz, Colin. "This Professor Can Tell from the Pixels That Your Photo's Been 'Shopped.'" *Smithsonian Magazine*, 19 September 2012. http://www.smithsonianmag.com/smart-news/this-professor-can-tell-from-the-pixels-that-your-photos-been-shopped-42457688.

Schultz, Reinhard, ed. *Tina Modotti: Photographien & Dokument.* Berlin: Sozialarchiv, n.d. [1989].

Schultz, Reinhard, and Andreas Hirsch, eds. *Tina Modotti: Photographer and Revolutionary.* Vienna: Kunst Haus Wein, 2010.

Schwartz, Dona. "To Tell the Truth: Codes of Objectivity in Photojournalism." *Communication* 13 (1992): 95–109.

Scruton, Roger. "Photography and Representation." *Critical Inquiry* 7: 3 (1981): 577–603.

Sekula, Alan. "The Body and the Archive." In *The Contest of Meaning: Critical Histories of Photography*, edited by Richard Bolton, 343–89. Cambridge: The MIT Press, 1989.

______. "Dismantling Modernism, Reinventing Documentary (Notes on the Politics of Representation)." *Massachusetts Review* 19:4 (1978): 859–83.

______. "Photography between Labour and Capital." In *Mining Photographs and Other Pictures, 1948–1968*, 193–268. Halifax: Nova Scotia College of Art & Design/Cape Breton University Press, 1983.

Sigüenza Orozco, Salvador and Fernando Mino Gracia. *Imágenes de un pionero del oficio fotográfico en Tlacolula.* Mexico City: Centro de Investigaciones y Estudios Superiores en Antropología Social, 2018.

Silverman, Jacob. "'Pics or It Didn't Happen': The Mantra of the Instagram Era." *Guardian*, 26 February 2015.

Silva, Armando. *Álbum de familia: La imagen de nosotros mismos.* Bogotá: Editorial Norma, 1998.

Silverman, Craig. "Three Ways to Spot If an Image Has Been Manipulated." *Poynter: A Global Leader in Journalism*, 24 May 2012. http://www.poynter.org/2012/three-ways-to-spot-if-an-image-has-been-manipulated/173387.

The Sokal Hoax: The Sham that Shook the Academy, edited by the editors of *Lingua Franca*. Lincoln: University of Nebraska Press, 2000.

Sokal, Alan, and Jean Bricmont. *Intellectual Imposters: Postmodern Philosophers' Abuse of Science*. London: Profile Books, 1998.

Solomon-Godeau, Abigail. *Photography after Photography: Gender, Genre History*, edited by Sarah Parsons. Durham, NC: Duke University Press, 2017.

______. *Photography at the Dock: Essays on Photographic history, Institutions, and Practices*. Minneapolis: University Minnesota Press,1991.

______. "Who Is Speaking Thus? Some Questions about Documentary Photography." In *The Event Horizon*, edited by Lorne Falk y Barbara Fischer, 193–214. Toronto, Coach House Press, 1987.

Solon, Olivia. "The Future of Fake News: Don't Believe Everything You Read, See or Hear." *Guardian*, 26 July 2017. https://www.theguardian.com/technology/2017/jul/26/fake-news-obama-video-trump-face2face-doctored-content.

Sontag, Susan. *On Photography*. New York: Delta, 1973.

______. *Regarding the Pain of Others*. New York: Picador, 2003.

Sorlin, Pierre. *The Film in History: Restaging the Past*. Totowa, New Jersey: Barnes & Noble, 1980.

Speed, Shannon. *Rights in Rebellion: Indigenous Struggle and Human Rights in Chiapas*. Palo Alto, CA: Stanford University Press, 2008.

St. Aubyn, Edward. *Mother's Milk*. London: Picador, 2005. Kindle Edition.

Stallabrass, Julian. "Sebastião Salgado and Fine Art Photojournalism." *New Left Review* 223 (1997): 131–61.

Starl, Timm. "A New World of Pictures: The Use and Spread of the Daguerreotype Process." In *A New History of Photography*, edited by Michel Frizot, 33–57. Cologne: Könemann, 1998.

Starr, Frederick. *In Indian Mexico: A Narrative of Travel and Labor*. Chicago: Forbes & Co., 1908.

Stasz, Clarice. "The Early History of Visual Sociology." In *Images of Information: Still Photography in the Social Sciences*, edited by Jon Wagner, 119–36. Beverly Hills, CA: Sage Publications 1979.

Stein, Sally. "Making Connections with the Camera: Photography and Social Mobility in the Career of Jacob Riis." *Afterimage* 10: 10 (1983): 9–16.

Stein, Steve J. "Visual Images of the Lower Classes in Early Twentieth-Century Peru: Soccer as a Window to Social Reality." In "Windows on Latin America: Understanding Society through Photographs," edited by Robert M. Levin. Special Issue, *South Eastern Latin Americanist*, June-Sept. 1987: 90–100.

Stephens, John Lloyd. *Incidents of Travel in Central America, Chiapas and Yucatan*, vol.1. New York: Harper and Brothers, 1841.

Stieglitz, Alfred. "Pictorial Photography" (1899). In *Classic Essays on Photography*, edited by Alan Trachtenberg, 115–23. New Haven, CT: Leete's Island 1980.

Stott, William. *Documentary Expression and Thirties America*. London: Oxford University Press, 1986.

Strauss, David Levi. "Photography and Propaganda: Richard Cross and John Hoagland in Central America and in the News." In David Levi Strauss, *Between the Eyes: Essays on Photography and Politics*, 12–41. New York: Aperture, 2003 [1988].

Szakowski, John. *Mirrors and Windows: American Photography since 1960*, Press Review, Museum of Modern Art, July 26, 1978. http://www.moma.org/pdfs/docs/press_archives/5624/releases/MOMA_1978_0060_56.pdf?2010.

Taracena Arriola, Arturo. *De la nostalgia por la memoria a la memoria nostálgica: La prensa literaria y la construcción del regionalismo yucateco en el siglo XIX*, Mexico City: UNAM, 2010.

______. "Photography in Guatemala as a Social Document." In *Images of Guatemala: 57 photographers from CIRMA Photography Archive and the Guatemalan photographic community*, edited by Arturo Taracena Arriola and Rosina Cazali, 5–36. Antigua: Centro de Investigaciones Regionales de Mesoamérica, 2005.

Tatard, Béatrice. "Julio de la Fuente: Trabajador social y fotógrafo." *Alquimia* 7 (1999): 44–45.

Tejedores de imágenes: Propuestas metodológicas de investigación y gestión del patrimonio fotográfico y audiovisual. Mexico City: Instituto Mora, 2014.

Thompson, Ginger. "The Rich, Famous and Aghast: A Peep-Show Book." *New York Times*, 25 September 2002.

Thord-Gray, I. *Gringo Rebel: Mexico 1913–1914*. Seguin, TX: Chiringa Press, 2010.

Tibbets, John. "The Incredible Stillness of Being: Motionless Pictures in the Films of Ken Burns." *American Studies* 37:1 (1996): 117–33.

Tidd, Rusula. "Telling the Truth in Simone de Beauvoir's Autobiography." *New Readings* (2011): 7–19. ojs.cf.ac.uk/index.php/newreadings/article/download/64/50.

Tirado Villegas, Gloria. *Quiero morir como nací*. Puebla: Benemérita Universidad Autónoma de Puebla, 1992.

Todorov, Tzvetan. "The Origen of Genres." *New Literary History* 8:1 (1976): 159–70.

______. "The Typology of Detective Fiction." In *The Poetics of Prose*, 42–52. Ithaca: Cornell University Press, 1977.

Toplin, Robert Brent, ed. *Ken Burns's* The Civil War: *Historians Respond*. Oxford: Oxford University Press, 1996.

Tovalín Ahumada, Alberto, et al. *Joaquín Santamaría: Sol de plata/Silver Sun*. Veracruz: Universidad Veracruzana-TAMSA-FONCA, 1998.

Triquell, Agustina. *Fotografías e historias: La construcción narrativa de la memoria y las identidades en el álbum fotográfico familiar*. Montevideo: Centro de Fotografía, 2011.
Turner, John Kenneth. *Barbarous Mexico*. Chicago: Charles Company Cooperative, 1911.
______. *Barbarous Mexico*. Austin, University of Texas Press, 1969.
Turok, Antonio. *Chiapas: El fin del silencio*. Mexico City: Era, 1998.
______. *Imágenes de Nicaragua*. Mexico City: Casa de las Imágenes, 1988.
Twain, Mark. *King Leopold's Soliloquy: A Defense of his Congo Rule*. New York: P. R. Warren, 1905.
Vallès, Edmon. *Història Gràfica de la Catalunya Contemporània: 1888/1931*. 3 vols. Barcelona: Edicions 62, 1991 [1974].
Valtierra, Pedro. *Nicaragua: Una noche afuera*. Mexico City: Cuartoscuro, 1991.
Vanderwood, Paul. Review of *Innovating Nicaragua* and *Made on Rails: A History of the Mexican Railroad Workers*. *Film & History* 19:2 (1989): 46–48.
Vázquez Olvera, Carlos. *El ropero de las señoritas Sámano Serrato: La fotografía familiar como fuente de investigación documental*. Mexico City: INAH, 2013.
Vélez Storey, Jaime. "Alegorías raciales de una mirada distante: Los retratos de Frederick Starr." In *De frente al perfil: Retratos raciales de Frederick Starr*, edited by Deborah Poole and Gabriela Zamorano Villarreal, 43–50. Michoacán: El Colegio de Michoacán, 2012.
Vélez Storey, Jaime, et al. *El ojo de vidrio: Cien años de fotografía del México indio*. Mexico City: Bancomext, 1993.
Vera, Luis Roberto. "Viajes a Tehuantepec: Entrevista a Manuel Álvarez Bravo." *Sábado*, supplement of *Unomásuno*, 23 September 1989, 1–2.
Vilches, Lorenzo. *Teoría de la imagen periodística*. Barcelona: Ediciones Paidós, 1987.
Villaseca Chávez, J. de Jesús. *Atenco rebelde: Imagen de un pueblo en lucha*. Mexico City: Editorial Latitudes, 2007.
______. "Prólogo." In *Sucumbe el abasto popular ante la ley del más fuerte*, 3–4. Mexico City: Talleres de Fotografía Jesús Villaseca, 2011,
______. "Prólogo." In *¡Ya basta! El camino a un Estado fallido*, 4–5. Mexico City: Talleres de Fotografía Jesús Villaseca, 2011.
Villela, Samuel. "Los Lupercio, fotógrafos jaliscienses." *Antropología* 48 (1997): 3–9.
______. *Sara Castrejón: Fotógrafa de la Revolución*. Mexico City, INAH, 2010.
Villoro, Juan. "Ricas, famosas y excesivas." *El País*, 9 June 2002.
Villoro, Luis. *Los grandes momentos del indigenismo en México*. Mexico City: El Colegio de México, 1950.
Walkowitz, Daniel. "Visual History: The Craft of the Historian-Filmmaker." *Public Historian* 7:1 (1985): 53–64.
Wallace, David Foster. *A Supposedly Fun Thing I'll Never Do Again*. New York: Little, Brown and Company, 1997.

Walton, Kendall. "Looking Again through Photographs: A Response to Edwin Martin." *Critical Inquiry* 12: 4 (1986): 801–808.

______. "Transparent Pictures: On the Nature of Photographic Realism." *Critical Inquiry* 11 (1984): 247–77.

Warburton, Nigel. "Varieties of Photographic Representation: Documentary, Pictorial and Quasi-documentary." *History of Photography* 15:3 (1991): 203–10.

Ware, Katherine C. "Photographs of Mexico, 1940." In *Paul Strand: Essays on his Life and Work*, edited by Maren Stange, 109–21. New York: Aperture, 1990.

Washington, Stacy. "African American Photographs as Political Resistance in a Postmodern Consumer Age." *Transit Circle* 1 (2002): 79–107.

Watzlawick, Paul, Janet Helmick Beavin, and Don Jackson, *Pragmatics of Human Communication*. New York: W. W. Norton, 1967.

Weaver, Mike. Review of *Revelaciones: The Art of Manuel Alvarez Bravo*; *Compañeras de México: Women Photograph Women*; and *Between Worlds: Contemporary Mexican Photography*. *History of Photography* 15:2 (1991): 154.

Westerbeck, Colin, and Joel Meyerowitz. *Bystander: A History of Street Photography*. London: Thames and Hudson, 1994.

Whelan, Richard. *Double Take: A Comparative Look at Photographs*. New York: Clarkson N. Potter, 1981.

White, Hayden. "Historiography and Historiophoty." *American Historical Review* 95, no. 5 (1988): 1193–99.

______. *Metahistory: The Historical Imagination in Nineteenth-Century Europe*. Baltimore: Johns Hopkins University Press, 1973.

Williams, Raymond. *Keywords: A Vocabulary of Culture and Society*. London: Fontana Press, 1976.

Willumson, Glenn W. *W. Eugene Smith and the Photographic Essay*. Cambridge: Cambridge University Press, 1992.

Wolf, Eric. *Sons of the Shaking Earth: The People of Mexico and Guatemala—Their Land, History, and Culture*. Chicago: University of Chicago Press, 1959.

Worth, Sol. "The Uses of Film in Education and Communication." In *Media and Symbols: The Forms of Expression, Communication, and Education; The Seventy-Third Yearbook of the National Society for the Study of Education*, edited by David Olson, 271–302. Chicago: University of Chicago Press, 1974.

Zamora, José. *Cholula: Memoria e identidad*. Cholula: Fototeca Municipal de San Pedro Cholula, 2017.

Zamorano Villarreal, Gabriela. *Indigenous Media and Political Imaginaries in Contemporary Bolivia*. Lincoln: University of Nebraska Press, 2017.

Zaragoza Luna, Samanta Norma. "Las neozapatistas en el fotoperiodismo (México, 1994–1996)." Doctoral Thesis, Ciencias Sociales, Universidad Autónoma Metropolitana-Xochilmilco, 2012.

______. *Alzando la Mirada: Las mujeres Zapatistas de Angeles Torrejón*. Puebla: Benemérita Universidad Autónoma de Puebla, 2018.

Zelich, C. "Portraiture, Social Documentation and Photojournalism." In *Idas & Chaos: Trends in Spanish Photography, 1920–1945*, 161–97. n. p., 1985.

CINEOGRAPHY

Burns, Ken. *The Civil War*, nine-part television series. United States: Public Broadcasting Service, 1990.

Father Knows Best, six-season television program. United States: Columbia Broadcasting System and National Broadcasting Company, 1954–1960.

Godard, Jean-Luc and Jean-Pierre Gorin. *Letter to Jane*. Paris: Dziga Vertov Group, 1972.

Griffin, Patrick, R. C. Raack, and William Malloch. *Goodbye Billy: America Goes to War*. United States: American Historical Association History Education Project, 1972.

Huston, John. *The Treasure of the Sierra Madre*. United States: Warner Brothers, 1948.

Moore, Michael. *Roger & Me*. United States: Warner Brothers, 1989.

Murià, Magí. *Alma torturada*. Barcelona, 1916.

Ophuls, Marcel. *The Sorrow and the Pity*. France: Télévision Rencontre, 1969.

Polley, Sarah. *Stories We Tell*. Canada: National Film board of Canada, 2012.

Roots, 8 episodes. United States: American Broadcasting Company, 1977.

Schub, Esfir, and Vsevolod Vishnevsky. *Spain*. USSR, 1939.

Victory at Sea, 26-part television series. United States: National Broadcasting Company, 1952–1953.

The World at War, 26-part television series. Great Britain: Thames Television, 1973–1974.

Wright, Basil. *Song of Ceylon*. Great Britain: Ceylon Tea Propaganda Board, 1934.

WORKS BY JOHN MRAZ

BOOKS AND ARTICLES

"Close-Up: An Interview with the Hermanos Mayo, Spanish-Mexican Photojournalists (1930s-Present)," *Studies in Latin American Popular Culture* 11 (1992): 195–218.

"De la fotografía histórica: Particularidad y nostalgia," *Nexos* 91 (1985): 9–12.

"'En calidad de esclavas': Obreras en los molinos de nixtamal, México, diciembre, 1919." *Historia Obrera* 6: 24 (1982): 2–14.

"Film and History in Revolutionary Cuba: 1965–1970." Doctoral Dissertation, History, UCSC, 1986.

"Foto Hermanos Mayo: A Mexican Collective." *History of Photography* 17:1 (1993): 81–89.

"Fotohistorias de la Revolución Mexicana." *Historias*, no. 107 (2020): forthcoming.

"From Robert Capa's 'Dying Republican Soldier' to Political Scandal in Contemporary Mexico: Reflections on Digitalization and Credibility" *Zonezero Magazine*, 2004. http://www.zonezero.com.

"Gringo." In *Iconic Mexico: An Encyclopedia from Acapulco to Zócalo*, edited by Eric Zolov, 265–71. Santa Barbara: ABC-CLIO, 2015.

"Los Hermanos Mayo: El Primero de Mayo y la fotografía de la clase obrera." *Boletín de investigación del movimiento obrero*, 11 (1988): 105–15.

"La lente emigrante de Walter Reuter." In *Walter Reuter: El viento limpia el alma*, 65–80. Barcelona: Lunwerg, 2009.

"Light and Sound: Teaching Latin American History with Media." *Proceedings of the Pacific Coast Council on Latin American Studies* 5 (1976): 121–34.

Looking for Mexico: Modern Visual Culture and National Identity. Durham: Duke University Press, 2009.

"*Lucía*: History and Film in Revolutionary Cuba." *Film & History* 5:1 (1975): 8–14, 18.

"*Lucía*: Visual Style and Historical Portrayal." *Jump Cut: A Review of Contemporary Media* 50 (2010), http://www.ejumpcut.org; originally published in *Jump Cut* 19 (1978): 21–27.

"*Memories of Underdevelopment*: Bourgeois Consciousness/Revolutionary Context." In *Revisioning History: Film and the Construction of a New Past*, edited by Robert Rosenstone, 102–14, 229–30. Princeton: Princeton University Press, 1995.

México en sus imágenes. Mexico City and Puebla: Artes de México-CONACULTA-ICSH-BUAP, 2014.

Nacho López: Mexican Photographer. Minneapolis, University of Minnesota Press, 2003.

"The New Photojournalism of Mexico." *History of Photography* 22:4 (1998): 313–65.

Photographing the Mexican Revolution: Commitments, Testimonies, Icons. Austin: University of Texas Press, 2012.

"Picturing Mexico's Past: Photography and *Historia Gráfica*." *South Central Review* 21:3 (2004): 24–45.

"'Querían fotos': Algunas inquietudes en torno a la antropología visual." In *Antropología visual*, edited by Ana María Salazar Peralta, 45–53. Mexico City: UNAM, 1997.

"Recasting Cuban Slavery: *The Other Francisco* and *The Last Supper*." In *Based on a True Story: Latin American History at the Movies*, edited by Donald E. Stevens, 103–22, 231–32. Wilmington (Delaware): Scholarly Resources, 1997.

"Representing the Mexican Revolution: Bending Photographs to the Will of *Historia Gráfica*." In *Photography and Writing in Latin America*, edited by Marcy Schwartz and Mary Beth Tierney-Tello, 21–39. Albuquerque: University of New Mexico Press, 2006.

"Retratos fotográficos." In *Los mexicanos: 2500 años de retrato*, 332–75. Mexico City: Fundación BBVA Bancomer, 2017,

Review of *Argentine, Mexican, and Guatemalan Photography*. *Journal of Latin American Studies*, 48:2 (2016): 410–12.

"The Revolution is History: Filming the Past in Mexico and Cuba." *Film Historia* 9:2 (1999): 147–67. Available online: http://revistes.ub.edu/index.php/filmhistoria.

"Santiago Alvarez: From Dramatic Form to Direct Cinema." In *The Social Documentary in Latin America*, edited by Julianne Burton, 131–49. Pittsburgh: University of Pittsburgh Press, 1990.

"Sara Castrejón: Photographing Revolution, Representing Women." In *Revolution & Ritual: The Photographs of Sara Castrejón, Graciela Iturbide, and Tatiana Parcero*, edited by Mary Davis MacNaughton, 22–38. Claremont, CA: Scripps College, 2017.

"Sebastião Salgado: Ways of Seeing Latin America," *Third Text* 16: 1 (2002): 15–30.

"Some Visual Notes Toward a Graphic History of the Mexican Working Class," *Journal of the West* 27:4 (1988): 64–74.

"El testimonio de los índices: Fotografía documental y fotoperiodismo." *Alquimia* 66 (2019): 63–68.

"Tina Modotti: En el camino hacia la realidad," *La Jornada Semanal* 7 (1989): 20–23.

"Today, Tomorrow and Always: The Golden Age of Illustrated Magazines in Mexico, 1937–1960." In *Fragments of a Golden Age: The Politics of Culture in Mexico Since 1940*, edited by Gilbert Joseph, Anne Rubenstein, and Eric Zolov, 116–57. Durham, NC: Duke University Press, 2001.

"Una storia che corre sui binari: Videostoria e classe operaia messicana." *Il Nuovo Spettatore* 14 (1992): 25–41.

"Universos: Pueblos indígenas," in *Nacho López. Fotógrafo de México*, edited by José Antonio Rodríguez and Alberto Tovalín, 221–51. Mexico City: Museo del Palacio de Bellas Artes, 2016.

"Video and Labor History: *Made on Rails* in Mexico." *Jump Cut: A Review of Contemporary Media* 54 (2012), http://www.ejumpcut.org; originally published in *Jump Cut* 39 (1994): 113–21.

"Video e historia obrera en México." *Voces y culturas: Revista de Comunicación* 5 (1993): 25–44.

"Visualizar el pasado mexicano: Someter fotografías a voluntad de la historia gráfica." In *Historia de la historiografía de América, 1950–2000*, edited by Boris Berenzon Gorn and Georgina Calderón Aragón, 371–420. Mexico City: UNAM and Instituto Panamericano de Geografía e Historia, 2009.

"War Is Hazardous for Your Health: Photographs and Testimonies about Deaths, Wounds, Disease and Medical Care during the Mexican Revolution." *História, Ciências, Saúde-Manguinhos* 18:3 (2011): 893–905.

"What's Documentary about Photography? From Directed to Digital Photojournalism," *Zonezero Magazine*, 2002. http://www.zonezero.com

COLLABORATIVE WRITINGS

Chiles, Frederic, and John Mraz. "The Historical Film Essay: *Todo es más sabroso con . . .*" *Proceedings of the Pacific Coast Council on Latin American Studies* 4 (1975): 183–86.

Leistner, Rita, and John Mraz. *Una historia moderna de imagines descolonizadoras: El proyecto Edward Curtis*. Puebla: Benemérita Universidad Autónoma de Puebla, 2018.

Mraz, John, and Ana Mauad, eds. *Fotografía e historia en América Latina*. Montevideo: Centro de Fotografía, 2015.

Mraz, John, and Raymond Tracy. "Classroom Production of an Historical Film Essay: Reflections and Guidelines." *History Teacher* 7:4 (1974): 540–51.

Mraz, John, and Jaime Vélez Storey. *Uprooted: Braceros in the Hermanos Mayo Lens*. Houston: Arte Público Press, 1996.

______. "Walter Reuter: Entrevistas realizadas en la Ciudad de México." In *Walter Reuter: El viento limpia el alma*, 13–23. Barcelona: Lundwerg, 2009.

Mraz, John, et al. *Walter Reuter: El viento limpia el alma*. Barcelona: Lundwerg, 2009.

Rocha, Gonzalo, and John Mraz. *La visión de los vendidos: Los héroes de la gran parodia nacional*. Mexico City: Ediciones Proceso, 2016.

JOURNAL ISSUES

Guest editor. "Cinema and History in Latin America." Special issue, *Film Historia* 9:2 (1999). http://revistes.ub.edu/index.php/filmhistoria.

Guest editor. "Mexican Photography." Special issue, *History of Photography* 20:3 (1996).

Guest editor. "Visual Culture in Latin America." Special issue, *Estudios Interdisciplinarios de América Latina y el Caribe* 9:1 (1998).

MODERN MEDIA PRODUCTIONS

BRACEROS Photographed by the Hermanos Mayo/BRACEROS fotografiados por los Hermanos Mayo. Photographic exhibit. Puebla: Centro Nacional para la Preservación del Patrimonio Cultural Ferrocarrilero, 2017.

Braceros vistos por los Hermanos Mayo. Photographic exhibit. Puebla: Centro Nacional para la Preservación del Patrimonio Cultural Ferrocarrilero, 2015.

Broken Spears: 1450–1783. Audiovisual production. University of California at Santa Barbara, 1974.

Dependency and Nationalism: 1885–1974. Audiovisual production. University of California at Santa Barbara, 1975.

The History of Mexico as Seen by the Muralists. Audiovisual production. University of California at Santa Barbara, 1971.

Julio Mayo: Bracero con cámara/Julio Mayo: Bracero with a Camera. Digital production. Puebla: Centro Nacional para la Preservación del Patrimonio Cultural Ferrocarrilero, 2015.

Made on Rails: A History of the Mexican Railroad Workers/ Hechos sobre los rieles: Una historia de los ferrocarrileros mexicanos. Videotape production, Puebla and Santa Cruz: Universidad Autónoma de Puebla and University of California at Santa Cruz, 1987/88. Distributed by The Cinema Guild, New York; Zafra/Macondo Video, Mexico City.

Magí Murià: Un pioner diletant/Magí Murià: Pioneer and Dilettante. Videotape production. Barcelona: TV Terrassa, 1993/94. Distributed by the Filmoteca de Catalunya.

El Movimiento Obrero Mexicano, 1857–1980. Photographic exhibit. Mexico City: CEHSMO, 1982.

Nicaragua innovando/Innovating Nicaragua. Videotape production, Managua and Puebla: Ministry of the Interior and UAP, 1986/87. Distributed by The Cinema Guild, New York; Zafra/Macondo Video, Mexico City; La Médiathèque des Trois Mondes, Paris.

Testimonios de una guerra. Fotografías de la Revolución Mexicana. Photographic exhibit. Mexico City: INAH, 2010.

"That's the medicine business for you, full of no guarantees": A Video-Essay on American Medicine and the Media. Videotape production. Santa Cruz: University of California at Santa Cruz, 1975.

Trabajo y trabajadores en México, 1940–1960, vistos por los Hermanos Mayo/Work and Workers in Mexico, 1940–1960, Seen by the Hermanos Mayo. Photographic exhibit. Puebla: CIHMO-UAP, 1984.

The Two Ways: 1775–1910. Audiovisual production. University of California at Santa Barbara, 1975.

COLLABORATIVE MODERN MEDIA PRODUCTIONS

Baker, Joyce, Perry Kaufman, and John Mraz. *Coming Apart: America in the 1960s*. Super 8mm film, University of California at Santa Barbara, 1972.

Chiles, Frederic, John Mraz, and Raymond Tracy. *The Great Depression*. Audiovisual production. University of California at Santa Barbara, 1975.

Chiles, Frederic, and John Mraz. *"Todo es más sabroso con . . .": An Historical Film-Essay on the Continuity of Neo-Colonialism in Mexico*. Super 8mm film. University of California at Santa Barbara, 1972.

Chiles, Frederic, Charles Churchill, John Mraz, and Raymond Tracy. *Visions of History*. Photographic exhibit. University of California at Santa Barbara, 1975.

Mraz, John, Roger Nelson, and Raymond Tracy. *Cracks in the Wall: America/the Fifties*. Super 8mm film. University of California at Santa Barbara, 1973.

www.ingramcontent.com/pod-product-compliance
Lightning Source LLC
LaVergne TN
LVHW041110080826
845145LV00007B/1759

* 9 7 8 0 8 2 6 5 0 1 4 4 8 *